Musical Aesthetics:
A Historical Reader

VOLUME I

From Antiquity
to the Eighteenth Century

EDITED BY

Edward A. Lippman

COLUMBIA UNIVERSITY

AESTHETICS IN MUSIC No. 4

PENDRAGON PRESS
NEW YORK

Other Titles in the Aesthetics in Music Series

No. 1   *Analysis and Value Judgment* by Carl Dahlhaus, Translated by
        Siegmund Levarie (1983)
        ISBN 0-918728-20-7

No. 2   *Arts, Sciences/Alloys: The Thesis Defense for his doctorat d'Etat* by Iannis
        Xenakis (1985)
        ISBN 0-918728-22-3

No.3   *Divining the Powers of Music: Aesthetic Theory and the Origins of Opera*
        by Ruth Katz (1986)
        ISBN 0-918728-48-7

No. 5   *Contemplating Music: Source Readings in Musical Aesthetics* Vol. I,
        Substance, selected and edited by Carl Dahlhaus and Ruth
        Katz (in press)
        ISBN 0-918728-60-6

Library of Congress Cataloging in Publication Data

Lippman, Edward.
    Musical aesthetics.

    (Aesthetics in music; no.4)
    Bibliography; p. 417
    1.Music—Philosophy and aesthetics—Addresses, essays, lectures.
I. Lippman, Edward A.
ML3845.M975 780'.1 85-28415
ISBN 0-918728-41-X (v. 1)

Contents

v

vi

PART NINE

THE AESTHETICS OF OPERA

vii

To Vi and our family

Introduction

Musical aesthetics is concerned with the beauty and expressiveness of music, and in particular with properties of this kind as they are perceived by hearing. It designates a field of philosophic thought that arose in the West largely during the course of the eighteenth century, reached its maturity in the nineteenth century, and has been considerably enlarged and transformed in the twentieth century. Although this is not to say that aesthetic concerns are absent at other times and places, yet the specific historical occurrence of a continuous and systematic area of investigation must obviously be distinguished from a universal but essentially implicit and undeveloped feature of human experience.

Leaving the aesthetic aspect of nature almost entirely out of consideration, musical aesthetics undertakes to account for the perceived properties of music. In addition, however, it presupposes the status of music as an art rather than as a field of expression altogether unique in character. But an art, in the light of the ancient and medieval conceptions of *technē* and *ars*, was an activity based on knowledge and skill. It was also one, in its higher forms, the meaning of which was determined by mimesis, or imitation—a property that identified aesthetic values with those of ethics and epistemology and thus obstructed the establishment of their independence. These two requirements—of theory and of imitation—were successively and successfully met by music, over a period extending from the Renaissance to the eighteenth century. It consequently was recognized as a higher art basically coordinate with others and thus amenable to the same considerations.

As an art of Antiquity, music was at one with the temporal and corporeal arts of poetry and dance; indeed the three were united to comprise a single composite art that was called "music" in a larger sense than ours. With the growing independence of each constituent art, music and dance obviously proved deficient in respect of a visual notation. It was notation, however, that endowed poetry and literature with the critically important values of workmanship and permanence. With the growing reliance during the Renaissance on notation and the musical score (the *res facta*), music could logically achieve artistic works that were fully comparable to those of verbal art—of poetry and literature and rhetoric. At the same time, this development in music made possible the growth of a body of theory. To be sure, music had always possessed a tradition of theoretical writings, but these belonged largely to the domain of mathematics and physics and acoustics and tuning: to the study of the musical system. There was also a tradition that recognized the role of genius and inspiration, for these were particularly prominent in the musical arts, where performance and improvisation and corporeal participation, especially as represented in the singing voice, emphasized the personal and creative powers of the individual. This was an aspect of art, however—vital though it was at various periods from the Renaissance onwards—that actually contradicted the predominant matter at issue, which was one of craft and theoretical science.

Essential to the establishment of music as an art, then, was not so much the presence of inspiration and personal genius, nor of a science of mathematical acoustics, but a knowledge and skill that pertained to counterpoint and composition—a theoretical foundation comparable to poetics and to the study of anatomy and perspective in sculpture and painting.

During the course of the sixteenth and seventeenth centuries the literary academy, which looked to Greece for its model, was duplicated by academies of painting and academies of music; and the fundamental equivalence of the arts permitted the rise of a field of aesthetic speculation common to them all. There was still another factor that abetted this development, however, for the common nature of the arts is realized best from the perspective of perception, especially of uninformed perception that is responsive to artistic effects but that in no way calls for an understanding of technical features of processes of construction. Thus it was logically during the Baroque, with its interest in an audience and in artistic impact on larger groups of people, that the similarities between the arts could most readily become apparent. The closer view of the expert and the connoisseur is one inevitably concerned with technical details, which serve to separate the arts more than to unite them.

An important early step in the development of aesthetics was the influence of ancient Greek art and artistic ideals on Renaissance thought and practice. This brought to the fore certain prominent issues which had to be re-examined and cleared away, so to speak, if aesthetics was to define its purposes and achieve its autonomy. Chief among these issues was the involvement of art with metaphysics and ethics, which was now brought into connection with the details of artistic quality and structure. So long as art was tied to the properties of the cosmos, to mathematics and science, to the problem of knowledge, to religious and moral values, and to medical influences, its specifically aesthetic comprehension could advance only slowly. These older traditions were strangely tenacious, however, doubtless for the reason that their connection with art was by no means simply a historical accident but the manifestation of an essential underlying interrelationship. Indeed it is the autonomy of aesthetics, and the con-comitant autonomy of art which it clearly mirrors, that appear as the historical accidents. And it is this circumstance, really, that comprises the essential limitation of the temporal and cultural spread of aesthetics as a branch of study. We are now turning back to these larger philosophic contexts, and away from the aestheticism which was the natural outcome of the intrinsic tendencies of an aesthetic outlook. At the same time the technical and constructive features of art have taken over much of the place of the more superficial perceptual qualities that distinguished our older aesthetic interest. Even beauty and expression have fallen into disrepute.

Music possessed its own traditions, of course, and its own striking peculiarities, and these persisted and will doubtless always persist in keeping its aesthetics partly distinct. We still speak of the fine arts *and* music, and music and art are still thought of as separate or contrasted areas of expression, a distinction that really extends to space art and time art in general. The special religious and moral and social powers of music still call for serious consideration, and even such apparently obsolete notions as the medical values of music and the presence of harmony in nature have not entirely disappeared from view. In the advent of dramatic style around 1600 and the development of an autonomous instrumental music during the succeeding two centuries music presented its own contributions to the problems of aesthetics that served to underline its idiosyncrasy. Instrumental music was in fact a phenomenon of the utmost moment to aesthetic theory in general, radically calling into question as it did the traditional axiom of imitation and the established notions of artistic meaning and truth; it also brought about the maturity of musical aesthetics in particular.

Enough will have been said to indicate that aesthetics is in a way surrounded by issues that belong more specifically to what we might call musical philosophy—issues of ontology, epistemology, and ethics. Revolving as they do around aesthetic matters, however, these can be included in our field, or at least on its peripheries, without arbitrariness or confusion. This is also to some extent the case with musical sociology, another ancient field of philosophy, that is now returning to currency in a new guise. It is important to keep in mind, however, that the field of aesthetics is open to its most telling criticism because of its astonishing neglect of social considerations (along with historical and cultural ones). Like the field itself, this omission reflects the contemporaneous isolation of art.

Other important fields related to musical aesthetics are musical criticism, musical theory, and musical psychology. Criticism is related to aesthetics ideally as practice is to theory, although it is rarely the case either that criticism is a conscious application of aesthetic principles or that aesthetics is a conscious critique of critical practices and evaluative statements. Musical theory is clearly more concerned with technical features of music than with its perceived qualities or its value or beauty or expressiveness. Yet as in the case of criticism, many theoretical tracts obviously involve aesthetic concerns. Musical psychology, finally, is concerned typically with elemental perceptual qualities such as those of intervals and chords rather than with larger musical contexts. For this reason it has been closely allied with auditory physiology, which remains very distant from the musical work as a whole. To the extent that psychology adopts more far-ranging goals, it devolves either into musical phenomenology or into a study of the creative process, both of which are logical parts of aesthetics also. What is usually meant by psychological aesthetics, however, is the investigation of the preferences of unselected subjects when they are presented with a variety of simple tonal relationships.

The relation of musical aesthetics to the study of style and genre is in part one of explicit to implicit values. To some extent, then, the two provide a natural mutual reinforcement, aesthetics giving us on occasion a distillation of the significance music possessed in its own time. Such a contemporaneous picture is obviously an indispensable basis for any understanding and evaluation of our own. The history of aesthetics is wihout doubt an important adjunct if not a part of the history of music. The reverse is to some extent true also, for the historical awareness and musical experience of the aesthetician go far to explain and account for his conceptions, with their particular virtues and limitations. It cannot be overlooked, however, that aesthetics and music are to a certain extent independent of one another; speculative thought has its own interest and autonomy and musical creation is often self-sustaining—an activity in its own right that is subject to few if any conscious theoretical preconceptions. This mutual independence is fostered not only by the occasional lack of speculative inclination on the part of composers and performers but also by the frequent lack of musical knowledge and experience on the part of aesthetical writers. Aestheticians indeed have the most varied background imaginable; the definition of the field, diffuse as it is, is considerably more precise than the circumscription of its practitioners. For as a glance at our List of Authors will reveal, these range from philosophers and scholars to critics and composers, with corresponding differences in the whole complexion of the ideas that are advanced and in their musical or intellectual sophistication.

Edward A. Lippman
Columbia University

Editor's Preface

The excellent translation of Book VI of St. Augustine's *De musica* is reprinted from *The Fathers of the Church*, Vol. 4, by kind permission of the translator, Robert Catesby Taliaferro. The excerpt from *Rameau's Nephew*, by Diderot, has been reprinted from the translation of L.W. Tancock by permission of Penguin Books, Ltd. The translation of Plato's *Laws*, by B. Jowett, and that of Augustine's *Confessions*, by E.B. Pusey, published by Simon and Schuster, are in the public domain. The remaining translations are the work of the Editor.

The original notes of the author of each selection are separated from the annotations of the Editor or of an earlier translator by the use of Arabic numbers for the former and lower-case letters for the latter.

This volume is the first of three which are designed to present the main trends of Western musical thought in the area of philosophy and aesthetics. The second volume is devoted to the nineteenth century and the third to the twentieth. Each section of the work, presenting the fundamental statements of a given aesthetic issue, has its own brief introduction defining and interrelating the relevant ideas, and concludes with its own special bibliography. The various sections, and their introductions in particular, seek to clarify the underlying historical continuities of thought.

PART ONE

Ancient Musical Ethics

The musical thought of Ancient Greece—and probably that of ancient civilizations in general—is rarely concerned with the aesthetic values of art as such, with artistic beauty and expressiveness for their own sake; for the creation and perception of art were almost invariably embedded in a larger social or ceremonial experience. Thus music is regarded in its relationship to Truth or to the Good: it is either a sensuous embodiment of ideal mathematical forms or, again pointing beyond itself, an influence on human character and behavior. The first of these philosophic conceptions is concerned not just with music, but with all harmonic structures: with the internal constitution of soul and body, of society, and of the cosmos. Plato has treated of its various aspects throughout the *Republic* and the *Timaeus*. The second conception, which is represented by the reading that follows, he treats at length in the *Republic* (Book III) and in the *Laws* (Books II and VII). This area of thought is concerned with the cultivation of the character of the individual, and since society is regarded as the individual in the large, of the character of society as well.

These two ancient divisions of musical thought—metaphysical and ethical—are not entirely separate. Indeed the second examines the dynamic or developmental process of which the first describes the ideal outcome, for the harmonious society, like the harmonious individual soul and body, is the product of a prolonged course of controlled education. Equally important is the involvement of aesthetics with both of these fields, for harmonic structure has an intrinsic beauty (There is an impressive instance of cosmic harmony in Book X of the *Republic*), while music approved for its educational value, as we learn in *Laws* Book II, must also give pleasure and be well constructed. Moral value remains primary, of course; music which is no more than play or harmless pleasure, which does not clearly imitate virtuous character and behavior, cannot really be taken seriously. There is an interpenetration of morality and aesthetics here which is foreign to the modern Western conception of art.

With the *Laws*, Plato's last and longest dialogue, the philosopher returns to his central interest, political theory, but with a practical intent and detail that were absent from the utopian project of the *Republic*. The discussion of musical education and of laws concerning music is both more comprehensive and more detailed than that of the earlier dialogue. The positive picture presented in Books II and VII may be supplemented here by the description of the dire results of musical license, which is found in Book III in connection with a discussion of excessive individual freedom in Athens:

> In the first place, let us speak of the laws about music—that is to say, such music as then existed—in order that we may trace the growth of the excess of freedom from the beginning. Now music was early divided among us into certain kinds and manners. One sort consisted of prayers to the gods, which

were called hymns; and there was another and opposite sort called lamentations, and another termed paeans, and another, celebrating the birth of Dionysus, called, I believe, "dithyrambs." And they used the actual word "laws," or *nomoi*, for another kind of song; and to this they added the term "citharoedic." All these and others were duly distinguished, nor were the performers allowed to confuse one style of music with another. And the authority which determined and gave judgment, and punished the disobedient, was not expressed in a hiss, nor in the most unmusical shouts of the multitude, as in our days, nor in applause and clapping of hands. But the directors of public instruction insisted that the spectators should listen in silence to the end; and boys and their tutors, and the multitude in general, were kept quiet by a hint from the stick. Such was the good order which the multitude were willing to observe; they would never have dared to give judgment by noisy cries. And then, as time went on, the poets themselves introduced the reign of vulgar and lawless innovation. They were men of genius, but they had no perception of what is just and lawful in music; raging like Bacchanals and possessed with inordinate delights—mingling lamentations with hymns, and paeans with dithyrambs; imitating the sounds of the aulos on the lyre, and making one general confusion; ignorantly affirming that music has no truth, and, whether good or bad, can only be judged of rightly by the pleasure of the hearer. And by composing such licentious works, and adding to them words as licentious, they have inspired the multitude with lawlessness and boldness, and made them fancy that they can judge for themselves about melody and song. And in this way the theatres from being mute have become vocal, as though they had understanding of good and bad in music and poetry; and instead of an aristocracy, an evil sort of theatrocracy has grown up. For if the democracy which judged had only consisted of educated persons, no fatal harm would have been done; but in music there first arose the universal conceit of omniscience and general lawlessness; freedom came following afterwards, and men, fancying that they knew what they did not know, had no longer any fear, and the absence of fear begets shamelessness. For what is this shamelessness, which is so evil a thing, but the insolent refusal to regard the opinion of the better by reason of an over-daring sort of liberty? Consequent upon this freedom comes the other freedom, of disobedience to rulers; and then the attempt to escape the control and exhortation of father, mother, elders, and when near the end, the control of the laws also; and at the very end there is a contempt of oaths and pledges, and no regard at all for the gods—herein they exhibit and imitate the old so-called Titanic nature, and come to the same point as the Titans when they rebelled against God, leading a life of endless evils [*Laws* 700-701c].

4

CHAPTER ONE

PLATO

Laws
(c. 350 B.C.)

BOOK II

ATHENIAN STRANGER. And now we have to consider whether the insight into human nature is the only benefit derived from well-ordered potations, or whether there are not other advantages great and much to be desired. The argument seems to imply that there are. But how and in what way these are to be attained, will have to be considered attentively, or we may be entangled in error.

CLEINIAS. Proceed.

ATH. Let me once more recall our doctrine of right education; which, if I am not mistaken, depends on the due regulation of convivial intercourse.

CLE. You talk rather grandly.

ATH. Pleasure and pain I maintain to be the first perceptions of children, and I say that they are the forms under which virtue and vice are originally present to them. As to wisdom and true and fixed opinions, happy is the man who acquires them, even when declining in years; and we may say that he who possesses them, and the blessings which are contained in them, is a perfect man. Now I mean by education that training which is given by suitable habits to the first instincts of virtue in children;—when pleasure, and friendship, and pain, and hatred are rightly implanted in souls not yet capable of understanding the nature of them, and who find them, after they have attained reason, to be in harmony with her. This harmony of the soul, taken as a whole, is virtue; but the particular training in respect of pleasure and pain, which leads

5

you always to hate what you ought to hate, and love what you ought to love, from the beginning of life to the end, may be separated off; and, in my view, will be rightly called education.

CLE. I think, stranger, that you are quite right in all that you have said and are saying about education.

ATH. I am glad to hear that you agree with me; for, indeed, the discipline of pleasure and pain which, when rightly ordered, is a principle of education, has been often relaxed and corrupted in human life. And the Gods, pitying the toils which our race is born to undergo, have appointed holy festivals, wherein men alternate rest with labour; and have given them the Muses and Apollo, the leader of the Muses, and Dionysus, to be companions in their revels, that these may be saved from degeneration, and men partake in spiritual nourishment in company with the Gods. I should like to know whether a common saying is in our opinion true to nature or not. For men to say that the young of all creatures cannot be quiet in their bodies or in their voices; they are always wanting to move and cry out; some leaping and skipping, and overflowing with sportiveness and delight at something, others uttering all sorts of cries. But, whereas the animals have no perception of order or disorder in their movements, that is, of rhythm or harmony, as they are called, to us the Gods, who, as we say, have been appointed to be our companions in the dance, have given the pleasurable sense of harmony and rhythm; and so they stir us into life, and we follow them, joining hands together in dances and songs; and these they call choruses, which is a term naturally expressive of cheerfulness.[a] Shall we begin, then, with the acknowledgement that education is first given through Apollo and the Muses? What do you say?

CLE. I assent.

ATH. And the uneducated is he who has not been trained in the chorus, and the educated is he who has been well trained?

CLE. Certainly.

ATH. And the chorus is made up of two parts, dance and song?

CLE. True.

ATH. Then he who is well educated will be able to sing and dance well?

CLE. I suppose that he will.

ATH. Let us see; what are we saying?

CLE. What?

ATH. He sings well and dances well; now must we add that he sings what is good and dances what is good?

CLE. Let us make the addition.

ATH. We will suppose that he knows the good to be good, and the bad to be bad, and makes use of them accordingly: which now is the better trained

---

[a]*choros*, erroneously connected with *chairein*. (Annotations are from the Jowett translation.)

in dancing and music—he who is able to move his body and use his voice in what he understands to be the right manner, but has no delight in good or hatred of evil; or he who is scarcely correct in gesture and voice and in understanding, but is right in his sense of pleasure and pain, and welcomes what is good, and is offended at what is evil?

CLE. There is a great difference, stranger, in the two kinds of education.

ATH. If we three know what is good in song and dance, then we truly know also who is educated and who is uneducated; but if not, then we certainly shall not know wherein lies the safeguard of education, and whether there is any or not.

CLE. True.

ATH. Let us follow the scent like hounds, and go in pursuit of beauty of figure, and melody, and song, and dance; if these escape us, there will be no use in talking about true education, whether Hellenic or barbarian.

CLE. Yes.

ATH. Now what is meant by beauty of figure, or beautiful melody? When a manly soul is in trouble, and when a cowardly soul is in similar case, are they likely to use the same figures and gestures, or to give utterance to the same sounds?

CLE. How can they, when the very colours of their faces differ?

ATH. Good, my friend; I may observe, however, in passing, that in music there certainly are figures and there are melodies: and music is concerned with harmony and rhythm, so that you may speak of a melody or figure having good rhythm or good harmony—the term is correct enough; but to speak metaphorically of a melody or figure having a 'good colour', as the masters of choruses do, is not allowable, although you can speak of the melodies or figures of the brave and the coward, praising the one and censuring the other. And not to be tedious, let us say that the figures and melodies which are expressive of virtue of soul or body, or of images of virtue, are without exception good, and those which are expressive of vice are the reverse of good.

CLE. Your suggestion is excellent; and let us answer that these things are so.

ATH. Once more, are all of us equally delighted with every sort of dance?

CLE. Far otherwise.

ATH. What, then, leads us astray? Are beautiful things not the same to us all, or are they the same in themselves, but not in our opinion of them? For no one will admit that forms of vice in the dance are more beautiful than forms of virtue, or that he himself delights in the forms of vice, and others in a muse of another character. And yet most persons say, that the excellence of music is to give pleasure to our souls. But this is intolerable and blasphemous; there is, however, a much more plausible account of the delusion.

CLE. What?

7

ATH. The adaptation of art to the characters of men. Choric movements are imitations of manners and the performers range over all the various actions and chances of life with characterization and mimicry; and those to whom the words, or songs, or dances are suited, either by nature or habit or both, cannot help feeling pleasure in them and applauding them, and calling them beautiful. But those whose natures, or ways, or habits are unsuited to them, cannot delight in them or applaud them, and they call them base. There are others, again, whose natures are right and their habits wrong, or whose habits are right and their natures wrong, and they praise one thing, but are pleased at another. For they say that all these imitations are pleasant, but not good. And in the presence of those whom they think wise, they are ashamed of dancing and singing in the baser manner, in a way which would indicate deliberate approval; and yet, they have a secret pleasure in them.

CLE. Very true.

ATH. And is any harm done to the lover of vicious dances or songs, or any good done to the approver of the opposite sort of pleasure?

CLE. I think that there is.

ATH. 'I think' is not the word, but I would say, rather, 'I am certain'. For must they not have the same effect as when a man associates with bad characters, whom he likes and approves rather than dislikes, and only censures playfully because he has but a suspicion of their badness? In that case, he who takes pleasure in them will surely become like those in whom he takes pleasure, even though he be ashamed to praise them. This result is quite certain; and what greater good or evil can a human being undergo?

CLE. I know of none.

ATH. Then in a city which has good laws, or in future ages is to have them, bearing in mind the instruction and amusement which are given by music, can we suppose that the poets are to be allowed to teach in the dance anything which they themselves like, in the way of rhythm, or melody, or words, to the young children of any well-conditioned parents? Is the poet to train his choruses as he pleases, without reference to virtue or vice?

CLE. That is surely quite unreasonable, and is not to be thought of.

ATH. And yet he may do this in almost any state with the exception of Egypt.

CLE. And what are the laws about music and dancing in Egypt?

CLE. You will wonder when I tell you: Long ago they appear to have recognized the very principle of which we are now speaking—that their young citizens must be habituated to forms and strains of virtue. These they fixed, and exhibited the patterns of them in their temples; and no painter, no other representative artist is allowed to innovate upon them, or to leave the traditional forms and invent new ones. To this day, no

8

alteration is allowed either in these arts, or in music at all. And you find that their works of art are painted or moulded in the same forms which they had ten thousand years ago;—this is literally true and no exaggeration,—their ancient paintings and sculptures are not a whit better or worse than the work of today, but are made with just the same skill.

CLE. How extraordinary!

ATH. I should rather say, How statesmanlike, how worthy of a legislator! I know that other things in Egypt are not so well. But what I am telling you about music is true and deserving of consideration, because showing that a lawgiver may institute melodies which have a natural truth and correctness without any fear of failure. To do this, however, must be the work of God, or of a divine person; in Egypt they have a tradition that their ancient chants which have been preserved for so many ages are the composition of the Goddess Isis. And therefore, as I was saying, if a person can only find in any way the natural melodies, he may confidently embody them in a fixed and legal form. For the love of novelty which arises out of pleasure in the new and weariness of the old, has not strength enough to corrupt the consecrated song and dance, under the plea that they have become antiquated. At any rate, they are far from being corrupted in Egypt.

CLE. Your arguments seem to prove your point.

ATH. May we not confidently say that the true use of music and of choral festivities is as follows: We rejoice when we think that we prosper, and again we think that we prosper when we rejoice?

CLE. Exactly.

ATH. And when rejoicing in our good fortune, we are unable to be still?

CLE. True.

ATH. Our young men break forth into dancing and singing, and we who are their elders deem that we are fulfilling our part in life when we look on at them. Having lost our agility, we delight in their sports and merry-making, because we love to think of our former selves; and gladly institute contests for those who are able to awaken in us the memory of our youth.

CLE. Very true.

ATH. Is it altogether unmeaning to say, as the common people do about festivals, that he should be adjudged the wisest of men, and the winner of the palm, who gives us the greatest amount of pleasure and mirth? For on such occasions, and when mirth is the order of the day, ought not he to be honoured most, and, as I was saying, bear the palm, who gives most mirth to the greatest number? Now is this a true way of speaking or of acting?

CLE. Possibly.

ATH. But, my dear friend, let us distinguish between different cases, and not be hasty in forming a judgement: One way of considering the question

9

will be to imagine a festival at which there are entertainments of all sorts, including gymnastic, musical, and equestrian contests: the citizens are assembled; prizes are offered, and proclamation is made that anyone who likes may enter the lists, and that he is to bear the palm who gives the most pleasure to the spectators—there is to be no regulation about the manner how; but he who is most successful in giving pleasure is to be crowned victor, and deemed to be the pleasantest of the candidates. What is likely to be the result of such a proclamation?

CLE. In what respect?

ATH. There would be various exhibitions: one man, like Homer, will exhibit a rhapsody, another a performance on the lyre; one will have a tragedy, and another a comedy. Nor would there be anything astonishing in someone imagining that he could gain the prize by exhibiting a puppet-show. Suppose these competitors to meet, and not these only, but innumerable others as well—can you tell me who ought to be the victor?

CLE. I do not see how anyone can answer you, or pretend to know, unless he has heard with his own ears the several competitors; the question is absurd.

ATH. Well, then, if neither of you can answer, shall I answer this question which you deem so absurd?

CLE. By all means.

ATH. If very small children are to determine the question, they will decide for the puppet-show.

CLE. Very likely.

ATH. And I believe that we old men would have the greatest pleasure in hearing a rhapsodist recite well the Iliad and Odyssey, or one of the Hesiodic poems, and would award an overwhelming victory to him. But, who would really be the victor?—that is the question.

CLE. Yes.

ATH. Clearly you and I will have to declare that those whom we old men adjudge victors ought to win; for our ways are far and away better than any which at present exist anywhere in the world.

CLE. Certainly.

ATH. Thus far I too should agree with the many, that the excellence of music is to be measured by pleasure. But the pleasure must not be that of chance persons; the fairest music is that which delights the best and best educated, and especially that which delights the one man who is pre-eminent in virtue and education. And therefore the judges must be men of character, for they will require wisdom and have still greater need of courage; the true judge must not draw his inspiration from the theatre, nor ought he to be unnerved by the clamour of the many and his own incapacity; nor again, knowing the truth, ought he through cowardice and unmanliness carelessly to deliver a lying judgment, with the very

10

same lips which have just appealed to the Gods before he judged. He is sitting not as the disciple of the theatre, but, in his proper place, as their instructor, and he ought to be the enemy of all pandering to the pleasure of the spectators. The ancient and common custom of Hellas was the reverse of that which now prevails in Italy and Sicily, where the judgement is left to the body of spectators, who determine the victor by show of hands. But this custom has been the destruction of the poets themselves; for they are now in the habit of composing with a view to please the bad taste of their judges, and the result is that the spectators instruct themselves;—and also it has been the ruin of the theatre; they ought to be having characters put before them better than their own, and so receiving a higher pleasure, but now by their own act the opposite result follows. What inference is to be drawn from all this? Shall I tell you?

CLE. What?

ATH. The inference at which we arrive for the third or fourth time is, that education is the constraining and directing of youth towards that right reason, which the law affirms, and which the experience of the eldest and best has agreed to be truly right. In order, then, that the soul of the child may not be habituated to feel joy and sorrow in a manner at variance with the law, and those who obey the law, but may rather follow the law and rejoice and sorrow at the same things as the aged—in order, I say, to produce this effect, chants appear to have been invented, which really enchant, and are designed to implant that harmony of which we speak. And, because the mind of the child is incapable of enduring serious training, they are called plays and songs, and are performed in play; just as when men are sick and ailing in their bodies, their attendants give them wholesome diet in pleasant meats and drinks, but unwholesome diet in disagreeable things, in order that they may learn, as they ought, to like the one, and to dislike the other. And similarly the true legislator will persuade, and, if he cannot persuade, will compel the poet to express, as he ought, by fair and noble words, in his rhythms, the figures, and in his melodies, the music of temperate and brave and in every way good men.

CLE. But do you really imagine, stranger, that this is the way in which poets generally compose in states at the present day? As far as I can observe, except among us and among the Lacedaemonians, there are no regulations like those of which you speak; in other places novelties are always being introduced in dancing and music, generally not under the authority of any law, but at the instigation of lawless pleasures; and these pleasures are so far from being stable and governed by principles, as are those of the Egyptians by your account, that they have no consistency at all.

ATH. Most true, Cleinias; and I dare say that I may have expressed myself obscurely, and so led you to imagine that I was speaking of some really existing state of things, whereas I was only saying what regulations I

11

would like to have about music; and hence there occurred a misapprehension on your part. For when evils are far gone and irremediable, the task of censuring them is never pleasant, although at times necessary. But as we do not really differ, will you let me ask you whether you consider such institutions to be more prevalent among the Cretans and Lacedaemonians than among the other Hellenes?

CLE. Certainly they are.

ATH. And if they were extended to the other Hellenes, would it be an improvement on the present state of things?

CLE. A very great improvement, if the customs which prevail among them were such as prevail among us and the Lacedaemonians, and such as you were just now saying ought to prevail.

ATH. Let us see whether we understand one another:—Are not the principles of education and music which prevail among you as follows: you compel your poets to say that the good man, if he be temperate and just, is fortunate and happy; and this whether he be great and strong or small and weak, and whether he be rich or poor; and, on the other hand, if he have a wealth passing that of Cinyras or Midas, and be unjust, he is wretched and lives in misery? As the poet says, and with truth: 'I sing not, I care not about him' who accomplishes all things reputed noble, not having justice; let him who 'draws near and stretches out his hand against his enemies' be a just man. But if he be unjust, I would not have him 'look calmly upon bloody death', nor surpass in swiftness 'Thracian Boreas'; and let no other thing that is called good ever be his. For the goods of which the many speak are not really good: first in the catalogue is placed health, beauty next, wealth third; and then innumerable others, as for example to have a keen eye or a quick ear, and in general to have all the senses perfect; or, again, to be a tyrant and do as you like; and the final consummation of happiness is to have acquired all these things, and when you have acquired them to become at once immortal. But you and I say, that while to the just and holy all these things are the best of possessions, to the unjust they are all, including even health, the greatest of evils. For in truth, to have sight, and hearing, and the use of the senses, or to live at all without justice and virtue, even though a man be rich in all the so-called goods of fortune, is the greatest of evils, if life be immortal; but not so great, if the bad man lives only a very short time. These are the truths which, if I am not mistaken, you will persuade or compel your poets to utter with suitable accompaniments of harmony and rhythm, and in these they must train up your youth. Am I not right? For I plainly declare that evils as they are termed are goods to the unjust, and only evils to the just, and that goods are truly good to the good, but evil to the evil. Let me ask again, Are you and I agreed about this?

CLE. I think that we partly agree, and partly are opposed.

ATH. When a man has health and wealth and a tyranny which lasts, and when he is pre-eminent in strength and courage, and has the gift of immortality, and none of the so-called evils which counterbalance these goods, but only the unjustice and insolence of his own nature—of such a one you are, I suspect, unwilling to believe that he is miserable rather than happy.

CLE. That is quite true.

ATH. Once more: Suppose that he be valiant and strong, and handsome and rich, and does throughout his whole life whatever he likes, still, if he be unrighteous and insolent, would not both of you agree that he will of necessity live basely? You will surely grant so much?

CLE. Certainly.

ATH. And an evil life too?

CLE. I am not equally disposed to grant that.

ATH. Will he not live painfully and to his own disadvantage?

CLE. How can I possibly say so?

ATH. How! Then may Heaven make us to be of one mind, for now we are of two. To me, dear Cleinias, the truth of what I am saying is as plain as the fact that Crete is an island. And, if I were a lawgiver, I would try to make the poets and all the citizens speak in this strain; and I would inflict the heaviest penalties on anyone in all the land who should dare to say that there are bad men who lead pleasant lives, or that the profitable and gainful is one thing, and the just another; and there are many other matters about which I should make my citizens speak in a manner different from the Cretans and Lacedaemonians of this age, and I may say, indeed, from the world in general. For tell me, my good friends, by Zeus and Apollo tell me, if I were to ask these same Gods who were your legislators,—Is not the most just life also the pleasantest? or are there two lives, one of which is the justest and the other the pleasantest?—and they were to reply that there are two; and thereupon I proceeded to ask (that would be the right way of pursuing the inquiry), Which are the happier— those who lead the justest, or those who lead the pleasantest life? and they replied, Those who lead the pleasantest—that would be a very strange answer, which I should not like to put into the mouth of the Gods. The words will come with more propriety from the lips of fathers and legislators, and therefore I will repeat my former questions to one of them, and suppose him to say again that he who leads the pleasantest life is the happiest. And to that I rejoin:—O my father, did you not wish me to live as happily as possible? And yet you also never ceased telling me that I should live as justly as possible. Now, here the giver of the rule, whether he be legislator or father, will be in a dilemma, and will in vain endeavour to be consistent with himself. But if he were to declare that the justest life is also the happiest, everyone hearing him would inquire, if I am not

13

mistaken, what is that good and noble principle in life which the law approves, and which is superior to pleasure. For what good can the just man have which is separated from pleasure? Shall we say that glory and fame, coming from Gods and men, though good and noble, are nevertheless unpleasant, and infamy pleasant? Certainly not, sweet legislator. Or shall we say that the not-doing of wrong and there being no wrong done is good and honourable, although there is no pleasure in it, and that the doing wrong is pleasant, but evil and base?

CLE. Impossible.

ATH. The view which identifies the pleasant and the just and the good and the noble has an excellent moral and religious tendency. And the opposite view is most at variance with the designs of the legislator, and is, in his opinion, infamous; for no one, if he can help, will be persuaded to do that which gives him more pain than pleasure. But as distant prospects are apt to make us dizzy, especially in childhood, the legislator will try to purge away the darkness and exhibit the truth; he will persuade the citizens, in some way or other, by customs and praises and words, that just and unjust are as illusory as a scene-painting, and that injustice, which seems opposed to justice, when contemplated by the unjust and evil man appears pleasant and the just most unpleasant; but that from the just man's point of view, the very opposite is the appearance of both of them.

CLE. True.

ATH. And which may be supposed to be the truer judgement—that of the inferior or of the better soul?

CLE. Surely, that of the better soul.

ATH. Then the unjust life must not only be more base and depraved, but also in truth more unpleasant than the just and holy life?

CLE. That seems to be implied in the present argument.

ATH. And even supposing this were otherwise, and not as the argument has proven, still the lawgiver, who is worth anything, if he ever ventures to tell a lie to the young for their good, could not invent a more useful lie than this, or one which will have a better effect in making them do what is right, not on compulsion but voluntarily.

CLE. Truth, stranger, is a noble thing and a lasting, but your lesson is one of which men will hardly be persuaded.

ATH. And yet the story of the Sidonian Cadmus, which is so improbable, has been readily believed, and also innumerable other tales.

CLE. What is that story?

ATH. The story of armed men springing up after the sowing of teeth, which the legislator may take as a proof that he can persuade the minds of the young of anything; so that he has only to reflect and find out what belief will be of the greatest public advantage, and then use all his efforts to make the whole community utter one and the same word in their songs and tales and discourses all their life long. But if you do not agree with me, there is no reason why you should not argue on the other side.

CLE. I do not see that any argument can fairly be raised by either of us against what you are now saying.

ATH. The next suggestion which I have to offer is, that all our three choruses shall sing to the young and tender souls of children, reciting in their strains all the noble thoughts of which we have already spoken, or are about to speak; and the sum of them shall be, that the life which is by the Gods deemed to be the happiest is also the best;—thus we shall both affirm what is most certainly true, and the minds of our young disciples will be more likely to receive these words of ours than any others which we might address to them.

CLE. I assent to what you say.

ATH. First will enter in their natural order the choir of the Muses, composed of children, which is to sing lustily the heaven-taught lay to the whole city. Next will follow the choir of young men under the age of thirty, who will call upon the God Paean to testify to the truth of their words, and will pray him to be gracious to the youth and to turn their hearts. Thirdly, the choir of elder men, who are from thirty to sixty years of age, will also sing. There remain those who are too old to sing, and they will tell stories, illustrating the same virtues, as with the voice of an oracle.

CLE. Who are those who compose the third choir, stranger? for I do not clearly understand what you mean to say about them.

ATH. And yet almost all that I have been saying has been said with a view to them.

CLE. Will you try to be a little plainer?

ATH. I was speaking at the commencement of our discourse, as you will remember, of the fiery nature of young creatures: I said that they were unable to keep quiet either in limb or voice, and that they called out and jumped about in a disorderly manner; and that no other animal attained to any perception of order in these two things, but man only. Now the order of motion is called rhythm, and the order of voice, in which high and low are duly mingled, is called harmony; and both together are termed choric song. And I said that the Gods had pity on us, and gave us Apollo and the Muses to be our play-fellows and leaders in the dance; and Dionysus, as I dare say that you will remember, was the third.

CLE. I quite remember.

ATH. Thus far have I spoken of the chorus of Apollo and the Muses; the third and remaining chorus must be called that of Dionysus.

CLE. How is that? There is something strange, at any rate on first hearing, in a Dionysiac chorus of old men, if you really mean that those who are above thirty, and may be fifty, or from fifty to sixty years of age, are to dance in his honour.

ATH. Very true; and therefore it must be shown that there is good reason for the proposal.

CLE. Certainly.

ATH. Are we agreed thus far?

CLE. About what?

ATH. That every man and boy, slave and free, both sexes, and the whole city, should never cease charming themselves with the strains of which we have spoken; and that there should be every sort of change and variation of them in order to take away the effect of sameness, so that the singers may always receive pleasure from their hymns, and may never weary of them?

CLE. Everyone will agree.

ATH. Where, then, will that best part of our city which, by reason of age and intelligence, has the greatest influence, sing these fairest of strains in such a way as to do most good? Shall we be so foolish as to neglect this regulation, which may have a decisive effect in making the songs most beautiful and useful?

CLE. But, says the argument, we cannot neglect it.

ATH. Then how can we carry out our purpose with decorum? Will this be the way?

CLE. What?

ATH. When a man is advancing in years, he is afraid and reluctant to sing;—he has no pleasure in his own performances; and if compulsion is used, he will be more and more ashamed, the older and more discreet he grows;—is not this true?

CLE. Certainly.

ATH. Well, and will he not be yet more ashamed if he has to stand up and sing in the theatre to a mixed audience?—and if moreover when he is required to do so, like the other choirs who contend for prizes, and have been trained under a singing master, he is pinched and hungry, he will certainly have a feeling of shame and discomfort which will make him very unwilling to perform.

CLE. No doubt.

ATH. How, then, shall we reassure him, and get him to sing? Shall we begin by enacting that boys shall not taste wine at all until they are eighteen years of age; we will tell them that fire must not be poured upon fire, whether in the body or in the soul, until they begin to go to work—this is a precaution which has to be taken against the excitableness of youth;—afterwards they may taste wine in moderation up to the age of thirty, but while a man is young he should abstain altogether from intoxication and from excess of wine; when, at length, he has reached forty years, after dinner at a public mess, he may invite not only the other Gods, but Dionysus above all, to the mystery and festivity of the elder men, making use of the wine which he has given men to lighten the sourness of old age; that in age we may renew our youth, and forget our sorrows; and also in order that the nature of the soul, like iron melted in the fire, may become softer and so more impressible. In the first place, will not anyone who is thus mellowed be more ready and less ashamed to sing,—I do not say before a large audience, but before a moderate company; nor yet among strangers, but among his familiars, and, as we have often said, to chant, and to enchant?

CLE. He will be far more ready.

ATH. There will be no impropriety in our using such a method of persuading them to join with us in song.

CLE. None at all.

ATH. And what strain will they sing, and what muse will they hymn? The music should clearly be of some kind suitable to them.

CLE. Certainly.

ATH. And what strain is suitable for heroes? Shall they sing a choric strain?

CLE. Truly, stranger, we of Crete and Lacedaemon know no strain other than that which we have learnt and been accustomed to sing in our chorus.

ATH. I dare say; for you have never acquired the knowledge of the most beautiful kind of song, in your military way of life, which is modelled after the camp, and is not like that of dwellers in cities; and you have your young men herding and feeding together like young colts. No one takes his own individual colt and drags him away from his fellows against his will, raging and foaming, and gives him a groom to attend to him alone, and soothes and rubs him down, and sees that nothing is missing in his education which will make him not only a good soldier, but also a governor of a state and of cities. Such a one, as we said at first, would be a greater warrior than he of whom Tyrtaeus sings; and he would honour courage everywhere, but always as the fourth, and not as the first part of virtue, either in individuals or states.

CLE. Once more, stranger, you somehow appear to depreciate our lawgivers.

ATH. Not intentionally, if at all, my good friend; but whither the argument leads, thither let us follow; for if there be indeed some strain of song more beautiful than that of the choruses or the public theatres, I should like to impart it to those who, as we say, are ashamed of these, and want to have the best.

CLE. Certainly.

ATH. When things have an accompanying charm, either the best thing in them is this very charm, or there is some rightness or utility possessed by them;—for example, I should say that eating and drinking, and the use of food in general, have an accompanying charm which we call pleasure; but that this rightness and utility is just the healthfulness of the things served up to us, which is their true rightness.

CLE. Just so.

ATH. Thus, too, I should say that learning has a certain accompanying charm which is the pleasure; but that the right and the profitable, the good and the noble, are qualities which the truth gives to it.

CLE. Exactly.

ATH. And so in the imitative arts,—if they succeed in making likenesses, and are accompanied by pleasure, may not their works be said to have a charm?

CLE. Yes.

ATH. But equal proportions, whether of quality or quantity, and not pleasure, speaking generally, would give them truth or rightness.

CLE. Yes.

ATH. Then that only can be rightly judged by the standard of pleasure, which makes or furnishes no utility or truth or likeness, nor on the other hand is productive of any hurtful quality, but exists solely for the sake of the accompanying charm; and the term 'pleasure' is most appropriately applied to it when these other qualities are absent.

CLE. You are speaking of harmless pleasure, are you not?

ATH. Yes; and this I term amusement, when doing neither harm nor good in any degree worth speaking of.

CLE. Very true.

ATH. Then, if such be our principles, we must assert that imitation is not judged of by pleasure and false opinion; and this is true of all equality, for the equal is not equal or the symmetrical symmetrical, because somebody thinks or likes something, but they are to be judged of by the standard of truth, and by no other whatever.

CLE. Quite true.

ATH. Do we not regard all music as representative and imitative?

CLE. Certainly.

ATH. Then, when anyone says that music is to be judged of by pleasure, his doctrine cannot be admitted; and if there be any music of which pleasure is the criterion, such music is not to be sought out or deemed to have any real excellence, but only that other kind of music which is an imitation of the good, and bears a resemblance to its original.

CLE. Very true.

ATH. And those who seek for the best kind of song and music ought not to seek for that which is pleasant, but for that which is true; and the truth of imitation consists, as we were saying, in rendering the thing imitated according to quantity and quality.

18

CLE. Certainly.

ATH. And everyone will admit that musical compositions are all imitative and representative. Will not poets and spectators and actors all agree in this?

CLE. They will.

ATH. Surely then he who would judge correctly must know what each composition is; for if he does not know what is the character and meaning of the piece, and what it actually represents, he will never discern whether the intention is correct or mistaken.

CLE. Certainly not.

ATH. And will he who does not know what is true be able to distinguish what is good and bad? My statement is not very clear; but perhaps you will understand me better if I put the matter in another way.

CLE. How?

ATH. There are ten thousand likenesses which we apprehend by sight?

CLE. Yes.

ATH. Even in their case, can he who does not know what the exact object is which is imitated, ever know whether the resemblance is truthfully executed? I mean, for example, whether a statue has the proportions of a body, and the true situation of the parts; what those proportions are, and how the parts fit into one another in due order; also their colours and conformations, or whether this is all confused in the execution: do you think that anyone can know about this, who does not know what the animal is which has been imitated?

CLE. Impossible.

ATH. But even if we know that the thing pictured or sculptured is man, who has received at the hand of the artist all his proper parts and colours and shapes, shall we therefore know at once, and of necessity, whether the work is beautiful or in any respect deficient in beauty?

CLE. If this were true, stranger, we should almost all of us be judges of beauty.

ATH. Very true; and may we not say that in everything imitated, whether in drawing, music, or any other art, he who is to be a competent judge must possess three things;—he must know, in the first place, of what the imitation is; secondly, he must know that it is true; and thirdly, that it has been well executed in words and melodies and rhythms?

CLE. Certainly.

ATH. Then let us not faint in discussing the peculiar difficulty of music. Music is more celebrated than any other kind of imitation, and therefore requires the greatest care of them all. For if a man makes a mistake here, he may do himself the greatest injury by welcoming evil dispositions, and the mistake may be very difficult to discern, because the poets are artists very inferior in character to the Muses themselves, who would never fall into the monstrous error of assigning to the words of men the intonation and song of women; nor after combining the melodies with the gestures of freemen would they add on the rhythms of slaves and men of the baser sort; nor, beginning with the rhythms and gestures of freemen, would they assign to them a melody or words which are of an opposite character; nor would they mix up the voices and sounds of animals and of men and instruments, and every other sort of noise, as if they were all one. But human poets are fond of introducing this sort of inconsistent mixture, and so make themselves ridiculous in the eyes of those who, as Orpheus says, 'are ripe for true pleasure'. The experienced see all this confusion, and yet the poets go on and make still further havoc by separating the rhythm and the figure of the dance from the melody, setting bare words to metre, and also separating the melody and the rhythm from the words, using the lyre or the aulos alone. For when there are no words, it is very difficult to recognize the meaning of the harmony and rhythm, or to see that any worthy object is imitated by them. And we must acknowledge that all this sort of thing, which aims at only swiftness and smoothness and a brutish noise, and uses the aulos and the lyre not as the mere accompaniments of the dance and song, is exceedingly coarse and tasteless. The use of either instrument, when unaccompanied, leads to every sort of irregularity and trickery. This is all rational enough. But we are considering not how our choristers, who are from thirty to fifty years of age, and may be over fifty, are not to use the Muses, but how they are to use them. And the considerations which we have urged seem to show that these fifty-years-old choristers who are to sing, will require something better than a mere choral training. For they need have a quick perception and knowledge of harmonies and rhythms; otherwise, how can they ever know whether a melody would be rightly sung to the Dorian mode, or to the rhythm which the poet has assigned to it?

CLE. Clearly they cannot.

ATH. The many are ridiculous in imagining that they know what is in proper harmony and rhythm, and what is not, when they can only be made by force to sing to the aulos and step in rhythm; it never occurs to them that they are ignorant of what they are doing. Now every melody is right when it has suitable harmony and rhythm, and wrong when unsuitable.

CLE. That is most certain.

ATH. But can a man who does not know a thing, as we were saying, know that the thing is right?

CLE. Impossible.

ATH. Then now, as would appear, we are making the discovery that our newly appointed choristers, whom we hereby invite and, although they are their own masters, compel to sing, must be educated to such an extent as to be able to follow the steps of the rhythm and the notes of the song, that they may review the harmonies and rhythms, and be able to select what are suitable for men of their age and character to sing; and may sing them, and have innocent pleasure from their own performance, and also lead younger men to receive the virtues of character with the welcome which they deserve. Having such training, they will attain a more accurate knowledge than falls to the lot of the common people, or even of the poets themselves. For the poet need not know the third point, viz. whether the imitation is good or not, though he can hardly help knowing the laws of melody and rhythm. But our critics must know all the three, that they may choose the best, and that which is nearest to the best; for otherwise they will never be able to charm the souls of young men in the way of virtue. And now the original design of the argument which was intended to show that we were wise to lend support to the chorus of Dionysus, has been accomplished to the best of our ability, and let us see whether we were right:—I should imagine that a drinking assembly is likely to become more and more tumultuous as the drinking goes on: this, as we were saying at first, will certainly be the case.

CLE. Certainly.

ATH. Every man has a more than natural elevation; his heart is glad within him, and he will say anything and will be restrained by nobody at such a time; he fancies that he is able to rule over himself and all mankind.

CLE. Quite true.

ATH. Were we not saying that on such occasions the souls of the drinkers become like iron heated in the fire, and grow softer and younger, and are easily moulded by him who knows how to educate and fashion them, just as when they were young, and that this fashioner of them is the same who prescribed for them in the days of their youth, viz. the good legislator; and that he ought to enact laws of the banquet, which, when a man is confident, bold, and impudent, and unwilling to wait his turn and have his share of silence and speech, and drinking and music, will change his character into the opposite—such laws as will infuse into him a just and noble fear, which will take up arms at the approach of insolence, being that divine fear which we have called reverence and shame?

CLE. True.

ATH. And the guardians of these laws and fellow workers with them are the calm and sober generals of the drinkers; and without their help there is greater difficulty in fighting against drink than in fighting against enemies when the commander of an army is not himself calm; and he who is unwilling to obey them, and the commanders of Dionysiac feasts who are more than sixty years of age, shall suffer a disgrace as great as he who disobeys military leaders, or even greater.

CLE. Right.

ATH. If, then, drinking and amusement were regulated in this way, would

21

not the companions of our revels be improved? they would part better friends than they were, and not, as now, enemies. Their whole intercourse would be regulated by law and observant of it, and the sober would be the leaders of the drunken.

CLE. I think so too, if drinking were regulated as you propose.

ATH. Let us not then simply censure the gift of Dionysus as bad and unfit to be received into the State. For wine has many excellences, and one pre-eminent one, about which there is a difficulty in speaking to the many, from a fear of their misconceiving and misunderstanding what is said.

CLE. To what do you refer?

ATH. There is a tradition or story, which has somehow crept about the world, that Dionysus was robbed of his wits by his stepmother Hera, and that out of revenge he inspires Bacchic furies and dancing madnesses in others; for which reason he gave men wine. Such traditions concerning the Gods I leave to those who think that they may be safely uttered; I only know that no animal at birth is mature or perfect in intelligence; and in the intermediate period, in which he has not yet acquired his own proper sense, he rages and roars without rhyme or reason; and when he has once got on his legs he jumps about without rhyme or reason; and this, as you will remember, has been already said by us to be the origin of music and gymnastic.

CLE. To be sure, I remember.

ATH. And did we not say that the sense of harmony and rhythm sprang from this beginning among men, and that Apollo and the Muses and Dionysus were the Gods whom we had to thank for them?

CLE. Certainly.

ATH. The other story implied that wine was given man out of revenge, and in order to make him mad; but our present doctrine, on the contrary, is, that wine was given him as a balm, and in order to implant modesty in the soul, and health and strength in the body.

CLE. That, stranger, is precisely what was said.

ATH. Then half the subject may now be considered to have been discussed; shall we proceed to the consideration of the other half?

CLE. What is the other half, and how do you divide the subject?

ATH. The whole choral art is also in our view the whole of education; and of this art, rhythms and harmonies form the part which has to do with the voice.

CLE. Yes.

ATH. The movement of the body has rhythm in common with the movement of the voice, but gesture is peculiar to it, whereas song is simply the movement of the voice.

CLE. Most true.

ATH. And the sound of the voice which reaches and educates the soul, we have ventured to term music.

CLE. We were right.

ATH. And the movement of the body, when regarded as an amusement, we termed dancing; but when extended and pursued with a view to the excellence of the body, this scientific training may be called gymnastic.

CLE. Exactly.

ATH. Music, which was one half of the choral art, may be said to have been completely discussed. Shall we proceed to the other half or not? What would you like?

CLE. My good friend, when you are talking with a Cretan and a Lacedae-monian, and we have discussed music and not gymnastic, what answer is either of us likely to make to such an inquiry?

ATH. An answer is contained in your question; and I understand and accept what you say not only as an answer, but also as a command to proceed with gymnastic.

CLE. You quite understand me; do as you say.

ATH. I will; and there will not be any difficulty in speaking intelligibly to you about a subject with which both of you are far more familiar than with music.

CLE. There will not.

ATH. Is not the origin of gymnastics, too, to be sought in the tendency to rapid motion which exists in all animals; man, as we were saying, having attained the sense of rhythm, created and invented dancing; and melody arousing and awakening rhythm, both united formed the choral art?

CLE. Very true.

ATH. And one part of this subject has already been discussed by us, and there still remains another to be discussed?

CLE. Exactly.

ATH. I have first a final word to add to my discourse about drink, if you will allow me to do so.

CLE. What more have you to say?

ATH. I should say that if a city seriously means to adopt the practice of drinking under due regulation and with a view to the enforcement of temperance, and in like manner, and on the same principle, will allow of other pleasures, designing to gain the victory over them—in this way all of them may be used. But if the State makes drinking an amusement only, and whoever likes may drink whenever he likes, and with whom he likes, and add to this any other indulgences, I shall never agree or allow that this city or this man should practise drinking. I would go farther than the Cretans and Lacedaemonians, and am disposed rather to the law of the Carthaginians, that no one while he is on a campaign should be allowed to taste wine at all, but that he should drink water during all that time, and that in the city no slave, male or female, should ever drink wine; and that no magistrates should drink during their year of office, nor should pilots of vessels or judges while on duty taste wine at all, nor anyone who is going to hold a consultation about any matter of importance; nor in the day-time at all, unless for the purpose of training or as medicine; nor again at night, when anyone, either man or woman, is minded to get children. There are numberless other cases also in which those who have good sense and good laws ought not to drink wine, so that if what I say is true, no city will need many vineyards. Their husbandry and their way of life in general will follow an appointed order, and their cultivation of the vine will be the most limited and the least common of their employments. and this, stranger, shall be the crown of my discourse about wine, if you agree.

CLE. Excellent: we agree.

Additional Reading

Abert, Hermann. *Die Lehre vom Ethos in der griechischen Musik.* Leipzig, 1899.

Anderson, Warren D. *Ethos and Education in Greek Music.* Cambridge, Mass., 1966.

Jaeger, Werner. *Paideia: the Ideals of Greek Culture.* 3 vols, New York, 1939-44.

Lippman, Edward A. *Musical Thought in Ancient Greece.* New York, 1964.

Lodge, Rupert C. *Plato's Theory of Art.* London, 1953.

The Dialogues of Plato. Tr. B. Jowett. 4th ed. 4 vols. Oxford, 1953.

PART TWO

Medieval Musical Philosophy

A theoretical treatise on music in Antiquity often contained a final section devoted to the musical aspect of number and nature, a field we now would call speculative theory, as opposed to the technical theory that preceded it. Augustine takes up this tradition in his *De musica*, devoting the sixth book, however, to considerations that are as much theological as metaphysical. This apparently novel character is accounted for by his conversion to Christianity. The work was begun in 387 in Milan, but the sixth book written in 391 in Africa, after his baptism. The classical poetry that served as a reference in the earlier books is replaced by a hymn verse in the final one, and the preceding technical treatise is even explicitly referred to as an undertaking of little value. Yet the liberal arts are retained in the new Christian outlook; if they are not really demanded for the comprehension of the scriptures they are at least needed to refute heretics; but conceived as a preparation for theology rather than for philosophy, their value was unmistakably slighter and they were dispensable instead of essential. The trivium fared better than the quadrivium in this transformation, for the importance of rhetoric was as great in theological disputation as it had been in the philosophical and political argumentation of Antiquity. It was the practical treatise on music—the study of composition and performance—that was related to the trivium, and thus to the ends of persuasion and morality and ethics. But theoretical treatises were also not devoid of an ethical character, at least in the case of music, which was regularly singled out as the one quadrivial study of which this was true (although astronomy, especially since it often included considerations of music—in a cosmic connection—also contained an ethical motif).[1] But the identification of truth with God intensifies the ethical force of Augustine's musical speculation, and indeed the sixth book as a whole becomes an ascent from the corporeal to the eternal rather than a neutral description of the arithmetic and cosmic nature of music.

This ascent is obviously very close to those described in Platonism and Neoplatonism, yet there seem to be significant differences. The Christian version devalues the role of sensible beauty, which always has an equivocal status in any tradition shaped or touched by Platonism. Although the empirical world continues to provide a path to the supernal, it also encumbers the soul and draws it downward in the patristic conception; it often represents evil rather than a lesser degree of beauty. But there is another feature of Augustine's thought that seems almost the opposite of his ethical intensification, and that is the objectivity of his description of the process of perception, of the physiology and psychology of hearing, which relates him to the pagan tradition of science. In this respect as in others there

---

[1] See my article on "The Place of Music in the System of Liberal Arts," which is listed in the bibliography for this section.

is a close resemblance to Plato's *Timaeus*. It is as though Augustine demonstrates God by science, as though science leads him to God.

The first five books of *De musica* comprise a treatise on rhythmics and metrics; Augustine intended to write a complementary treatise on harmonics, the third division of the technical theory of music, but he never did so, perhaps because his conversion made the liberal arts less important to him, and perhaps also because he had passed beyond the stage of propaedeutic interests. He was in any event concerned more with time than with space, and this concern is fully expressed in the last book of the *De musica*, which deals with the temporal aspect of number and thus with proportions of duration rather than with proportions of length or with the spatial aspects of cosmic harmony, both of which topics are found in the final section of treatises on harmonics.

In books X and XI of the *Confessions* Augustine returns to problems of memory and time, and these books are consequently a natural complement of the last book of *De musica*. The approach has changed somewhat; it has become subjective rather than objective, or what we would now call, doubtless with greater precision, phenomenological. Augustine no longer stands outside the processes of perception and consciousness; instead he seeks to describe the contents of consciousness in their own terms. And the religious motivation has become more fervent; Augustine's power of subtle and sensitive analysis is compounded with deep feeling.

The musical views of Augustine are very different, then, from what we would normally think of as aesthetic. Not that aesthetics, considered now in its self-conscious development, is not ultimately connected with metaphysics and ethics, but that it is more closely focussed on the properties of sensible appearance in its own right, and on the feelings related to these properties. Augustine's view—indeed the musical outlook of Antiquity and of the Middle Ages in general—is less restricted, more broadly philosophical. His deliberations in the last book of his *De musica*, which are really a temporal version of the metaphysics of harmony, belong to the speculative theory of music, which is an aspect of quadrivial science, or of "natural philosophy." Such a study, fused with philosophy in Plato and with theology in Augustine, has little direct connection with musical practice, while musical ethics (which as we have seen in Plato's *Laws*, was closely connected with aesthetic properties) involved the specific ethical values of the various modes and rhythms, and the morally good and bad, and clearly rested on the concrete practices of composition and performance. There is a short section (par. 33) in Book X of the *Confessions* in which Augustine deals with the problematical field of music rather than with musical theory. His sensitivity to sensuous beauty, here experienced with compelling immediacy, subjects him to a powerful attraction that conflicts with an appreciation of the meaning of the sung text, and he remains torn between the two very different demands, unable to reconcile them:

Thus I fluctuate between peril of pleasure and approved wholesomeness; inclined the rather (though not as pronouncing an irrevocable opinion) to approve of the usage of singing in the church; that so by the delight of the ears the weaker minds may rise to the feeling of devotion. Yet when it befalls me to be more moved with the voice than the words sung, I confess to have sinned penally, and then had rather not hear music.

Music can somehow stir up the various affections of the spirit, and in this way, it would seem, kindle in the mind a more religious and ardent flame of devotion than spoken words alone. But the correct relationship between melody and words is a precarious one. Augustine conceives it in terms of body and soul. The melody is a contentment of the flesh that enervates the mind; it is often beguiling, the sense not going along with the reason in such a way as to come behind it patiently, but even though it has gained admission for the sake of reason, striving to run ahead and be the leader. Should music be banished from the church entirely? Augustine wonders (seeming almost to echo Plato), or should it be restricted to a simple style that is closer to speech than to song?

If the theory of music is a powerful adjunct of philosophy and theology, music in its sounding actuality is a far less tractable instrument, for it contains a power for harm as well as for good.

CHAPTER TWO

AUGUSTINE

De musica VI
(391)

BOOK SIX

*The mind is raised from the consideration of changeable numbers in inferior things
to unchangeable numbers in unchangeable truth itself.*

Chapter I

(1) *Master.* We have delayed long enough and very childishly, too,
through five books, in those number-traces belonging to time-intervals. And
let's hope a dutiful labor will readily excuse our triviality in the eyes of
benevolent men. For we only thought it ought to be undertaken so
adolescents, or men of any age God has endowed with a good natural
capacity, might with reason guiding be torn away, not quickly but gradually,
from the fleshly senses and letters it is difficult for them not to stick to, and
adhere with the love of unchangeable truth to one God and Master of all
things who with no mean term whatsoever directs human minds. And so,
whoever reads those first books will find us dwelling with grammatical and
poetical minds, not through choice of permanent company, but through
necessity of wayfaring. But when he comes to this book, if, as I hope and
pray, one God and Lord has governed my purpose and will and led it to what
it was intent upon, he will understand this trifling way is not of trifling value,
this way we, too, not very strong ourselves, have preferred to walk, in
company with lighter persons, rather than to rush with weaker wings
through the freer air. So, as far as I can see, he will judge either we haven't

31

sinned at all or very little, if only he is of the number of spiritual men. For if by chance the other crowd from the schools, with tumultuous tongues taking vulgar delight in the noise of rhythm-dancers, should chance upon these writings, they will either despise all or consider those first five books sufficient. But this one the very fruit of those is found in, they will either throw aside as not necessary, or put off as over and above the necessary. But, brother-fashion, I warn those others not educated to understand these things, if, steeped in the sacraments of Christian purity and glowing with the highest charity for the one and true God, they have passed over all these childish things, for fear they descend to them and, having begun to labor here, bewail their backwardness, not knowing they can pass over difficult roads and obstacles in their path, even if unknown, by flying. But, if those read who because of infirm or untrained steps cannot walk here, having no wings of piety to disregard and fly by these things with, let them not mix themselves up with an improper business, but nourish their wings with the precepts of the most salutary religion and in the nest of the Christian faith, and carried over by these let them leave behind the labor and dust of this road, more intent on the fatherland itself than on these tortuous paths. For these books are written for those who, given up to secular letters, are involved in great errors and waste their natural good qualities in vanities, not knowing what their charm is. And if they would notice it, they would see how to escape those snares, and what is the place of happiest freedom.[a]

Chapter 2

(2) And so you, my friend, sharing reason with me, that we may pass from corporeal to incorporeal things, tell me if you will, when we recite this verse, *Deus creator omnium*, where you think the four iambs and twelve times are it consists of. Is it to be said these numbers are only in the sound heard or also in the hearer's sense belonging to the ears, or also in the act of the reciter, or, because the verse is known, in our memory too?

Disciple. In all of them, I think.

M. Nowhere else?

D. I don't see what else there is, unless, perhaps, there is some interior and superior power these proceed from.

M. I am not asking for what is to be merely suspected. And so if these four kinds are so apparent to you, you see no others equally evident, then let us

---

[a]Because of the passages of Letters 101 to Memorius, Marrou conjectures that this first chapter of Book 6 a self-sufficient unit. For this was the only Book he sent to Memorius. *Sextum sane librum quem emendatum reperi, ubi est omnis fructus caeterorum, non distuli mittere Charitati tuae* (*Epist.* 101.4). See Marrou, *St. Augustin et la fin de la culture antique* (*Bibl. des Ecoles d'Athènes et de Rome*, cvix, 1939) 580-83. (Annotations are from the Taliaferro translation.)

look at them, if you will, separately one by one and see whether any one of them can be without any other. For I am sure you won't deny the possibility of a sound's beating the air by the drop of liquid or the shock of bodies, with pauses and limits of this sort, and existing where no hearer is present. And when this takes place, of the four there is only this first kind where the sound has the numbers.

D. I don't see any other.

(3) M. What about this other kind in the sense of the hearer? Can it be if nothing sounds? For I am not asking whether the ears have, if something sounds, a power [vis] of perceiving they don't lack even if the sound is wanting. For, even when there is a silence, they differ somewhat from deaf ears. But I am asking whether they have the numbers themselves, even if nothing is sounding. For it is one thing to have the number, another to be able to sense the harmonious sound. For if you should touch with your fingers a sentient place in the body, the number of times it's touched is sensed by the sense of touch. And when it is sensed, the sensor possesses it. But it is likewise a question whether, not the sensing, but the number is in the sensor, when nothing is touching.

D. I couldn't easily say the sense is lacking in such numbers determined in themselves, even before anything sounds; otherwise it would neither be charmed by their harmony nor offended by their absurdity. And so, whatever it is we either approve or disapprove by when something sounds, when we do so not by reason but by nature, that I call the number of the sense. For this power of approval and disapproval is not created in my ears, when I hear the sound. The ears are certainly not otherwise accessible to good sounds than to bad ones.

M. Watch out you don't confuse the following two things. For, if any verse is sometimes pronounced shorter, sometimes longer, it cannot occupy the same interval of time, although the same ratio of feet may be preserved. And so, pleasing the ears by its peculiar kind of harmony is the doing of that power we accept harmonious things and reject disagreeable ones by. But its being perceived in a shorter time when it is spoken more quickly than when it is spoken more slowly makes no difference except how long the ears are touched by sound. So this affection of the ears when they are touched with sound is in no way such as if they should not be so touched. For as hearing differs from not hearing, so hearing this tone differs from hearing another. Therefore, this affection is neither prolonged beyond nor restrained to less, since it is the measure of the sound producing it. So it is one thing in the iamb, another in the tribrach, longer in the longer iamb, shorter in the shorter, nothing in a rest. And if it is produced by an harmonious sound, it must be harmonious. Nor can it be except when its author, the sound, is present; for it is like a trace imprinted in water, not found before your pressing a body into it, and not remaining when you have taken it away. But the natural power, belonging to the judiciary, you might say, present in the ears, is still there during the rest, and the sound does not bring it into us, but is rather received by it to be approved of or disapproved of. And so, if I am not mistaken, these two must be distinguished, and it must be admitted the numbers in the passion of the ears when something is heard are brought in by the sound and taken away by the rest. And it is inferred the numbers in the sound itself can be without those in the hearing, although these last cannot be without the first.

Chapter 3

(4) D. I agree.

M. Notice, then, this third kind, being in the practice and operation of the person pronouncing, and see whether these numbers can be without those in the memory. For silent within ourselves we can also by thinking go through certain numbers in the amount of time they would be gone through by the voice. It is evident these are in a certain operation of the mind which, since it produces no sound and visits no passion on the ear, shows this kind of number can be without the other two, namely, the one in the sound, the other in the hearer when he hears. But we ask if it would be without the memory's accompanying it. Yet, if the soul produces the numbers we find in the beat of the veins, the question is solved. For it is clear they are in the operation and we are no whit helped with them by the memory. And if it is not sure in the case of these whether they belong to the soul operating, certainly about those we produce in recurrent breathing, there is no doubt there are numbers in its time-intervals, and the soul so operates them they can also be changed in many ways when the will is applied. Nor is there need of any memory for their production.

D. It seems to me this kind of number can be without the other three. For, although I don't doubt the various veinbeats and respiration-intervals are created for the equilibrium [temperatio] of bodies, yet who would so much as deny they are created by the soul in operation? And if the flow, according to the diversity of bodies, is faster for some, slower for others, yet, unless there is a soul to produce it, there is none.

M. Consider, too, the fourth class, that is, the class of those numbers in the memory. For, if we draw them out by recollection, and, when we are carried away to other thoughts, we again leave them as if hidden in their own hiding places, I don't think it is difficult to see they can be without the others.

D. I don't doubt they can be without the others. But just the same, unless they were heard or thought, they could not be sent on to the memory. And so, although they remain at the death of those that are heard or thought, yet they are imprinted by them.

34

Chapter 4

(5) *M.* I don't contradict you, and I should like now to ask which of these four kinds you judge the principal one. Except, I believe, while we were discussing these things, a fifth kind appeared from somewhere, a kind in the natural judgment of perceiving when we are delighted by the equality of numbers or offended at a flaw in them. For I am mindful of your opinion our sense could have in no way done this without certain numbers latent in it. Or do you, perhaps, think a great power like this belongs to some one of those four?

D. On the contrary. I think this kind is to be distinguished from all of them. For it is one thing to sound and this is attributed to a body; another to hear, and in the body the soul is passive to this from sounds; another to produce numbers either more slow or less so; another to remember them; and another, by accepting or rejecting, to give sentence on them all as if by some natural right.

(6) *M.* Come, now, tell me which if these five is the most excellent.

D. The fifth, I think.

M. You are right, for, unless it excelled, it could not bring judgment on them. But again, I want to know of the other four which you judge the greatest.

D. The kind in the memory, certainly. For I see those numbers are of greater duration than when they sound or are heard or are produced.

M. Then you prefer things made to things making. For you said a while ago those in the memory are imprinted by the others.

D. I should rather not prefer them. But still, how can I not prefer those of greater duration to those of less, I don't see.

M. Don't let this disturb you. For not as eternal things to temporal are those decaying through a longer time to be preferred to those passing away in a shorter time. Because one day's sanity is to be preferred to many days' folly. And if we compare desirable things, one day's reading is better than many days' writing, if the same thing is read in one day, written in many. So numbers in the memory, although they remain longer than those they are imprinted by, yet it is not proper to prefer them to those we cause, not in the body, but in the soul. For they both pass away, one by cessation, others by forgetting. But those we operate seem to be snatched from us, even though we have not yet stopped, by the succession of those immediately following, when the first by disappearing give place to the second, the second to the third, and continuously those before to those after, until a complete stop destroys the last. But in the case of forgetting, several numbers are wiped away together, even though by degrees. For they do not remain entire for any time. For what is not found in the memory after a year, for instance, is also already less after a day's time. But this decrease is not sensed, yet it is not

35

therefore falsely conjectured. Because the whole does not disappear suddenly the day before the year is finished, and so the understanding grants it begins to lapse from the time it comes into the memory. That is why we often say, 'I vaguely remember,' whenever we repeat something, recalling it after a time before its complete destruction. And, therefore, both these kinds of numbers are mortal. But things making are by right preferred to those made.

D. I accept and approve.

(7) M. Now, then, consider the other three, and explain which of them is the best, and so to be preferred to the others.

D. That's not easy. For, according to the rule things making are to be preferred to those made, I am forced to give the prize to the sounding numbers. For, when we hear we sense them, and when we sense them we are passive to them. And so, these last make those others existing in the ear's affection when we hear, but, again, these we have by sensing produce in the memory others they are rightly preferred to, since they are produced by them. But here, because sensing and remembering both belong to the soul, I am not disturbed if I should prefer something produced in the soul to something else likewise produced in it. But I am disturbed how the sounding numbers, certainly corporeal or somehow in a body, are to be considered of more worth than those found in the soul when we sense. And yet, again, it is disturbing how these last are not rather to be more highly considered since they make, and the others are made by them.

M. Be rather amazed at the body's being able to make anything in the soul. For it could not, perhaps, if the body the soul used to animate and govern without trouble and with the greatest ease, changed for the worse by the first sin, were not subject to death and corruption. And yet, it has a beauty of its own, and in this way it sets its dignity off to fair advantage in the eyes of the soul! And neither its wound nor its disease has deserved to be without the honor of some ornament. And the highest Wisdom of God designed to assume this wound, by means of a wonderful and ineffable sacrament, when He took upon Himself man without sin, but not without the condition of sin. For He was willing to be humanly born, to suffer, and to die. None of these things was accomplished by our merit, but by this most excellent goodness, in order we might rather look to the pride we most deservingly fell into those things by, than to the humiliations He undeservingly suffered, and so with calm mind we might pay the death owed, if He, too, was able to bear it unowed on our account, and anything else more secret and more atoned for in such a sacrament to be understood by saintly and more holy people. And so it is not surprising a soul operating in mortal flesh feels the passion of bodies. And not because it is better than the

36

body ought all taking place in it be considered better than all taking place in the body. I suppose you think the true is to be preferred to the false.

D. Who wouldn't.

M. But what we see in our sleep isn't a tree?

D. Not at all.

M. But its form is in the soul. And the form of what we now see has been made in the body. And so, since the true is better than the false, and although the soul is better than the body, the true in the body is better than the false in the soul. But as the latter is better in so far as it is true, not in so far as it is made in the body, so the former is worse in so far as it is false, not in so far as it is made in the soul. Have you anything to say about this?

D. Nothing, certainly.

M. Listen, then, to this other thing, nearer to the mark, I believe, than 'better.' For you won't deny what is proper is better than what is not proper.

D. I certainly admit that.

M. But no one doubts a man would be improper in the same clothes a woman would be proper in.

D. That's evident.

M. Well, then, it isn't to be greatly wondered at, is it, if this form of numbers is proper in the sounds falling on the ears, and improper in the soul when it has them by sensing and being passive?

D. I don't think so.

M. Why, then, do we hesitate to prefer sounding and corporeal numbers to those made by them, even though they are made in the soul which is better than the body? Because we are preferring numbers to numbers, producers to produced, not the body to the soul. For bodies are the better the more harmonious [numerosiora] they are by means of these numbers. But the soul is made better through lack of those numbers it receives through the body, when it turns away from the carnal senses and is reformed by the divine numbers of wisdom. So it is truly said in the Holy Scriptures, 'I have gone the rounds, to know and consider and seek wisdom and number.'[b] And you are in no way to think this was said about those numbers shameful theaters resound with, but about those, I believe, the soul does not receive from the body, but receiving from God on high it rather impresses on the body. And what kind of thing this is, is not to be considered in this place.

Chapter 5

(8) But, lest it turn out the life of a tree is better than our own, because it doesn't receive numbers from the body by sensing (for it has no sense), it

[b]Eccle. 7.26.

must be carefully considered if there is really nothing called hearing unless something is produced in the soul by the body. But it is very absurd to subordinate the soul like a matter to the body as an artisan. For the soul is never inferior to the body, and all matter is inferior to the artisan. The soul, then, is in no way a matter subordinated to the body as an artisan. But it would be, if the body worked numbers in it. Therefore, when we hear, numbers are not made in the soul by those we know in sounds. Or do you think otherwise?

D. What happens, then, when a person hears?

M. Whatever it is—and perhaps we cannot find or explain it—it won't result, will it, in our denying the soul's being better than the body? And when we admit this, can we subordinate it to the body working and imposing numbers, so the body is an artisan but the soul a matter something harmonious is made from and in? And, if we believe this, we must believe the soul is inferior to the body. And what more miserable and detestable thing than this can be believed? And since things are thus, I shall try as much as God will help me to conjecture at and discuss whatever lies there. But if, because of the infirmity of either or both of us, the result should be less that we wish, either we ourselves shall investigate it at another time when we are less agitated, or we shall leave it to more intelligent people to examine, or, unworried, we shall leave it unsolved. But we must not for that reason let these other more certain things slip from our hands.

D. I shall hold that as unshaken if I can, and yet I shouldn't wish that secret place to remain impenetrable to us.

(9) M. I shall say right away what I think. But you must either follow or go ahead of me, if you can, when you see me stop and hesitate. For I think the body is animated by the soul only to the purpose of the doer. Nor do I think it is affected in any way by the body, but it acts *through* it and *in* it as something divinely subjected to its dominion. But at times it acts with ease, at times with difficulty, according as, proportionately to its merits, the corporeal nature yields more or less to it. And so, whatever corporeal things are taken into this body or come into contact with it from without, have in the body itself, not in the soul, some effect either opposed to its operation or agreeing with it. And so, when it fights the body's opposition and with difficulty throws the matter subjected to it into the ways of its operation, it becomes more attentive to the actions because of the difficulty. And this difficulty on account of the attention, when not unobserved, is called feeling, and this is named pain or trouble. But when what is taken in or touches it easily agrees, all that or as much as is necessary is projected into the course of its operation. And this action of the soul by which it joins its body to an outside body harmonizing with it, since it is accomplished more attentively because of an unusualness, is not unobserved, but because of the harmony is felt with

38

pleasure. But when those things the soul uses to mend the wear and tear in the body are lacking, need follows. And when the soul becomes more attentive on account of the difficulty of the action and this operation does not pass unobserved, then this is called hunger or thirst or some such thing. But when there is a superfluity of things taken in, from the burden of these is born a difficulty of operation and an awareness accompanies the issue. And since this action does not pass unobserved, indigestion is felt. It also operates with attention when it gets rid of the superfluity; if smoothly, with pleasure; if roughly, with pain. The soul also occupies itself attentively with any sickly disturbance of the body, desiring to succor it as it declines and disintegrates. And when this action does not pass unobserved, it is said to feel sickness and illness.

(10)   In short, it seems to me the soul, when it has sensations in the body, is not affected in any way by it, but it pays more attention to the passions of the body. But this sense, even while we do not sense, being nevertheless in the body, is an instrument of the body directed by the soul for its ordering so the soul may be more prepared to act on the passions of the body with attention to the end of joining like things to like and of repelling what is harmful. Further, I think, it operates something luminous in the eyes, a most clear and mobile air in ears, something misty in the nose, something damp in the mouth, something earthy and muddy you might say in the touch. But whether these are put together in this way or by some other distribution, the soul acts quietly if the things within are in unity of health as if they agreed to some domestic pact. But when things affecting the body, you might say with otherness, are applied, it exerts more attentive actions accomodated to certain places and instruments. Then it is said to see or hear or smell or taste or touch. And by such actions it willingly associates proper things and resists improper ones. I think the soul, then, when it senses, produces these actions on the passions of the body, but does not receive these passions.

(11)   And so, when we now examine the numbers of sounds and the sense of hearing is called into doubt, it isn't necessary to digress any longer. Let's return, then, to the question, and see if sound causes anything in the ear. Or do you deny that it does?

D. Not at all.

M. Well, you agree ears are an animated member?

D. I do.

M. Since, then, what in this member is like air is moved when the air is moved, we don't believe, do we, the soul, with a vital motion quickening in silence the body of the ears before this sound, can either stop from the work of moving what it animates, or can move the air of the ear now moved extrinsically in the same way it moved before the sound slipped in?

D. It seems it must be in another way.

M. Then, to move it in another way, mustn't it be said to act, not to be acted on?

D. That's true.

M. So we are not absurd in believing the movements of the soul, or its actions or operations—find any easier name you can—do not escape the soul's notice when it senses.

(12)   But these operations are applied to these passions of the body either as when figures interrupt the light of our eyes, or sound enters the ears, or odors move into the nostrils, or savors to the palate, and to the rest of the body solid and bodily things; or as when something runs and crosses from place to place in the body itself; or as when the whole body is moved by its own weight or that of another. These are operations the soul applies to these passions of the body, delighting the soul when it agrees with them, offending it when it opposes them. But when it is affected by its own operations, it is affected by itself, not by the body. But clearly when it adapts itself to the body, it is less with itself, because the body is always less than it is.

(13)   And so, when the soul is turned from its God to its servant, it is necessarily deficient; but, when it is turned from its servant to its God, it necessarily progresses and furnishes its servant a very easy life, and, therefore, the least laborious and full of business, no attention being given it in its surpassing peace. Just so is the bodily affection called health. Indeed, it needs none of our attention, not because the soul then does nothing in the body, but because it does nothing more easily. For in all our operations the greater the difficulty we operate with, the more attentively we do it. But this health will be the most firm and certain when this body will have been restored to its former stability, in its own time and order. And this its resurrection is properly believed before it is fully understood. For the soul must be ruled by the superior, and rule the inferior. But God alone is superior to it, and only body is inferior to it, if you mean the soul whole and entire. And so as it cannot be entire without the Lord, so it cannot excel without a servant. But as its Lord is greater than it, so its servant is less. And so, intent on its Lord, it understands His eternal things and is greater, and its servant, too, is greater in its kind through the soul itself. But when the Lord is neglected, intent on its servant with the carnal concupiscence it is seduced by, the soul feels the movements it gives its servant, and is less; yet not so inferior as its servant, even when it is at the lowest in its own nature. But the body by this offense of its mistress is much less than it was, since she was much greater before it.

40

(14)   And so, for one now mortal and fragile, it is dominated with great difficulty and attention. And from there does this error fall upon the soul that it esteems the body's pleasure because the matter yields to its attention, more than it esteems its health needing no attention. No wonder it is involved in troubles, preferring unquiet to security. But a greater unquiet arises for one turning back to God for fear he be turned away. And it is so until the push of carnal business, excited by daily habit and inserting itself into the heart of the conversion by disorderly memories, comes to rest. When a man's movements that carry him away into outside things have been in this way quieted, then he enjoys an interior freedom of peace signified by the sabbath. So he knows God alone is his Lord, and He is served with the greatest freedom. But, although he starts those carnal movements as he wishes, he does not stop them as he wishes. For, again, the reward of sin is not in his power as sin itself is. For, indeed, this soul is a thing of great worth, and yet it doesn't remain apt for suppressing its own lascivious movements. For it sins in its strength, and by divine law made weaker after sin it is less able to undo what it has done. 'Unhappy man I am, who will deliver me from the body of this death? The grace of God through Jesus Christ our Lord.'[c] Then a movement of the soul, conserving its force and not yet extinct, is said to be in the memory. And, when the mind is intent on something else, it is as if that previous movement were not in the mind and were lost, except, before it dies away, it be renewed by some affinity of similar things.

(15)   But have you anything to say to the contrary?

D. You seem to me to say what is probable, and I shouldn't dare oppose.

M. Since, then, feeling itself is a moving the body against the movement made in it, don't you think then we do not feel when bones and nails and hair are cut, not because these are not at all alive in us, for otherwise they would neither be held together nor be fed nor grow, nor show their strength in begetting their kind. But because they are penetrated with an air less free or mobile than is necessary for the soul's causing a movement there so rapid as that movement it is against when it's said to feel. Although some such life is understood in trees and other vegetation, it is nowise proper to prefer it, not only to our own life exceeding it in reason, but also to that of brutes. For it is one thing not to sense because of very great solidity, and another not to sense because of very great health of body. For in the one case the instruments moving relatively to the passions of the body are lacking, and in the other these passions themselves are lacking.

D. I approve and agree.

[c] Rom. 7.24-25.

Chapter 6

(16) *M.* Let's get back to the problem proposed, and tell me, of the three kinds of numbers, one in the memory, the other in sensing, and another in sound, which of these seems to you the most excellent.

D. I put sound after these other two, both in the soul and in some sense living. But of these last two I am uncertain which I consider superior. But, perhaps, since we said those in action are to be preferred to those in the memory only because the ones are active and the others are caused by them, so for the same reason it is proper to prefer also those in the soul while we are listening to those in the memory caused by them. That's the way it seemed to me before.

M. I don't think your reply absurd. But since it has been argued those numbers in sensing are also operations of the soul, how do you distinguish them from those we see to be in act even when the soul in silence and not remembering performs something harmonious through intervals of time? Or do the ones belong to the soul moving itself with respect to its body, while those others inhering belong to the soul moving itself with respect to the body's passions?

D. I accept this distinction.

M. Well, do you think it acceptable those relative to the body be judged superior to those relative to the body's passions?

D. Those existing in silence seem to me to be freer than those exerted not only on the body but also on the body's passions.

M. It seems we have distinguished five kinds of numbers and ordered them in some sort of scale of merits. And if you will, we shall impose names proper to them, to avoid in the rest of our discourse using more words than things.

D. Very willingly.

M. Then let the first be named judicial, the second advancing [*progressores*], the third reacting [*occursores*],[d] the fourth memorial, the fifth sounding.

D. I understand and I am glad to use these names.

Chapter 7

(17) *M.* Come now, tell me, which of these seems to you undying, or do you think they all fall in their time and die?

D. I think the judicial alone are undying. For the others, I see, either pass away when they are made or are stricken out of the memory by forgetfulness.

---

[d]*Occursores* is here translated as 'reacting,' but with the understanding, of course, that the sounding numbers cause the reacting numbers only as something like occasional causes.

M. You are just as certain, then, of the immortality of the first as you are of the destruction of the others? Or is it proper to inquire more diligently whether they are undying?

D. Let's look into the matter thoroughly.

M. Say, then, when I pronounce a verse sometimes longer, sometimes shorter, provided I comply with the law of times putting feet in a one-two ratio, I don't offend the judgment of your senses with any kind of hitch or fraud, do I?

D. Not at all.

M. Well, but that sound, given out in shorter and, you might say, faster syllables, it can't occupy more time than it sounds, can it?

D. How can it?

M. Then, if those judicial numbers are time-bound in just the interval the sounding numbers were disposed in, can they hope to judge those other sounds based on the same iambic law, but slower?

D. In no way.

M. Then it appears those judicial numbers are not confined to a span of time.

D. It certainly appears so.

(18) *M.* You are right in agreeing. But if they are confined to no interval, then no matter how slowly I should emit iambic sounds in regular intervals, they could still be used for judging. But now, if I should say a syllable of such a stretch as three steps in walking (to make it small), and another syllable double that, and if I should order the succeeding iambs at such a pace, then the law of one to two would nevertheless be preserved. And yet we couldn't apply that natural judgment to confirming these measurements, could we?

D. I can't deny you seem right, for my opinion of the matter is very simple.

M. Then the judicial numbers are also confined to certain limits of time-spans they cannot exceed in their judgments. And whatever exceeds these intervals, they find no way to judge. And if they should be confined in this way, I do not see how they are immortal.

D. And I don't see what I can say to that. Although now I shall be less forward in presuming on their immortality, yet I do not understand how they are in this way proved mortal. For it is possible whatever intervals they can judge they can always judge, since I cannot say they are destroyed as the others by forgetfulness, or their length of time is so long as a sound's movement, or of such a stretch as reacting numbers, or as the numbers we have called advancing, impelled in time and prolonged in length. For each of these passes away with the time of its operation. But the judicial remain certainly in the nature of man, whether also in the soul I do not know, to pass judgment on things given even if varied within certain lengths, by approving harmonies in them and rejecting discords.

(19) *M.* At least you concede some men are more quickly offended by discordant numbers, some more slowly, and most judge them defective only by the comparison with sound ones on hearing them agree and disagree.

D. I agree to that.

M. Well, what do you think this difference arises from, if not from nature or practice or both?

D. That's true.

M. Then, I want to know if someone at sometime could pass judgment on and approve longer intervals than another could.

D. I believe that's possible.

M. Well, anyone who can't, if he should practice properly and should not be really dull, could, couldn't he?

D. Certainly he could.

M. But he couldn't go so far as to judge even longer intervals, comprehending in that judicial sense intervals in the ratio of one to two hours or days or months or years (for they'd at least be hindered by sleep) and approving them as iambs of motion.

D. They can't.

M. Why can't they do so? Unless it's because to each living thing in its proper kind and in its proportion with the universe is given a sense of places and times, so that even as its body is so much in proportion to the body of the universe whose part it is, and its age so much in proportion to the age of the universe whose part it is, so its sensing complies with the action it pursues in proportion to the movement of the universe whose part it is? So this world, often called in Sacred Scriptures by the name of heaven and earth, is great by containing all things whose parts being all diminished in proportion it remains just as large, or increased in proportion it still remains just as large. For nothing is large or itself in space and time-stretches, but with respect to something shorter; and again nothing is small of itself, but with respect to something larger.[e] And so, if there is attributed to human nature for the actions of carnal life a sense such that it cannot pass judgment on greater stretches of times than the intervals pertaining to the use of such a life demand, then, since this nature of man is mortal, so I think also this sense is mortal. For it is not for nothing custom is called a sort of second and fitted-on nature. But we see new senses in the judging of this kind of corporeal things, built up by custom, by another custom disappear.

---

[e]Just as the thing rhythmed was considered only as a matrix for ratios, so here the extended world is such a matrix, and so is the sensible life of man. Being then belongs more to the relations than to the relata and this doctrine will find its keystone in the Trinity where the distinction of Persons involves a certain primacy of relations. It is interesting to note in this connection that Boethius, who mentions Augustine, carefully pointed this out in his discussion of the categories of Aristotle in his *De Trinitate*.

Chapter 8

(20)   But whatever kind of thing these judicial numbers may be, they are certainly superior to any other in this, that we doubt and with difficulty find out if they are mortal. But of the other four kinds there is no question they are mortal. And although they do not embrace some members of these four classes because they have been extended beyond their laws, yet they appropriate the kinds themselves for their very consideration. For even the advancing numbers, when they seek a certain harmonious operation in the body, are modified by the secret will of the judicial numbers. For whatever restrains and keeps us from walking with unequal steps, or from beating out in unequal intervals, or from eating or drinking with uneven motions of the jaw, and from scratching with unequal motions of the nails, or to be brief, from unequal movements in any application of ourselves to doing something with our bodily members, and tacitly demands a certain equality, that very thing is something judicial, I don't know what, introducing God the builder of the animal, properly believed to be the author of all fittingness and agreement.

(21)   And these reacting numbers, brought forth certainly not according to their own will, but in virtue of the body's passions, in so far as the memory can keep their intervals, just so far they given over the judgment of the judicial are numbers and are judged. For the number consisting in time-intervals can in no way be judged by us unless we are aided in the judging by memory. For any syllable, no matter how short, since it begins and stops, has its beginning at one time and its ending at another. Then it is stretched over some little interval of time and stretches from its beginning through its middle to an end. So reason finds spatial as well as temporal intervals have an infinite division and so no syllable's end is heard with its beginning. And so, even in hearing the shortest syllable, unless memory help us have in the soul that motion made when the beginning sounded, at the very moment when no longer the beginning but the end of the syllable is sounding, then we cannot say we have heard anything. And from this it often comes about, being occupied with another thought, we do not in conversation seem to have heard even ourselves. This is not because the soul does not at that time put in motion those reacting numbers, since certainly the sound reaches the ears, and the soul cannot be idle at its body's passion and since it cannot move differently than if that passion of the body should occur, but because the impetus of the motion is immediately blotted out by the attention [*intentio*] on something else, an impetus which, if it remained, would remain in the memory so we would also know and feel we had heard. But if a rather slow mind follows not too easily what reason discovers in the case of a short syllable, in the case of two syllables there's certainly no doubt no soul can

45

hear both at the same time. For the second does not sound unless the first stops. For how can what cannot sound together be heard together? Then, as the diffusion of rays shining out into the open from tiny pupils of the eye, and belonging therefore to our body, in such a way that, although the things we see are placed at a distance, they are yet quickened by the soul, so, just as we are helped by their effusion in comprehending place-spans, the memory too, because it is somehow the light of time-spans, so far comprehends these time-spans as in its own way it too can be projected. But when a sound beats a longer time on the ears, in no way articulated and again another, double it, or equal it, is added on from some stopping place or another, then that motion of the mind, created by its attention on the past and finished sound in its transition, is repressed by its attention on the continuously succeeding sound, and so it does not remain in the memory. And so mustn't these judicial numbers be thought of as extended in a certain interval of time? For they can't judge the numbers situated in the time-spans unless the memory should come to their assistance, with the exception of the advancing numbers whose very advance they regulate. But there intervene the time-spans where we forget or remember what they judge. And so we cannot judge round or square or any other solid definite things in those bodily forms which are properly objects of the eyes, unless we turn them around to the eyes. But when one part is seen, if for that reason it should blot out what is seen in another, then the attention of the person judging would be in vain, because it, too, is accomplished in a certain time-span. And it is up to memory to see to this diversity.

(22)   But it is much more evident we judge memorial numbers by judicial when the memory itself presents them. For, if reacting numbers are judged in so far as they are presented by it, much more are those found to live in the memory itself which are brought back by memory itself as if they had been stored up by other applications of our attention. For what else do we do when we recall to memory except examine somehow what we've stored up? But a motion of the mind, not destroyed, runs back into our cogitation on the occasion of similar ones, and it's this that's called remembering. And so, either in thought alone or also in the movement of our members, we enact numbers we have already enacted sometime or other. But for that reason we know they haven't just come, but come back into our cogitation, because whenever they were being committed to memory, they were repeated with difficulty, and we needed prior practice in order to follow through. And with this difficulty overcome, when the numbers offer themselves without trouble and at will, comformably to the times and in their proper order, so easily, indeed, those inhering more forcibly come forth as if of their own will even while we are thinking of something else, we then feel they are not new. There is also another thing, I

46

think, giving us to feel the present motion of the mind has already existed at some time: that is, to recognize when we compare by an interior light of some sort the recent, and certainly more lively, movements of the action we are in the midst of when we remember, with the now more composed memorial numbers. And such knowledge is recognition and remembering. Then the memorial numbers are also judged by these judicial numbers, never alone, but along with active or reacting numbers or with both, bringing them from their hiding-places to the light, and recalling these numbers, lost before and now brought to life again. So, since the reacting numbers are judged in so far as the memory presents them to those judging, in turn the memorial numbers can be judged as the reacting numbers exhibit them. So this is the difference: for the reacting numbers to be judged, the memory presents what might be called recent traces of their flight, but when we hear and judge the memorial numbers, the same traces relive with the passage of the reacting numbers. Now, why do we need to say anything further about the sounding numbers, since, if they are heard, they are judged in the reacting numbers? But if they should where they can't be heard, who doubts they can't be judged by us? And just as in sounds with the ears as instruments, so in dancing and other visible motions, we judge, by means of these same judicial numbers with the help of the memory, whatever pertains to temporal numbers.

Chapter 9

(23)   Since things are so, let us try if we can and transcend those judicial numbers and see if there are any superior to them. Although in the case of these judicial numbers we now see a minimum of time-spans, yet they are only applied for judging those things in a time-span, and not even all such, but only those articulated memory-wise. Do you object to this?

D. The force and power of these judicial numbers moves me to the utmost. For its seems to me it's to them the functions of all the senses are referred. And so, I don't know whether among numbers any thing more excellent than these can be found.

M. There is nothing lost in our looking more carefully. For, either we shall find in the human soul superior ones, or, if it should be clear there are none in it higher, we shall confirm these to be the highest in it. For it is one thing not to be, and another not to be capable of being found either by us or any man. But I think when that verse *Deus creator omnium* we quoted is sung, we hear it through reacting numbers, recognize it through memorial numbers, pronounce it through advancing numbers, are delighted through judicial numbers, and appraise it by still others, and in accordance with these more hidden numbers we bring another judgment on this delight, a kind of judgment on the judicial numbers. Do you think it's the same thing to be delighted by sense and to appraise by reason?

D. I admit they are different. But I am disturbed first by the name. Why aren't those called judicial numbers where reason rather than where delight resides? Second, I fear this appraisal of reason is only a more diligent judgment of judicial numbers concerning themselves. Not one kind of number in delight and another in reason, but one and the same kind of number judges at one time those produced in the body when memory presents them as we just proved, and at the other times of themselves, in a purer manner and more remote from the body.

(24) M. Don't worry about names; the thing is in the meaning [potestas]. Names are imposed by convention, not by nature. But your thinking them the same and not wishing to accept them as two kinds of number—the same soul's doing both, I guess, wrings that out of you. But you must notice in advancing numbers the same soul[f] moves the body or moves to the body, and in reacting numbers the same soul goes to meet its passions, and in memorial numbers it fluctuates in motions, you might say, until they somehow subside. And so we see the motions and affections of one nature, that is, the soul, in these kinds which are necessarily enumerated and distinguished. And, therefore, if, as it is one thing to be moved to those things the body is passive to, and this is done in sensing; another, to move oneself to the body, and this is done in operating; another, to hold in the soul what is gotten from these motions, and that is to remember; so it is one thing to accept or reject these motions either when they are first produced or when revived by the memory, and this is done in the delight at the fitness or in the distaste at the absurdity of such movements or affections; and another thing to appraise whether they delight rightly or not, and this is done by reasoning—if all this is true, then we must admit these last are of two kinds just as the first are of three kinds. And, if we have been right in our judgment, the very sense of delight could not have been favorable to equal intervals and rejected perturbed ones, unless it itself were imbued with numbers; then, too, the reason laid upon this delight cannot at all judge of the numbers it has under it, without more powerful numbers. And, if these things are true, it appears five kinds of numbers have been found in the soul, and, when you add to these those corporeal numbers we have called sounding, you will see six kinds of numbers in rank and order. And now, if you will, let those that tried to take first place be called sensuous, and those found to be more excellent receive the name of judicial numbers, since that is more honorable. And again I think the name of sounding numbers ought to be changed, since, if they should be called corporeal, they will also evidently

[f]I read *eamdem animam* for *eadem animam* in Migne, an obvious misprint not in Benedictine Edition.

signify those involved in dancing and in any other visible motion. Do you approve, then, of what's been said?

D. I do. For it seems to me both true and evident. And I am willing to accept your corrections in vocabulary.

Chapter 10

(25) M. Well, now examine the force and power of reason in so far as we can examine it in its works. For reason itself, to mention the most extraordinary thing it attains in its operation, first has considered what is good mensuration, and seen it to be in a free movement, and directed it to the end of its own beauty. Then it saw there was something in the movements of bodies varying in the brevity and length of time, in so far as it was greater or less in time, and something else varying in the beat of spatial intervals in certain degrees of swiftness and slowness. After this division, it articulated into different numbers whatever was in a time-stretch by means of moderate intervals convenient to the human senses, and followed through their kinds and order to the measurements of verses. Lastly, it turned its attention to what the soul it's the head of would do in the measuring, operating, sensing, and retaining of these things. And it separated all these numbers of the soul from bodies. And it saw itself could not notice, distinguish or rightly enumerate all these things without certain numbers of its own, and it set them above the others as of an inferior order, by means of a kind of judicial appraisal.

(26) And now of its own delight, that looks so closely into the balancings of times and shows its decisions in measuring these numbers, it asks this question: 'What is it we love in sensible harmony?' Nothing but a sort of equality and equally measured intervals, isn't it so? Does the pyrrhic foot or spondaic or anapestic or dactylic or proceleusmatic or dispondaic delight us for any other reason than its comparing the one of its parts to the other by an equal division of itself? And what beauty does the iamb, trochee, or tribrach have if not the division of their greater part into two such as their lesser? And, too, do the six-time feet sound more smooth and gay except through their division according to either law: that is, either into two equal parts with three times each, or into one part single and the other double; that is, so the greater part is twice the less and is in this way divided equally by it, since the four times are measured off and cut in two by the two times? What about the five and seven-time feet? How is it they seem more adapted to prose than to verse, if not because their smaller part does not divide their larger in two? And yet, whence are they themselves admitted in the order of their own kind to the numberliness of times, if not because the smaller part also in the five-time foot has two such sub-parts as the greater has three, and in seven-

time feet the smaller three such as the greater four? So in all feet, no measuring net marks off any least part others as many as possible are not equal to.

(27) Consider in the case of feet joined together, whether this conjoining be continued on as far as one wishes as in rhythms, or whether it be restrained by some definite end as in meters, or whether it be divided into two members symmetrical to one another by some law as in verses—by what now other than equality is one foot in accord with another? And how is it the molossus' and ionic's middle syllable, a long one, can be divided, not by division, but by the will of the person reciting and beating time, into two equal moments, so even the whole foot is in harmony with each three-time part when it is added to others divided in the same way? Isn't it only because the law of equality dominates, that is, because it's equal to its sides, each of two times, and it itself is of two times? Why can't the same thing be done in the case of the amphibrach when it is added to other four-time feet, if it isn't because an equality of this sort isn't found there, the middle syllable being double and the sides single? Why in rests isn't our sense offended by a deficiency, if not because what is due that same law of equality, although not in sound, is yet made up in spread of time?[8] Why, too, is a short syllable taken for a long one when followed by a rest—and not by convention, but by natural consideration directing the ears—if not because by the same law of

[8]There is more in this sentence than meets the eye. In the first place we have here the appearance in rhythm of the being of non-being. The rest, the absence of a sensible motion, is itself the object of the time-count and plays its role on the same level as a sensible sound. Its absence is counted by the 'spread of time' (spatium temporis). This is the forerunner of the distentio animi of the Confessions, all of which is certainly tied in with Plotinus' doctrine of tó parakoloúthema in his treatise On Time and Eternity: 'What it means then to say [time] is the accompaniment of movement . . . .' (III. 7.10.1-2), For the essential point of Plotinus' attack on Aristotle's 'Time-is-the-number-of-movement' theory is that there is something like the synthesis of the constantly recurring motions which necessitates an intellectual accompaniment of the motion. For, without this there would be no unity of the past and present, no one magnitude to be numbered. Nor can the movement itself establish its own homogeneity so that it can be said for instance that the daily motion of the heavens is always equal to itself. It is the intellectual accompaniment which in view of equality considers one or another cyclic movement in the sensible world as equal one cycle to another and so perceives an order there. 'For on the one hand one will refer a body moving for such and such a time to the [uniform] movement of such and such magnitude (for it is the principle) and to its time. But the time of this movement, on the other hand, one will refer to the movement of the soul which divides out the equal intervals' (Enn. III. 7.13.58-62). So in mechanical theories the choice of equal motions is made with a view to the convenient ordering of all the others. One should hasten to add this does not reduce time to a purely psychological being. Any thing perceived by an act of the intellect is an object in its own right.

It is not too far-fetched, perhaps, to consider along with these texts of Plotinus and Augustine a text of Aristoxenus: 'It is clear that the comprehending of melody is the accompanying with hearing and understanding of the notes gone by in their every difference (For melody like the other parts of music is in becoming) . . . For the comprehension of music consists of these two, sensing and memory. For we must sense what is becoming and remember the become. There is no other way to follow the things of music' (Harmonica II 38, 29-39.3).

equality we are prevented, in a longer time-span, from forcing the sound into a shorter time? And so the nature of hearing and passing over in silence allows the lengthening of a syllable beyond two times: so what is also filled with rest can be filled with sound. But for a syllable to occupy less than two times, with a span left and rests at will, is a sort of deception of equality, because there can be no equality in less than two. And finally in the case of that equality of members, the circuits the Greeks call *períodoi* are varied by and verses are formed by, how is a return made somehow to the same equality unless the members joined together as unequals be found to have a force of equality so that in the circuit the shorter member harmonize in beat with the greater by equal feet, and in the verse by a more subtle consideration of numbers?

(28)   And so reason wonders and asks the sensuous delight of the soul which reserves to itself the judicial role whether, when an equality in the number of time-spans pleases it, any two short syllables one hears are really equal, or could it be one of them is pronounced longer, not to the long syllable's measure, but a little under, yet enough to exceed its like. You can't deny this is possible, can you, when the soul's delight does not sense these differences, but delights in unequals as equals? And what is worse than this error and inequality? And so we are advised to turn away from the enjoyment of things imitating equality. For we cannot perceive whether they perfectly fill out their time, although we can perhaps perceive they do not perfectly do so. And yet in so far as they imitate we cannot deny they are beautiful in their kind and order.

Chapter 11

(29)   Let's not, then, be envious of things inferior to ourselves, and let us, our Lord and God helping, order ourselves between those below us and those above us, so we are not troubled by lower, and take delight only in higher things. For delight is a kind of weight in the soul. Therefore, delight orders the soul. 'For where your treasure is, there will your heart be also.'[h] Where delight, there the treasure; where the heart, there happiness or misery. But what are the higher things, if not those where the highest unchangeable undisturbed and eternal equality resides? Where there is no time, because there is no change, and from where times are made and

---

The doctrine of Augustine certainly starts with these same terms and insights. Obviously, the doctrine of creation *ex nihilo* and of the Incarnation will force him to more intellectualist conclusions. See Guitton, *Le temps et l'éternité chez Plotin et St. Augustin* (Paris 1933), which, however, does not treat the problem profoundly enough.
[h]Matt. 6.21.

ordered and changed, imitating eternity as they do when the turn of the heavens comes back to the same state, and the heavenly bodies to the same place, and in days and months and years and centuries and other revolutions of the stars obey the laws of equality, unity, and order. So terrestrial things are subject to celestial, and their time circuits join together in harmonious succession for a poem of the universe.

(30)   And so many of these things seem to us disordered and perturbed, because we have been sewn into their order according to our merits, not knowing what beautiful thing Divine Providence purposes for us. For, if someone should be put as a statue in an angle of the most spacious and beautiful building, he could not perceive the beauty of the building he himself is a part of. Nor can the soldier in the front line of battle get the order of the whole army. And in a poem, if syllables should live and perceive only so long as they sound, the harmony and beauty of the connected work would in no way please them. For they could not see or approve the whole, since it would be fashioned and perfectly by the very passing away of these singulars. So God has ordered the man who sins as vicious, but not viciously. For he has been made vicious by will, thus losing the whole he who obeyed God's precepts possessed, and has been ordered in part so who did not will to fulfill the law has been fulfilled by the law. But whatever is fulfilled by the law is also fulfilled justly; and whatever justly is not fulfilled viciously, because so far as he is man he is something good. But whatever is unchaste in so far as it is unchaste is a bad work. But man for the most part is born of unchastity, that is to say, from man's bad work, God's good work.

(31)   And so, to return to the subject all this was said for, these numbers are pre-eminent by virtue of the beauty of ratio. And if we were absolutely separated from them, then, whenever we should be disposed to the body, the advancing numbers would not alter the sensuous numbers. But by moving bodies they produce the sensible beauties of times. And so reacting numbers are also made opposed to sounding numbers. And the same soul receiving all its own motions multiplies, you might say, in itself, and makes them subject to recall. And this force it has is called memory, a great help in the everyday business of this life.

(32)   Then whatever this memory contains from the motions of the mind brought to bear on the passions of the body are called *phantasíai* in Greek. And I don't find in Latin anything I should rather call them. And the life of opinion consists in having them instead of things known and things perceived, and such a life is at the very entrance of error. But when these motions react with each other, and boil up, you might say, with various and conflicting winds of purpose, they generate one motion from another; not indeed those impressed from the senses and gotten from the reactions to the

body's passions, but like images of images, to which we give the name phantasms. For my father I have often seen I know, in one way, and my grandfather I have never seen, another way. The first of these is a phantasia, the other phantasm. The first I find in my memory, the last in that notion of my mind born of those the memory has. But it is difficult both to find out and to explain how they are born. Yet, I think, if I had never seen human bodies, I could nowise imagine them by thinking with a visible form. But what I make from what I've seen, I make by memory. Yet it's one thing to find a phantasia in the memory and another to make a phantasm out of the memory. And a power of the soul can do all these things. But it is the greatest error to hold even true phantasms for things known, although in both kinds there is that we say, not absurdly, we know, that is, we have sensed such and such things, or imagined them. After all, I am not afraid to say I had a father and a grandfather. But I should be made to say it is they themselves my mind holds in the phantasia or phantasm. But some follow their phantasms so headlong the only ground for all false opinions is to hold phantasias or phantasms for things known, known by the senses. And so let us resist them as much as we can, nor so fit our mind to them that, while our thinking is on them, we believe we see them with the understanding.

(33)   And this is why, if numbers of this kind, coming to be in a soul given over to temporal things, have a beauty of their own, yet, even though they continually effect it by passing away, this beauty is grudged by a Divine Providence born of our punishable mortality merited by God's most just law, where yet He has not so forsaken us we may not turn back and be fetched again from the delight of the carnal senses, under the spread of His merciful hands. For such a delight strongly fixes in the memory what it brings from the slippery senses. And this habit of the soul made with flesh, through carnal affection, in the Holy Scriptures is called the flesh. And it is struggling with such a mind in that apostolic sentence: 'In mind I serve the law of God, but in flesh the law of sin.'[i] But when the mind is raised to spiritual things and remains fixed there, the push of this habit is broken, too, and, being little by little repressed, is destroyed. For it was greater when we followed along with it; not altogether nothing, but certainly less when we check it. And so with a determined retreat from every wanton movement where lies the fault of the soul's essence, and with a restored delight in reason's numbers, our whole life is turned to God, giving numbers of health to the body, not taking pleasure from it; which happens when the exterior man is corrupt, even when there is a change for the better.

[i]Rom. 7.25.

Chapter 12

(34)   But the memory not only takes in the carnal motions of the mind, and we have already spoken of these numbers, but also the spiritual motions I shall now speak of briefly. For in so far as they are simpler, they demand fewer words, and the greatest possible serenity of mind. That equality we could not find sure and fixed in sensible numbers, but yet we knew shadowed and fleeting, the mind could never indeed desire unless it were known somewhere. But this could be nowhere in the spans of places and times; for those swell up and these pass away. Where, then, do you think, tell me, if possible. For you don't think it's in the forms of bodies, and you'll never dare say they are equal by pure experiment; nor in intervals of times where we do not know whether they are insensibly longer or shorter than they should be. I want to know where you think that equality is on seeing which we desire certain bodies or motions of bodies to be equal and on more careful consideration we dare not trust them.

D.   There, I think, where it is more excellent than bodies, but whether it is in the soul itself or above the soul I do not know.

(35)   M.   If, then, we look for that rhythmical or metrical art we use for making verses, do you think it possesses the numbers verses are made by?

D.   I can't suppose anything else.

M.   Whatever these numbers are, do they seem to you to pass away with the verses or to remain?

D.   To remain, certainly.

M.   Therefore, it must be agreed some things that pass away are made from some numbers that remain?

D.   Reason forces me to agree.

M.   Well, you don't think this art is other than some affection of the artisan's minds, do you?

D.   So I believe.

M.   Do you believe this affection also to be in the unskilled in this art?

D.   Nowise.

M.   And in the one having forgotten it?

D.   Not even in the one himself unskilled even though he has been skilled at some time or other.

M.   Well, if anyone reminds him by questioning, do you think those numbers return to him from the persons questioning, or he moves himself to something within his own mind whence returns to him what he had lost?

D.   I think he does it within himself.

M.   You don't think, by questioning, he could also be forcibly reminded which syllable is short or which is long if he has forgotten completely, do you? Since by an old agreement and custom of man, to some syllables a lesser, to others a greater stretch is given. For indeed if it were by nature or by discipline fixed and stable, then the learned men of our time would not have lengthened some syllables the ancients shortened, nor shortened some they lengthened.

D. I believe this can be so, since however much is forgotten can again be brought to memory by a remindful questioning.

M. I can't believe you think anyone by questioning could get you to remember what you ate a year ago.

D. I confess I couldn't, and I don't think now I could be reminded about syllables whose spans were completely forgotten.

M. Why so, except because, in the noun *Italia*, the first syllable by the will of certain men is shortened, and now by the will of others lengthened? But that one and two should not be three and that two should not be the double of one, none of the dead or living or of those to be can bring it about.

D. Evidently not.

M. What, then, if we ask very clearly all the other things pertaining to numbers the way we have with one and two, and if one were questioned, unskilled, not by forgetting, but because he had never learned? Don't you think then he could likewise know this art except for the syllables?

D. How doubt it?

M. How, then, do you think he would move himself so these numbers may be impressed on his mind, and make that affection called art? Or will the questioner give them to him?

D. I think he does it within himself this way that he understands the things asked to be true and replies.

(36) M. Come, tell me now whether these numbers under discussion seem to you to be changeable?

D. Nowise.

M. Then you don't deny they're eternal.

D. I admit it.

M. Well, is there no lingering fear some inequality won't spoil them?

D. Nothing at all is surer for me than their equality.

M. From where, then, must we believe what is eternal and unchangeable to be given the soul if not from the eternal and unchangeable God?

D. I don't see what else to believe.

M. Well, then, isn't it evident he, who under another's questioning moves himself within to God to know the unchangeable truth, cannot be reminded by any outside warning to see that truth, unless his memory hold his own same movement?

D. It's evident.

Chapter 13

(37) *M.* I wonder, then, how he falls away from the contemplation of these things to need another's recalling it to his memory. Or must the mind even when intent on it be thought to require such a return?

D. I think so.

M. Let us see, if you will, what this could be that could so incite to turn away from the contemplation of the highest and unchangeable equality. For I only see three kinds. For the mind is either intent upon something equal when it is turned away or something higher or lower.

D. There is need only to discuss two of them, for I see nothing superior to eternal equality.

M. Then, do you see anything could be equal to it and yet other?

D. I don't.

M. It only remains, then, to inquire what the lower is. But don't you think first of the soul avowing that equality to be certainly unchangeable, but knowing it itself changes from its intuiting at one time this equality and at another time something else and so following the variety of time, not found in eternal and unchangeable things, works this and that?

D. I agree.

M. Then this affection or motion of the soul by which it understands eternal things and counts temporal things below them even within itself and knows these higher things are rather to be desired than those lower, don't you think that's prudence?

D. I certainly do.

(38) *M.* Well, then, don't you think it worth pondering, at once there's not in the soul the inhering in eternal things, there's yet in it the knowing they should be inhered in?

D. I want us very much to ponder this, and I want to know how it comes about.

M. You will easily see, if you notice the things we direct the mind to most, and have the greatest care for. For I think they're those we very much love, isn't that so?

D. No others.

M. Say, then, we can only love beautiful things, can't we? For, although some people seem to love ugly things, those the Greeks commonly call *saprophíloi*, it is yet a matter of how much less beautiful they are than those things pleasing most people. For, clearly, no one loves those things whose foulness his sense is offended by.

D. It's as you say.

M. These beautiful things, then, please by number, where we have shown equality is sought. For this is found not only in that beauty belonging to the

56

ears or in the motion of bodies, but also in the very visible forms where beauty is more usually said to be. Don't you think it's only equality when equal numbers reply to equal numbers in twos, but in ones, when they have a mean place so equal intervals are kept for them on each side?

D. I certainly do.

M. What is it in light itself holding the origin of all colors (for color also delights us in the forms of bodies), what is it in light and colors we seek if not what suits the eye? For we turn away from too great a flare, and we are unwilling to face things too dark, just as also in sounds we shrink from things too loud, and do not like whispering things. And this is not in the time-intervals, but in the sound itself, the light, you might say, of such numbers, whose contrary is silence, as darkness to colors. When, then, we seek things suitable for the way of our nature and reject things unsuitable we yet know are suitable to other living things, aren't we here, too, rejoicing in some law of equality when we recognize equals allotted in more subtle ways? This can be seen in smells and tastes and in the sense of touch—and for this a long time to follow out more clearly but very easy to explore. For there's not one of these sensibles doesn't please us from equality or likeness. But where equality and likeness, there numberliness [*numerositas*]. In fact, nothing is so equal or like as one and one, isn't that so?

D. I agree completely.

(39) M. Well, didn't we persuade ourselves a while ago the soul effects these things in bodies, and doesn't suffer from bodies?

D. We did.

M. Then the love of acting on the stream of its bodily passions turns the soul away from the contemplation of eternal things, diverting its attention with the care of sensible pleasure; it does this with reacting numbers. But the love of operating on bodies also turns it away, and makes it restless; this it does with advancing numbers. The phantasias and phantasms turn it away; these it does with memorial numbers. Finally, the love of the vainest knowledge of such things turns it away; this it does with sensible numbers where lie rules of an art, as if glad in their imitation. And from these is born curiosity by its very care an enemy of peace, and in its vanity impotent over truth.

(40) But the general love of action turning away from the true arises from pride by which vice the soul has preferred imitating God to serving God. And so it is rightly written in Holy Scripture: 'The beginning of man's pride is to fall from God,'[j] and 'The beginning of all sin is pride.' What pride is could not have been better shown than where it is said: 'What does earth and ashes take pride in, since in its own life it gives up its inmost things?' For

[j]Eccli. 10. 14, 15, 9, 10.

since the soul is nothing through itself—for it would not otherwise be changeable and suffer a flight from essence—since then through itself it is nothing, but whatever it is is from God, staying in its order, it is quickened in mind and conscience by the presence of God Himself. And so it has this good inmost. And so to puff with pride is to go forth to the outermost and, we might say, to become empty, that is to be less and less. But to go forth into the outermost what is that but giving up the inmost things, that is, putting yourself away from God, not in the span of places, but in affect of mind?

(41) But that appetite of the soul is to have under it other souls; not of beasts as conceded by divine law, but rational ones, that is, your neighbors, fellows and companions under the same law. But the proud soul desires to operate on them, and as much as every soul is better than every body, just so much does the action on them seem more excellent than on bodies. But God alone can operate on rational souls, not through a body, but through Himself. But such is the state of sin that souls are allowed to act upon souls moving them by signifying by one or the other body, or by natural signs as look or nod, or by conventional signs as words. For they act with signs by commanding or persuading, and if there is any other way besides command and persuasion, souls act with or upon souls. But by rights it has come about those souls wishing to be over others command their own parts and bodies with difficulty and pain, in part being foolish in themselves, in part, oppressed by mortal members. And so with these numbers and motions souls set upon souls by, with the desire of honor and praise they are turned away from the sight of that pure and entire truth. For God alone honors the soul making it blessed in secret when it lives justly and piously before Him.

(42) The motions the soul thrusts upon those cleaving to it and servant to it, then, are like the advancing ones, for it acts as if on its own body. But those motions it thrusts out, wishing to attach some to itself or to enslave, are counted as reacting motions. For it acts as if in the senses forcing a thing moving up outside to become one with it, and a thing not able to do so to be kept out. And the memory takes in both these motions, and makes them memorial, likewise boiling up in tumultuous fashion with the phantasias and phantasms of these acts. Nor are there lacking the corresponding judicial numbers seeing what moves suitably and unsuitably in these acts, not wrongly to be called sensible, for it is by sensible signs souls act toward souls. What wonder if the soul wound up in so many and great concerns is turned away from the contemplation of the truth? And it sees it in so far as it breathes free of them. But, because it has not yet turned them out, it cannot remain there. And so it is the soul has not at once the knowledge of where it ought to be and the power to be there. Do you agree?

D. Nothing, I daresay, to the contrary.

Chapter 14

(43) M. What's left, then? Since we have considered as far as possible that stain and oppression of the soul, isn't it to see what action is divinely commanded it for its return, after purgation and forgiveness, to peace, and for its entry into the joy of its Master?

D. Yes.

M. And what more do you think there's for me to say when Holy Scripture, in so many volumes endowed with such authority and holiness, exhorts us only to love our God and Lord with all our heart, with all our soul, and with all our mind, and to love our neighbor as ourself? If, then, we refer all those motions and numbers of human action to this end, we shall certainly be cleansed. Isn't it so?

D. It certainly is, but how short this is to hear, and how hard and arduous to do.

(44) M. What, then, is easy? To love colors and voices and sweets and roses and soft bodies? It is then easy for the soul to love these things where it only desires equality and likeness, yet, considering a little more carefully, knows hardly the last shadow and trace of them? And is it difficult for the soul to love God thinking upon whom, as thoughts till then upon mean and sickly things allow, it finds these nothing unequal, nothing unlike, nothing divided in places, nothing changed in time? Or is there rather delight in throwing up a vast extent of building and passing the time in works of this kind where if the numbers please—there's nothing else—what can there be called equal and like, the discipline's reason would not laugh to scorn? And if this is so, why then does it sink from the truest height of equality to these things, and build up earthly machines in its own ruins? Was this not promised by Him who knows not to deceive? 'For my yoke,' He says, 'is light.'[k] The love of this world is more wearisome. For, what the soul seeks in it, constancy and eternity, it does not find, since the lowest beauty is finished out with the passage of things, and what there imitates constancy is thrown through the soul by the highest God. For the form [species] changeable only in time is prior to that changeable both in time and place. And just as souls have been told by the Lord what to love, so they are told through the Apostle John what not to love. 'Do not love this world,' he says' 'because all things in the world are concupiscence of the flesh, concupiscence of the eyes, and secular ambition.'[l]

(45) But what manner of man do you think this is, referring all those numbers from the body and over against the body's passions and held from

[k]Matt. 11.30.
[l]I John 2.15,16.

them by memory, not to carnal pleasure, but only to the body's health? A man referring all those numbers operating on souls bound to him or those numbers put out to bind them, and therefore sticking within the memory, not to his own proud excelling, but to the usefulness of those souls themselves? A man also using those numbers in either kind as directing, in the role of moderators and examiners of things passing in the senses, not for an idle or harmful curiosity but for a necessary approval or disapproval? Doesn't such a man work all these numbers and yet not get caught in them? For he only chooses the body's health not to be hindered, and refers all those actions to the good of that neighbor he has been bidden to love as himself in the natural tie of common right.

D. You talk of a great and very manlike man.

(46) M. It's not those numbers below reason and beautiful in their kind do soil the soul, then, but the love of lower beauty. And whenever the soul finds to love in it not only equality, concerning which we have said enough for this work, but also order, it has lost its own order. Nor yet does it depart from the order of things even at this point, and so it is whenever and however a thing is, it is highly ordered. For it is one thing to keep order and another to be kept by order. That soul keeps order that, with its whole self, loves Him above itself, that is, God and fellow souls as itself. In virtue of this love it orders lower things and suffers no disorder from them. And what degrades it is not evil, for the body also is a creature of God and is adorned in its own beauty, although of the lowest kind, but in view of the soul's dignity is lightly esteemed, just as the value of gold is degraded by a mixture with the finest silver. And so whatever numbers result from our criminal mortality, we shall not except them from the making of Divine Providence, since they are beautiful in their own kind, but let us not love them to become happy in their enjoyment. For we shall keep free of them since they are temporal, by using them well, as with a board in a flood by not throwing them aside as burdensome and not grasping them as stable. But the love of our neighbor commanded us in our most certain ascent to inhere in God and not so much to be kept by His ordering as to keep our own order firm and sure.

(47) Or perhaps the soul does not love order as even those sensible numbers attest? But how, then, is the first foot a pyrrhic, the second an iamb, the third a trochee, and so on? But in this law you will have rather told the following of reason, not of sense. Well, isn't this so of sensible numbers that when say eight long syllables take up as much time as sixteen short ones, yet the shorts look rather to be mixed with the longs? And when reason judges of sense and for it proceleusmatic feet are declared equal to the spondaic, it finds here only the power of ordering, because long syllables are only long in comparison with short syllables, and again short syllables are only short

in comparison with long. And so the iambic verse, no matter how long it's pronounced, if it does not lose the rule of one and two, does not lose its name. But that verse consisting of pyrrhic feet with the gradual lengthening of its enunciation becomes suddenly spondaic, if you consult not grammar with music. But if it is dactylic or anapestic, since longs are perceived by comparison with shorts mixed in, no matter how long its enunciation, it keeps its name. Why are additions of half feet not to be kept with the same law, in the beginning as at the end; nor all used, although fitting the same beat? Why the sometime placing of two shorts rather than one long at the end? Aren't they measured off by sense itself? Nor in these is there found an equality-number, suffering no change, but only a bond of order. It would take too long to go over all the other things like this having to do with the numbers of times. But even the senses reject visible forms, either leaning the wrong way or upside down, and like things, where it's not the inequality— for the equality of the parts remains—but the perverseness that's condemned. And finally in all our senses and works when we familiarize many unusual and therefore unpleasing things by gradual steps to our taste, we first accept them with a kind of toleration and then gladly, haven't we kept our pleasure with order, and don't we turn from them unless the first are harmoniously bound with the middle, and the middle with the last?

(48)   And so, let us put our joy neither in carnal pleasure, nor in the honors and praises of men, nor in the exploring of things touching the body from without, having God within where all we love is sure and unchangeable. And in this way it comes to be, when temporal things are present, yet are we not involved in them, and those things outside the body can be absent without sense of pain, and the body itself taken away with little or no sense of pain and brought back transformed by the death of its nature. For the soul's attention in the direction of the body contracts endless business, and the love of some special work to the neglect of universal law, a work yet inseparable from the universe of God's rule. And so who loves not the law is subject to the law.

Chapter 15

(49)   For if, for the most part, thinking intently on things incorporeal and being always what they are, we meanwhile effect temporal numbers in some bodily movement, easy and useful, by walking or singing, then they pass straight through us unnoticed, although they would not be were we not acting. And then, if, when we are occupied in our empty phantasms, likewise these, too, pass by as we act without feeling, how much more and more constantly 'when this corruptible has put on incorruption, and this mortal

has put on immortality,'ᵐ that is, to speak plainly, when God has vivified our mortal bodies, as the Apostle says,'for the spirit remaining in us.'ⁿ How much more, then, intent on one God and manifest truth, face to face, as it's said, shall we feel with no unquietness and rejoice in the numbers we move bodies by. Unless perhaps one is to believe the soul, although it can rejoice in things good through it, cannot rejoice in the things its good from.

(50)   But this action the soul, its God and Master willing, extracts itself from the love of an inferior beauty by fighting and downing its own habit that wars against it; on that point of victory within itself over the powers of this alloy from whose envious desire to entangle it, it soars to God—its support and station—isn't such an action for you called the virtue temperance?

D. I see and understand.

M. Well, when it advances along this way, now divining eternal joys nor quite grasping them, no loss of temporal things nor any death can deter it from saying to weaker fellows, can it: 'It is good I be dissolved and be with Christ; but for your sakes it is necessary to remain in the flesh'?ᵒ

D. So I think.

M. And this disposition where it fears neither adversity nor death, that can only be called fortitude, can't it?

D. I see that.

M. Now, this ordering itself, according to which it serves only one God, desires to be co-equal to only the purest souls and to have dominion only over animal and corporeal nature, what virtue do you think that is?

D. Who doesn't know that's justice?

M. Right.

Chapter 16

(51)   But now I want to know, when we decided a while ago among ourselves prudence to be the virtue the soul knows its proper station by, its ascent to it being through temperance, that is, conversion of love to God called charity, and aversion from this world attended by fortitude and justice, I want to know whether you think when it will have come to the fruit of its delight and zeal by perfect sanctification, by that perfect vivification, too, of its body, and, the swarm of phantasms wiped from its memory, will have begun to live with God Himself for God alone, when will have been fulfilled that divinely promised us in these words: 'Beloved, now we are sons of God, and it has not yet appeared what we shall be. We know when

ᵐI Cor. 15.53.
ⁿRom. 8.11.
ᵒPhil. 1.23,24.

He will have appeared we shall be like Him, since we shall see Him as He is',[p]—I want to know then whether you think these virtues we've recalled will then be there too.

D. I don't see, when those things the fight's about have passed by, how either prudence can be there, only choosing what to follow in opposition, or temperance, only turning love from things opposed, or fortitude, only bearing up under things opposed, or justice, only desiring to be equal to the most blessed souls and to master its lower nature in opposition, that is, not yet in possession of that it desires.

(52) *M.* Your reply is not absurd so far. And I don't deny it has seemed this way to certain learned men. But I, on consulting the books whose authority none surpasses, found this said, 'Taste and see, since the Lord is sweet.'[q] The Apostle Peter also puts it this way: 'If yet you have tasted, since the Lord is sweet.'[r] I think this is what is effected in those virtues purging the soul by conversion. For the love of temporal things could only be dislodged by some sweetness of eternal things. But when it has come to what is sung, 'But the sons of men will hope under the cover of your wings; they will be drunk of the abundance of your house, and you will give them to drink in a torrent of pleasure; for in you is the fountain of life,' it does not say the Lord will be sweet to taste, but you see what a flood and flow is said of the eternal fountain; even a drunkenness follows on it. And by this name is wonderfully signified, it seems to me, that forgetfulness of secular vanities and phantasms. Then the rest follows, and it says, 'In your light we shall see light. Stretch forth your mercy to those knowing you.' 'In light' is to be taken as in Christ, who is the Wisdom of God, and is often called light. When therefore it is said 'We see,' and 'knowing you,' it can't be denied there'll be prudence there. Or do you think the true good of the soul can be known where there's no prudence?

D. I now understand.

(53) *M.* Well, can there be those right in heart without justice?

D. I know justice is very often signified by this name.

M. Then isn't it that the same prophet later says when he sings, 'And your justice to those who are of right heart'?

D. Evidently.

M. Come, then, recall if you will we have already sufficiently expounded the soul lapses by pride into certain actions of its own power, and neglecting universal law has fallen into doing certain things private to itself, and this is called turning away from God.

D. I remember, certainly.

[p]I John 3.2.
[q]Ps. 33.9.
[r]I Peter 2.3.

M. When, therefore, it acts, so this never again delights it, doesn't it seem to you to fix its love in God and to live most temperately and chastely and securely away from all filth?

D. It seems to be.

M. See, then, too, how the prophet goes on saying, 'Let not the foot of pride come upon me.' For, saying 'foot' he signifies the distraction or fall, and in freedom from this the soul inheres in God and lives eternally.

D. I agree and follow.

(54) *M.* Then fortitude remains. But as temperance against the lapse in the free will, so fortitude avails against the force anyone can be broken by if less strong in the face of attackers or if wretchedly lying down. And this force is usually well signified in the Scriptures by the name of hand. Then who besides sinners try to apply this force? Well, in so far as the soul is barricaded through this very thing and secured by God's support so nothing befalls it from anywhere, it sustains an enduring and you might say impassible power called fortitude; and I think this is said when it is added, 'Nor let the hand of sinners disturb me.'[s]

(55) But whether this or something else is to be understood by these words, will you deny the soul fixed in that perfection and blessedness sees the truth, remains unspotted, suffers no harm, is subject to the one God, and rises above other natures?

D. I don't see how it can otherwise be absolutely perfect and blessed.

M. Then, either this contemplation, sanctification, impassibleness, and ordering of it are those four virtues perfected and consummated, or, not to split hairs over names when the things fit, instead of these virtues the soul in labor uses, some such powers are to be hoped for it in eternal life.

Chapter 17

(56) We have only recalled what belongs most to this present discussion, that all this is done by God's Providence He has created and rules all things through, so even the sinful and miserable soul may be moved by numbers and set numbers moving even to the lowest corruption of the flesh. And these numbers can be less and less beautiful, but they can't lack beauty entirely. But God, most good and most just, grudges no beauty whether fashioned by the soul's damnation, retreat, or perseverance. But number also begins from one, and is beautiful in equality and likeness, and bound by order. And so, whoever confesses there's no nature of any kind, but desires unity, and tries as much as it can to be like itself, and holds its salvation as a

[s]Ps. 35.8-12.

proper order in place or time or weight of body, must confess all things whatever and of any size are made from the beginning through a form equal to it and like to the riches of His goodness, by which they are joined together in charity as one and one gift from one.[t]

(57) And so that verse proposed by us, 'Deus creator omnium,' sounds with the harmony of number not only to the ears, but even more is most pleasing in truth and wholeness to the soul's sentiment. Unless, perhaps, you are moved by the stupidity, to speak mildly, of those denying anything can be made from nothing, even though God Almighty be said to have made it. Or is it rather the artisan can operate the sensible numbers of his habit by the reasonable numbers of his art, and by sensible numbers those advancing numbers, his numbers in their operation move by, and time-spans belong to; and from these again he can fashion visible forms in wood numbered with place-spans; and the nature of things serving God's will cannot make this wood from earth and other elements; and could not even make these final things from nothing? In fact the time-numbers of a tree must precede its place-numbers. For there's no stem does not in fixed time-measures spring up to replace its seed, germinate, break out into the air, unfold its leaves, become strong, and bring back either fruit or, by very subtle numbers of the wood itself, the force of the seed. And how much more the bodies of animals where the placing of the members presents a much more numbered equalness to sight. Can these be made of the elements and these elements not have been made of nothing? For which among them is more ordinary and lowly than earth. Yet first it has the general form of body where, unity and numbers and order are clearly shown to be. For any part of it, no matter how small, must be extended from an indivisible point in length, third takes on breadth, and fourth height, to fill the body. From where, then, is the measure of this progression of one to four? And from where, too, the

---

[t]For Augustine the doctrine of creation from nothing is not only an article of faith, but a dialectical truth which follows from a sound doctrine of oneness. It rests on the recognition of beings, objects of the human intellect but independent of it. A scrutiny of these beings leads immediately to the further recognition that their very being as object supposes an absolute sufficiency in itself participated in by all the others. This is oneness in itself, the ground of all recognition and knowledge. For Plato and Augustine, as soon as one understands what it means to know, one is forced to admit oneness in itself. Any proof which proceeds only from premises to conclusion by the methods of discursive knowledge is insufficient. For one can always deny premises. To find that without which one cannot even deny premises is the task of the upward dialectic.

Since for Augustine time is a kind of unity and order contemplated by the human intellect by which the sensible things existing seemingly only at this moment and hardly existing then take on significance and have a history, it therefore is more than the sensible things themselves, and the acuity of such a question as that of the eternity of motion is greatly diminished and perhaps has little meaning. The appearance here of the phrase 'Creator of all things' and its constant appearance throughout the book is indicative that the great problem of time is to give the sensible world meaning and being rather than to save us from the intellectual horror of self-perpetuating 'eternal' moving things of which time is only an abstraction.

equality of the parts found in length, breadth, and height? From where a corrationality (for so I have chosen to call proportion), so the ratio length has to the indivisible point, breadth has to length, and height to breadth? Where, I ask, do these things come from, if not from the highest and eternal rule of numbers, likeness,equality, and order? And if you abstract these things from earth, it will be nothing. And therefore God Almighty has made earth, and earth is made from nothing.

(58)   Then, too, this form earth is differentiated from the other elements by, doesn't it present something one in so far as it has received it, and no part of it is unlike the whole? And doesn't it have the soundest final ground in its kind by the connection and agreement of the same parts? And the nature of water extends above it, itself abounding in unity, more beautiful and more pellucid because of the greater likeness of its parts, keeping the place of order and its own soundness. And what shall I say of the nature of air, sweeping to unity with a greater reach and as much more beautiful than water is than earth, and so much higher in worth. And what about the supreme circuit of the heavens where the whole universe of visible bodies ends, the highest beauty in its kind, and the soundest excellence of place? Now all these things we've enumerated with the help of the carnal senses, and all things in them, can only receive and hold local numbers seemingly in a kind of rest, if temporal numbers, in motion, precede within and in silence. Likewise, a vital movement measures off and precedes these as they move in time-spans, a vital movement serving the Master of all things, having in its numbers no temporal spans divided out, but with a power providing times.[u] And above this power, the rational and intellectual numbers of the blessed and saintly souls[v] transmit the very law of God no leaf-fall breaks and our hairs are numbered by, to the judgments of earth and hell, without toll from any nature between.

(59)   I in my littleness have gathered with you what I could and as I could on such great matters. But, if any read this talk of ours committed to writing, they must know these things have been written by persons much weaker than those who, having followed the authority of two Testaments, by believing, hoping, and loving, venerate and worship the consubstantial and

---

[u]Augustine seems to be saying that the root of all dispersion is the temporal and that the spatial dispersion depends upon it. He then proceeds to enumerate the hierarchy of numbers. As Svoboda has pointed out, we can consider this as a hierarchy of rhythms since *numerus* is an ambiguous word. Conceptually it makes little difference, but rhetorically this systematic ambiguity may have great effect. Time has much the same position in the system of Kant as in that of Augustine: it is the mediating principle between the intelligibles and the sensible world. So it is, too, for Plotinus.

[v]'The rational and intellectual numbers of the blessed and saintly souls' refer, as Augustine points out in *Retractationes* 1.11.3, to the angels. He finds the word 'souls' inappropriately used.

This whole book is a bold development of the traditional Platonic phrase stemming from Xenocrates: *psyché arithmós autón kinòn*-"The soul is a self-moving number.'

unchangeable Trinity of the one highest God from whom, through whom, and in whom are all things. For they are purified, not by flashing human reasoning, but by the effective and burning fire of charity. And while we do not think those the heretics deceive with the promises of reason and false science ought to be neglected, yet, in the consideration of the ways themselves, we go more slowly than holy men who deign not to wait in their flying ascent. And yet we should dare not do this if we did not see that many pious sons of that best of mothers, the Catholic Church, who in their youthful studies have sufficiently developed the faculty of speaking and arguing, have, for the confuting of heretics, done this same thing.

CHAPTER THREE

AUGUSTINE

Confessions
(c. 397)

BOOK XI

5. I would hear and understand, how "In the Beginning Thou madest the heaven and earth." Moses wrote this, wrote and departed, passed hence from Thee to Thee; nor is he now before me. For if he were, I would hold him and ask him, and beseech him by Thee to open these things unto me, and would lay the ears of my body to the sounds bursting out of his mouth. And should he speak Hebrew, in vain will it strike on my senses, nor would aught of it touch my mind; but if Latin, I should know what he said. But whence should I know, whether he spake truth? Yea, and if I knew this also, should I know it from him? Truly within me, within, in the chamber of my thoughts, Truth, neither Hebrew, nor Greek, nor Latin, nor barbarian, without organs of voice or tongue, or sound of syllables, would say "It is truth," and I forthwith should say confidently to that man of Thine, "thou sayest truly." Whereas then I cannot enquire of him, Thee, Thee I beseech, O Truth, full of Whom he spake truth, Thee, my God, I beseech, forgive my sins; and Thou, who gavest him Thy servant to speak these things, give to me also to understand them.

6. Behold, the heavens and the earth are; they proclaim that they were created; for they change and vary. Whereas whatsoever hath not been made, and yet is, hath nothing in it, which before it had not; and this it is, to change and vary. They proclaim also, that they made not themselves; "therefore we are, because we have been made; we were not therefore, before we were, so as to make ourselves." Now the evidence of the thing, is the voice of the

speakers. Thou therefore, Lord, madest them; who art beautiful, for they are beautiful; who art good, for they are good; who Art, for they are; yet are they not beautiful nor good, nor are they, as Thou their Creator art; compared with Whom, they are neither beautiful, nor good, nor are. This we know, thanks be to Thee. And our knowledge, compared with Thy knowledge, is ignorance.

7. But how didst Thou *make the heaven and the earth?* and what the engine of Thy so mighty fabric? For it was not as a human artificer, forming one body from another, according to the discretion of his mind, which can in some way invest with such a form, as it seeth in itself by its inward eye. And whence should he be able to do this, unless Thou hadst made that mind? and he invests with a form what already existeth, and hath a being, as clay, or stone, or wood, or gold, or the like. And whence should they be, hadst not Thou appointed them? Thou madest the artificer his body, Thou the mind commanding the limbs, Thou the matter whereof he makes any thing; Thou the apprehension whereby to take in his art, and see within what he doth without; Thou the sense of his body, whereby, as by an interpreter, he may from mind to matter, convey that which he doth, and report to his mind what is done; that it within may consult the truth, which presideth over itself, whether it be well done or no. All these praise Thee, the Creator of all. But how dost Thou make them? how, O God, didst Thou *make heaven and earth?* Verily, neither in the heaven, nor in the earth, didst Thou *make heaven and earth*; nor in the air, or waters, seeing these also belong to *the heaven and the earth;* nor in the whole world didst Thou make the whole world; because there was no place where to make it, before it was made, that it might be. Nor didst Thou hold any thing in Thy hand, whereof to make heaven and earth. For whence shouldest Thou have this, which Thou hadst not made, thereof to make any thing? For what is, but because Thou art? Therefore *Thou spakest, and they were made,* and *in Thy Word Thou madest them.*

8. But how didst Thou speak? In the way that the *voice* came *out of the cloud, saying, This is my beloved Son?* For that voice passed by and passed away, began and ended; the syllables sounded and passed away, the second after the first, the third after the second, and so forth in order, until the last after the rest, and silence after the last. Whence it is abundantly clear and plain that the motion of a creature expressed it, itself temporal, serving Thy eternal will. And these Thy words, created for a time, the outward ear reported to the intelligent soul, whose inward ear lay listening to Thy Eternal Word. But she compared these words sounding in time, with that Thy Eternal Word in silence, and said "It is different, far different. These words are far beneath me, nor are they, because they flee and pass away; but the *Word of* my *Lord abideth* above me *for ever."* If then in sounding and passing words Thou saidst that *heaven and earth should be made,* and so *madest heaven and earth,* there was a corporeal creature before heaven and earth, by

whose motions in time that voice might take his course in time. But there was nought corporeal before *heaven and earth;* or if there were, surely thou hadst, without such a passing voice, created that, whereof to make this passing voice, by which to say, *Let the heaven and the earth be made.* For whatsoever that were, whereof such a voice were made, unless by Thee it were made, it could not be at all. By what Word then didst Thou speak, that a body might be made, whereby these words again might be made?

9. Thou callest us then to understand the *Word, God, with* Thee *God,* Which is spoken eternally, and by It are all things spoken eternally. For what was spoken was not spoken successively, one thing concluded that the next might be spoken, but all things together and eternally.[a] Else have we time and change; and not a true eternity nor true immortality. This I know, O my God, and give thanks. I know, I confess to Thee, O Lord, and with me there knows and blesses Thee, whoso is not unthankful to assured Truth. We know, Lord, we know; since inasmuch as any thing is not which was, and is, which was not, so far forth it dieth and ariseth. Nothing then of Thy Word doth give place or replace, because It is truly immortal and eternal. And therefore unto the Word coeternal with Thee Thou dost at once and eternally say all that Thou dost say; and whatever Thou sayest shall be made is made; nor dost Thou make, otherwise than by saying; and yet are not all things made together, or everlasting, which Thou makest by saying.

10. Why, I beseech Thee, O Lord my God? I see it in a way; but how to express it, I know not, unless it be, that whatsoever begins to be, and leaves off to be, begins then, and leaves off then, when in Thy eternal Reason it is known, that it ought to begin or leave off; in which Reason nothing beginneth or leaveth off. This is Thy Word, which is also "the Beginning;[b] because also It speaketh unto us." Thus in the Gospel He speaketh through the flesh; and this sounded outwardly in the ears of men; that it might be believed and sought inwardly, and found in the eternal Verity; where the *good* and only *Master* teacheth all His disciples. There, Lord, hear I Thy voice speaking unto me; because He speaketh unto us, who teacheth us; but He that teacheth us not, though He speaketh, to us He speaketh not. Who now teacheth us, but the unchangeable Truth? for even when we are admonished

[a]"For in the Eternal, speaking properly, there is neither any thing past, as though it had passed away, nor any thing future, as though it were not as yet, but whatsoever is, only is." Aug. lib. 83. quaest. qu. 19. (Annotations are from the Pusey translation.)
[b]"He saith 'The Beginning, because also I speak unto you,' Believe me to be the Beginning, lest ye die in your sins. For as though in what they said, 'Who art Thou?' they had said no other than, 'What shall we believe Thee to be,' He answereth, 'The Beginning,' i.e. believe me to be the Beginning. For if the Beginning remained as He is, with the Father, not taking the form of a servant, or speaking, as man to man, how should they believe in Him, since feeble hearts could not hear the Intelligible Word without the intervention of a sensible voice. 'Therefore' He saith, 'believe me to be the Beginning, *because* that ye may believe, I not only am, but also speak unto you.' " Aug. ad loc.

through a changeable creature; we are but led to the unchangeable Truth; where we learn truly, *while we stand and hear Him,* and *rejoice greatly because of the Bridegroom's voice,* restoring us to Him, from Whom we are. And therefore the Beginning, because unless It abided, there should not, when we went astray, be whither to return.[c] But when we return from error, it is through knowing that we return; and that we may know, He teacheth us, *because* He is *the Beginning, and speaking unto us.*

11. In this *Beginning,* O God, *hast Thou made heaven and earth,* in Thy Word, in Thy Son, in Thy Power, in Thy Wisdom, in Thy Truth; wondrously speaking, and wondrously making. Who shall comprehend? Who declare it? What is that which gleams through me, and strikes my heart without hurting it; and I shudder and kindle? I shudder, inasmuch as I am unlike it; I kindle, inasmuch as I am like it. It is Wisdom, Wisdom's self which gleameth through me; severing my cloudiness which yet again mantles over me, fainting from it, through the darkness which for my punishment gathers upon me. For *my strength is brought down in need,* so that I cannot support my blessings, till Thou, Lord, Who hast been *gracious to all mine iniquities,* shalt *heal all my infirmities.* For *Thou shalt also redeem my life from corruption, and crown me with loving kindness and tender mercies, and shalt satisfy my desire with good things, because my youth shall be renewed like an eagle's.* For *in hope we are saved,* wherefore *we through patience wait for* Thy promises. Let him that is able, Hear Thee inwardly discoursing out of Thy oracle: I will boldly cry out, *How wonderful are Thy works, O Lord, in Wisdom hast Thou made them all;* and this *Wisdom* is the *Beginning,* and in that *Beginning* didst Thou *make heaven and earth.*

12. Lo are they not full of their old leaven, who say to us, "What was God doing before *He made heaven and earth?*" "For if (say they) He were unemployed and wrought not, why does He not also henceforth, and for ever, as He did heretofore? For did any new motion arise in God, and a new will to make a creature, which He had never before made, how then would that be a true eternity, where there ariseth a will, which was not? For the will of God is not a creature, but before the creature; seeing nothing could be created, unless the will of the Creator had preceded. The will of God then belongeth to His very Substance. And if aught have arisen in God's Substance, which before was not, that Substance cannot be truly called eternal. But if the will of God has been from eternity that the creature should be, why was not the creature also from eternity?"

---

[c]"Whither should the mind return, to become good, but to The Good, when it loves and desires and obtains It? Whence if it turn away again, and become not good, thereby, that it doth turn away from the Good, unless that Good, whence it turns away abode in Itself, it would not have whither to turn, if it would amend." Aug. de Trin. 1. viii. c. 3. "Arché and Principium, signifying "the first Principle" as well as "Beginning" have a force, which cannot be expressed by our corresponding Scriptural term.

13. Who speak thus, do not yet understand Thee, O Wisdom of God, Light of souls, understand not yet how the things be made, which by Thee, and in Thee are made: yet they strive to comprehend things eternal, whilst their heart fluttereth between the motions of things past and to come, and is still unstable. Who shall hold it, and fix it, that it be settled awhile, and awhile catch the glory of that ever-fixed Eternity, and compare it with the times which are never fixed, and see that it cannot be compared; and that a long time cannot become long, but out of many motions passing by, which cannot be prolonged altogether; but that in the Eternal nothing passeth, but the whole is present; whereas no time is all at once present: and that all time past, is driven on by time to come, and all to come followeth upon the past; and all past and to come, is created, and flows out of that which is ever present? Who shall hold the heart of man, that it may stand still, and see how eternity ever still-standing, neither past nor to come, uttereth the times past and to come? Can my hand do this, or the hand of my mouth by speech bring about a thing so great?

14. See. I answer him that asketh, "What did God before He *made heaven and earth?*" I answer not as one is said to have done merrily, (eluding the pressure of the question,) "He was preparing hell (saith he) for pryers into mysteries." It is one thing to answer enquiries, another to make sport of enquirers. So I answer not; for rather had I answer, "I know not," what I know not, than so as to raise a laugh at him who asketh deep things and gain praise for one who answereth false things. But I say that Thou, our God, art the Creator of every creature: and if by the name "heaven and earth," every creature be understood; I boldly say, "that before God made heaven and earth, He did not make any thing." For if He made, what did He make but a creature? And would I knew whatsoever I desire to know to my profit, as I know, that no creature was made, before there was made any creature.

15. But if any excursive brain rove over the images of forepassed times, and wonder that Thou the God Almighty and All-creating and All-supporting, Maker of heaven and earth, didst for innumerable ages forbear from so great a work, before Thou wouldest make it; let him awake and consider, that he wonders at false conceits. For whence could innumerable ages pass by, which Thou madest not, Thou the Author and Creator of all ages? or what times should there be, which were not made by Thee? or how should they pass by, if they never were? Seeing then Thou are the Creator of all times, if any time was before Thou *madest heaven and earth,* why say they that Thou didst forego working? For that very time didst Thou make, nor could times pass by, before Thou madest those times. But if before *heaven and earth* there was no time, why is it demanded, what Thou then didst? For there was no "then," when there was no time.

16. Nor dost Thou by time, precede time: else shouldest Thou not precede all times. But Thou precedest all things past, by the sublimity of an

everpresent eternity; and surpassest all future because they are future, and when they come, they shall be past; *but Thou art the Same, and Thy years fail not.* Thy years neither come nor go; whereas ours both come and go, that they all may come. Thy years stand together, because they do stand; nor are departing thrust out by coming years, for they pass not away; but ours shall all be, when they shall no more be. Thy years are one day; and Thy day is not daily, but To-day, seeing Thy To-day gives not place unto to-morrow, for neither doth it replace yesterday. Thy To-day, is Eternity;[d] therefore didst Thou beget The Coeternal, to whom Thou saidst, *This day have I begotten Thee.* Thou hast made all things; and before all times Thou art: neither in any time was time not.

17. At no time then hadst Thou not made any thing, because time itself Thou madest. And no times are coeternal with Thee, because Thou abidest; but if they abode, they should not be times. For what is time? Who can readily and briefly explain this? Who can even in thought comprehend it, so as to utter a word about it? But what in discourse do we mention more familiarly and knowingly, than time? And, we understand, when we speak of it; we understand also, when we hear it spoken of by another. What then is time? If no one asks me, I know: if I wish to explain it to one that asketh, I know not: yet I say boldly, that I know, that if nothing passed away, time past were not; and if nothing were coming, a time to come were not; and if nothing were, time present were not. Those two times then, past and to come, how are they, seeing the past now is not, and that to come is not yet? But the present, should it always be present, and never pass into time past, verily it should not be time, but eternity. If time present (if it is to be time) only cometh into existence, because it passeth into time past, how can we say that either this is, whose cause of being is, that it shall not be; so, namely, that we cannot truly say that time is, but because it is tending not to be?

18. And yet we say, "a long time" and "a short time;" still, only of time past or to come. A long time past (for example) we call an hundred years since; and a long time to come, an hundred years hence. But a short time past, we call (suppose) ten days since; and a short time to come, ten days hence. But in what sense is that long or short, which is not? For the past, is not now; and the future, is not yet. Let us not then say, "it is long;" but of the past, "it hath been long;" and of the future, "it will be long." O my Lord, my Light, shall not here also Thy Truth mock at man? For that past time which was long, was it long when it was now past, or when it was yet present? For then might it be long, when there was, what could be long; but when past, it was no longer; wherefore neither could that be long, which was not at all. Let us not then say, "time past hath been long:" for we shall not find what hath been long,

---

[d]"For where the day neither commences with the end of yesterday, nor is ended by the commencement of the morrow, it is ever To-day." Aug. Enchir. 49.

seeing that since it was past, it is no more; but let us say, "that present time was long;" because, when it was present, it was long. For it had not yet passed away, so as not to be; and therefore there was, what could be long; but after it was past, that ceased also to be long, which ceased to be.

19. Let us see then, thou soul of man, whether present time can be long: for to thee it is given to feel and to measure length of time. What wilt thou answer me? Are an hundred years, when present, a long time? See first, whether an hundred years can be present. For if the first of these years be now current, it is present, but the other ninety and nine are to come, and therefore are not yet, but if the second year be current, one is now past, another present, the rest to come. And so if we assume any middle year of this hundred to be present, all before it, are past; all after it, to come; wherefore an hundred years cannot be present. But see at least whether that one which is now current, itself is present; for if the current month be its first, the rest are to come; if the second, the first is already past, and the rest are not yet. Therefore, neither is the year now current present; and if not present as a whole, then is not the year present. For twelve months are a year; of which whatever be the current month is present; the rest past, or to come. Although neither is that current month present; but one day only; the rest being to come, if it be the first; past, if the last; if any of the middle, then amid past and to come.

20. See how the present time, which alone we found could be called long, is abridged to the length scarce of one day. But let us examine that also; because neither is one day present as a whole. For it is made up of four and twenty hours of night and day: of which, the first hath the rest to come; the last hath them past; and any of the middle hath those before it past, those behind it to come. Yea, that one hour passeth away in flying particles. Whatsoever of it hath flown away, is past; whatsoever remaineth, is to come. If an instant of time be conceived, which cannot be divided into the smallest particles of moments, that alone is it, which may be called present. Which yet flies with such speed from future to past, as not to be lengthened out with the least stay. For if it be, it is divided into past and future. The present hath no space. Where then is the time, which we may call long? Is it to come? Of it we do not say, "it is long;" because it is not yet, so as to be long; but we say, "it will be long." When therefore will it be? For if even then, when it is yet to come, it shall not be long, (because what can be long, as yet is not,) and so it shall then be long, when from future which as yet is not, it shall begin now to be, and have become present, that so there should exist what may be long; then does time present cry out in the words above, that it cannot be long.

21. And yet, Lord, we perceive intervals of times, and compare them, and say, some are shorter, and others longer. We measure also, how much longer or shorter this time is than that; and we answer, "This is double, or treble; and that, but once, or only just so much as that." But we measure

times as they are passing, by perceiving them; but past, which now are not, or the future, which are not yet, who can measure? unless a man shall presume to say, that can be measured, which is not. When then time is passing, it may be perceived and measured; but when it is past, it cannot, because it is not.

22. I ask, Father, I affirm not: O my God, rule and guide me. "Who will tell me that there are not three times, (as we learned when boys, and taught boys,) past, present, and future; but present only, because those two are not? Or are they also; and when from future it becometh present, doth it come out of some secret place; and so, when retiring, from present it becometh past? For where did they, who foretold things to come, see them, if as yet they be not? For that which is not, cannot be seen. And they who relate things past, could not relate them, if in mind they did not discern them, and if they were not, they could no way be discerned. Things then past and to come are."

23. Permit me, Lord, to seek further. O my hope, let not my purpose be confounded. For if times past and to come be, I would know where they be. Which yet if I cannot, yet I know, wherever they be, they are not there as future, or past, but present. For if there also they be future, they are not yet there; if there also they be past, they are no longer there. Wheresoever then is whatsoever is, it is only as present. Although when past facts are related, there are drawn out of the memory, not the things themselves which are past, but words which, conceived by the images of the things, they, in passing, have through the senses left as traces in the mind. Thus my childhood, which now is not, is in time past, which now is not: but now when I recall its image, and tell of it, I behold it in the present, because it is still in my memory. Whether there be a like cause of foretelling things to come also; that of things which as yet are not, the images may be perceived before, already existing, I confess, O my God, I know not. This indeed I know, that we generally think before on our future actions, and that that forethinking is present, but the action whereof we forethink is not yet, because it is to come. Which, when we have set upon, and have begun to do what we were forethinking, then shall that action be; because then it is no longer future, but present.

24. Which way soever then this secret fore-perceiving of things to come be; that only can be seen, which is. But what now is, is not future, but present. When then things to come are said to be seen, it is not themselves which as yet are not, (that is, which are to be,) but their causes perchance or signs are seen, which already are. Therefore they are not future but present to those who now see that, from which the future, being fore-conceived in the mind, is foretold. Which fore-conceptions again now are; and those who foretell those things, do behold the conceptions present before them. Let now the numerous variety of things furnish me some example. I behold the day-break, I foreshew, that the sun is about to rise. What I behold, is present;

what I foresignify, to come; not the sun, which already is; but the sun-rising, which is not yet. And yet did I not in my mind imagine the sun-rising itself, (as now while I speak of it,) I could not fortell it. But neither is that day-break which I discern in the sky, the sun-rising, although it goes before it; nor that imagination of my mind; which two are seen now present, that the other which is to be may be foretold. Future things then are not yet: and if they be not yet, they are not: and if they are not, they cannot be seen; yet foretold they may be from things present, which are already, and are seen.

25. Thou then, Ruler of Thy creation, by what way dost Thou teach souls things to come? For Thou didst teach Thy Prophets. By what way dost Thou, to whom nothing is to come, teach things to come; or rather of the future, dost teach things present? For, what is not, neither can it be taught. Too far is this way out of my ken: *it is too mighty for me, I cannot attain unto it;* but from Thee I can, when Thou shalt vouchsafe it, O sweet light of my hidden eyes.

26. What now is clear and plain is, that neither things to come nor past are. Nor is it properly said, "there be three times, past, present, and to come:" yet perchance it might be properly said, "there be three times; a present of things past, a present of things present, and a present of things future." For these three do exist in some sort, in the soul, but otherwhere do I not see them; present of things past, memory; present of things present, sight; present of things future, expectation. If thus we be permitted to speak, I see three times, and I confess there are three. Let it be said too, "there be three times, past, present, and to come:" in our incorrect way. See, I object not, nor gainsay, nor find fault, if what is so said be but understood, that neither what is to be, now is, nor what is past. For but few things are there, which we speak properly, most things improperly; still the things intended are understood.

27. I said then even now, we measure times as they pass, in order to be able to say, this time is twice so much as that one; or, this is just so much as that; and so of any other parts of time, which be measurable. Wherefore, as I said, we measure times as they pass. And if any should ask me, "How knowest thou?" I might answer, "I know, that we do measure, nor can we measure things that are not; and things past and to come, are not." But time present how do we measure, seeing it hath no space? It is measured while passing, but when it shall have passed, it is not measured; for there will be nothing to be measured. But whence, by what way, and whither passes it while it is a measuring? whence, but from the future? Which way, but through the present? whither, but into the past? From that therefore, which is not yet, through that, which hath no space, into that, which now is not. Yet what do we measure, if not time which now is not. Yet what do we measure, if not time in some space? For we do not say, single, and double, and triple, and equal, or any other like way that we speak of time, except of spaces of times. In what space then do we measure time passing? In the future, whence it passeth through? But what is not yet, we measure not. Or in the

present, by which it passes? but no space, we do not measure: or in the past, to which it passes? But neither do we measure that, which now is not.

28. My soul is on fire to know this most intricate enigma. Shut it not up, O Lord my God, good Father; through Christ I beseech Thee, do not shut up these usual, yet hidden things, from my desire, that it be hindered from piercing into them; but let them dawn through Thy enlightening mercy, O Lord. Whom shall I enquire of concerning these things? and to whom shall I more fruitfully confess my ignorance, than to Thee, to Whom these my studies, so vehemently kindled toward Thy Scriptures, are not troublesome? Give what I love; for I do love, and this hast Thou given me. Give, Father, Who *truly knowest to give good gifts unto Thy children.* Give, because I have taken upon me to know, and trouble is before me until Thou openest it. By Christ I beseech Thee, in His Name, Holy of holies, let no man disturb me. For *I believed, and therefore do I speak.* This is my hope, for this do I live, that *I may contemplate the delights of the Lord.* Behold, *Thou hast made my days* old, and they pass away, and how, I know not. And we talk of time, and time, and times, and times, "How long time is it since he said this;" "how long time since he did this;" and "how long time since I saw that;" and "this syllable hath double time to that single short syllable." These words we speak, and these we hear, and are understood, and understand. Most manifest and ordinary they are, and the self-same things again are but too deeply hidden, and the discovery of them were new.

29. I heard once from a learned man, that the motions of the sun, moon, and stars, constituted time, and I assented not. For why should not the motions of all bodies rather be times? Or, if the lights of heaven should cease, and a potter's wheel run round, should there be no time by which we might measure those whirlings, and say, that either it moved with equal pauses, or if it turned sometimes slower, otherwhiles quicker, that some rounds were longer, others shorter? Or, while we were saying this, should we not also be speaking in time? Or, should there in our words be some syllables short, others long, but because those sounded in a shorter time, these in a longer? God, grant to men to see in a small thing notices common to things great and small. The stars and lights of heaven, are also *for signs, and for seasons, and for years, and for days;* they are; yet neither should I say, that the going round of that wooden wheel was a day, nor yet he, that it was therefore no time.

30. I desire to know the force and nature of time, by which we measure the motions of bodies, and say (for example) this motion is twice as long as that. For I ask, Seeing "day" denotes not the stay only of the sun upon the earth, (according to which day is one thing, night another;) but also its whole circuit from east to east again; according to which we say, "there passed so many days," the night being included when we say, "so many days," and the nights not reckoned apart;—seeing then a day is completed by the motion of

the sun and by his circuit from east to east again, I ask, does the motion alone make the day, or the stay in which that motion is completed, or both? For if the first be the day; then should we have a day, although the sun should finish that course in so small a space of time, as one hour comes to. If the second, then should not that make a day, if between one sun-rise and another, there were but so short a stay, as one hour comes to; but the sun must go four and twenty times about, to complete one day. If both, then neither could that be called a day, if the sun should run his whole round in the space of one hour; nor that, if, while the sun stood still, so much time should overpass, as the sun usually makes his whole course in, from morning to morning. I will not therefore now ask, what that is which is called day; but, what time is, whereby we, measuring the circuit of the sun, should say that it was finished in half the time it was wont, if so be it was finished in so small a space as twelve hours; and comparing both times, should call this a single time, that a double time; even supposing the sun to run his round from east to east, sometimes in that single, sometimes in that double time. Let no man then tell me, that the motions of the heavenly bodies constitute times, because, when at the prayer of one, the sun had stood still, till he could achieve his victorious battle, the sun stood still, but time went on. For in its own allotted space of time was that battle waged and ended. I perceive time then to be a certain extension. But do I perceive it, or seem to perceive it? Thou, Light and Truth, wilt shew me.

31. Dost Thou bid me assent, if any define time to be "motion of a body?" Thou dost not bid me. For that no body is moved, but in time, I hear; this Thou sayest; but that the motion of a body is time, I hear not; Thou sayest it not. For when a body is moved, I by time measure, how long it moveth, from the time it began to move, until it left off. And if I did not see whence it began; and it continue to move so that I see not when it ends, I cannot measure, save perchance from the time I began, until I cease to see. And if I look long, I can only pronounce it to be a long time, but not how long; because when we say "how long," we do it by comparison; as, "this is as long as that," or "twice so long as that," or the like. But when we can mark the distances of the places, whence and whither goeth the body moved, or his parts, if it moved as in a lathe, then can we say precisely, in how much time the motion of that body or his part, from this place unto that, was finished. Seeing therefore the motion of a body is one thing, that by which we measure how long it is, another; who sees not, which of the two is rather to be called time? For and if a body be sometimes moved, sometimes stands still, then we measure, not his motion only, but his standing still too by time; and we say, "it stood still, as much as it moved;" or "it stood still twice or thrice so long as it moved;" or any other space which our measuring hath either ascertained, or guessed; more or less, as we use to say. Time then is not the motion of a body.

32. And I confess to Thee, O Lord, that I yet know not what time is, and again I confess unto Thee, O Lord, that I know that I speak this in time, and that having long spoken of time, that very "long" is not long, but by the pause of time. How then know I this, seeing I know not what time is? or is it perchance that I know not how to express what I know? Woe is me, that do not even know, what I know not. Behold, O my God, before Thee I lie not; but as I speak, so is my heart. *Thou shalt light my candle; Thou, O Lord my God, wilt enlighten my darkness.*

33. Does not my soul most truly confess unto Thee, that I do measure times? Do I then measure, O my God, and know not what I measure? I measure the motion of a body in time; and the time itself do I not measure? Or could I indeed measure the motion of a body how long it were, and in how long space it could come from this to that, without measuring the time in which it is moved? This same time then, how do I measure? do we by a shorter time measure a longer, as by the space of a cubit, the space of a rood? for so indeed we seem by the space of a short syllable, to measure the space of a long syllable, and to say that this is double the other. Thus measure we the spaces of stanzas, by the spaces of the verses, and the spaces of the verses, by the spaces of the feet, and the spaces of the feet, by the spaces of the syllables, and the spaces of long, by the spaces of short syllables, not measuring by pages, (for then we measure spaces, not times;) but when we utter the words and they pass by, and we say "it is a long stanza, because composed of so many verses; long verses, because consisting of so many feet; long feet, because prolonged by so many syllables; a long syllable because double to a short one." But neither do we this way obtain any certain measure of time; because it may be, that a shorter verse, pronounced more fully, may take up more time than a longer, pronounced hurriedly. And so for a verse, a foot, a syllable. Whence it seemed to me, that time is nothing else than protraction; but of what, I know not; and I marvel, if it be not of the mind itself? For what I beseech Thee, I my God, do I measure, when I say, either indefinitely "this is a longer time than that," or definitely "this is double that?" That I measure time, I know; and yet I measure not time to come, for it is not yet; nor present, because it is not protracted by any space; nor past, because it now is not. What then do I measure? Times passing, not past? for so I said.

34. Courage, my mind, and press on mightily. God is our helper, He *made us, and not we ourselves.* Press on where truth begins to dawn. Suppose, now, the voice of a body begins to sound, and does sound, and sounds on, and list, it ceases; it is silence now, and that voice is past, and is no more a voice. Before it sounded, it was to come, and could not be measured, because as yet it was not, and now it cannot, because it is no longer. Then therefore while it sounded, it might; because there then was what might be measured. But yet even then it was not at a stay; for it was passing on, and passing away. Could

it be measured the rather, for that? For while passing, it was being extended into some space of time, so that it might be measured, since the present hath no space. If therefore then it might, then, lo, suppose another voice hath began to sound, and still soundeth in one continued tenor without any interruption; let us measure it while it sounds; seeing when it hath left sounding, it will then be past, and nothing left to be measured; let us measure it verily, and tell how much it is. But it sounds still, nor can it be measured but from the instant it began in, unto the end it left in. For the very space between is the thing we measure, namely, from some beginning unto some end. Wherefore, a voice that is not yet ended, cannot be measured, so that it may be said how long, or short it is; nor can it be called equal to another, or double to a single, or the like. But when ended, it not longer is. How may it then be measured? And yet we measure times; but yet neither those which are not yet, nor those which no longer are, nor those which are not lengthened out by some pause, nor those which have no bounds. We measure neither times to come, nor past, nor present, nor passing; and yet we do measure times.

35. "Deus Creator omnium," this verse of eight syllables alternates between short and long syllables. The four short then, the first, third, fifth, and seventh are but single, in respect of the four long, the second, fourth, sixth, and eighth. Every one of these, to every one of those, hath a double time: I pronounce them, report on them, and find it so, as one's plain sense perceives. By plain sense then, I measure a long syllable by a short, and I sensibly find it to have twice so much; but when one sounds after the other, if the former be short, the latter long, how shall I detain the short one, and how, measuring, shall I apply it to the long, that I may find this to have twice so much; seeing the long does not begin to sound, unless the short leaves sounding? And that very long one do I measure at present, seeing I measure it not till it be ended? Now his ending is his passing away. What then is it I measure? where is the short syllable by which I measure? where the long which I measure? Both have sounded, have flown, passed away, are no more; and yet I measure, and confidently answer (so far as is presumed on a practised sense) that as to space of time this syllable is but single, that double. And yet I could not do this, unless they were already past and ended. It is then themselves, which now are not, that I measure, but something in my memory, which there remains fixed.

36. It is in thee, my mind, that I measure times. Interrupt me not, that is, interrupt not thyself with the tumults of thy impressions. In thee I measure times; the impression, which things as they pass by cause in thee, remains even when they are gone; this it is which still present, I measure, not the things which pass by to make this impression. This I measure, when I measure times. Either then this is time, or I do not measure times. What when we measure silence, and say that this silence hath held as long time as

did that voice? do we not stretch out our thought to the measure of a voice, as if it sounded that so we may be able to report of the intervals of silence in a given space of time? For though both voice and tongue be still, yet in thought we go over poems, and verses, and any other discourse, or dimensions of motions, and report as to the spaces of times, how much this is in respect of that, no otherwise than if vocally we did pronounce them. If a man would utter a lengthened sound, and had settled in thought how long it should be, he hath in silence already gone through a space of time, and committing it to memory, begins to utter that speech, which sounds on, until it be brought unto the end proposed. Yea it hath sounded, and will sound; for so much of it as is finished, hath sounded already, and the rest will sound. And thus passeth it on, until the present intent conveys over the future into the past; the past increasing by the diminution of the future, until by the consumption of the future, all is past.

37. But how is that future diminished or consumed, which as yet is not? or how that past increased, which is now no longer, save that in the mind which enacteth this, there be three things done? for it expects, it considers, it remembers; that so that which it expecteth, through that which it considereth, passeth into that which it remembereth. Who therefore denieth, that things to come are not as yet? and yet, there is in the mind an expectation of things to come. And who denies past things to be now no longer? and yet is there still in the mind a memory of things past. And who denieth that the present time hath no space, because it passeth away in a moment? and yet our consideration continueth, through which that which shall be present proceedeth to become absent. It is not then future time, that is long, for as yet it is not: but a "long future," is "a long expectation of the future," nor is it time past, which now is not, that is long; but a long past, is "a long memory of the past."

38. I am about to repeat a Psalm that I know. Before I begin, my expectation is extended over the whole; but when I have begun, how much soever of it I shall separate off into the past, is extended along my memory; thus the life of this action of mine is divided between my memory as to what I have repeated, and expectation as to what I am about to repeat; but "consideration" is present with me, that through it what was future, may be conveyed over, so as to become past. Which the more it is done again and again, so much the more the expectation being shortened, is the memory enlarged; till the whole expectation be at length exhausted, when that whole action being ended, shall have passed into memory. And this which takes place in the whole Psalm, the same takes place in each several portion of it, and each several syllable; the same holds in that longer action, whereof this Psalm may be a part; the same holds in the whole life of man, whereof all the actions of man are parts; the same holds through the whole age of the sons of men, whereof all the lives of men are parts.

39. But because *Thy loving kindness is better than* all *lives,* behold, my life is but a distraction, and *Thy right hand upheld me,* in my Lord the *Son of man,* the *Mediator betwixt Thee,* The One, and us many, many[e] also through our manifold distractions amid many things, that by Him *I may apprehend in Whom I have been apprehended,* and may be re-collected from my old conversation, to follow The One, *forgetting what is behind, and* not distended but *extended,* not to things which shall be and shall pass away, but *to those things which are before,* not distractedly but intently, *I follow on for the prize of my heavenly calling,* where I may *hear the voice of* Thy *praise,* and *contemplate* Thy *delights,* neither to come, nor to pass away. But now *are my years spent in mourning.* And Thou, O Lord, art my comfort, my Father everlasting, but I have been severed amid times, whose order I know not; and my thoughts, even the inmost bowels of my soul, are rent and mangled with tumultuous varieties, until I flow together into Thee, purified and molten by the fire of Thy love.

40. And now will I stand, and become firm in Thee, in my mould, Thy truth; nor will I endure the questions of men, who by a penal disease thirst for more than they can contain, and say, "what did God before He *made heaven and earth?"* "Or, how came it into His mind to make any thing, having never before made any thing?" Give them, O Lord, well to bethink themselves what they say, and to find, that "never" cannot be predicated, when "time" is not. This then that He is said "never to have made;" what else is it to say, than "in 'no time' to have made?" Let them see therefore, that time cannot be without created being,[f] and cease to *speak* that *vanity.* May they also be *extended towards those things which are before;* and understand Thee before all times, the eternal Creator of all times, and that no times be coeternal with Thee, nor any creature, even if there be any creature before all times.

41. O Lord my God, what a depth is that recess of Thy mysteries, and how far from it have the consequences of my transgressions cast me! Heal mine eyes, that I may share the joy of Thy light. Certainly, if there be a mind gifted with such vast knowledge and foreknowledge, as to know all things past and to come, as I know one well-known Psalm, truly that mind is passing wonderful, and fearfully amazing; in that nothing past, nothing to come in after-ages, is any more hidden from him, than when I sung that Psalm, was hidden from me what, and how much of it had passed away from the beginning, what, and how much there remained unto the end. But far be it

---

[e] "Before we arrive at the One, we need many things. Let the One extended us on, lest the many distend us, and break us off from the One" Aug. Serm. 255. c. 6.

[f] "For if eternity and time are rightly distinguished, in that time exists not without a varying changeableness, whereas in eternity is no change, who seeth not that times could not have been, had no creature come into existence, which should vary something by some change?" Aug. de Civ. Dei, b. xi. c. 6. end.

that Thou the Creator of the Universe, the Creator of souls and bodies, far be it, that Thou shouldest in such wise know all things past and to come. Far, far more wonderfully, and far more mysteriously, dost thou know them. For not, as the feelings of one who singeth what he knoweth, or heareth some well-known song, are through expectation of the words to come, and the remembering of those that are past, varied, and his senses divided,—not so doth any thing happen unto Thee, unchangeably eternal, that is, the eternal[g] Creator of minds. Like then as Thou *in the Beginning* knewest *the heaven and the earth*, without any variety of Thy knowledge, so *madest* Thou *in the Beginning heaven and earth*, without any distraction of Thy action. Whoso understandeth, let him confess unto Thee; and whoso understandeth not, let him confess unto Thee. Oh how high art Thou, and yet the humble in heart are Thy dwelling-place; for Thou *raisest up those that are bowed down, and they fall not, whose elevation Thou art.*

Additional Reading

Abert, Hermann. *Die Musikanschauung des Mittelalters.* Halle, 1905.

Bruyne, Edgar de. *Etudes d'esthétique médiévale.* 3 vols. Bruges, 1946.

Chapman, Emmanuel. *Saint Augustine's Philosophy of Beauty.* New York & London, 1939.

Davenson, Henri (Henri Irénée Marrou). *Traité de la musique selon l'esprit de Saint Augustin.* Neuchatel, 1944.

Edelstein, Heinz. *Die Musikanschauung Augustinus nach seiner Schrift "De musica."* Ohlau, 1929.

Gérold, Théodore. *Les Pères de l'église et al musique.* Paris, 1931. (reprint: Geneva 1973.)

Hoffmann, Wilhelm. *Philosophische Interpretation der Augustinusschrift "De arte musica."* Marburg, 1931.

Jaeger, Werner. *Early Christianity and Greek Paideia.* Cambridge, Mass., 1961.

Lippman, Edward A. "The Place of Music in the System of Liberal Arts." In: *Aspects of Medieval and Renaissance Music.* Ed. Jan La Rue. New York, 1966.

---

[g]"In God, all things are ordered and fixed; nor doth He any thing, as by a sudden counsel, which He did not from eternity foreknow that He should do; but in the movements of the creature, which He wonderfully governeth, Himself not moved in time, in time is said to have done, as by a sudden will, what He disposed through the ordered causes of things in the unchangeableness of His most hidden counsels, whereby each several thing, which in its appointed time comes to [our] knowledge, He both makes, when present, and, when future, had already made." Aug. in Ps. 105, 45. sec. 35.

Pietzsch, Gerhard. *Die Musik im Erziehungs- und Bildungsideal des ausgehenden Altertums und frühen Mittelalters.* Halle, 1932.

St. Augustine. "On Music." Tr. R.C. Taliaferro. In: Vol. 4 of *The Fathers of the Church.* New York, 1947.

Schrade, Leo. "Music in the Philosophy of Boethius" *Musical Quarterly* 33, 1947.

Svoboda, K. *L'Esthétique de St. Augustin et ses sources.* Brno, 1933.

85

PART THREE

The Contest of Ancient and Modern

During the course of the sixteenth century in Italy a growing musical expressiveness contrasted more and more with the traditional imitative style. To some extent this was a contrast of secular and sacred, of poetic texts in Italian with liturgical ones in Latin, although church music also sought expressive impact through enhanced sonority, the use of polychoirs, and the adoption of figures modeled on those of rhetoric. But another important and more radical factor was the new interest in the music of ancient Greece and in its emotional and moral effects. The influence of Aristotle replaced that of Neoplatonism, with its accumulated mystic concern with numbers and with cosmic relationships, and the catharsis that Aristotle's *Poetics* specified as the effect of tragedy became the first influential model for musical aesthetics. Thus the appearance of musical aesthetics was centered in the contest of ancient and modern, where "modern" stood for the established Renaissance polyphonic style and "ancient" for expressive monody. The underlying aesthetic contrast of principles was one of feeling and effects as opposed to the "modern" ideal of euphony and auditory pleasure. In its simplest terms it was the adoption of expression in place of beauty. While music remained a mathematical science of harmonics and rhythmics, it was concerned also with the study of composition and performance; in terms of the liberal arts, it added to the subject-matter prescribed by the quadrivium an interest in the trivium, in the properties of rhetoric, in which music had always played a constitutive role.[1] It thereby set out on that journey that was to make it a fine art even more than a liberal art, a journey on which the principle of imitation was its companion throughout, having been joined to it originally in Plato's *Republic* and then in the *Poetics* and the *Politics* of Aristotle (although in the last of these music is said to "resemble" rather than to imitate its object).

Mei's Letter of 1572 is an important and influential document of this change. It furnished the underlying rationale for Giovanni de' Bardi's Camerata, and thus played an important part in the origin of opera. What it helped to formulate was really a new conception of music which is essentially aesthetic. At the same time, this new conception also represents a new corpus of practical theory that is concerned with composition and performance, with musical poetics and oratory. The value and even the relevance of mathematics is called into question in a series of disputes that continues for centuries, as simplicity is set against complexity, melody against counterpoint (or harmony), and South against North. The argument for melody is initially a plea for emotional impact, but it subsequently serves the ideals of natural expressiveness and of morals and religion. It constitutes a preliminary kind of aesthetics (or later a traditional kind) in that it is

---

[1]See my article on the liberal arts, which is listed again in the bibliography for the present section.

directed chiefly to the *effects* of music—a field that encompasses medicine and magic and morals as well as emotions—rather than to the properties and qualities of music itself.

CHAPTER FOUR

GIROLAMO MEI

Letter on Ancient and Modern Music
(1572)

.... The singing of the ancients was a solo melody in all their songs, as we hear the psalmody in church today in the reciting of the Divine Office, and especially in solemn services; also the chorus of singers was of many voices among the ancients, as in the tragedies, where by law it had to be definitely of fifteen, or as in the ancient comedies, where it had been restricted in the same way to the number of twenty-four. Then as to the chorus of the satires and that of dithyrambs and other customary hymns sung in that religion by multitudes of singers combined, I have not been able to note the number of those who might have sung in them. I have spoken solely of choruses, because concerning the characters on the stage both in the tragedy and in the comedy and the satire, or those who might have sung whatever manner of poems, either to the lira or to the aulos or some other instrument, this doubt does not occur, because the voice being solo, it necessarily could not sing any other than a solo melody. Then as to whether the melody of the voice was the same as the melody of the instrument that accompanied it, and whether the notes of the melody that was sung by the voice were the same as those of the instrument with respect to high and low as well as with respect to the rapidity and slowness of their number or rhythm, will be discussed in its place. What chiefly impelled me and made me arrive at this belief that the whole chorus sang the same melody was the observation that the music of the ancients was considered a powerful means of exciting the affections, as one discovers through the many incidents related to us by their authors, and

91

the observation that that of our musicians is, as is commonly said, more readily adapted to everything else. Now all this is necessarily a power which arises from the opposed and contrary qualities which each of them possesses by nature, of which those of ancient music are adapted and naturally suitable to accomplish what they do, and in contrast, those of modern music to impede it. And it is necessary that these foundations and principles be natural and firm, and not invented by somebody, and variable. Now considering that music as far as it pertains to song is concerned with the qualities of the voice, particularly in regard to its being high, medium, or low, I began to see that primarily its virtue must of necessity have its principal foundation in these, and then, that each of these passions of the voice not being the same, it was also not reasonable that each would have the same faculty, but that just as they were contrary among themselves, and arising from contrary movement, so also it was necessary that each have contrary properties, which would likewise have the power of producing necessarily contrary effects. Now because the voice had been given by nature to animate beings and to man especially for the signification of inner thoughts, it was similarly reasonable that all these diverse qualities of it, being all definitely distinct, were appropriate to express distinctly, each taken for itself, the affection of some determinate ones, and it was at the same time necessary that each express suitably its own and not those of another. Whence the high voice would not be able to express properly the affections of the medium and far less those of the low, nor the low in the opposite way those of the medium and far less those of the high, nor the medium none of those of the high or of the low; rather the quality of the one must necessarily, being its opposite and contrary, be an impediment to the operation of the other. Now on the basis of these thought and principles I began to argue that if the music of the ancients had sounded many melodies confusedly together in the same song as our musicians do with their bass, tenor, contralto, and soprano, or with more parts than these or with fewer, at the same time, it would have been without doubt impossible for it ever to have been able to excite so vigorously in the auditor the affections it desired, as one reads it did at every turn in so many accounts and testimonies of great and worthy authors.

Now to see the truth of this conclusion more distinctly and as though face to face we can first observe, resuming the principles and true foundations indicated above, where they of necessity lead us when they are accompanied by the other conditions that must necessarily intervene, and then examine this with the authority of what one may delineate of it by what one reads of it in those who have left us some notice of it in their writings. It is a certainty, then, that the high and the low of the diastematic and, as we say, intervallic voice, which is the proper subject of music, as qualities that arise from diverse and in every way opposite causes (the first coming from the speed and the second from the slowness of the motion with which it is produced), are the signs and marks of diverse and in every way contrary affections of the animated being, of which each sign expresses naturally its own affection. In the same way it is clear that the affections are excited in the souls of others when they represent to themselves as though present (either as fact or as memory) those certain affections which through these certain signs are made manifest to them. Now to do this with the voice is not possible other than with the quality of it, whether low or high or medium, which has been provided by nature for this effect, and which is the proper and natural mark of the one that somebody wishes to arouse in the listener. Similarly it is well known that the tones intermediate between the extremely high and the extremely low are suitable to show a calm and moderate disposition of affection, and the very high are marks of a soul highly agitated and stirred up, and the very low of thoughts both abject and dispirited; and in the same way, that rhythm intermediate between speed and slowness shows a tranquil soul, and speed an aroused one, and slowness an indolent and dull one: and all together it is clear that all these qualities both of harmony and of number have through their intrinsic nature the faculty of exciting affections each similar to itself. Whence very high and very low tones were rejected by the Platonists in their Republic,[a] the former being plaintive and the latter mournful, and only the middle ones accepted; as again was done by them in connection with numbers and rhythms. Furthermore all contrary qualities, whether they be natural or acquired, in being mixed and confounded together become weakened and in a certain way blunt the forces of one another, equally if they are equal, proportionately to the power and vigor of each if they are not equal; whence it arises that each of them mixed with another diverse one acts in itself relatively to the other either imperfectly or very little. So that if we mixed with an equal quantity of boiling water as much again of iced, as distant in its excess cold from being temperate as the boiling in its excess heat, not only would the force of each not be efficacious either in surplus of cold or in surplus of heat, but both would be reduced to an intermediate disposition, not adapted in its nature either to chill or to warm, unless perhaps through some quality of the person in question that some one else might not possess; if he were in himself, let us say, more disposed to this than to that excess, it would appear able to effect much more the one than the other. Now since all the things proposed are indubitably true, it was a necessity that when the music of the ancients was heard, it produced affections so vigorous in excitation, since one reads that it availed itself solely of those properties that were adapted to awaken those affections, without otherwise mixing in with any of them some contrary thing which might impede it or weaken its force in acting. It is then

---

[a] Plato *Republic* iii. 398c. (Annotations are from the Palisca edition.)

necessary, therefore, that all the singers together sang not only the same words, but the same mode and the same melody, with the same quantity of measure and with the same quality of number and rhythm, all of which things together were by their intrinsic nature adapted to produce the effect that the artificer strove and intended to induce; and this could not be other than a united and fixed song completely together, and completely directed to that same end by its sole natural and suitable means. Now up to this point the discourse founded in the natural principles set out above conducts us. But that it really in fact was such a manner of singing, an argument sufficient for us, besides many others that could be cited, would have to be this in particular, that among the ancient authors (allowing to remain to one side for the present Plato, Aristotle, Athenaeus, Proclus, Pollux, Vitruvius, and many others, who in several places incidentally, if indeed at length and rather diffusely, have spoken of this faculty because by chance some one might be able to think and say that there did not appear in them, as not to the purpose, the narration of every particular of it), in the very ones most learned and most accurate who wrote expressly and diligently of the art (of whom among the Greeks and Latins I have read a good fifteen such),[b] in no one is there found any name which appears even to correspond to any of those that have been called by musicians since one hundred fifty years ago (at which time one reckons that the music of our times may have had its origin)[c] bass, tenor, contralto, and soprano, a thing which, if in those times past one had ever sung many melodies together as subsequently became the practice, we neither can nor should with justice believe could ever have happened. Add to this, then, what our musicians call imperfect consonances, like the minor third, the major third, the minor sixth or the major, and all the other such with which all their songs are heard to be replete; there is not found among the ancients any record of consonances; which without doubt—by him who is desirous of discoursing justly on the matter—should not be nor reasonably can be believed to have come about for another reason than manifestly because they did not make use of them, and therefore did not know them in practice nor in their imperfection esteem them; and it is reasonable that their not making use of them arose because, all of them singing a single melody and having in this a goal totally diverse from that of the moderns, they did not have that need for them which our musicians have. Because the latter have received and approved them only

[b]Mei provided Galilei with a list of sources he had read on the reverse of the last page of this letter (fol. 24v).
[c]Mei believed that the history of polyphonic music did not extent further back than about 1420. Galilei, who made a similar statement in his *Dialogo*, p. 80 [See the bibliography for this section], evidently accepted this. Such a view seems to have been prevalent, since Sebaldus Heyden considered the earliest preserved part-music to be no older than a hundred years: *De arte canendi* (Norimbergae, apud I. Petreium, 1540; 1st ed. Nuremberg, 1537), fol. A2 verso.

through the necessity which clearly they are charged with to vary the harmonies of these so diverse, combined melodies of theirs; because otherwise, without this concern, this style of theirs with perfect consonances alone, having rid them very little of excessive tedium to the ear (whose delight without any other outside purpose—either to penetrate with their concept more efficaciously to the mind or to arouse in others more this than that affection—is today alone the aim of their singing), of which tedium they have so much fear and put so much excessive diligence into avoidance and with so much nicety that it is therefore accepted among them by law even as being a great fault when two perfect consonances of the same species follow one another directly. And with the ancients their lack of discussion and of practice arose from lack of use and not from the imperfection alone (as some one perhaps may think himself able to argue), which manifestly may be judged and almost seen directly from the observation that they have discussed many other qualities of these same intervals and of many other imperfect ones (to call them so for the present), like the enharmonic dieses, the two chromatic ones, the lemma and semitone, and the sequialtera and tone, all of them called by the same name dissonant although apt for song; because those really in fact not making use of any of them, unless simply for such intervals of the voice and not by some pact about consonances, would not have any taste for such a quality, nor therefore was it at all necessary to them to consider their essence and accidents and virtues. It thus appears quite clear from what has been said that music among the ancients (meaning the singing of their songs either by many or by few voices) was a single song and melody. Whence it should not further appear strange if in the moving of others it produced its affections so vigorously as one reads, when it was composed, as we say, by a fine master, arranged with judicious artifice, and then executed by skilled people and appropriate voices. Because the same melody in a simple mode being sung by all, and among the best with a small number of notes, in a manner that with its ascents and leaps did not exceed at all the natural confines of that affection which its words revealed it sought to express, making use at the same time of number and rhythm either rapid or slow or moderate, following what from the sense of its thought it was planned to express, there could not fail to result to the greatest extent possible to it all that which anyone proposed. Nor similarly, by way of contrast, should it appear something at all out of place (as we say) or strange if the music of our times does not effect a single one of these marvels, because carrying in a certain propitious manner into the soul of the listener at the same time diverse and contrary signs of affections while it mixes indistinctly together melodies and tones most dissimilar and contrary in nature to one another, although each of these things in itself naturally might have its own quality and force adapted to awaken and move with its similarity its proper affection, it can not generally in itself excite the same one, but rather to him who soberly considers it, can manifestly appear on the contrary not to have a style of its own, at least, that can reasonably be imagined, because it being necessary that the force and virtue of the melody and of the high tones weaken and blunt the vigor and power of the low ones, and assume in the opposite way the natural quality of these reciprocally weakened and debilitated ones, the distracted mind of him who listens at the same time and as though at once in diverse and contrary parts through the mixture of the diverse notes that properly represent to it diverse and contrary affections together, can not in addition, by the force of whichever of them, be as though thrust more to this than to that, since from that very one to which the one force in a definite way violently draws it, the other with equal strength draws it back, not otherwise than would be confirmed by a column, which was perched equally throughout on its base, if some one in order to cast it to the ground harnessed it in the location of the capital with two or more equal ropes, each drawn in an opposed direction and at an equal distance by equal forces. Because this, with all the forces that might be exerted upon it, would not be displaced at all from its position, even if it perhaps of itself were not hindered by some part through its own defect, since the opposite force would resist the opposed violence. But if some one with all the same arrangements and with all the same forces attacked it, pulling on one part alone, it would not, I maintain, be at all a marvelous thing if all this force together was of such power that it cast it to the ground.[d] Add then in the music of our composers beyond all the things mentioned that the sense of the continued refinement of their chords and consonances and a hundred other excessive manners of artifice that they have almost fired away at, so to say, seeking to entice the ears, is of great hindrance to exciting the mind to any affection, occupied with and as though bound principally to these little deceits of pleasure so produced, all things different from if not contrary to that which in the affection and in the practice needs to be a simple and natural thing or at least to appear thus made, and to have for an aim only the desire to excite itself in another, a token of which may be that if anyone happens upon a group where some are weeping, some are laughing, others are talking quietly, others are acting boisterous together, others are leaping through drunkenness, and others may be doing something else: not having in himself by chance a particular inclination to some one of these affections, he will therefore not depart from his state, except perhaps in remaining confused by the situation: but if in contrast anyone happens upon a company where either everyone is lamenting or everyone is celebrating, it will be a very great composure, either natural or of the mind, that is not moved and not arranged in some way in accordance with those affections. Add to this the great variety of the use of many strings outside of every

[d]Compare this passage with Galilei's paraphrase, *Dialogo*, p. 82.

natural appropriateness (it being understood that either we intend in all the parts together a single body, as it were, or in each of them taken in itself), a thing always censured among the ancients by all men of judgment, among whom one perhaps hears no complaint more frequent against the insolence and foolishness of the musicians of their times than: it is not at all natural, rather in fact against the whole nature of the affection, because as everyone can hear, generally one who complains never departs from the high notes, and on the contrary one who is sorrowful never departs from the low, unless by such a little distance as would never, because it would not be accommodated nor appropriate to such a purpose, reach the medium position, much less cross over it as we hear the melodies of these musicians of ours do, who not only arrive there with the entire body of all these melodies of theirs mixed together, but also very often with a single one, whether it be soprano or tenor, leaping now upwards, now downwards, off the staff either mediately or immediately by eleven or twelve notes at such a time. Nor in the meantime must we omit the incredible carelessness of our musicians with respect to number and rhythm in all the parts, each one considered in itself or the whole body of them together, which numberless times if not always in all these things is contrary to the nature of the matter that the concept signified by the words seeks to express, which reasonably it should be above every other consideration to follow, and is without some proper characteristic in each part, but rather by chance that of the one part diverse from that of the other, so that many times in the same tempo the soprano will scarcely move when the tenor flies, and the bass will go strolling along as though in new-soled shoes, or indeed the opposite, which is the cause of so many imperfections; and no matter how much force is applied through these means to the expression of the affection, it is not necessary to discuss it further,[e] it being a matter that may be seen easily, as we say, by minnows, not to mention by one who desires to consider prudently the nature of each affection, because who is of so slow an intelligence as not to be able to comprehend easily, if he sets about considering the truth, that one who is infuriated speaks with a different speed and the supplicant commends himself with a different slowness than the man who is of calm mind discourses! besides which carelessness of number there may be arrogated as though for good measure the excessive diminution of the tempo, introduced outside of every natural reason and convenience of movement of the voice, commencing from the notes called by these people "maxima" and decreasing up to those that are called by the same "semicromes," over all of which infirmities almost as a head there must be set particularly the disordered perturbation and mixture and chopping of

[e]Paraphrased in Galilei, *Dialogo*, p. 82. The same complaint is made also by Bardi in "Discorso sopra la musica antica," *Lyra Barberina*, II, 241; trans. in Strunk, *Source Readings*, p. 294.

the words, whence there is not permitted to penetrate to the intelligence of the one who listens the virtue of the concept that may be efficaciously expressed in them, as very often even the very ones who sing them do not take it in, which notwithstanding, if it were well understood, could be apt in itself alone to excite and generate an affection in others. But what shall we say beyond this of that other perverse affront, namely, that the soprano many times may sing the beginning of the words of a concept, or their repetitions, and the tenor be in the middle of them, and the bass in the final and other parts elsewhere; or they may differ between them in their pronunciation![f] so that indeed this also draws them down to that same characteristic as all the other things set out above, which is to distract the mind by diverse, and if it so happens, contrary parts; which distraction, making all these points, as it were, strike disunitedly and not at the same center, not having therefore sufficient value or force, but rather the one being openly of hindrance to the other, does not make a penetration into it and does not enter and thus does not awaken an affection there, quite contrary to what is said according to the proverb about the dripping of water, which continuously and unitedly striking the same place in the stone finally hollows it out.

Now for all these causes adduced up to this point, leaving out every other authority and argumentation that could be added to them by one who minutely and with greater subtlety went searching through everything; leaving these out, I say, through not wanting excessively and without purpose to be still more tedious in a matter which by this time it appears is sufficiently certain to one who does not desire, disputing at every turn, to be obstinate about the truth, I believe it to be obviously true that the music and singing of the ancients was without further doubt a definite melody, which therefore well controlled and well conducted could accomplish with its qualities in a reasonable and natural way all those things that we hear recounted, which is not at all possible if for the most part it has been shown to agree somewhat with the music and the singing of our times.

But perhaps it may appear to some one that from the things thus concluded there necessarily follow two that are, let us say, inappropriate: the first is that if ancient music was truly as has been shown a definite melody, it can hardly not appear at once, in its simplicity, a very homely thing, so to say, and therefore not to have been held in such esteem as one always hears it to be by all the great men, as a thing which in its peculiarity is very easy to acquire and of which every modest talent could easily be capable. The other is that since it did not practice the use of the consonances in singing because everyone sang the same melody, to what end is such diligence and noisy resentment brought to bear by its writers concerning

[f]Compare *Dialogo*, p. 82.

98

them? in the desire of the one to defend the reasonableness of some of them against the authority of others, who did not accept it and condemned it?

Additional Reading

Galilei, Vincenzo. *Dialogo della musica antica e moderna.* Florence, 1581. (facsimiles: Rome, 1934; New York, 1967; reprint: Milan, 1947; partial translation in Strunk, *Source Readings.*)

Lippman, Edward A. "The Place of Music in the System of Liberal Arts." In: *Aspects of Medieval and Renaissance Music.* Ed. Jan LaRue. New York, 1966.

Mei Girolamo. *Letters on Ancient and Modern Music.* Ed. Claude Palisca. American Institute of Musicology, 1960.

Palisca, Claude. "Girolamo Mei: Mentor to the Florentine Camerata." *Musical Quarterly* 40, 1954.

Pirotta, Nino. "Temperaments and Tendencies in the Florentine Camerata." *Musical Quarterly* 40, 1954.

PART FOUR

The Ideal
of Universality

Both the broad scope of Mersenne's thought and his effort to reduce it to a systematic form are characteristic of seventeenth-century scholars and philosophers; they are found in thinkers as diverse as Kepler, Fludd, Kircher, Spinoza, Descartes, Hobbes, and Gassendi. They have a typical manifestation in the large encyclopedic treatise, somewhat like a revival of the medieval *summa*. It is as though the rapid expansion of empirical knowledge called for some unifying force to contain it and give it sense, and this was found variously in the new axiomatic certainty of Descartes, or in a geometric form of exposition, or in the appeal to a universal science of mathematics (either in its traditional Pythagorean form or in a novel one), or in a religious view of the world as a unity created by God. Ancient and medieval conceptions of cosmic harmony inevitably played a role in such synthetic views, and music was frequently regarded as the most direct manifestation of divinity.

But the universal scope of musical treatises brought together the most diverse contents, in which old and new were juxtaposed in a rich and complex texture. One extreme of this diversity was occupied by physical science and technology; the other by mathematical metaphysics and theology. Between these were ranged traditional contrapuntal theory (now gradually expanded to encompass expressive dissonance), more recent musical poetics centered in musical figures, a ramified scheme of musical effects that extended from medicine to the affections and was complemented by a materialistic conception of human temperaments based on bodily fluids, complex typologies of musical style, and comprehensive enumerations and descriptions of musical instruments. Many of these matters were incipient varieties of aesthetics that were not elaborated from that point of view. Others, such as the growing awareness of vibrations, of the physical nature of sound, and of the inequality of function between the two tones making up an interval, were of the utmost consequence for the future of tonal and musical perception. Acoustics and theology stand side by side in Mersenne. They also may have a bearing on aesthetics, but in very different ways, the first being relevant only to the elements of aesthetics and the second fundamentally equivocal in its implications.

The argument Mersenne presents in the book on consonance for the superiority of the unison over the octave is essentially repeated in the book on composition for the superiority of monophony over polyphony. Both discussions are in a strange way related to the argument of Girolamo Mei, but the standard has shifted from emotional impact to theological value. They are also more tangibly related to the eighteenth-century defense of melody against counterpoint and harmony, although the point of view then becomes a specifically aesthetic one.

Mersenne was an indefatigable correspondent, and the letters he exchanged with Descartes and others reveal how painstaking he was in his deliberations. The *Harmonie universelle* similarly examines its subjects from every point of view conceivable to its author, and the arguments tend to become so exhaustive that they often touch upon properly aesthetic matters even though they are in general directed to other issues. But if Mersenne continually sought advice through his correspondence, he was also quite original in many areas, laying the ground in musical theory for future conceptions of consonance and tonality.

CHAPTER FIVE

MARIN MERSENNE

Harmonie universelle
(1636)

VOL. 2 TREATISES ON THE CONSONANCES, THE DISSONANCES, THE GENERA, THE MODES, AND ON COMPOSITION

BOOK ONE, ON THE CONSONANCES

PROPOSITION IV.

To determine if the unison is a consonance, and if it is sweeter and more pleasing than the octave.

Those who maintain that the unison among consonances is what unity is among numbers deny that it should be called a consonance, because it has no diversity of sound with respect to low and high: but those who believe the unison is the queen of the consonances are of the opposite opinion, inasmuch as it suffices that the tones be different in number to make a consonance, and the blending of the tones being the formal cause of the said consonances, that the blending which unites them so perfectly that they are heard as being almost a single tone should not be deprived of the name that it gives to the others. Which one can confirm by the names that we give to God when we call him Being, Goodness, Beauty, etc., for although God does not have the being, the goodness, or the beauty that we have, but has these perfections in a degree infinitely more perfect, nevertheless it is permissible to speak of him in this manner, which the holy Scripture makes use of for our instruction; and consequently the unison being the exemplary cause and the aim of the consonances, since they all tend towards the said unison, from which they take their origin as the ratios of inequality take theirs from the ratio of equality, it is not without justification for one to maintain that it is the first consonance.

Now the unison is considered in two ways, for it can continue on the same tone, that is to say, on a single string, as happens when one sings without raising or lowering one's voice in the chorus of the monks who use no plainchant at all; which one can call *ison*—that is, "level"—singing, and in which the continuation is similar to the beginning, and all the parts are in unison.

The other type of unison is that of plainchant, which makes use of all kinds of degrees for ascending or descending, and which has more variety than the other, which is like a voice that holds firmly to the same note and that has no distinction at all other than that which comes from the different syllables or from a few interruptions, rests, and pauses to take breath, to breathe, and to relieve the voice and the chest.

These two sorts of unison are different in that the first has only a single type of voice or of sounds while the second has a number of types as great as is the difference of high or low; this is why the first unison is simpler than the second; and each is a consonance, since they are the union of two or of several sounds which is pleasing to the ear although they have no other difference at all other than their particular and individual nature, which is the least difference of those that exist between substances.

For this difference suffices to establish the ratio of equality, which is distinct from that of identity, which is simpler, even though Aristotle may say in the 39th problem of his Section 19[a] that the octave is more pleasing than the unison because this is only a simple sound. And in Book II of his *Politics*, Chapter V, that he who places the unison among the consonances is like the one who introduces the community of all things in republics and who confounds verses with the foot. But Jean de Muris in Book II of his *Speculum musicae*,[b] Chapter X, maintains that it is a consonance, with which all those will remain in agreement who love to follow reason and experience more than authority. And so to the community of the republics, which Aristotle opposed to contradict his master, it is very desirable; but it is not to be hoped for as long as diversity is preferred to equality; for all the most excellent things suit us to that equality and communion of goods, since in nature, the earth, the air, and the heavens are equally made for the whole world, since in the state of grace there is only a single joy, a single hope, the

---

[a] The reference is to the Pseudo-Aristotle *Problems*, which were compiled about 100 A.D.

[b] Now believed to have been written by Jacob of Liége.

same commandments, and a single law; and in that of glory only a single God, who will be everything to everyone, *omnia in omnibus*, since all things will be subject to him, and they will have abandoned diversity, which is the source of corruption. So that one may say that Plato, whose spirit, it seems, attained the greatest illumination of nature, was contemplating the beauty of the eternal Ideas when he proposed the happy communion of the blessed, which his disciple is constrained to embrace when he avows that the blessings of friends should be common. Now all men should be friends, since they are brothers, and children of the same father, and since the true religion teaches us that the faithful should be a single body and a single spirit, since they all have the love and the glory of God for their ultimate end. From this it comes that all the holy Scripture has no purpose other than to make us embrace the communion of the blessed both of the spirit and of the body, and to unite us with God for ever, so that the unison, which does not have here the esteem that it should have, triumphs over the diversity from which error proceeds and enjoys eternally the prerogatives of which it is desired to deprive it by the differences of time and movement that one makes use of at present.

As to the second part of the proposition, to learn if the unison is sweeter and more pleasing than the octave, I say first of all that there is no doubt that it be sweeter, since it unites the tones more often and more easily, for the unison being one to one, all the pulsations of the air are united at each impulse, instead of which the pulsations of the octave are united every two impulses; and one will always find in the operations of all the senses that that which unites most easily is the sweetest; but it does not follow that it be the most pleasing: for even though sugar and honey be very sweet, they are nevertheless not pleasing to those who prefer sour and bitter things: that is why it is necessary to see if the unison is more pleasing than the octave.

I say then secondly that it seems that the unison is more pleasing than the octave because it flatters the ear more, and it is understood more easily by the imagination, which is the principal seat of pleasure.

And if one wishes to use comparisons to confirm this truth, nature furnishes us with them in all the sciences, for the great pleasure of algebra consists in finding all sorts of equations which occur by means of equality. The science of mechanics has its foundation in equilibrium, which is a certain kind of unison. And medicine apparently has no aim or speculation more exalted than the temperament of bodies reduced to the equality of the humors. And if it is permissible to ascend higher, we shall find an eternal unison in the divinity, since the three persons are only a single nature, and have only a single will, a single power, and a single goodness, although they may be in reality distinct. Which perhaps will be the reason that the Blessed will always sing at the unison, so that their song may be conformable to the equality of the three persons, and to the state of equality, which takes its

107

origin from eternal beatitude, which is susceptible of no alteration, and which, being very simple, requires very simple songs, which can not be simpler when several are singing than when they sing at the unison.

One can confirm the same thing again by the beginning and the end of compositions, which nearly always form a unison, which is the end of music, since experiment shows that all the consonances tend towards the unison, as I demonstrate elsewhere. And if one compares the force that the unison of plainchant has with that of the musical consonances, one will find that it is more powerful, and that it makes a stronger impression on the mind which is in no way distracted by the variety of the consonances and dissonances, and which begins to enjoy the music of the Blessed when it hears the unison, which makes it remember its origin, and the beatitude that it hopes for and that it awaits.

The power of the unison not only imprints its effects on the spirit and on the soul but also on inanimate bodies; for as often as one touches a string of the lute, of the viol, or of some other instrument, it sets into motion the other strings that are disposed to and tend to the unison, and makes them vibrate; and consequently it can serve to make all sorts of machines move, and to set off a cannon: So that one may lay siege to and conquer cities by means of the unison, as it is said that Orpheus[c] built them with the sound of his harp. But we must reserve this discourse for the treatise on the sounds that are used in war.

Now one of the strongest reasons that persuade us that the unison is more pleasing and more natural than the octave is drawn from the experience that shows that we become bored much more in hearing singing at the octave than in unison, which one hears in churches with pleasure for a period of several hours: and although children sing naturally at the octave with men, nevertheless their intention is to sing in unison, to which all voices tend, which are conserved and fortified by their likes; for resemblance is the source of love, and the conservation of the being and of the nature of each thing, which is conserved better by uniformity than by deformity. Now the movements that our spirits receive from the unison are perfectly uniform and equal, and those from the octave are unequal, since the one are two times more rapid than the other.

And if we compare sounds with the objects of touch, we shall find that the ear receives as much pleasure in hearing singing in unison as the sense of touch in handling polished, soft, and smooth things, such as satins are, and a thousand other similar things. From this it comes that dissonances are called hard and rough, because their sounds resemble hard, rough, and uneven

---

[c]Mersenne means Amphion, who built a city wall if not a city with the sound of a lyre if not a harp.

bodies, which wound the hand, and which break up the spirits that serve the sense of touch.

Yet many believe that the octave and the other consonances are more pleasing than the unison, the more especially as they have variety in their union, and as nature likes diversity, as we have proved in a particular proposition: and if one reflects about the harmonies that enchant the spirit in concerts, one will be constrained to avow that there are sometimes certain places that ravish the listener; which never happens so powerfully with the unison.

Moreover the different voices of music that are doubled are so many unisons that are enriched and enhanced by the diversity of consonances; so that if they are good and pleasing being all alone, they should be still better and more pleasing when they are joined to the said harmonies.

As to the great equality and union of the tones that make up the unison, it seems it is too simple to give pleasure, since one experiences in several things, and particularly in the visible, that what is too simple, and what is not composed of several parts, is not esteemed pleasing. Now the unison is similar to lines that are entirely alone, just as the tone is similar to the point and to unity.

To which one may add that it is not possible to distinguish the unison from the simple tone when it is perfect, that is to say, when the voices that make up the unison are perfectly equal; and consequently that it is not more pleasing than one voice, since it is heard in the same way as if there were only a single one.

One may also report here all the reasons I have made use of elsewhere to prove that diversity pleases the senses, and the comparison Zarlino uses in Book III of his *Institutions*, Chapter 8, where he holds that the unison and the octave are similar to the extreme colors, that is to say, to white and black; and the other intermediate consonances, namely the fifth, the fourth, and the thirds, to the intermediate colors, that is to say, to green, to red, and to blue, and consequently that the unison and the octave are not so pleasing as the other consonances, since white and black are less pleasing than the mixed or intermediate colors. Which does not prevent one from concluding nevertheless that the unison would please all sorts of men more if they were in the state of perfection, which it seems shrinks from diversity, pleasure in which testifies to our indigence and our imperfection. For since all music exists only for the sake of the unison which is its end, why do we not value it more highly than all the other harmonies? Is not the end better and more pleasing than the means we employ to arrive at it? But those who take more pleasure in the other harmonies than in the unison are like those who love somber and overcast weather in broad daylight more than the pure light of the sun; and who prefer the colors that partake of darkness, as they are the intermediates, to white, which is the image of light and which serves as the color of the garments in which the angels are clothed to appear to men, and which our Savior made use of in his transfiguration, for his garments were white like snow and brilliant like light. In effect those who think more highly of green and of the other composite colors than of white, and of the imperfect consonances than of the unison, are like those whose eye cannot endure light and who receive more contentment from speculation on particular truths than on the universal one that resides in God, and who love to rejoice in creatures and in passing delights more than in the creator and in eternal pleasures.

As to those who have risen above all that is created, and who have experienced a thousand times the aversion that one has towards all the truths of mathematics and of physics when they have been discovered, from which one receives almost no contentment except in the labor one undergoes in searching for them, they receive no contentment from concerts, and love to hear singing at the unison more than in several parts, as much as the unison represents to them the abode of the blessed, and the perfect union of the three divine persons who are in the unison of a perfect equality.

And because the unisons that are produced here are not perfect, those who rise above all that is corporeal, and who begin to be united by an ardent love with God, receive no contentment from unisons except when they have some text that they make use of to be entranced in the contemplation of the supreme being; and they are more comfortable not to hear singing at all in order not to be in any way distracted from the thought they entertain of the uncreated unity, to which they are so fastened that no worldly thing can separate them from it.[d]

I estimate then that the unison is more pleasing than the consonances, and that we must show compassion for the fragility and inconstancy of men who do not have this feeling, and who think much more highly of diversity and inequality than of unity and equality, inasmuch as they do not judge things because they possess more simplicity and more excellence, but by what contributes best to their appetite and to their phantasy.

Now one may confirm this truth by a weighty consideration of everything that renders things pleasing, that is to say, of that which gives them being, faculties, and action; for we must in no way doubt that what renders things pleasing is not still more pleasing than the said things, since they possess nothing that they have not borrowed, and that they are pleasing only

---

[d]Here theology joins Platonism and Neoplatonism, as the aesthetics of melody and simplicity and effect which was discussed in the introduction to Part III is now reduced to the still higher "aesthetics" of silence and the ideal. The preferred number of musical parts, which Mersenne characteristically takes to be one, is reduced for a time to zero. Echoes of Augustine, of the passage of the *Confessions* cited in the introduction to Part II, are unmistakable. The argument increases in complexity, however, in what follows.

through what they have borrowed from the source from which they have taken their origin.

Lines, figures, and bodies have nothing except what they have borrowed from the point, since the line is nothing other than the movement of the point, just as figures and bodies are only the movement of lines and of planes; for if one removes all the points nothing remains over, so that if one contemplates the beauty and the perfection of the point one will avow that it has the beauty of lines and of figures in eminence and in perfection.

And all creatures, who do not depend less on God than lines depend on the point, have no beauty nor anything pleasing except what they receive from the presence of God, who recreates them perpetually; so that there is nothing perfect in creatures except God. From this it comes that the greatest beauty of creatures is the greatest assistance that God gives them, and the greatest quantity of his light that he alots to them, and with which he illumines them: just as those numbers are the greatest to which unity sends the greatest multitude of its rays, and to which it communicates itself more amply; so that one may say that all possible numbers are nothing other than unity communicated, or the love, the perfection and communication of unity, without which no number can subsist.

Now consonances depend on the unison, like lines on the point, numbers on unity, and creatures on God, and that is why they are the sweeter the more they approach it, for they have nothing sweet nor pleasing except what they borrow from the union of their tones, which is the greater as they partake more of the nature of the unison: although several do not receive from it so great a pleasure as from the other consonances, more especially as they do not have a sufficiently strong or elevated spirit to contemplate the point and unity in their simplicity, or to stop in contemplation before the sole presence of the divinity considered without any relation to visible things. For the spirit of the majority of men is so enclosed within the body, and restricted by phantasms, that it can not raise itself above the senses; and if it happens that they elevate themselves as far as the center of the divinity that the cabalists call the occult Aleph, the En-Sof, they find themselves entirely lost in the midst of the shadows that take hold of their understanding, more especially as the phantasms that gave them some appearance of light no longer accompany them, which constrains them to fall again into the false light that eclipses the rays of the intelligible sun, and that steals from us the true beauty in order to feed us on a false beauty which brings no pleasure that is solid and permanent. Which Saint Augustine remarked in the third chapter of his book on the knowledge one should have of the true life, in which having shown the power of dialectic, he adds, "Dialectica namque disserendi potens, potenter quoque dubia definiens, cunctas scripturas evibrans, et eviscerans, cunctam humanam sapientiam annihilans, cùm in divinitatem intendit, tantâ maiestatis luce repercussa pavidum caput

111

tremefacta reflectit, atque in abdita mundanae sapientiae fugiens delitescit, dissolutisque syllogismorum nexibus stulta abmutescit."[e]

So that all the wisdom and the capacity of human understanding can by no means disclose to us the light of the first truth, and make us avow that perfect contentment consists in perfect simplicity, which one never enjoys sufficiently except when one contemplates it in itself, and when one abandons diversity entirely in order to embrace the divine unity, to which the Royal Prophet aspired, when he sang those words, "Satiabor cùm apparuerit gloria tua."[f]

Nevertheless when one knows the art and the usage of meditation on the true pleasure, one easily discovers that the eternal ideas are its sole and its genuine object, and consequently that we are mistaken when we believe that beauty has its seat in the being of creatures separated and distinct from the being of the creator; for beauty, and that which we call pleasing in sensible or intelligible things, depends on uncreated being, just as numbers depend on unity, lines on the point, time on the moment, movement on immobility, and the consonances on the unison.

Now numbers have nothing in them but unity which renders them lesser or greater in proportion as it communicates itself more or less; for example, the number one thousand is ten times greater than the number one hundred, because unity communicates itself ten times more to one thousand than to one hundred; but it has an infinite power that is so proper to it that it can not communicate it, since it cannot render number infinite, just as God can not communicate his infinity nor his independence: from which one may conclude that it is necessary to consider the creator in creatures, like unity in numbers, and like the unison in the consonances.

In effect one experiences that those consonances are two, three, or four times better and more excellent to which the unison communicates itself two, three, or four times more, as I shall demonstrate in a special discussion; for when it communicates to them two degrees of union, they are two times better than when it communicates only one degree to them, and so forth, then, until they are reduced to the unison by the subtraction of degrees of the variety that determines the material of the consonances, as union determines their form; for if inequality and diversity serve as body for the consonances, equality and union are their soul and spirit, as we shall see in the treatise on the Divisions, and in that on the Suppositions of each

---

[e]"For dialectics, having command of discussion, determining efficaciously also what is uncertain, throwing over and eviscerating all the scriptures, annihilating all human wisdom: when it is directed towards divinity, bends its fearful head, driven back trembling by the light of such great majesty, takes refuge in the secrets of worldly wisdom, and enervated by the entwinings of syllogisms, becomes mute and foolish." (*De cognitione verae vitae liber unus.*)

[f]"I shall be satisfied when Thy glory appeareth." This verse is not found in the Book of Psalms.

consonance,[g] where I demonstrate that of all the divisions of each consonance, that one is the sweetest and the most pleasing which unites the tones most perfectly; and that of two or several suppositions of a single consonance, or of several, be it upward or downward, that one is the best and the most natural of which the union is greatest.

And when we shall have divested creatures of their differences, and of their variety, and when the veil of exterior and finite appearances shall be lifted from them, we shall perceive the divine spirit which makes them move, and then we shall be a single spirit with God, in accordance with the beautiful word of the Apostle, "Qui adhaeret Deo, unus spiritus est cùm eo";[h] for as soon as we shall see that there is no goodness or beauty in creatures but divine goodness and beauty, our spirit will attach itself so powerfully to that object which enraptures the blessed, that it will seem to be a single thing with it, just as the objects understood and the understanding are no more than a single thing in the school of the Peripatetics.

But just as we suffer patiently in the imperfection of the state in which we are, when our ears are beaten by the variety of the consonances in awaiting the abode in which we shall be enraptured by the perfect unison, of which we can not perfectly comprehend the beauty while we have need of the diversity for our conservation: in the same way, we can not understand divine beauty and excellence until it has opened our eyes, and it has explained the enigma that hides it from us, and that shuts off the view of it from us, as very thick mists and clouds shut off that of the sun. From thence it comes that consommés and jellies do not yield so strong, so useful, and so pleasing a nourishment to those who feel well, as bread, flesh, and the other foods that are not divested of their different imperfections at all, especially as the body of man has several different parts, of which each one requires a different nutriment: so that the potable gold, or the elixir on which the chemists and the cabalists pride themselves, is not proper for nourishment, because it is too simple and too pure.

Moreover, experience makes us see that we cannot subsist here for a long time without the variety of the different actions and passions, of which each tires us, and at once displeases us: for example, when one is weary one takes pleasure in sitting down, but as soon as one has remained two or three hours sitting one finds oneself just as weary as before, and one prefers to recommence work until there is a new weariness, rather than to remain seated still longer. Which proves clearly that the pleasure of man can not subsist without variety, while he is in a variable state; and consequently that the continuation of the unison can not be so pleasing to him as when it is

---

[g]The division of a consonance is produced by adding a proportional intermediate tone, the supposition by adding a proportional tone above or below the consonance.
[h]"He who adheres to God is one spirit with him."

interrupted by other consonances, or even by dissonances: although this diversity does not at all keep the unison from being more pleasing than the other consonances when it is made use of in the places in which it is required or permitted according to the rules of art.

Now that state of variety in which we are, is the reason that we avoid the unison as much as we can, because it is too sweet and too excellent for this life. Thence it comes that we prefer to finish music with the octave, the fifth, the third, or their replicates than with the unison; and when we finish with it, we accompany it with other consonances, because while the spirit is subject to material which subjects it to phantasms, to shades, and to error, it does not dare to raise itself, so to speak, to the perfection of unity, which is entirely divested of the variety and the unequality encountered in the other consonances; by which it testifies that the unison is as though outside of music, as God is beyond his creatures, and that when we hear the unison, we must remember that the least pleasure of divine harmony is more excellent than the perfect knowledge of the harmony of which we make use, as one may infer from this beautiful line of Saint Augustine, "Incomparabili felicitate praestantius est Deum ex quantulacunque particulâ pia mente sentire, quàm quae facta sunt universa comprehendere," in the fifth book of his word-by-word commentary on Genesis, Chapter 16.[i] From which one may conclude: in proportion as the pleasure that the spirit separated from error and from phantasm receives from the unison surpasses all the contentments that come from the other consonances, since it is the image of divine harmony, and the source of the said pleasures.

But one may still raise an objection which seems to divest the unison of the prerogative that we give it, to wit, that the spirit takes more pleasure in conceiving the things which augment its knowledge. Thence it comes that nature likes diversity, as I have proved through this same reason in a special discussion. Now one learns nothing in considering the unison, since it contains no interval, and since all the tones are only a single thing: and one learns in the other consonances the difference of low and high tones, and the contentment that proceeds from their mixture; and consequently the unison is the poorest and the least pleasing concord of all the consonances, since it gives no new knowledge.

And then, if the greater union of its tone is the cause of a greater contentment, it follows that there is more contentment in seeing a room whose walls touch, or are very slightly distant, and a little house, than in seeing a large royal palace, because the parts of the little house are more united than those

---

[i]"It is more excellent to perceive God with incomparable ease in however small a particle, through a pious mind, than to comprehend all fabricated things in entirety." To make the meaning of his citation more self-contained, Mersenne substitutes "God" for "him" and "fabricated things" for "those things." (*De genesi ad litteram libri XII.*)

of a large palace. One may say the same thing of all that is grand and magnificent, and that may be abridged and shortened, because the reductions bring it about that the parts of the things that one reduces are more united than when they have a greater extension.

Finally, the difference of all creatures will be completely preserved in heaven, where it will please all the saints more than if they were all only a single thing, and they had no difference between them; for it seems that all the pleasure of the knowledge of creatures consists in the relationship and the comparison that one makes of them to God, and of some with the others.

But it is easy to respond to these objections, since they suppose the imperfect state of men, whose knowledge will be much more perfect when they see clearly the great union of all creatures, and when they recognize that the diversity of objects exercises a great tyranny over our spirits, that it diverts us from contemplation and from thoughts that convey us to unity, to which one may attain only in divesting creatures of their diversity, in order to encounter there the unity that reigns absolutely, and not to see there more than the root of being, and the center of sovereign reason, as one does not see more than the root terms of the harmonic, arithmetic, and geometric proportions when one has divested the larger numbers of what they had that was superfluous and useless, and as one does not perceive more than spirits, and the quintessence of the mixed, when one has rejected the terrestrial, and all that rendered them subject to corruption, and to different alterations.

As to the greater knowledge that comes from the other consonances, one may compare it to the light of several little candles, or to that of glow-worms: but that of unity and the unison is similar to the light of the sun, which obscures all the others by its presence, as the grace and the excellence of the unison makes that of the other consonances vanish; for although we do not enjoy here all the pleasure that may come from the unison, because of the distractions which the diversity of the consonances presents to us, nevertheless the little attention that we bring to bear in order to consider its excellence gives us a knowledge much more noble and elevated than is that of the other consonances; just as the little knowledge that we have of heaven is much more excellent than that of the elements, although [this is] larger and more certain.

It nevertheless does not follow that a confined room is more pleasing than a large hall, or that a little house is more beautiful than a large palace, more especially as one does not measure the beauty of edifices by the union, but by the relationship and the symmetry of their parts, as one measures that of the consonances by the union of their tones. And as to the diversity of the bodies and of the spirits of paradise, it will be so tempered by union, that some may hold that all the bodies of the blessed will be comprised by the humanity of Jesus Christ, as their spirits will be engulfed in his divinity, so that God is all things in all, and so that he reigns absolutely in the being of all creatures, who can succeed to a higher degree of perfection only in entering into the perfect unison of the created being with the uncreated, which consists in no longer having knowledge or love except of the divinity.

One can also prove that the unison is more excellent than the other consonances by astrology, which finds the consonances in the aspects of the stars, more especially as conjunction is the most powerful and the most excellent of all the aspects; and many deny that it merits the name of aspect, just as they deny that the unison is of the number of the consonances. In effect, if the conjunction of the stars represents the unison, just as they maintain that opposition represents the octave, the trine aspect the fifth, the quartile the fourth, and the sextile the thirds and the sixths, and that the said conjunction is more powerful than the other aspects, one may say that it has a great conformity to the unison. But I shall explain the aspects of the stars in the first book of string instruments: and it suffices now to consider that all things are inclined with as much affection and inclination to union as they are inclined to their preservation.

Thence it comes that man does all that he can to unite himself with all sorts of goods, from which he hopes some advantage to his comfort, and to the preservation and augmentation of his being; and that the greatest good which may enter into the spirit of man, to wit, eternal glory, consists in the union that men will have with God as to the spirit, and with the humanity of our Savior as to the body, as Saint Paul teaches in chapter 4 of his Epistle to the Ephesians, whom he consoles in the hope that all Christians must have of the change of their bodies which are now subject to all sorts of variety, into another perfect body with which we shall encounter Jesus Christ, of whom the years will serve as a symbol establishing us in the springtime of a very pleasant and very perfect age, "Denec occurramus ei in virum perfectum, in mensuram aetatis plenitudinis Christi."[j] Now all these considerations bring us to recognize that the unison is the most perfect and the most pleasing consonance of music, since it participates more abundantly in that which renders it sweet and pleasing; and since there is only a single imperfection of the variety that preoccupies us, and that makes us prefer what is more similar to our frailty and our misery, which is not able to subsist here without diversity, which is the mother of corruption, although we would aspire to the unison and to unity. Which is represented to us by that excellent verse of the Evangelist, "Porrò unum est necessarium."[k]

Now if music serves for something in this world, one should particularly make use of it to recall the memory of one part of these considerations, so that it not be said in eternity that men who make a profession of reason, and

[j]Verse 13: "Till we all come . . . unto a perfect man, unto the measure of the stature [i.e., the age] of the fulness of Christ." (King James version.)
[k]"For oneness is necessary."

who should make use of recreations and of speculations for the end to which God destined them, have abused the chaste and rational pleasure of music, and have imitated some musicians, who do not at all raise themselves higher than to the passion and the action of the senses, and to the pleasure of the ear, which should serve solely as a channel to provide free entrance to the contemplation of eternal things, and to the pleasure that comes from the thought of the final end, of which true philosophers should converse incessantly. But it is time to speak of the other difficulties that are encountered in the unison, of which the definition is explained in the proposition that follows, after the five corollaries which I am adding in order to anticipate a quantity of difficulties and of objections that are grounded in the prejudices of musicians, and of other persons who imagine several things that are not; and in order to shape the spirit of those who sing or who love music to make use of harmony to elevate themselves to God, and to contemplate the grandeur of his goodness, and the sweetnes of his benedictions and of his mercy which all those enjoy of whom the Royal Prophet speaks in that first verse of Psalm 72. "Quàm bonus Israël Deus his qui recto sunt corde."[1]

Additional Reading

Lenoble, Robert. *Mersenne ou la naissance du mécanisme.* Paris, 1943.

Ludwig, Hellmut. *Marin Mersenne und seine Musiklehre.* Halle/Saale & Berlin, 1935.

Mersenne, Marin. *Harmonie universelle.* Paris, 1636.

Otto, Irmgard. *Deutsche Musikauffassung im 17. Jahrhundert.* Berlin, 1937.

Palisca, Claude V. "Scientific Empiricism in Musical Thought." In: H.H. Rhys, ed. *Seventeenth-Century Science and Art.* Princeton, 1961.

Roth, L., ed. *Correspondence of Descartes and Constantyn Huygens, 1635-1647.* Oxford, 1926.

[1] "Truly God is good to Israel, even to such as are of a clean heart." Psalm 73 in the King James version.

PART FIVE

Musical Poetics
in Germany

It was as a natural consequence of the conception of the musical work of art, which was formulated during the sixteenth century, that the field of musical thought dealing with composition found its first explicit form in the later part of the century, under the head of *musica poetica*. It was created when a series of musical figures was added to the established principles of modal counterpoint. These figures derived from rhetoric, and consisted mostly of homophonic sections and various types of repetition of these sections, any of which produced an expressive impact when it was set into a context of continuous imitative polyphony that is essentially non-repetitive. To this core there was added a mechanical explanation of affections, the stereotyped "feelings" that were symbolized by intervallic and rhythmical melodic patterns. The affections were aroused in the listener when the tonal patterns to which they were correlated produced analogous motions in the corporeal fluids, or "vital spirits." Finally *musica poetica* did not comprise simply a technique of composition, the way counterpoint did, but affected the form and style of the whole musical work, which was often thought of as a kind of oration.

Treatises on musical poetics became a German specialty, doubtless because of the prominence of rhetoric in German education. In the stylistic and formal discussions they included, the anti-Baroque aesthetics of the eighteenth century found its fullest expression. In Leipzig and Hamburg and Berlin, the ideals of this aesthetics were the same as those of France: simplicity and clarity. The full range of such compositional aesthetics, in which the model of rhetoric affects every aspect of musical poetics, can be seen in *Der vollkommene Capellmeister*, the major work of the prominent Hamburg composer and theorist Johann Mattheson. The reality of the musical feelings was particularly evident in performance, which had the same relationship to composition as oratory had to rhetoric, and the aesthetics of performance was therefore a kind of corollary of the theory of composition and could easily be incorporated into the same treatise, especially since the composer and the performer were regularly one and the same person. The underpinning of this aesthetics was the theory of imitation, and speech was the chief object to be imitated. Thus vocal music was preferred to instrumental, for it could more adequately embody the ideals of imitation and clarity.

This preference is even more obvious in the treatise of Krause, a principal figure in Berlin aesthetics, since he is concerned with the composition of poetry that is to be set to music. In the section of the treatise given below, Krause presents a prolonged and ingenious series of arguments to justify musical complexity, appealing among other things to the theory of temperaments and to the rhetorical conception of appropriateness; but it is obvious throughout where his true preference lies.

Like Mattheson, Krause represents the eighteenth-century version of the recurrent conflict of complexity and simplicity, of cerebration and spontaneity. These are manifested respectively in two different compositional techniques of securing musical definiteness, the one through the repetition that is associated with thematic manipulation and counterpoint, and the other through purely melodic expansiveness and variety. The argument leads inevitably from feeling to virtue, and from there to the imprecision of meaning that was seen as a fundamental deficiency of music in comparison to language. Krause concludes with an impressive rationale of the coupling and cooperation of music and words, of the power of their association, and of the vital role music plays in their moral influence.

As we can see in the writings of Mattheson and Krause, and in much the same way in those of Rousseau as well, it was melody that became the focal point of musical aesthetics in the eighteenth century. For melody—with vocal melody as an ideal—was a manifestation in which all the major aesthetic ideas found their most characteristic and striking embodiment: ideas of the imitation of nature, of national style and taste, of the elaborate, middle, and plain style of rhetoric, of simplicity and clarity, of affective and persuasive quality, of the impact of music on the vital spirits, and of the expansion of its social appeal. The basic principles of *galant* aesthetics, the control of music by reason and the restriction of feeling to the sphere of polite sentiment and sentimentality, were revised only in the last three decades of the century. (See Part IX below).

CHAPTER SIX

JOHANN MATTHESON

Der vollkommene Capellmeister
(1739)

PART II
CHAPTER 5

On the Art of Composing a Good Melody

1. Melodic composition is an effective skill[1] in the invention and working out of singable pieces such as give pleasure to the hearing.

2. This art of composing a good melody includes what is most essential in music. It is therefore greatly to be wondered at that such a central matter on which indeed the greatest accomplishment rests has been neglected up to this very day by nearly every teacher. So little, in fact, has this been thought about that even the most prominent masters, and among these the most copious[2] and the most recent, must admit *that it is almost impossible to give definite rules about the matter,* with the pretext that it depends for the most part on good taste. Yet by this too the most fundamental rules can and must be

---

[1]Melopoeia est facultas, vel habitus effectivus conficiendi cantum. Aristides Quintilianus, *De musica, Liber I,* pp. 28 and 29 [of Vol. II of the Meibom ed. (Mattheson's citation is put together from two separated statements)].
[2]As Monsieur Rameau and those of his lights are. I have recently seen something of his musical work for clavier, which I liked far more than his incomprehensible ruminations. From the former one remarks that he must be a good organist, from the latter that he must be an unnatural composer: although the Jesuits at present turn him into a wonder. *Traité de l'harmonie,* p. 142.

given; for true understanding let us ask only skilled chefs, for allegories the teachers of morals, orators,[3] and poets.

3. Thus concerning the all-necessary matter of melodic science these authors expose their weaknesses and poor insight more than enough to the light of day. Others, by way of contrast, who nevertheless otherwise profess to know everything, act somewhat more cleverly in this case, since in their thick books they prefer to be entirely silent about it.

4. I keep insisting, then, *before all else*, on an individual, pure melody, as the most beautiful and natural thing in the world, and I am indisputably the first who has publicly presented specifications and rational instructions for it; perhaps these, like my other innovations, will also serve now or some day for another to boast of without even mentioning the originator. No one else, to my knowledge, has written of melody systematically and with due attention. Everything devolves alike on polyphonic texture, and the most experienced composers of all occasionally lack nothing in their work so much as melody because they always hitch the horses up behind the wagon in their endeavors and write away with from four to ten voices before they have learned to do justice to one or to impart true grace to it.

5. We place melody, in contrast, at the foundation of the entire art of composition, and cannot comprehend at all why the clear difference between simple and manifold harmony, which was mentioned long ago in my writings for good reasons, is never taken into consideration appropriately, when, for example, it is insistently maintained against all reason *that melody arises*[4] *from harmony and all rules for the first must be derived from the second.*

6. But melody is in fact nothing other than the original, true, and simple harmony itself, in which all the intervals follow *after, upon,* and *behind one another,* just as precisely the same intervals and no others[5] are perceived in polyphonic texture *together, at once,* and *with one another,* and consequently bring a *multiple* harmony[6] into being. Good taste, to be sure, must rule in both; otherwise they are not worth a straw.

[3]See J.H. König's treatise on good taste.

[4]See the *Traité de l'harmonie* of M. Rameau, Bk. II, Ch. 19, p. 139; Ch. 21, p. 147. The best thing is that one writes that harmony is engendered first. I will grant it: but what is engendered must have parents.

[5]Thus it is quite absurd when one wishes to devise an essential difference between harmonic and melodic intervals. Rameau, *loc. cit.*

[6]Zarlino, *Istitutione* Part II, Ch. 12, p. 96f. and *Sopplimenti* Bk. 8, Ch. 2, p. 279, where he teaches "what harmony was among the ancients," N.B., "the third part of melody" [i.e., of the flow of music, the other two parts being melody in the present-day sense, and words]. See Johannes Magirus (a very learned clergyman and excellent musician), *Artis musicae* [Frankfurt 1596; 2nd ed., Braunschweig 1611], Bk. II, Ch. 24, p. 98, *De harmonia simplici,* and also Ch. 27, p. 105, *De harmonia composita.* My edition of this book is of 1592, figuring by the dedication: although the title-page is missing, which I remember because the Walther Dictionary [J.G. Walther, *Musikalisches Lexicon,* Leipzig, 1732] states that the first edition appeared in 1596. Plato also treats of this simple harmony in Book III of the *Republic,* and the true ancients knew of no other.

7. This fundamental distinction and explanation probably ends all strife over the question, because everyone must grant that the first elements from which a many-voiced texture is created consist simply in the tonal intervals, just as when they succeed one another, and then, that in natural philosophy, which a solid musician must be thoroughly acquainted with, the statement will remain incontestably correct, *that the simple was prior to the composite and consequently is its source or root.*

8. Now he who wishes to set up a correct division must first well consider and comprehend the whole context in all its parts. This pronouncement can be subject to no doubt; therefore I turn it to account in the following form: No one will know what a third, fifth, octave, and so on means, who has not previously felt, heard, seen, and found it to be the case that the first consists of three, the second of five, and the third of eight tones, as of so many simple elements and essential basic melodic parts, which are attached to each other in accordance with certain regular steps.

9. Such fitting together of tonal steps is called, properly and before all else, *harmonia, compages* [joining together], which can be demonstrated with the rational ancient Greeks, who accomplished all their musical wonders with simple harmony.

10. No one can set up the division of a string, therefore, or even of an octave, until and before he has considered, grasped, sung, or played the whole tonal scale, step by step, degree after degree, without the slightest omission. And that is already melody.

11. As then the following examples are to demonstrate sufficiently and to make self-evident: all and every polyphonic texture lies hidden in the melodic scale; multiple harmony derives its rules from melody; a piece for one voice even without accompaniment can very well exist, but a so-called harmony without melody is only an empty sound and no vocal piece at all; all arrangement of sound without imitation means little or nothing, but this imitation is grounded in individual melodies whether it be in fugues, concertos, or other genres; every theme always simply carries a melody, upon which, as upon the ground, the multiple harmony afterwards constructs its embroidery and outline, and also in accordance with which it regulates itself either wholly or at least in part; everyone must previously study his part alone before he can sing together in the chorus; and finally, even apart from this, it remains difficult enough anyway for beginners not to make mistakes in a harmony where there are many different melodies, even though they otherwise can carry their own part fairly well. It follows from all of this that the former, in a certain light, is more difficult than the latter.

Canon at the unison for four voices.

Mol- to   pia -   ce   Onor;   ma non tan-   to   quan-to   Amor.

12. Here the simple diatonic scale, with its steps rising and falling in a direct line, already makes in a completely natural context such a simple and noble melody that a complete four-voiced harmony with all the imaginable consonances is correctly contained in it along with all the appropriate minor and major intervals—seconds, thirds, fourths, fifths, sixths, sevenths, and octaves—without a single note being changed.

13. I present further this Scottish dance, and ask how miserable the bass to it would turn out if it were not arranged imitatively with respect to the main melody, and how good in contrast even only a twofold harmony proves when the accompanying voice takes its pattern, so to speak, from the ruling one, and follows or opposes it in the most friendly way in almost all the same melodic passages and turns. Everything that this harmony has flows indisputably from the melody, which is imitated by the former and must be taken as an original.

Ecossoise

14. Yet ask solid dancing masters s'ils commencent leurs lécons par des entrechats, ou par la Demarche de la Danse?—whether they first teach their

pupils entrechats but afterwards a measured walk? One indeed cannot at once demand skilled leaps with both feet from anyone before he has learned to walk correctly, just as little as anyone is able to present the third part of a thing who knows nothing of the first and second. The one refers unavoidably here to the other.

15. My next, incontestable assertion runs as follows: *Natural patterns give rise to artistic ones.* Art is a servant of nature and appointed for its imitation. Even if it were possible to strike or to divide separate thirds, fifths, and so on deliberately and arbitrarily without knowing, counting, measuring, and investigating the sounds lying between their limits, yet natural singing was previous to playing in man (I say in man), and the beautiful native instrument of the throat still produces a single sound at a time. In an orderly way.

16. If therefore we speak of intervals, we must understand in this regard chiefly that use in which their terminal tones are heard successively and only produce at one time a single sound or simple tone, not, however, the way they affect the ear simultaneously and constitute a composite entity: for only the former alone can arise in a regular way from one man and thus for this reason stands higher, because purely melodic song is simpler and naturally older than full-voiced texture;[7] the latter in contrast calls for more people or for imitative instruments.

17. The strongest and strictest rules of multiple harmony are based on the above-mentioned counting along and secret computation[a] of the steps and sounds lying in between in the case of disjunct intervals. For why is it incorrect and severely forbidden to write the following?

---

[7]Quia cantus simplicior concentui et prior natura ["Because melody is simpler than harmony and prior in nature."] G.J. Vossius, *De artis poeticae natura ac constitutione* [Amsterdam, 1647. Mattheson obviously quotes from memory, giving a slightly variant title and omitting a page reference.]

[a]Mattheson's idea and his manner of expression here seem to take as their model Leibnitz's well known characterization of music as an *exercitium arithmeticae occultum nescientis se numerare animi* (an "unconscious exercise in arithmetic in which the mind does not know it is counting"). *Epistolae ad diversos*, 4 vols., ed. Christian Kortholt, Leipzig, 1734-42; letter 154.

matter and the highest peak of musical *perfection*.[10] At the same time they ask forgiveness for having uncovered such a mystery, confess their inability in melody, and acknowledge themselves as defeated. What more can one want?

22. Kindly permit me another few questions before I move ahead to the work in hand. The first is then whether music disposed in accordance with certain self-devised harmonic rules can always be good, without regard, if worst comes to worst, to whether it infringes against the order of the melody, of the song, of the rhythm, of prosodic quantity, of fine taste, and so on.[11] The second is: Whether such theories as these, since they both come from *Rameau*, can co-exist and be compatible with the one above concerning the priority of melody. If these two questions have been fundamentally answered with yes, and my preceding rational conclusions (not to mention the other experiential bases adduced) have been truly contradicted with no: then I will not waste a word more in all my days on behalf of melody.

23. Among the scholars the unique *Donius* indeed noted in the preceding century that there were people by the dozens who could not make a true distinction between melody and symphony nor separate the creation of melody from symphonic composition. He says: although full-voiced texture has great power either to increase or to diminish the tones, yet this is a matter that is entirely foreign and not peculiar to the nature of the modes, because we must consider such things in an unadorned, simple vocal melody, and when this has happened we may only then speak of accords. His own words deserve to find a place below.[12]

[10]La Melodie n'a pas moins de force dans les expressions que l'Harmonie mais it est presque impossible de pouvoir en donner des regles certaines, en ce que le bon gout y a plus de part que le reste: ainsi nous laisserons aux heureux genies le plaisir de se distinguer dans ce genre, dont depend presque toute la force des sentimens, et nous esperons que les habiles gens, pour qui nous n'avons rien dit de nouveau ne nous sauront pas mauvais gré d'avoir declaré des secrets, dont its auroient peutêtre souhaité être les seuls depositaires, puisque notre peu de lumiere ne nous permet pas de leur disputer *ce dernier degré de perfection, sans lequel la plus belle Harmonie devient quelques fois insipide,* et par où ils sont toujours en etat de surpasser les autres. ["Melody does not have less force in expression than harmony but it is almost impossible to be able to give secure rules for it, in that good taste plays a greater role here than everything else: thus we shall leave to the fortunate geniuses the pleasure of distinguishing themselves in this genre, on which all the force of feeling depends, and we hope that the capable people for whom we have said nothing new will not be ill-disposed towards us for having announced secrets of which they may have wished to be the sole possessors, since our small enlightenment does not permit us to argue with them over *that last degree of perfection without which the most beautiful harmony sometimes becomes insipid,* and through which they are always in a position to surpass others."] Rameau, *loc. cit.*

[11]Rameau, *ibid.*, p. 137.

[12]Musici da Dozzina, che non fanno distinguere la Melodia della Sinfonia e la Melopoeia della Sinfoniurgia: perche se bene il Concento ha gran forza d'accrescere o dimuire la proprietà dei Modi; tuttia, come hò detto tante volte, questa è cosa estrinseca alla natura loro, i quali s'hanno di considerare fondamentale in una *semplice Aria,* e poi parlare delle Consonanze. G.B. Doni, *Sopra i Toni o Modi veri,* p. 123 [The title seems to be Mattheson's version of the title of one of the tracts included in Doni's *Annotazioni . . . ,* Rome, 1640].

Truly for no other reason than because the tonal steps of the melodic scale lying between these leaps, which we always have in mind during them although they are not expressly written out, betray covered fifths and octaves. Now does this knowledge derive from harmony or from melody? Then we also have here an exhibition of harmonic rules that flow from melody, and there are many more such.

18. Therefore we employ each and every interval in melody in a natural way, just as we employ them in harmony in an artificial and composite way. We can indeed accomplish just as little in full-voiced texture by means of mere octaves, or mere thirds, fourths, and so on, as in melody or in individual song; such a procedure in many-voiced harmony would also be just as foolish, indeed still more foolish, than in melody; yet we derive from this a one-sided and very shallow argument. Seconds belong prominently to both, and change in everything provides the greatest delight.

19. From the two axioms adduced there accordingly follows irresistibly the conclusion *that the correct beginning in composition must be made with pure melody*; for in all instruction only a single good method or type of teaching exists, namely that we proceed from the simple things to the compound and from the more familiar to the less familiar.

20. Although one who likes all manner of intermixed foods will not know how good a simple dish tastes no matter how much health and the discreet Horace[8] recommend it. Why then does such a thing not taste good to him? Answer: He does not take succulent meat for dinner, which always contains its own gravy, but rather sets out bad fish which devour a great deal of seasoning, many dissonances.

21. There are cooks of a type who to be sure acknowledge quite gladly in print *that often even the most beautiful harmony is insipid without melody;*[9] on that account I give them precisely here a comparison with taste and with foods; they affirm of their own will that almost all the force of ideas, passions, and their expressions are dependent on no other thing than simple melody, promise also boldly in titles and superscripts, in plain and clear language, to teach *everything* in their books and chapters that can in any way make a musical work perfect; and to make things work out accordingly, the sheer *impossibility* of giving rules for melody is offered as an excuse, since they themselves cannot really deny that precisely this melody is the principal

[8]Ut noceant homini credas, memor illius *escae* Quae *simplex* olim tibi sederit.
["For how harmful to a man a variety of dishes is, you may realize if you recall that plain fare which agreed with you in other days."] Horace, Liber II, *Satira* 2 [verses 72 and 73. The italics are Mattheson's].
[9]Rameau, *op. cit.*, p. 142.

24. But the good *Doni*, although he wrote a tract of his own on melody, which however had a totally different purpose[13] than our present work, indeed perceived the evil and yet did not remedy it at all, much less provide means and ways by which some one might arrive at the composition of pleasant melodies.

25. It is impossible, for one thing, that with *many voices much melody*, and indeed *really good* melody, may be found at the same time, because the latter must be divided up much too much and thus loses in the long run all apt coherence. I say in the long run, for with short movements it is much more practicable, if a solid harmonist deals with them, and indeed especially in instrumental things. But where words are to be sung they become imperceptible when all the voices are to be provided with equal elaboration; the melody of the principal voice, in whatever place it may be, becomes unclear, and the lack of freedom makes even the full texture offensive.

26. The hearing, by contrast, often takes greater pleasure in a single well-ordered voice that carries a fine melody in all natural freedom than in four and twenty in which the same is torn apart to such a degree in order to be imparted to all that we don't know what is supposed to be going on. *Mere melody moves hearts with its noble simplicity, clarity, and distinctness in such a fashion that it excels all the harmonic arts*; these are the words of a very learned, former Strassburg theologian.[14]

27. But if we want to allot, perhaps, to one or two voices alone the predominance and fine song, as is quite correct in certain circumstances and genres, the others must unavoidably then be somewhat the losers, and what makes the former good neglects the latter altogether. It takes a true master to attend to three or four voices equally well with apt passages and voice leading, and how indeed can this be done by a person who has still not learned to lay out a single voice that is melodically correct?

28. Harmony is really nothing other, or should correctly be nothing other, than a fitting together of different melodies, although these cannot all be

---

[13]*Discorso sopra la Perfettione delle Melodie* (the general title-page has "de' Concenti" [i.e., "of harmony" rather than "of melody"]), as a supplement to the *Compendio del Tratto de' Generi e Modi* . . . [Rome, 1635] amounts to four sheets, whose beginning at once gives a notion of the content, with these words: Non è mio intendimento di trattare in questo luogo che cosa sia propriamente Melodia, e quante le sue specie,—mi son proposto solamente, di scoprire alcuni mie pensieri intorno le Musiche a una voce sola—equelle di più voci si compongono ["It is not my intention to treat in this place what Melodia properly may be, and what its species are; I have undertaken solely to make known some of my thoughts concerning pieces for solo voice, and those that are composed of more voices"], etc., pp. 95-96.

[14]Nuda Melodia tantopere corda commovet simplicitate, luculentia et perspicuitate sua, ut nonnunquam artificium vincere harmonicum aestimetur. Johannes Lippius, in *Disputatio musica III* [Wittenberg, 1610].

perfectly beautiful to the highest degree. For this reason the Greeks called their composition a *melopoetics*, that is, the making of melody; in this there consisted for them almost the whole of music, and with it they accomplished the greatest of miracles, as we are reliably informed, although they thought little of polyphony or at any rate certainly used none such as is in the present day customary with us.

29. Now if we wish our procedure to be truly orderly, we must first describe this melody fundamentally and in a way that circumscribes it; that it is, namely:

> *A cultivated song in which only single tones follow one another in so correct and desired a manner that sensitive minds are moved thereby.*

30. It is accordingly not merely high and low tones (for they also belong in common to polyphony) but really *single* tones that are the true material of melody in particular.

31. For another thing, the desired succession of such tones, as the form of the melody, consists not only in steps or in a stepwise progression but also in certain leaps that have a correct relationship with one another which is precisely our simple one, as the true source of all multiple accordance, in which property, to be sure, it will well find a place in our elucidation but not in a limited description.

32. Thirdly, if that which is to move sensitive minds must be before all things *simple, clear, flowing, and lovely*, then for this final purpose the natural and sublime as well as the calculated organization come into consideration. For nothing can be clear that contains no order; nothing can flow that is unnatural, and so on.

33. This intent, however, in moving sensitive souls the melody indeed can and must convey and achieve, although it might not always do so alone to such a degree and with such brilliance and strength as when polyphony comes to its aid; and thereby certainly hearts which otherwise know little of delicate things and the number of which is without doubt the greatest are then also often moved.

34. Ancient and recent history, daily experience, nature, and reason testify that mere melody entirely alone can awaken and express certain inclinations of the heart exceedingly well and move attentive listeners.

35. But because these motions themselves are not all of one and the same kind, they will also be excited quite differently by the connection of harmony with the melody than when this last acts only alone without

assistance, for an attractive accompaniment, even if it is only a bass but much more if it is a full-voiced texture, helps particularly to represent with greater emphasis that which is proper, for example, to a friendly meeting, a most blissful embrace, a hearty agreement, to sportive game and contest, to splendor, majesty, and similar things. In contrast to this, simple melody in certain circumstances can very well excite really all the more sensitive inclinations, such as love, hope, fear, and so on, entirely alone.

36. Yet with what means did the learned ancient Greeks accomplish their musical wonders? What moved Augustine's heart in the Ambrosian congregation? What penetrated so deeply into the soul in the Protestant Reformation? What is it still nowadays that promptly forces tears from the eyes[b] of many people in great churches, and promptly excites the tongue to exultation? With what means are infants put to sleep? What takes hold of a bird and seems to compel it to imitate someone who whistles to it? Was and is it indeed anything other than mere unaccompanied melody?

37. One of the most powerful and astonishing effects of this melody is probably in dancing, in which few trouble even about whether only a bass is present or any accompaniment at all; indeed the most experienced dancing masters gladly dispense with such an accompaniment and the English say of their country dances that a two-voice setting would sound elegant, to be sure, but would give little emphasis to the main part, and that middle parts or full-voiced settings would stand in the way of all dancing pleasure, whereas a simple melody, if it is stated five or six times, for appropriateness, on a single cello, is easily more than sufficient.

38. Now to people who do not feel such great effects of unaccompanied melody one might reasonably hold up the familiar scriptural words: We have whistled for you and you have not danced. There is really no lack of such souls, but they are commonly counted among the coarsest and cannot detract from the force of unaccompanied song but can indeed deprive themselves completely of the pleasure to be obtained from it.

39. I am reminded here of an aria which I myself formerly sang on the stage in the person of a dreamer and which began in this way: *Yet appear to me soon, etc.*, and likewise of another on the words: *All, all is finished*, in a Passion, both of which without the slightest accompaniment brought about more attention or stir than if they had been provided with the finest harmonic settings. But singers are also required for this such as need no particular instrumental mask.

---

[b]A corollary of the rhetorical conception of music is the unmistakably real character of the affections aroused. Emotions so conceived fit very well into their traditional "pre-aesthetic" context of the effects of music—magical, medical, physical, and so on.

40. A certain air from one of the newest Parisian ballets, with the opening words: *Les trésors de la fortune ne font pas un parfait bonheur*, was sung not long ago by a distinguished gentleman without a single accompaniment and with such grace that it really enchanted the listeners, and those, in fact, who are very well accustomed to praise something full-voiced; then the same gentleman played exactly this melody on an alto transverse flute and in truth it came forth so lamentingly and movingly that it caused an actual sadness among the bystanders.[c] There are examples from all styles.

41. Also finally, since music consists of melody and harmony, but the former is by far the most prominent part and the latter only an artful collection or connection of many melodic sounds, so we indeed can nevermore justly deny to simple song, according to the prescriptions of sound reason also, at least its considerable participation in the expressive agitation of sensitive hearts.

42. As far as invention is concerned, through which the beginning[15] of all songs, tonal and other speeches that are to be constructed must always be made (just as it also usually occupies at once the first or second section in books on rhetoric), this has found no place in our above description of melody but has rather found its own chapter because it really belongs to the explanation of melopoetics.[d] How this is distinguished from melody, however—that the best Greek theorist of melodic composition teaches us.[16]

43. In the meantime it is to be wondered at that really no one who had written about music before the completion of the *melodic Kern*[e] was public knowledge, gave us a thorough and precise definition of melody. There is a great difference between grasping a thing in general and describing it thoroughly in particular. In pedagogy it will not do to opine: What melody is one doubtless need not say to a musician.[17]

---

[c]Instrumental music is accordingly capable of producing the same literal emotional effect as vocal, although it always looks to vocal melody as a model, and must therefore avoid "a throng of variegated notes" (paragraph 109).

[15]See Orchestre I [Mattheson's *Das Neu-Eröffnete Orchestre*, Hamburg, 1713], pp. 40, 202.

[d]During the elaborate discussion of the *Vollkommene Capellmeister*, every aspect of rhetoric is found as a matter of course to have its musical counterpart, from invention and organization to the various types of figures. Oratory is similarly a model for performance. Grammar is also occasionally called upon, and at times, particularly in the discussion of meter, poetics. These are the branches of knowledge that have taken the place of the quadrivium in the study of music.

[16]Aristides Quintilianus [ed. Meibom], p. 29. Differt melopoeia a melodia: quod haec fit cantus iudicium; illa habitus effectivus ["Melodic composition differs from melody: because the latter is produced by the disclosure of singing, the former by the effective skill"].

[e]Mattheson's *Kern melodischer Wissenschaft*, Hamburg, 1737, which presented the entire melodic aesthetics that was incorporated into the *Vollkommene Capellmeister* two years afterwards.

[17]Heinichen, on p. 543 of his recent method. [Johann David Heinichen, *Neu erfundene und gruendliche Anweisung* . . . Hamburg, 1711; 2nd ed., Dresden, 1728.] If this is to be called *scolding*, it is nevertheless *sensible scolding*. Let it be noted in the record.

44. And if indeed something of this sort may have come to light, it was either incorrect in a systematic way concerning material, form, and final purpose in that it was deficient now in the one and now in the other, or there also grew out of it loose discourses such as hardly can be surveyed with a yardstick and yet such as say in many words very little, indeed nothing definite at all, but rather correspond with more than one thing.

45. I had occasion long ago, to be sure, to deal with this matter thoroughly in the *Musicalische Critic*,[f] and at that time the *Vollkommene Capellmeister* was already in process; but I was reluctant to withdraw from this work such material, which truly belonged to it, and hoped things would move along somewhat more quickly with its publication. Now that in the meantime this did not happen sooner, several ideas have also become still somewhat more mature since then, and no instruction comes too late so long as it conveys something good.

46. From the above correct description and its elucidation alone, then, a good basis for useful melodic rules can already be derived, and the imagined impossibility of the same easily eliminated. For if only first of all we properly consider the four properties: *simple, distinct, flowing,* and *lovely,* and place them before us for further investigation, then four classes or divisions of such rules will yield themselves automatically.

47. If we consider secondly an *affecting or moving nature* as the only one in which true melodic beauty consists[g] and to which the four above-mentioned properties are only subservient and helpful, than we have before us the entire theory of the natural inclinations of the heart, and no lack of good rules will be uncovered, but perhaps of their intelligent application. This is not the place to develop this last point, which belongs to practical knowledge as well as to natural philosophy in particular, but only to go through the four properties in question diligently.

48. In pursuance of this, the following can furnish a good postulate for the rules deriving from *simplicity*:

> *We can take no pleasure in a thing in which we do not participate at all.* Seven rules are readily drawn from this:
> 1. That in all melodies there must be something that is familiar to nearly everybody.
> 2. All that is forced, far-fetched, and difficult in nature must be avoided.
> 3. Nature must be followed mostly, custom sometimes.
> 4. Great artifice is to be set aside or very much concealed.

[f]Mattheson's *Critica musica*, 2 vols., Hamburg, 1722, 1725. He is doubtless referring here to Part IV (Vol. I) and Part VIII (Vol. II).
[g]It is evident here that the emotional effect of music has become the empirical manifestation and criterion of the older value, "beauty."

5. The French are to be imitated in this more than the Italians.
6. The melody must have certain limits that can be reached by everyone.
7. Brevity is preferred to length.

49. The French taste is given the preference in the point of simplicity in that it calls for a high-spirited, lively intelligence that is a friend of appropriate jest and an enemy of all that has the air of effort and work.[18] Although judicious Italians also, such as Marcello[h] and his likes (which, however, may not be numerous at all), hold untoward difficulties in contempt.

50. With *clarity* much is said, and also more laws are demanded by it than by the other properties. We will cite only ten for examination.

1. The caesuras and sections are to be exactly attended to, not only in vocal things, but also in instrumental.
2. One must always take a certain passion as the aim.
3. No meter must be changed without reason, need, and interruption.
4. The number of meters is to be kept within bounds.
5. No cadence is to occur in contradiction to the regular division of the measure.
6. The verbal accent is to be carefully observed.
7. One must avoid embellishment with great caution.
8. Strive for a noble simplicity in expression.
9. Comprehend exactly and differentiate the type of style.
10. Direct one's intent not to words but to their sense and understanding; see not to variegated notes but to expressive tones.

51. A knowledge of the jurisdiction of each key is indispensable to a *flowing quality*. The *Orchestre* teaches what kind of a meaning this word *jurisdiction* has here.[19] Most of this has to do primarily with cadences, pauses, and sections, which are otherwise not unjustly called clauses. Now if a melody necessarily loses its flowing property through frequent stoppages, it is self-understood that we have a reason not to introduce such a halt often. Eight rules serve for this purpose:

1. The regularity of the tonal feet or rhythms is to be kept diligently in view.
2. Also the geometric relation of certain similar phrases, or the *numerum musicum* (i.e., the melodic numerical proportion), is to be exactly preserved.

[18]La superiorité du gout françois et ce genie vif, ami d'un badinage gracieux, enemi de tout ce qui porte l'air du travail. *Discours sur l'harmonie* [an anonymous work, as Mattheson tells us in Paragraph 63], p. 82.
[h]Benedetto Marcello (1686-1739). See Strunk's *Source Readings* for a section of his *Teatro alla moda*.
[19]First Eröffnung [Mattheson's *Neu-eröffnete Orchestre* again], p. 106, under the name *étendue* ["compass"], and also p. 147, under the designation *ambitus*. Some call it the "extension."

3. The fewer *formal* cadences a melody has, the more flowing it is without question.
4. The cadences must be sought out and the voice well conducted around them before one progresses to the points of rest.
5. In the course or movement of the melody the few intermediate points of rest must have a certain connection with what follows them.
6. An overly dotted character *in singing* is to be shunned; it requires a special circumstance.
7. The paths and avenues of the melody may not be negotiated with many abrupt impulses, with little chromatic steps.
8. No theme must hinder or interrupt the melody in its natural progress.

52. What now after this concerns *loveliness*[20] may be abetted by means of these eight rules:

1. Even and small intervals are to be preferred in this regard to large leaps.
2. Such small steps are to be judiciously varied.
3. All kinds of unsingable phrases to be compiled in order to guard against similar things.
4. Well sounding ones in contrast to be selected and collected as models.
5. The conduct of all phrases, sections, and divisions to be well observed.
6. Good repetitions, yet not too frequent, to be introduced.
7. The beginning to be made in straightforward tones related to the key.
8. Moderate runs or variegated figures to be used.

53. Now anyone who gives the matter the slightest consideration can easily comprehend that these rules could still experience a great amplification if it had been undertaken to increase further their number of thirty-three. For me they are already too numerous, and I also wanted to make the very first attempt to clear a path with them in the firm belief that he who really masters the adduced axioms of melody can already draw additional useful consequences from them in time, and if he justly takes experience as an aid, can pursue the matter more and more to its artistic perfection.

54. A mass of rules makes a science difficult; few and good ones make it simple and pleasant. No rules at all forebode its decline. And nevertheless, because it also does not end the matter by far if one knows merely the briefly formulated rules, but rather it would seem to be highly necessary for their practical use to impart an explanation of them, I will go through them in order and discuss them as briefly as possible.

55. As to what accordingly concerns the presupposition *That in a good melody there must be something, an indefinable something, with which the whole world, so*

---

[20]In loveliness or cajoling style the Italians have priority over the French, according to the avowal of the latter themselves.

to speak, is acquainted: by this we do not say at all that one might introduce cleverly many worn out things and old hackneyed little formulas, not by any means. Rather we mean much more this: that one not go entirely too far with his newly concocted inventions, not become an eccentric, and in the process make his melody not only strange but also difficult and disagreeable.

56. Hearing always desires to have *something* with which it already in some degree is acquainted, be it as little as it may; otherwise nothing can be heard by it *easily*, much less please it. The more rarely one treads between known passages of this kind and the more one knows how to mix them with other, more foreign yet apt sections, the better the work will turn out.

57. The second rule of *simplicity* arises from the first: For just as on the one hand we may not completely set aside everything familiar, so again, on the other hand, everything *forced, pretentious, and altogether too far-fetched must be avoided diligently*. What is meant by this can be more fittingly discerned and heard in the work of composers given to affectation than described in words. In this case the examples are odious; otherwise many of them could be cited.

58. Commonly when good people are lacking in pleasing inventions and in spirit yet at the same time do not wish conspicuously to plagiarize or steal from other composers, they usually become true eccentrics and take refuge in outright willful whims, seeking thus to substitute astonishing oddities for the failure of natural fertility. As difficult as this may become for authors, it also comes to be annoying to listeners—with some few dandies excepted who wish to be regarded as though they truly understood something of it.

59. The third rule, *that we should follow nature mostly, but custom only in some things,* proceeds equally from the grounds previously established and is rightly connected with them. The natural vocalizing of one who is theoretically inexperienced will yield the best melody, and indeed so much the more because it is distant from all artificial constraints and only related to custom in some measure; but such a person must have heard a great deal that is good in his day and possess an inborn capacity.

60. Nothing can be *simpler* and more comfortable than what nature itself puts into our hand, and nothing will prove difficult that custom and habit call good. Therefore a composer must at times in the fabrication of his melodies—if they are to be *simple*—conduct himself like a mere amateur, and learn from him, as it were, the essence of nature, which he will seek in vain in high art.

61. Fourthly, if we *reject artificiality*, this is not to be applied to true art; but to employ this skillfully and to hide it or clothe it modestly—that is precisely the very difficult point. My advice was to the effect that even the most artistic composer of all might rely just as little on his actual weaving tricks as a skilled fencer on his feints.

62. Since the fifth rule directs us to the French and counsels us *to follow them more than the Italians in melodic simplicity*, we can not do better than to put *Lully's* work before us and the work of several renowned composers after him; for the more recent Frenchmen in part ape the Italians entirely too much, and desire against their natural disposition to be great artists, but in this way spoil the *simplicity* otherwise indisputably peculiar to them and inherent, by which they unnecessarily make matters difficult for others as well as for themselves. Such did their own countryman, the unnamed author of *L'Histoire de la Musique*, give them to understand quite clearly and emphatically in his last two volumes, which do not originate with *Bonnet.*

63. The able but also unnamed author of a tract already cited[21] discusses this as follows: "If we find a rival in Italian music we must not therefore immediately *banish it into a dismal exile,* but also not *in a foolish manner prefer it,* but rather avoid everything extreme and *enrich* ourselves *with its compositions.* For although we Frenchmen now and then take Italian teachers for the sake of high art, yet the Italians conversely, for the sake of grace and loveliness, also may frequently draw upon the harmony of our land for help in order to come the nearer to beloved nature; this is always simple, always true; and uncovers no beauty where compulsion rules, no delicacy where art plays the master."

64. All too great and forced art (I can not say too much about this) is a loathsome artificiality and takes from nature its noble simplicity. If nature at first blush seems to transmit many things extremely shapeless, this supposed ugliness nevertheless concerns only the external aspect, not the inner essence. Nature never lacks beauty, naked beauty; she only hides this at times under a discreet cover or playful mask. Our stone cutters can polish the diamond, but give it in this no other gleam, no other limpidity, than what it already possesses by nature. Ministering art accordingly presents no beauty to nature at all and does not even increase it by a hair's breadth, but rather, through its effort, only places it in a true light, which quite certainly must be more darkened than brightened where a despotic art issues the commands.

65. It contributes greatly to *simplicity* if, in consequence of the sixth rule, we *set certain bounds* to our melody that every moderate voice can reach. For if a song moves either very much too high or very much too low it becomes *difficult* for many people because of this and must be transposed now in one

---

[21]Si l'Ausonie nous offre une Rivale, sans la proscrire tristement, sans la proferer follement, fuyant tout extrême, enrichons nous de ses beautez. Et si pour le sublime de l'Art nous ecoutons quelque fois ses leçons, que pour le gracieux de la belle Nature, elle consulte souvent l'Harmonie de nos bords: celle-ci toujours simple, toujours vraie, ne trouve point la beauté où regne l'Affectation ni la tendresse où regne l'Art. *Discours sur l'harmonie,* p. 80.

way, now in another, which causes downright inconvenience. Those who are good singers will at least find no difficulty in reaching an octave, yet who knows what unusual advantage may often be involved if one sets these boundaries for himself still more narrowly, perhaps at a seventh or a sixth; for the more a composer attempts too much here the more he accustoms himself to melodic passages that are poorly connected with one another, wandering, and detached. One rambles about in a presumed freedom and brings nothing forth that impresses the heart as well fitted together or artistic.

66. I do not speak here of such practised composers as are masters of melody, find before them capable people for performance, and pride themselves on using their freedom in the right place; for these one cannot set such exact bounds. But I would want to advise a beginning maker of melodies that at first he choose for himself the range of a sixth or octave, yet in such a way that even a peasant not notice it. Certainly it will contribute a great deal to make his melodies *simple* and *convenient*. For of what special service is it to me that this or that person alone is able to perform an aria which extends, for example, over two octaves? I might want—even if only mentally—to sing with him; in this there consists the greatest pleasure; but that is not permitted to me: the composition is too difficult.

67. The last rule of this first section is not the least, namely, *that one is to prefer brevity to length*. But this needs the less clarification the more we can comprehend that a concise and not too widely spread out melody is *simpler* to retain than a long and stretched out one.

68. With which, however, it is not said that a short aria is *simpler* to compose, for along with brevity we also include worth. The simplicity here applies only to the listeners, not the composer, although to the former a thing will rarely *seem* simple that to the latter, in a certain laborious or painstaking sense, has become truly difficult.

69. I say *seem*. For there are certain composers all of whose work, effort, and revisions really serve only in that they eliminate everything which does not *demonstrate an unusual simplicity* or have such an appearance, and the more they inspect their works in such a manner or pass them in review the more often they bring about in the same a naturalness and simplicity. But these minds are rarely to be met with, and in their efforts they may with every right make use of the Italian proverb: *Questo facile quanto è difficile! How difficult for us is this apparently simple thing!* We must make it as elegantly as if it were only child's play,[22] although often a secret perspiration breaks out in us in doing so, which nevertheless no one must notice or else he would perspire with us

[22]Ludentis speciem dabit; et torquebitur. Horace, *Ars poetica*, v. 124. [i.e. Epistles II.ii.124, "He will wear the look of being at play, and yet be on the rack."]

in fellowship like that Sybarite who came upon a ragamuffin in bitter, thoughtless labor.

70. "I do not mean, then, *simplicity* of composition, which can often be fortunate but must always be suspicious. I mean only the simplicity that a listener finds in such works as have been already composed and have been as difficult for the composer as anything in the world. One might compare them with those artful gardens which are put together with turf and grass esplanades, and the costliness of which one does not detect, regarding them instead as something accidental and a work of nature only, although they were purchased for millions."[23]

71. I recently read a master's conclusion to the following effect: *What I have been able to achieve through diligence and practice, that another also must be able to achieve who has only half way the disposition and aptitude.* At the same time I thought that if this were true, how then could such a master be the sole one in the world and no one equal him? Pieces that are difficult to play can be excused well in another way, to be sure,[24] but because for all that most people actually lack if not the will, yet the desired aptitude and skill for the purpose *completely*, hard work of such kind will be useful to very few of them. This is incontestably true, and confirmed by unfortunate experience.

72. The second principal property of a well disposed melody is *clarity*; in this the first rule, *that one is to observe exactly the caesuras of the text*, stated a great deal with few words. It is almost not believable how even the greatest masters so often offend in this, as they usually apply all their powers to drive the ears to rebellion with furious and rushing figures; yet the understanding is by no means satisfied with this, and much less can the heart feel anything genuine.

73. The most astonishing thing is that everyone adheres to the idea that no such remarks are needed in the case of instrumental music, but it shall be demonstrated plainly and clearly further on below that all instrumental melodies, large as well as small, must have their correct *commata, cola,* periods [i.e., phrases, clauses, sentences], etc., not differently than, but just the same as does song with human voices, because it otherwise is impossible to find a *clarity* in them.

---

[23] Je n'entens pas la facilité de composer, elle peut quelques fois etre heureuse; mais elle doit toujours etre suspecte. J'entens la facilité que les Auditeurs trouvent dans les compositions deja faites, qui a eté souvent pour l'Auteur une des plus difficiles choses du Monde: de sorte qu'on pourroit la comparer à ces jardins enterrasses, dont la depense est cachèe, et qui, apres avoir coutè des millions, semblent n'etre que le pur ouvrage du hazard et de la Nature. Pelisson, in the Preface of the *Oeuvres* of Sarrazin.

[24] e.g., All excellent things have their certain difficulty; but all difficult things are therefore not excellent: Things with which no difficulty is connected do not serve as a test, and so on.

74. To such clarity one will also never truly succeed if the following guideline is not observed, through which *in each melody we must set up an emotion* (if not more than one) *as our principal goal.*

75. Just as a judicious painter always provides one or the other of his elegant figures (where many of them are presented) with particularly exalted colors so that it stands out noticeably among the other depictions, the composer accordingly must also in his melodic compositions direct his intent continuously and *particularly* to one or another passion, and so observe or express the same that it has far more meaning than all the remaining attendant circumstances.

76. We may also, in connection with painting, bear this in mind: that an able painter's purpose is not merely directed, let us say, to painting a pair of black or blue eyes, a noble nose, and a small red mouth, but rather he always strives to represent in such facial features one or another inner impulse and applies all his numerous ideas to the end that the viewer might say, for example: Something amorous lies hidden in the eyes, there is something magnanimous about the nose, and something scornful about the mouth.

77. Just as little, then, must a composer of melody also be satisfied only with painting away at beautiful variegated notes, diligently making a parade of his intervals and other implements, and decorating the whole in addition with the most splendid adjectives; instead he must really strive to see that a dominant emotion rules his construction. Now if he does not feel this himself or does not know how to imitate it naturally, how is it possible for him to excite it in others?[i]

78. But when nothing of this sort is expressed in a melody, it possesses little or almost nothing at all that is *clear,* and the attentive listener can make nothing of it other than an empty singing and sounding. This rule lays down for us only the highest necessity of representing such a passion, and points out the urgent reasons; how one must proceed with this, however, belongs in another place.

79. In the meantime it is to be wondered at that in pieces which are supposed to be directed simply to instruction, we praise primarily the seriousness, the greatest emphasis and most exact expression of the words, the harmony, the skill, and the concertizing manner, and desire to amplify the teachings and vigorous ideas much more than to deal with emotions and passions.

80. Indeed the greatest emphasis, the vigorous ideas, and the most exact observation of the words, that is, of the intelligence residing in the words,

[i] Evidence of the reality of the emotions in music, and at the same time of the essential place of imitation in musical aesthetics.

arise originally from the emotions and passions, and can exist without the same just as little as a wagon can without wheels: if it does not have these it is a sleigh or a sled. Let us take an application from true and long experience, and so it will reveal itself to be.

81. What do our teachers in the pulpit do; do they not become indignant; do they not perspire; do they not rejoice; do they not weep; do they not clap their hands together; do they not threaten? Who will say that this belongs much more to mere cold instruction than to vital emotion? Who can contradict Plato and David in this? If we wish to give vigorous ideas and teachings a supplementation, and still more an exalted supplementation, this can not proceed half-heartedly.

82. Precisely seriousness in itself is an extremely important affection and such a national mark of distinction as a Spaniard would not for all the world willingly do without. In sum, everything that occurs without commendable affections amounts to nothing, does nothing, is worth nothing, be it where, how, and when it will. Teachings without emotion are of the kind that were celebrated thus in song:

> Those good teachings let me own,
>   As also asks each mother's child
>   Who is of the very mind as I:
>   They can convert us and console.[j]

83. The simplest children's game is never without passion, not only in an incidental way, but in a primary one; no infant can be absolved from it. And if, for example, a teacher has no *eager interest* in imparting something sound to the one entrusted to him or if he feels no *joy* when he teaches something solid, of what profit is it to both? But are eager interest and joy not emotions, and does the unlocked mouth of a student not indicate desire? But let us continue!

84. When the French alter the measure in almost every line of their *recitative* and also very often in the *airs*, they take the trouble almost in vain, and could with less expense follow the Italians in this if their changeable pronunciation would tolerate it, as the Italians, with us, observe no measured beat at all in singing recitative, even in a metrical passage. It is almost the same thing, however, to have no measure or to have a new one every instant.

85. But because recitative really cannot be called melody, and in melodic compositions, by contrast, insofar as they are to be *clear*, too frequent alteration of the beat is to be avoided, it is then evident that the *soul of the*

> Ich lobe mir die guten Lehren,
>   Und so thut ieder Mutter-Kind,
>   Das eben so wie ich gesinnt:
>   Sie können trösten und bekehren.

142

melody, namely the measure, *must be only single.* And this was the third rule for furthering clarity. But if the rhyme structure or an unexpected affection demands the alteration of the beat, then need knows no command, to be sure; yet in my opinion the poet should not lightly make a noticeable change in his syllabic rhythm in an aria, for it would be as though he also wanted to arouse at the same time another passion in an unexpected way (*ex abrupto*).

86. The fourth rule of *clarity* rests on the *number of units in the measure,* which are otherwise called mensurations. Now although the same relations in large and long movements may not be so easily recognized by everyone, nevertheless their comfortable and comprehensible arrangement will give the song not a little *clarity,* even though many a person does not know to what it is due; in short and lively melodies, by contrast (*airs de mouvement*), such caution is unremittingly necessary, because otherwise a cheerful vocal tune will meet no other fate than a pair of arms, let us say, of which one has two hands but the other three or more.

87. Now it is indeed nothing difficult to establish to some degree the actual number of these mensurations in certain styles, as for example in the hyporchematic and choraic;[k] but in other styles it proves that much more difficult. Where there is much activity, the melos must exhibit the very greatest correctness of division in the piece; where on the contrary things go along indolently and prolixly or also merely seriously and slowly, there more exception can be made in consideration of the uniformity, because the departure is not so noticeable.

88. Generally one does best, in the broadest *adagio* also, if he chooses an even number of measures rather than an uneven one. So much is certain: that a nimble song should *never* have an uneven number of measures; and precisely all these *airs de mouvement* may be taken with complete security as a basis in this, and regarded as a model; for as we have said, they are among all types of melody, with regard to this characteristic, the most correct and the *clearest.*

89. *The observation of the regular division of each measure,* namely the so-called *caesura,* gives us the fifth rule of clarity. Such a division always falls either on the down-beat or on the up-beat when the mensuration is even, never on the second and the last quarter. In uneven measure, however, this division occurs nowhere but on the down-beat alone, or to speak more correctly, no division at all really takes place, because the caesura lies simply on the first note of the segment.

90. To introduce a cadence or any other noticeable fall and pause of the voice in contradiction to this nature of the meters is just such a mistake in the

[k]Styles of ancient Greek dance songs, the hyporchematic of Cretan origin and the choraic belonging to the tragedy.

art of composition as when a Latin poet ends the syllabic feet with the words and thus allows the caesura to enter, which may only occur at the end of a verse.

91. The chief cause of this frequently encountered evil in the art of melodic composition doubtless arises mostly because the usual four-quarter measure is carelessly mixed with that which calls only for two halves. The former obviously has four different members but the latter only two, which in both kinds amounts to no more than two parts and consequently also permits just this many cadences or pauses in the melody, namely in each part, not in each member, when a part has more than two of these: for in such a case pauses must be made only on the first and third beats, where the parts begin, but not on the second and fourth, where they end. More about this can be found in the first volume of the *Musicalische Critick*, p. 32f.

92. The following example of an otherwise excellent master shows how easily one can commit an error in this. It will also show at the same time how easily mistakes of this kind may be prevented, and indeed right at the start: for otherwise they roll on more and more and increase like snowballs.

Incorrect

Correct

93. It is necessary to make a small exception in this, namely that in a few dancelike and melismatic[1] things in uneven measures the last beat must now and then also serve to a certain degree as a caesura: when a special uniformity is sought and continued throughout in the same way. But let such a thing occur with diligence and not approximately or through ignorance of the rule. For example:

[1]Mattheson's conception of "melismatic" is doubtless the same as Kircher's, so that it would designate a style of vocal music which is lively, strictly homophonic, and usually secular.

94. Just as the *accent* in the pronunciation of words can make a text clear or unclear in accordance with whether it is introduced in the correct or the incorrect place, so also can the sound, in accordance with whether it is accented well or poorly, make the melos clear and unclear, and from this arises the sixth rule of clarity.

95. Both kinds of accent, of text as well as of sound, a composer must understand exactly, so that he does not violate the long and short of the syllables in vocal things or the tonal prosody in instrumental pieces. But what kind of significance this has, and what kind of value its skillful application has, can be learned along with more things in the cited section of the *Critick*.

96. With this we also include the actual *stress*, or the *emphasis*, because that word which is supplied with such always demands a certain kind of musical accent. Only it depends on one's knowing how to judge correctly just which these emphatic words are. And there is no better counsel here than that we investigate all manner of delivery, especially in prose, and endeavor to find the properly deserving word, perhaps by the following means:

97. If I wanted to know, for example, where the verbal stress may lie in this sentence: *Our life is a journey,* then I would only need to cast the proposition as question and answer, namely: *What is our life? A journey.* Accordingly it is revealed here that the emphasis falls on the word journey; and if the composer projects such a word through his tones in one or another unconstrained manner he will be *clear.*

98. Because what we are dealing with here is of considerable importance, an additional few cases will displease no one; for example, *He who presumes to sit here in the world in quiet peace is very much deluded.* Then the framing of the question will be determined, which in my opinion must go as follows: Is not he deceived who presumes to sit in quiet peace in the world? Answer: *Very much so!* Accordingly the true stress would fall on the adverb of intention, and on nothing else; in the genesis of this modifier, however, the verb *deluded* [*betrogen*] must carry the greatest emphasis. It is to be noted in this connection that precisely these adverbs often have the most to say in speech, and the stress lies on them frequently, especially when they signify a magnitude, attribute, extent, comparison, explanation, and so on.

99. One more example: *The path to heaven is overgrown with thorns.* There is asked, as it were, in this case: *With what is the path to heaven overgrown?* and answered: *With thorns.* For if this single word is removed no intelligence at all will remain over, or the utterance does not say what it purports to say, which is a sign by which one may equally note the place of stress.

100. At times the place seems to be ambiguous, so that the emphasis can readily affect more than one word, according to the intention. For example,

My angel, are you there? Here either the person or the location is asked about and thus with the first intent the stress is placed on *you* and with the second on *there*. The context must decide the issue. In such form everyone can go on to practice this himself, and sharpen his understanding.

101. The seventh rule of *clarity* teaches us *to apply all embellishments and figures with great discretion*. Daily experience shows what kind of atrocious little patches are pasted to the face through the neglect of this precept of melodic beauty. An unnamed author recently wrote about this as follows: "The arias are so variegated and so frilled that one becomes impatient before the end comes. The composer is satisfied when he sets down only senseless notes, which the singers, through a thousand contortions, make still more insipid. They laugh during the most tragic performance and their Italian prolixities always come in the wrong place. The arias that the excellent T. has composed are much too orderly: their passages are always filled out with such frenzies, which are suitable for flattering throats but not for the mind."

102. This kind of embroidered work, be it produced by a composer of corrupted taste or by an exuberant singer, seems to me not different from an altogether too ornamented livery for pages or trumpeters, in which everything is covered to such an extent with gold and silver brocade that one can recognize in it neither the cloth nor the color of the cloth. Even this comparison is much too favorable. But since such excess in decorations should not be approved of, a sensible composer finds so much the more reason to guard against them the more easily a bad habit or fashion in many people can grow out of depraved taste.

103. These are precisely the ruinous extravagances about which *Quintilian* even in his time was able to sing a ditty in which he expressly acknowledged that he could not in any way sanction what was undertaken at the time with music in the theater, where namely the *effeminate and voluptuous manner of singing* contributed not a little to suppress and stifle entirely what still perhaps existed in some hearts of masculinity and virtue.[25]

104. Now we come to conscious *simplicity*, of which the eighth rule of *clarity* treats, and which is to be understood, however, not as something dull, foolish, or common, but much more as something noble, undecorated, and really singular. This simplicity constitutes the most important point of all in writing and speaking as well as in singing and playing, indeed in the whole

---

[25]Apertius profitendum puto, non hanc musicam a me praecipi, quae nunc in Scenis effoeminata et impudicis modis fracta, non ex parte minima, si quid in nobis virilis roboris manebat, excidit. ["I think it should be stated openly that I do not teach this effeminate and lewd music of the stage which has in no small measure taken away whatever manly strength remained in us."] Quintilian, *Institutiones*, Book I, Ch. 10:31.

146

of human intercourse; and if ever inborn characteristics were to be acknowledged, here would certainly be the right place for them.

105. So much is doubtless beyond dispute, that men also in this respect have some prior endowment, one above the other, in accordance with which the construction of the body and the mixture of the humors are regularly or irregularly disposed and consequently susceptible or insusceptible of impression.[m] Noble thoughts always have a certain simplicity, something uncontrived, and only a single aim. Now he who imagines things of this kind without any compulsion, in accordance simply with natural laws, will best succeed.

106. If we wish to have examples and models, we have only to look at old painting and sculpture and medallions. What strong features, majestic visages, and energetic postures do we not encounter? in which, nevertheless, even the very slightest, superfluous ornament is not conveyed, but rather the most beautiful simplicity and most pleasing bareness stand forth. This bareness is not wretched, however, but noble minded and modest; not loathsome, but delightful, because it stands in its true light. Just in such a way, then, should our melodies also be constituted.

107. We now have two more rules of *clarity* left to explain: the ninth, which commends us *to distinguish the manners of composing well from one another.* This seeks briefly to say much: we are not to mix with one another the vocal and instrumental styles in the church, in the theater, and in the chamber; not to set down a petition where a prescription should stand; not to require the voice to do things that are suitable for violins; not to score military recruiting pieces for lutes,[n] and other similar things of which something has already been called to mind above.

108. The tenth rule of *clarity* is indeed by chance the last, but in respect of content almost the most important. For in pursuance of the same, if we want to direct *our chief intent not to the words, but rather to the understanding and to the thoughts contained in them,* then no limited insight into the affection contained in such words will be requisite for this, which it will be necessary to consider in more detail in another place.

109. This rule, moreover, has two parts, of which one deals with human voices but the other with instruments, and most strongly recommends to us

---

[m]The doctrine of temperaments, descended from ancient medicine, and providing the basis for the various effects of the different musical intervals, rhythms, styles, and so on, which acted mechanically on the vital spirits to produce the affections. This was the underlying machinery of Baroque musical aesthetics.

[n]This of course takes a stand in opposition to the Baroque delight in stylistic transfer as well as to Baroque exuberance and sophistication in general. It really represents a galant aesthetic, which with the emphasis it places on simplicity, also frequently adumbrates the later eighteenth-century conception of classical Antiquity (See paragraph 106, for example).

more *clarity* and expressive tones, not a throng of variegated notes. For that not a single melody should be without sense, without intent, without emotion, even if without words, is confirmed by this and by the laws of nature itself. So much for the second class of elucidation of our fundamental melodic rules.

110. The third property of a good melody was, then, that it must be *flowing*. This will be abetted, first of all, if one keeps steadily in view the rhythmical agreement and correct alteration of the arithmetical relation of certain tonal feet. With this we do not say that one must in fact retain the same kind of rhythm, which would produce a discomfort and an aversion; rather one must necessarily exchange various tonal feet with one another just as this occurs in its own way in Latin poetry. But in melody those rhythms that have occurred before in one place must again appear in another and correct place so that they answer one another, as it were, and make the melody flowing.

111. The order that is observed in such introduction and change of the tonal feet one calls a geometric relation, for as the arithmetic relation considers these feet on which the melody walks along, as it were, in and for themselves, so in contrast the geometric relation shows how they are fitted together and must correctly give an account of their individualization. For example:

a is a certain tonal foot of three notes which are different in intrinsic value; *b* is again one of the same number of notes but all of the same duration. There is in each of these a particular arithmetical constitution. In contrast, *c* and *d*, both taken together, represent the orderly alternation of the preceding feet and make of them a whole geometric section.

112. On this occasion no one may be ashamed to take the hand of prosody and to make himself a catalogue of all the feet in poetry in order to compare such with the melodic ones, among which many will then be mentioned that are strangers in poetry, because music surpasses it in riches here and also eveything that the former has arises originally from the latter. Actually this material belongs to rhythmical composition, which calls for study in its own right if one wishes to pursue it with technical correctness. In the following chapter we will go through it.

113. The third rule for the promotion of a *flowing* constitution in melody, as well as the fourth, concerns the cadences or closes. For since it naturally is well established that many closes and sections obstruct the course of a song,

so it is easy to imagine that a truly flowing melos must have only few, only few formal cadences.

114. It is true, to be sure, that themes sometimes occur which have cadences one right after the other, and follow a sound intention expressly through these; and that similarly our chorales, of which several indeed have very beautiful melodies although they often scarcely reach the limits of a fifth (like the German Gloria), consist of almost nothing but cadences; but here we are not speaking of this, namely of the stylistic properties of fugues and odes, but of the poverty that is evident when one is able to present in other things nothing but cadences. Even in fugues they must be avoided or concealed.

115. The worst thing of all in this regard is when such closes are in addition very poorly chosen, against and in opposition to the fourth rule, and the song strides to a premature rest even before it has yet acquitted itself of the slightest expressive turn or can have any reason for tiredness. It is good, pleasing, and beautiful if immediately at the beginning a principal cadence on the final note is heard, for example:

With this the listener at once obtains an account of the entire key and of the manner in which the composer plans to progress further when once he has taken such a firm step; this is pleasing. But the untimely makers of cadences do not follow such an intention at all; with minor keys they immediately fall into a cadence on the third, and with major into the close on the fifth, for these lie closest at hand for them. There is the end of the matter; then they simply no longer know what to do.

116. To this elucidation we can also add the advantage that accrues to a melody in its *flowing* nature when the divided triad is sounded in a skillful way right at the beginning, for the listener obtains from this a still greater capacity of judging the region within which his ears will be conducted. Everyone very much likes knowing beforehand and judging; thus a procedure of this kind is pleasing.

117. If also overly dotted character, especially in vocal things, can bring with it little or nothing *flowing*, the sixth rule counsels us in this case to discard such. In preluding and fantasizing, where precisely no properly flowing melody is called for, this need not be taken so literally; in the whole of instrumental music, to speak of it in general, also not; indeed in entrées and

similar noble dances, just as at times in overtures, it will be expressly necessary to introduce much dotted rhythm; it sounds very fresh and lively, and expresses various, cheerful, and also some vehement emotions very well, but it nevertheless nowhere *flows*.

118. Continuity or skillful connection helps melodic flow a great deal; therefore one has to see in the fifth place, especially at certain pauses or closes, that nothing is blurted out, but rather that all things are suited to one another and fitted together without long delay, by means of convenient approaches and progressions, as occurs in a good oration through transitions. The French pursue this almost entirely too diligently in their music, and because of it give their compositions much that resembles an organ grinder. For this reason moderation also must be preserved here, for that which is all too flowing becomes slippery and easily steals away.

119. The everlasting pulling and dragging through half-tones and dissonances with which many are so much infatuated has its time and its place, to be sure, as circumstances permit it or demand it; but he who desires to compose something *flowing* may not seek such twisted chromatic paths. Where there is not such an intent, however, everyone has a free hand in this respect. I will constrain no one.

120. Now just as good, unforced coherence in which one does not proceed too anxiously does not make a phrase with its following one less *flowing* because of their connection, so in contrast a great hindrance arises in this property if perhaps to suit one or another theme, one interrupts the song, the lyrical constitution, in its natural course with inept pauses, and holds the melody back in its progress; for then, indeed, it cannot possibly *flow*.

121. We understand here, however, the theme of a bass or secondary voice, not of a subject in a fugal piece: that is to say, if the bass or the violins, say, wanted to come into particular prominence in an aria, so that in the mean time the most important or vocal part had to suffer and wait only in order that the former might also take hold of the theme (be it constituted as it may)—which runs contrary to all reason and yet occurs daily.

122. The class of *loveliness* is more considerable than the three preceding ones, just as these, in contrast, are more necessary. Now in so far as the eight rules imparted on this require clarification, the first is to the effect that one must employ more degrees or steps and in general more small intervals than large leaps if the melody is to sound *lovely*.

123. He who wishes to find examples of this and arrange them in order can place them like *locos communes*° under certain general and particular headings, from which no inconsiderable utility is to be expected. We will

°A reference to the rhetorical "commonplaces."

make a little outline and indicate to the industrious inquirer by means of it how he might possibly proceed in this case:

First general heading, of the ascending half-tone, supplied with selected examples:

Ver- süs- se mein-en Schmerz etc.

Son las- sa, si, son las- sa etc.

Second general heading, of the descending half-tone, with selected examples:

Ach! en- de mei- ne Qua- len etc.

Tor- na o sol, tor- na a me, tor- na tor- na etc.

To both of which might be appended: *Two special headings of the small half-tones, ascending as well as descending, for example:*

Herr, Hö- re mich, mein Kö- nig und mein Gott, Ver-

nimm mein Schrei- en.

Third general heading, in which are contained well chosen samples of the ascending minor third:

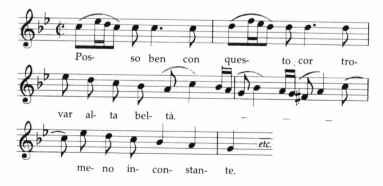

Pos- so ben con ques- to cor tro-

var al- ta bel- tà.

me- no in- con- stan- te.

151

Fourth general heading, of the descending third, and so on, up to the fourth.

124. Now even if we observe the previous rule and to further the *loveliness* of a melody proceed more by steps than by leaps, the following axiom still demands: *that one also judiciously alternate such steps and small intervals,* that is to say that one should not take simply steps, simply thirds, much less simply fourths, and also not set down many intervals of one and the same kind in continuous succession, but rather delight the hearing with more frequent change, by which the song will become the loveliest of all.

125. Of half tones, for example, three or four in succession, provided no special intention is hidden in them, will already be too many, especially of small semitones. Five to six steps are also somewhat disagreeable, diatonic ones particularly, unless the words or circumstances, or as we said, a special procedure, a theme, a run, and similar things expressly call for more. We are speaking here only of the *loveliness* of a melody in general, not of unusual occurrences, when every rule suffers exception.

126. Of thirds, two or three in succession can be allowed, and not more of one and the same kind without damaging *loveliness*; of fourths, however, seldom more than two, if they are accentuated. The down-beat and up-beat of the measure make for some doubt here, to be sure, yet it is not of the importance that would destroy the rule in itself or invalidate it. He who wishes to take the trouble to go through pieces of music for this purpose with understanding will discover the truth; for example:

These three fourths would not sound lovely: But these two are good:

127. By this we shall be led imperceptibly to the third rule of *loveliness*, in virtue of which one *is to seek out industriously unmelodic or unsingable passages,* place such under certain headings, take note of wherein their poor sound consists, investigate the causes of the same, and painstakingly avoid similar things.

128. One does not have to seek far for such things, because the bad is usually met with more often than the good, but with those who make a craft of counterpoints more than with others, one comes upon a remarkable treasure of inept and contrary passages, and here one can easily become rather clever through their mistakes.

129. When, for example, some one writes the following:

everyone who had any concept whatever of a *lovely* melody would have to admit readily that such an ascending minor third b-d, which is followed by an accented half-tone cannot at all sound natural, not to mention *pleasing*.

130. Now one might say: I hear such a thing very well, but do not know how to offer any reason for it; for him the account will serve that the terminal notes b and e-flat make a harsh dissonance, namely a diminished fourth, that they are both accented, and sound still worse than otherwise because of the intermediate "d," on account of the irregular division. In this resides the reason.

131. For if the middle note "d" remained absent, and a half-note beat were made of the "b," one would not notice the unpleasant sound so strongly by far, because the "b" then would acquire a pause or stay and might the more easily be forgotten. There would also not be so bad an effect on the composition of the aforesaid diminished fourth even if it occurred in shorter notes of equal value, provided only that the two terminal notes had no accent, but rather one of them was represented as the fourth member of the measure. For example:

Yet here also a certain ornament would be called for in the execution as a concealment, the slur, which we have indicated with dots; one would not need this, on the other hand, if the defective fourth descended instead of ascending.

132. Under the entry on the judicious alternation of intervals, the following unmelodious example could stand in the bad series:

Here, however, the reason is not in dissonance but rather in the untimely empty leap of the major third b-flat to d, which has no community with either the preceding or the following intervals, and accordingly is not at all suitable for alternation.

133. The intervals, that is to say, contain a strange order: two ascending steps, an ascending major third, and an ascending half step. That all four of these intervals ascend, many might think, is indeed something uniform and good; but we answer: the ascent is arranged in such uneven steps that precisely because of it the alleged uniformity falls away entirely, and a hindrance is presented to a lovely alternation. If the third were only filled in, the passage would at once be tolerable, but it would be still better if instead of the ascending third a descending one were introduced, thus:

134. From such a close examination of poorly laid out passages many special rules will infallibly arise, of which we now wish to give only a small sample. According to the introductory guide above it is evident:

1. That an ascending half step which is followed by an ascending major third with another ascending half step does not make a good melody.
2. That two ascending fourths, when they are accented, and still less three of them, can hardly sound good, for a poorly mediated seventh will be produced in the melody.
3. That a third and a second, when they come after one another in the following way:

are extremely lame and unmelodic. And whether accents on the first part or dots on the second can much improve things here is really to be doubted. The reason is that our ears, after the falling third and rising second, prefer to hear another large interval downward and not a smaller one, since the former would expand the vital spirits that are restricted by the seconds,[P] for example:

[P]A reference to the fundamental causal explanation of the affections (the predecessor of today's electro-chemical neural processes).

135. Just such natural reasons exist also for the example cited in paragraph 129, namely that the expansion is pleasing when a constriction precedes. Thus:

If this succession is reversed, it will also have the opposite effect; that is, all restriction is that much more depressing when an expansion has preceded. It is better, therefore, to guard against such passages, unless they are in uneven measure, with a certain addition that introduces a connection or an appealing manner, for example:

where the unmelodic example given in paragraph 134 secures a completely different form because of the accent and likewise because of the down-beat and up-beat as well as the arpeggiation and ornaments. In all phrases of this kind, however, that which precedes and follows will come significantly into consideration.

136. We will add another few remarks or rules concerning *unlovely* passages, namely:

4. Two seconds with an empty space between, one after another, will produce nothing lovely either after them or before them, in this fashion:

for after the perceived step g-f, we would like to hear a continuation of this diatonic type of step in descending or to perceive an extension upwards, but there follows here a gap; the melody breaks off and becomes unsingable. Now nothing will help here except the filling in of the rift.

5. A descending fourth followed by an ascending major third produces much that is unpleasant; the reasons are a poor separation and the accent, together with the equal value of these three sounds, as is to be discerned from a better separation of them, a more correct accent, and a varied value:

(unnatural)   (completely natural)

137. Now just as one must seek out bad passages in order to avoid them and to investigate their causes, so on the other hand one *has to take notice of well sounding ones as models*, which is the fourth rule by which one can bring about a loveliness in one's melodies.

138. *Bononcini* the younger is a lovely composer; *Telemann* also; and indeed I would especially propose these two, without offense to anyone, to a person eager to teach, so that he might draw from their widely known melodies the *most graceful* passages, and after close investigation, make particular comments on them. We find, for example, in the cantatas of the first this pleasing phrase:

139. From this one could set himself some such following rule: *A dactyl within a minor third downward, followed by a fifth leaping upward and then back again,* produces a beautiful effect, especially if, as here, the final note is heard three times, the third and fifth once each, and the ornamental sound of the half-tone below also once, for in this way one immediately has a perfect concept of the whole key.

140. If this phrase afterwards occurs again, through repetition, at the third above the tonic, its loveliness will be doubled, and indeed through the natural cause above, by virtue of which an expansion proves pleasant when a constriction has preceded. Above the third was minor; here it is major.

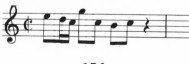

141. Here a new, special rule for the *lovely* conduct of the voice could find its place along with others, to the effect that after three or more such leaps of a fifth, many steps may be heard gladly and with pleasure because of the love of change, like such that directly follow.

142. In Telemann's works one comes upon an excellent stock of such beautiful passages, of which we will set down, only as a sample, merely the beginning of an aria, the words of which express heavenly grandeur very majestically and sonorously, since in so few notes not only a complete concept of the key is to be heard, but also, along with the exceptional *loveliness*, considerable exaltation:

Wel-   che   Pracht, be- glück-   tes   Au-. ge etc.

143. One sees here how gracefully the steps and leaps alternate with one another, how the falling, ascending, and progressing are so prudently intermixed. Certain pieces of this outstanding composer I was not able years ago to tire of singing; in particular he has elaborated the chorale, *Ach! Gott vom Himmel sieh darein* for organ with a bass viol in so richly melodic a fashion that there is nothing which surpasses it. This chorale may be found in the published smaller works of Herr *Telemann*, and I may well say, without being a forceful orator, that an organist who is not familiar with it is lacking in an eminent delight.

144. The fifth rule of *loveliness* consists in the *exact observation of the correct relation of all the parts of a melody with respect to one another.* Our previous interest concerned only the relation of the intervals, which one must indeed distinguish well from what is now in question, inasmuch as the parts themselves are compared.

145. The present rule aims not alone to have, for example, the second principal part of an aria stand in an alliance, so to speak, or on good terms with the first, but also to have the other smaller secondary parts display their required uniformity. Now in opposition to this, most galant composers manage in such a way that one would often think one part of their melody properly at home in Japan and the other in Morocco.

157

146. No one, to be sure, may proceed in this so very strictly as to take up a compass and measuring stick for the purpose; yet gross inequality and an untoward relation of the parts produce just such an injury to *loveliness*, indeed at times to the required *clarity* itself, as a large head and short legs to the beauty of the body. If in the first part, for example, this measure had been put forward:

It could then not fail to be pleasing if in the second part answer were made perhaps in the following form, proper understanding continued, and the relatedness of both parts accordingly sustained:

147. The sixth rule of *loveliness* demands that one contrive pleasing repetitions and imitations, but by no means too frequently. Commonly, true repetitions have their place more at the beginning of a melody than in its continuation, for there they often follow one another directly, and also without transposition, but later something always comes between them.

148. Of recurrence and how it may contribute a great deal to the apt relationship of the parts we have already spoken above, and therefore know what may be said in this regard. When we come to figures the matter will be still further explained. Here one may note merely the difference that simple repetition takes one and the same tones as a basis, but that recurrence and imitation bring to bear now higher tones and now lower ones. Of the first, this small passage can provide a sample, and indeed, because of the final descending tone, a really good one:

Oc- chi vez- zo- si, io non mi pen-to,

It would not be so pleasing if the voice held to an exact repetition with the word *pento*, and omitted the descent.

149. Not only in the last principal part of a melody, when we compare it with the first, will it appear *lovely* to apply recurrence skillfully, but it will also

sound very pleasing in the sections and connecting passages of each individual part in itself, if reason and moderation are drawn upon for counsel in this.

150. In what precedes we have been instructed in general about the conduct of whole parts of a melody; in this section, by way of contrast, and in the following one, we shall investigate in particular a few aids and circumstances that contribute a great deal to our purpose. For first it is to be remarked that repetitions in the beginning of an aria are adopted not out of deficiency or poverty but rather for the sake of *loveliness* and gracefulness, which are the more noticeable when sometimes, as above, one or another note is altered as though by chance and yet with careful deliberation. Anyone could easily set something new to the words *io non mi pento*, but it would not by far fall upon the ear in as lovely a way as the repetition.

151. After this it also sounds very lovely when in the beginning as well as in the continuation of the melody the repetitions and recurrences are well intermixed, and of this I want to present the following extract as a model. The beginning is as follows:

After this the composer continues the melody and cadences on the fifth, pauses for a couple of measures, then takes up the *repetition* of the beginning after he has secured the understanding of the text with complete satisfaction, and moves on to the end of the first part. The second part he commences with a recurrence and presents it in a twofold way: first at the sixth and then at the third, all of which sounds quite lovely, especially as the words rhyme in addition, for a recurrence never sounds better than in circumstances such as *vezzosetta, semplicetta*.

152. No one who has a mind to study can with the present musical wealth of the world be without all manner of diverse things and excellent examples, but what is doubtless lacking mostly is that not everyone knows what he is to

seek for and investigate in such things that is really serviceable to his purpose. For this the present instruction now furnishes some guidance without it being necessary to accumulate examples further.

153. Many old and new composers may pay me secret thanks that I am not bringing so many of their treasures into currency as I might have when I mentioned unmelodic passages above; of gold plate, however, I shall have on occasion neither cause nor desire to speak with such restraint as was well the case previously.

154. *That every beginning of a good melody is made with such tones as either present the key itself or are else closely related to it:* such is the requirement of the seventh rule of *loveliness*. Once more we need not seek far for examples, but only consider the one that has just preceded, in which the first four notes at once sound the complete chord of the key even more than is necessary.

155. Now this indeed occurs in the cited place simply in leaps and does not sound so well behaved as if it were accomplished in steps: yet such can not be observed all the time on account of the subject, and one must attend a great deal not only to the love of change, but also distinguish whether the sense of the words is fresh and cheerful or whether it is suffering and calm. An example of the latter is placed at our disposal by the following, in which the significance of patient suffering is expressed very naturally through steps alone, and indeed small ones, but nevertheless the key sufficiently displayed at the same time.

Sof-   fro   in   pa-   ce

156. A sparkling, flirtatious, and exuberant constitution in melodic composition nowadays has the greatest approval, and also mine insofar as I would not lightly advise anyone to swim against the stream. Now he who harbors this intent to please the largest mass of people, and no other, must at times set aside to a certain extent the gracefulness and other more essential properties of song. I am acquainted with several who know how to wear their coat in this case somewhat according to the wind; yet they finally swing again and again into the saddle and hold fast to good taste.

157. The last of our melodic rules will be that for the furtherance of *loveliness* one *use only moderate melisma or running figures*. Here we shall not investigate the passages or words to which ornaments of this kind are well or poorly suited, for that belongs to the most necessary part of the intelligibility and clarity already discussed. Now we shall consider only the simple form of the

melody without a special interest in its varying amenability to the observation of such decorations, and we say accordingly that melismas, when they are immoderately applied or extended too widely, obstruct *loveliness* and arouse aversion. This example is good:

repetition

158. Of contrary examples and unlovely passages there is indeed precisely no shortage; yet in the face of every danger I will set one down that as well as the former one comes from *Bononcini*, for great people also make mistakes.

a te più non ver- rà

— — — — — a te più non ver- rà.

159. In the last example I have diligently underlaid the words, which mean nothing special and are not at all worth such frippery, and I believe that one of those cases has presented itself here which were mentioned in paragraph 156.

160. One can still remark besides in connection with recurrences that these same, if things are to move along correctly in fugues and church pieces, must always answer major keys with major and minor with minor, which in the madrigal and dramatic manner of composition, in cantatas, arias, and so on, is optional, as is to be seen from the examples above.

161. At times a composer has singers and especially female singers before him to whom he either will gladly give as much to do as they can execute—that is, he will in every way bring about an advantage to them over others because they possess the skill for it and they are his favorites—or on the other hand they harass, worry, and molest him until he satisfies their foolish desire and not seldom must write things down that he himself disapproves

of, because they are opposed to reason, only so that he may keep them in a good mood and hence prevent them from fishing something out of their own brain that is ten times worse, throwing his aria before his feet, and saying it is not composed for their voice.

162. It happens, then, doubtless for this reason, that in works which carry the name of a great and famous master one oftentimes meets with *passaggi* or running figures which contain so little in the way of lovely moderation that they can with every right be called basically rude if not something worse.

163. In either case one must judge these things discreetly if marks of the good taste of the composer are otherwise found; but it is necessary for no one to imitate the thing if precisely the same causes are not operative for him as for the most part, however, are at home with the Italians. For a Frenchman, on account of the character of his subordinates in so far as they are compatriots, will downright never be forced to such extravagances by them, because the Italian flexibility and the rapid disposition of the throat is not bestowed upon the French by nature. Although among the newest composers in France there are some who wish to exceed themselves in this but also only make themselves the more laughable the more they compel their disposition, otherwise inclined to loveliness, to such excesses. Perhaps there will be occasion further on to mention more of this.

164. In the meantime the ice should have been broken a little here in that we have appended some explanations to our previous rules of melody which in part can serve instrumental music, but mostly belong to the singing voice, in which the source and the root of all melodic constitution is to be sought, so that henceforth it might be an easy matter to carry out this treatise further, to distinguish one from the other still more exactly, to provide them with more examples, and to offer a supplement to the things that have been discovered.

CHAPTER SEVEN

CHRISTIAN GOTTFRIED KRAUSE

Von der Musikalischen Poesie
(1752)

CHAPTER II
What Kind of Ideas Music Arouses

Which sounds and tones alone can truly be called music. Not every discourse is capable of being joined to music. Demonstration that music moves us. How the listener's body comports itself at that time. Music awakens obscene ideas. Digression on fugues and on pieces that are very rich in harmonic beauties. Which of the fugues is in proper use. Whether a musical piece is faulty because it is difficult. Music produces an intuitive knowledge. The effects and the uses of music. It makes us capable of gentle feelings; but it does not extend our knowledge. How it is surpassed in this by poetry. How music is nevertheless useful to us through mere amusement.

Not all sounds, indeed not all tones, that delight us are music. There are persons who are greatly pleased by the neighing of horses and similar things. Many find the greatest pleasure in the whistling of the wind, in the noise of a waterfall, in the rippling of a brook, and in the singing, whistling, and chirping of a nightingale. But as it is really not understanding according to which the American hamster and the bees proceed in their artlike toils because they do everything from an instinct and without alteration, which is the inseparable property of understanding, so we also cannot call the chirping and whistling of a nightingale a true music, because such tones doubtless please the ears but by no means are capable of the pervasive

163

inflections and changing harmonious adjustments by which the heart is moved and which alone really cause motions of the soul. Music calls for a thinking being. Each tone is a thought, and a true music must simultaneously move and delight. If some one wishes to object that he is no more moved by a number of outstanding passages that can occur in a flute or violin solo than by the artfully mixed tones that the throat of a nightingale brings forth, I need only admit that many a connection of tones simply delights but does not at the same time strongly move. And we will really not be able to make such an assertion about entire Quantz and Benda solos.

If it had to be done, we could write a melody to every discourse. Indeed we pronounce all words with certain sounds, and these sounds must also by no means be left out of account in vocal pieces. It is said of Lulli that he took great counsel from the sound of discourse in his compositions, and repeated and articulated the words often before he composed. It therefore seems as if music could be connected with each and every thought expressed in words. But since its nature consists principally in the delightful and the moving, and it arouses no other ideas than these, then also not every discourse but rather only moving words will be susceptible of union with music.

Every tone and every connection of tones sounds either pleasant or unpleasant to our ears. We feel in this an enjoyment of the senses because we would not have the enjoyment without hearing. But this enjoyment does not remain merely in the ears; it imparts itself also to the soul, which to be sure is conscious of it, but yet does not clearly analyze what takes place inwardly at that time. Tones, melodies, and music thus produce sensuous ideas that are quite delightful and for the most part moving. Such things can be elaborated still further, only I must first recall the following. Many people have a natural antipathy to certain things. Mr. Voltaire says there are people who possess understanding and reason but whose senses are so little affected by all harmony that music seems to their ears to be only a noise and poetry an artfully concocted foolishness. Furthermore if something is to make an impression, our acquiescence to it is required. We must not pay attention at the same time to other things. The most skilled and fiery orator does not move us when we are distracted. Besides this acquiescence, that which is to affect us must also not be in any way so sublime that neither our senses nor our understanding can grasp it. Let us conduct a person who has still never seen any pictures at all to a collection of paintings. The bright colors of a poor painting will perhaps please him more than the finest traits of a masterpiece. In the same way a farmer will often be less delighted or moved by a really beautiful opera aria than by a dance piece of his fiddler. I therefore take a person who in fact has not yet heard much music and still less knows it rules, but who nevertheless has no antipathy towards it, is not ill bred, and has a sound ear. I have this person hear a piece that is either played on instruments only or sung in a foreign language. If it is joyous his

164

blood begins to move more rapidly than before, he comes out of the inactive state which let us say he was in, his eyes and gestures change, he speaks more cheerfully and loudly, he forgets what he otherwise had to do, and is not aware of much that goes on around him. Merely things that happen to us when we are in an affective state.

With less cheerful music other conditions occur in his body, which just as much as the former, however, are accompaniments of the passions. He perceives the tones without being able to say anything further about them than that he likes them. People who have the greatest understanding of music often think of nothing else during very moving pieces. They are quite conscious of the ideas contained in them, but their spirit is so filled with them that they cannot make them clear but only feel them clearly. Now the philosophers say about clarity in ideas that it can be increased in a twofold way, the one according to extent, when this consists of many parts and when the mass of characteristics increases, and the other by means of the greater clarity of the characteristics. In the latter case the parts are developed and made more apparent; we learn to comprehend them more. This happens in a musical piece that is elaborately developed from a theme of several measures. At first we comprehend only generally how the succession of tones is constituted in the theme. In the repetition of this theme, however, although in other contexts, the melody becomes more familiar, clearer; we learn to see into it more, and probably even by heart. If the theme is given again and again in one and the same context, it will soon become clear to us. But then the charm falls away that the new, the unexpected brings. Also the musicians forbid such uniformity in their rules of composition. Now provided only that this kind of growing clarity does not increase to the point of distinctness, it can also contribute somewhat to the passions; but yet it does not suffice to move the spirit.

On the other hand one often finds that an aria the theme of which is worked out only to a very small degree according to the actual harmonic rules of the composers is nevertheless very moving. There then accrue to the theme as the principal idea continually new, moving characteristics which yet, however, are so appropriate to it that our feeling remarks no contradiction among them; that is, the clarity becomes greater with the extension, and the spirit very moved by it. In contrast, another piece, of which those knowledgeable in music say it is painstakingly worked out and its clarity of intention is great, is not so very affecting. In tonal connections of this artful kind there is also an external reason that they are less moving. If the composer wants to introduce his theme or parts of it really too often, the melody will readily cease to be noticed because of this, and without intelligibility no melody can either delight or move. Thus those musicians do best who combine both kinds of clarity in their works. By a painstaking working out of the theme they satisfy their musical rules, and it uncommonly delights the listener when he becomes aware, in the more frequent introduction of the principal section, how so much is made from little. The composers are then also certain that they do not completely stray from their principal idea and the feelings that belong to it. But they know well, by virtue of their experience and knowledge of the entire nature of music, that simply through this they will not arrive at the true goal; therefore they connect with the theme so many other ideas, until they are certain in good conscience of their aim. Granted that a great deal still remains left over for their skill to accomplish in setting forth the intention of the principal idea, they will prefer to be pleasing rather than learned musicians. So long, therefore, as a composition still produces emotion or even enjoyment, then that long also is harmonic art acceptable in it. For the most part, however, it is not so much musicians, but rather only musical amateurs who must be taken as judges of this; amateurs who, to be sure, can have heard a lot of music and can also have good taste, but who neither know much of the rules of harmony nor are biased in any other way. They must leave things to the decision of their ears, and for such listeners music is normally made. What pleases them or even moves them will also please and move the musicians themselves. These latter, however, have a certain intellectual music, if such a thing can be asserted, which they enjoy when they perceive that the composer was able to put many beauties of harmony into the piece before them. The more of these he heaps up and the less one expects it, the better is the piece. But the more it has of these kinds of perfections the less it will please mere amateurs, who judge only the impressions of the ears and of the heart.

This state of affairs was arrived at in the following fashion. It was seen that many melodic passages could also be introduced in the bass. There was an awareness that it sounds pleasing when various voices take up a given theme and through its repetition and segmentation set up a competition over it among themselves. It was noticed that when all the voices are active, as the musicians say, this expresses a grandeur, an astonishment, a general delight, and a great zeal, and the heart is filled by it with certain elevated and strong feelings. Musicians moreover found the opportunity to show their skills and their diligence. They went so far in this, however, that they wanted to express all the other affections and not only those we have mentioned, or in their concern they even forgot the affections altogether. What happened was the same as in architecture. Because some one saw there that four ornaments looked appropriate he added four more to these and some one else increased them even to twelve. From this there arose a Gothic excess in decorations. There are certain countries and places in which we find more taste for pieces that are harmonically filled out than for those that carry us along by means of melody, perhaps because in those places people look only to the ostensibly large and splendid in other things also, and do not know much of the natural and nobly simple. But an eminent man knowledgeable in music, who listened to an opera with me in which throughout all the arias were heavily elaborated in such a way, assures me that during it he did not feel the desired pleasure and enjoyment, so true is it that most of these artful musical pieces do not much involve the heart. The musicians cannot deny this if they want to be sincere, although their understanding may take much pleasure in such musical works. With a beautiful melodic aria, on the other hand, they will be moved just as well as those who understand nothing of music.

Yet those artful pieces are nevertheless something admirable if they are brought in at the right time, in the right place, in splendid pieces of church music, in circumstances appropriate to them, with the moderation required, and in such a manner that the chief end of music, affection, is not absent from them. In addition, however, they call for their own listeners, who are very practiced in music, just as Milton's *Paradise* does not easily please women who have not yet read any other poems at all, even though they otherwise may have quite enough natural refinement of understanding. Musical pieces that are so very worked out must also usually be played several times before they are fittingly understood, and even the ear of the listener can not grasp the beauties that appear in them the first time. It must be acquainted beforehand with these difficult tonal relationships, although these last are also found in many musical pieces that certainly have no excess of harmonic beauties. For just as even musicians who are not unskilled must first get many passages of the melodies into their fingers, as we say, so passages of this kind must also be heard correctly, as it were, before they can delight or move the soul; and it is not simply a mistake if such new melodic passages, somewhat difficult to comprehend, occur in a piece. Certain feelings cannot be depicted without them. In such pieces more wit, penetration, and enthusiasm are contained than feelings of gentler affections, and they are always somewhat more difficult to perform and to understand. But what is grasped instantly is liked rapidly, to be sure, and by many persons, but it is not at all on that account to be preferred to those difficult things. In music just as in poetry there are many kinds of ideas, and moreover expression differs according to the differing disposition of poets and musicians. Horace and Juvenal wrote satires, Canitz and Haller odes to their dead wives, Hagedorn and Gellert fables and stories. But let us set these poems before a connoisseur of poetry, or even before some one who still has not developed a perfected taste for it. One will please him more than the other, according as the disposition of the poet agrees more or less with the disposition of the reader. Let us give him further an Anacreontic song to read, an epigram, a didactic poem, a heroic poem, and ask him whether one is not easier to understand than the other. If we apply this to music it will become clear that a clavier concerto of the estimable Berlin Bach is by no means less perfect than one of the worthy Capellmeister Graun, although this last might immediately please more listeners (soon and without effort, I may say) than the first, provided—to make the comparison correct—both concertos are set properly for the clavier and arranged according to the capacity of the one who plays them.

But if now a piece has been played for me with the required manner and facility, especially one such as has many harmonic perfections, and it nevertheless does not move lovers of music or please them in a sensuous way, then it is a merely intellectual music, which however still finds its fanciers, since one can prize something merely for the reason that it requires effort. Above all such works are to be judged according to their destination. They are not intended, like an opera aria, to please all people and as though at once. They are made for such lovers and connoisseurs of music as take pains to hear them often enough, to play them, and so to say, to study them, and it is noteworthy that those who know music are for the most part already tired of a light aria when it is played repeatedly just when a very learned piece would really begin to please them. But with music that is supposed to be for everyone the main rule is: as soon as the melody becomes difficult for the ear to understand or unpleasant to it, through art and the beauties of harmony, one must at once desist from these things. An idea can hardly find its way to the heart or please it when the expression of the same injures a delicate ear. *Nihil intrare potest in affectum, quod in aure velut quodam vestibulo statim offendit.* (Quintilian.) The irksome impression of too many untoward dissonances robs the understanding of the freedom to follow the thoughts and to imagine that which is denoted by them. The ear is one of the most arrogant judges, and delivers its verdict on the spur of the moment. No idea has an effect on it, and neither explanation nor account can be given of its pronouncements. A professor of arts is of this opinion, with respect to poetic expression; how much more will the same be true in music, which is made far more for the ear, which desires to be thoroughly flattered by it? Thus we see why melodious and especially vocal things that excell in such a way are so generally liked, although besides the adduced reasons for this the following cause can also be given, namely, that since even the poorest composer is held by the words to a certain definite affection, therefore vocal pieces are necessarily more moving than others in which one has not properly proposed to express a certain passion.

I return again to my musical piece and its listener. He is moved, for he receives a sensuously certain knowledge of the melody. He can like it even if he has just heard from some one who understands music, perhaps, that the aria is not worth much. Doubt is not prejudicial here; in the productions of the mind we depend principally on the sensible impressions that they make on us. We know that a piece of music can violate many rules of composition and yet move us. It is then moving, only not to everyone, perhaps, or not strongly enough, or not in the way it should be moving according to the circumstances of the place and the time. To the extent that something is sonorous, pleasing, and moving, to that extent it also has this effect with most people. Nature itself has made us that way, although doubtless not even all good pieces please all people equally greatly. Very much depends upon temperament, just as many a poem would not delight us so much if its material were not so in keeping with our views and inclinations.

If finally the knowledge that is to move us must be active, then it will easily be perceived in the case of my listener that the same ideas are aroused in him. An impenetrable darkness must enshroud his heart if it is not cheered and cleansed by a joyful piece. If the melody is sad, he would have to be very volatile if he does not at least seem to become reflective. And let us also just undertake the following experiment. Let us have him note at the same time the motion of the players, or look with us at the part, and let us show him how the notes are patterned when the music goes rapidly and when it goes slowly. During the exceptionally beautiful passages of the piece he will certainly lose sight of and awareness of the musician together with his arm and his notes. That means his knowledge is more intuitive than symbolic, and this is a certain demonstration that he has been moved.

It has accordingly with justice been said of music for a long time that it calms those who are angry, lifts up those who are downcast, chases away grievous cares, numbing sadness, and irksome bad humor (the opposite of affability and affection), sets the heart at peace, and instills all the gentle motions, love, satisfaction, hope, and sympathy. It lends the heart a cheerfulness that makes one affectionate, sociable, and affable, and experience teaches that those who love music are seldom severe, spiteful, and uncompanionable. The soft feelings of bewitching tones make morals firm, the understanding more flexible, and the heart more sensitive. Their impressions further the facility, fondness, kindness, and sympathy of feeling, and give our passions the expedient moderation in which the true nature of virtue consists. Through the pleasure they cause, the emotional inclinations are shaped, and the desires purified and directed. To virtue there belongs in every way a very sensitive heart. Without this one doubtless can possess considerable reason, but not be virtuous. The soft and flexible souls in the world are the best and most useful; the defiant ones are too little fit for really noble things. *Faciles motus mens generosa capit.* The greatest heroes have been lovers of music, indeed musicians. If many musicians are vile, many other sorts of people are no less so. For virtue there are demanded inclinations and desires that aim at the benefit of mankind. It is not a matter all the time of deep insight into truths; proper reason perhaps accomplishes only little in the world. Love of kindred, concern for descendants, love of social intercourse, sympathy, charity—all these virtues

169

derive from natural inclinations which we gladly satisfy for the reason that we feel a gentle pleasure in doing so; and music makes us more susceptible of this pleasure and thus also makes its own contribution to virtue.

As useful and as valuable to us as musical delights are, however, tones are nevertheless not able by far to arouse in us all the ideas that words can awaken. With these last we connect not only general but also particular and individual concepts. Therefore an orator can arouse not only satisfaction in general but also in particular my satisfaction with my circumstances. But the musician produces in me only general ideas. An adagio makes me sad, an allegro joyful; but I know not why and over what. Several special varieties of affection also can be remarked well in melodies; for example, hope in God is otherwise expressed than that with which a lover flatters himself that he is fortunate. The musician characterizes what I hope to achieve in particular cases through various tones, and God always through such as declare at the same time his greatness and the respect therefore to be paid, and similar things. Tones are also rather intelligible when the goal of the affection represented is likewise a noticeably strong passion susceptible of musical expression. Thus the musician can characterize well the desire of a lover, but not the longing of a miser. And into the individual circumstances of each single affection and of the one experiencing it the musician in his tones will not be able to descend. If music accordingly through repeated gentle feelings at once roots out the wildness of the spirit and in such a way purifies the passions, it nevertheless cannot improve the understanding, if this word is taken to designate clear insight into things or the widening of our knowledge. An understanding that does not permit itself to descend into individual things is not very useful. Never has anyone become through a concert more learned, intelligent, or prudent. No one says: that was an instructive piece of music. The most adept musician will not be able to express merely in tones the sentence: A patient man is better than a strong one. Strive as you will to convince some one in tones that he is to love his neighbor; you will not be successful. You do not have for the purpose the means of the orator, whose listener thinks of a true concept with each word of this sentence; and our understanding really is so astonishingly practised in this respect that we usually are no longer aware that it is operating. But the more things we already have connected each word with—and this happens very often, for speech is given to us both out of necessity and for the sake of its delightfulness—the more the same word gives us to think of when we hear it. All these relationships the poet can turn to use, and nevertheless, in the event he fears his reader might not connect with a word the concept he wants to have, he prefers to use a circumlocution and shows his image in an aspect that has a necessary connection with the desired thought. By contrast, in hearing a tone we naturally and first of all think of nothing except whether it sounds pleasant or unpleasant, although there is present also the factor that the more one deals with tones the more he learns to think of also with them. Otherwise, however, they contain a language, to be sure, but only the language of the desires and passions, and in spite of all our efforts we do not know as well and as clearly what they are trying to say as we do with words because we cannot descend with them into individual things.

At the same time, if the purpose of all imitation is either to make us attend to its representations and to instruct us, or to prejudice and stir us with favor or aversion towards the things represented, then music, to be sure, can not teach us in the way we are instructed by a science. But its representations nonetheless satisfy our innate understanding and our desire to learn, and the varied arrangement of the tones gives just as much pleasure to the spirit as the beautiful arrangement of a poem. Granted, then, that many pieces also do no more than please, yet we are indeed determined by what appears pleasant to us. *Delectatio quasi pondus est animae: delectatio ordinat animam.* And how great is not this delight? Shaftesbury maintains as something undeniable that the admiration and love of order and proportion, be it where it may, naturally improves the character, is productive of social inclination, and offers a very great aid to virtue, which last is itself nothing other than love of order and beauty in society; in the smallest things in the world the sight of order takes possession of the soul and draws our inclination after it. In none of the fine arts is there so much order and excellent relationship as in music. Directed to inward things, to thoughts and their movement and arrangement, in the arousal of affections and in the effort to please it is grounded in rules that are thoroughly conformable to nature. Whereas eloquence and poetry can move us through prejudices and deceptions that run counter to the totality of order in the world. And in its external disposition music has as much symmetry as only architecture can have, and much more than poetry.

In melodic passages it is not merely a matter of such an equivalence as we observe in the rhyme structures and the similar lines of poetic stanzas. Mostly all the sections, periods, clauses, and phrases have quite exact and yet very different proportions among themselves. All conjunctions of tone, in harmony as well as in melody, are measured out and measured off. Thus music delights quite exceptionally, indeed it moves, although we often do not clearly recognize its object. But because our understanding always seeks to be active along with the movements of the soul, and accordingly distinct thoughts seek to participate also in music, we connect words and tones with one another. Instructive, fiery words still more exalted by a persuasive melody are of great benefit and of incomparable effect. If the former illuminate the understanding and at once in themselves besiege the heart, the latter come to their aid with their ravishing power; and through this the truth is made more pleasant, more forcible, and the love of virtue stronger. The text contains the ideas in a vocal piece, and their sequence and arrangement in general. The music as well as the words works towards the clarification of the ideas and towards the persuasion and activation of the listeners, and it lends to words to which many hearts are closed such charms as unlock the heart and provide an entrance to truth. In this there also consists the greatest superiority that vocal music has over instrumental music.

Additional Readings

Abert, Hermann. "Wort und Ton in der Musik des 18. Jahrhunderts." In his: *Gesammelte Schriften und Vorträge*, ed. Friedrich Blume. Halle, 1929.

Beaujean, Joseph. *Christian Gottfried Krause*. Dillingen, 1930.

Cannon, Beekman Cox. *Johann Mattheson, Spectator in Music*. New Haven, 1947.

Dammann, Rolf. *Der Musikbegriff im deutschen Barock*. Cologne, 1967.

Deditius, Annemarie. *Theorien über die Verbindung von Poesie und Musik: Moses Mendelssohn, Lessing*. Liegnitz, 1918.

Engelke, Bernhard. "Neues zur Geschichte der Berliner Liederschule." In: *Riemann-Festschrift*. Leipzig, 1909.

Frotscher, Gotthold. "Die Ästhetik des Berliner Liedes in ihren Hauptproblemen." *Zeitschrift für Musikwissenschaft* 6, 1923-24.

Gross, Karl Josef. *Sulzers allgemeine Theorie der schönen Künste*. Berlin, 1905.

Krause, Christian Gottfried. *Von der Musikalischen Poesie*. Berlin, 1952.

Marks, Paul F. "The Rhetorical Element in Musical *Sturm und Drang:* Christian Gottfried Krause's *Von der Musikalischen Poesie.*" *International Review* 2, 1971.

Mattheson, Johann. *Der vollkommene Capellmeister*. Hamburg, 1739.

Schäfke, Rudolf. "Quantz als Ästhetiker: Eine Einführung in die Musikästhetik des galanten Stils." *Archiv für Musikwissenschaft* 6, 1924.

Schering, Arnold. "Christian Gottfried Krause." *Zeitschrift für Ästhetik und allgemeine Kunstwissenschaft* 2, 1907.

_____ "Die Musikästhetik der deutschen Aufklärung." *Zeitschrift der internationalen Musikgesellschaft* 8, 1906-07.

Serauky, Walter. *Die musikalische Nachahmungsästhetik im Zeitraum von 1700 bis 1850*. Münster, 1929.

Stege, Fritz. "Die deutsche Musikkritik des 18. Jahrhunderts unter dem Einfluss der Affektenlehre." *Zeitschrift für Musikwissenschaft* 10, 1927.

Unger, Hans-Heinrich. *Die Beziehungen zwischen Musik und Rhetorik im 16.-18. Jahrhundert*. Würzburg, 1941.

PART SIX

English Views of Imitation and Expression

In undertaking to characterize music as one of the arts, English tracts of the eighteenth century had recourse primarily to the idea of imitation. For this there was the powerful authority of Aristotle's *Poetics*, which occasionally became the explicit basis of the argument, but in any case was not open to question. Now when imitation was regarded more closely it turned out to present peculiar difficulties in connection with music in particular, not to mention that in general it referred to an object external to art as a basis of definition and suggested that the value of art would reside in its fidelity to this object. As a matter of common experience, however, the intrinsic property of music seemed to be expressiveness, or the provocation of some kind of feeling. This was evident entirely without and prior to any comparison to rhetoric, while its imitative capacity was far from obvious, and in Antiquity, might have been simply a consequence of its association with poetry.

It was indeed in the context of a comparison of poetry and music that English musical aesthetics existed, an understandable framework in view of the historical connection of the two arts, and one quite suited also to represent the conception of music as a fine art rather than a liberal art. Treatises on two or more arts were thus in a sense the successors of those on the quadrivium. But this new membership of music rested essentially on imitation, which Batteux had established in 1743 as the single principle of all the arts. The imitative capacity of music thus became an issue crucial to its new status.

Sorting out these problems (in spite of the confusion of music in its own right with the "music" of poetry and with the combination of music and poetry), establishing the relationship between imitation and expression, taking into account the variety of objects and types of musical imitation, and attempting some closer approach to a description of the emotive effects of music (which in England made no use of elaborate systems of rhetorical figures)—these were the tasks addressed successively by Harris (1744), Avison (1752), Webb (1769), William Jones (1772), Beattie (1776), Twining (1789), and Adam Smith (1795), who represent a cohesive tradition of thought, presented with refreshing simplicity and clarity.

CHAPTER EIGHT

JAMES HARRIS

Three Treatises Concerning Art
(1744)

A DISCOURSE ON MUSIC, PAINTING,
AND POETRY

CHAPTER I.

Introduction.—Design and Distribution of the Whole.—Preparation for the following Chapters.

All Arts have this in common, that *they respect Human Life*. Some contribute to its *Necessities*, as Medicine and Agriculture; others to its *Elegance*, as Music, Painting, and Poetry.

Now, with respect to these two different *Species*, the *necessary* Arts seem to have been *prior in time*; if it be probable, that Men consulted how *to live* and *to support themselves*, before they began to deliberate how *to render Life agreeable*. Nor is this indeed unconfirmed by Fact, there being no Nation known so barbarous and ignorant, as where the Rudiments of these *necessary* Arts are not in some degree cultivated. And hence possibly they may appear to be the *more excellent and worthy*, as having claim to a *Preference*, derived from their *Seniority*.

The Arts however of *Elegance* cannot be said to want Pretensions, if it be true, that nature framed us for *something more than mere Existence*. Nay, farther, if *Well-being* be clearly preferable to *Mere-being*, and this without it be but a thing contemptible, they may have reason perhaps to aspire even to a *Superiority*. But enough of this, to come to our Purpose.

§ 2. The Design of this Discourse is to treat of Music, Painting, and Poetry; to consider in what they *agree*, and in what they *differ*; and which upon the whole, is more excellent than the other two.

In entering upon this Inquiry, it is first to be observed, that the Mind is made conscious of the *natural World* and its Affections, and of other *Minds* and their Affections, by the several *Organs of the Senses*.[1] By the *same Organs*, these Arts exhibit to the Mind *Imitations*, and imitate either Parts or Affections of this *natural World*, or else the Passions, Energies, and other Affections of *Minds*. There is this Difference however between these *Arts* and *Nature*; that Nature passes to the Percipient thro' *all* the Senses; whereas these Arts use *only two* of them, that of Seeing and that of Hearing. And hence it is that the *sensible Objects* or *Media*, thro' which[2] they imitate, can be *such only*, as these two Senses are framed capable of perceiving; and these Media are *Motion, Sound, Colour*, and *Figure*.

Painting, having the *Eye* for its *Organ*, cannot be conceived to imitate, but thro' the Media of *visible* Objects. And farther, its Mode of imitating being always *motionless*, there must be subtracted from these the Medium of *Motion*. It remains then, that *Colour* and *Figure* are the only Media, thro' which Painting imitates.

Music, passing to the Mind thro' the *Organ* of the *Ear*, can imitate only by *Sounds and Motions*.

Poetry, having the *Ear* also for its *Organ*, as far as *Words* are considered to be no more than *mere Sounds*, can go no farther in Imitating, than may be performed by *Sound* and *Motion*. But then, as *these its Sounds stand by Compact for the various Ideas with which the Mind is fraught*, it is enabled by this means to imitate, *as far as Language can express*; and that it is evident will, in a manner, include all things.

Now from hence my be seen, how these Arts *agree*, and how they *differ*.

They *agree*, by being *all* Mimetic, or Imitative.

They *differ*, as they imitate by *different Media*; Painting by *Figure* and *Colour*;

---

[1]To explain some future Observations, it will be proper here to remark, that the Mind *from these Materials thus brought together, and from its own Operations on them, and in consequence of them, becomes fraught with* Ideas—and that many Minds *so fraught, by a sort of* Compact *assigning to* each Idea *some* Sound *to be its* Mark *or* Symbol, *were the first* Inventors *and* Founders *of* Language.
[2]To prevent Confusion it must be observed, that in all these Arts there is a Difference between the *sensible Media, thro' which they imitate*, and the *Subjects* imitated. The sensible Media, thro' which they imitate, must be always *relative to that Sense, by which the particular Art applies to the Mind*; but the Subject imitated may be *foreign to that Sense, and beyond the Power of its Perception*. Painting, for instance, (as is shewn in this Chapter) has *no sensible Media*, thro' which it operates, except *Colour* and *Figure*: But as to *Subjects*, it may have Motions, Sounds, moral Affections and Actions; *none of which* are either *Colours* or *Figures*, but which however are *all capable of being imitated thro' them*. See Chapter the second, Notes 5, 6, 7.

Music, by *Sound* and *Motion*; Painting and Music, by *Media which are Natural*; Poetry, for the greatest Part, by a *Medium which is Artificial*.[3]

§ 3. As to that Art, which upon the whole is *most excellent of the three*; it must be observed, that among these various *Media* of imitating, some will naturally be *more* accurate, some *less*; some will *best* imitate one Subject; some, another. Again, among the Number of *Subjects* there will be naturally also a Difference, as to *Merit* and *De-merit*. There will be some *sublime*, and some *low*; some *copious*, and some *short*; some *pathetic*, and others *void of Passion*; some formed to *instruct*, and others *not capable* of it.

Now, from these *two* Circumstances; that is to say, from the *Accuracy of the Imitation*, and the *Merit of the Subject imitated*, the Question concerning *which Art is most excellent*, must be tried and determined.

This however cannot be done, without a *Detail of Particulars*, that so there may be formed, on every part, just and accurate *Comparisons*.

To begin therefore with Painting.

CHAPTER II.

On the Subjects which Painting imitates.—On the Subjects which Music imitates.— Comparison of Music with Painting.

The fittest Subjects for Painting, are all such Things, and Incidents, *as are peculiarly characterised by* Figure *and* Colour.

Of this kind are the whole Mass[4] of *Things inanimate and vegetable*; such as Flowers, Fruits, Buildings, Landskips—The various Tribes of *Animal Figures*; such as Birds, Beasts, Herds, Flocks—The *Motions* and *Sounds peculiar* to each Animal Species, when accompanied with *Configurations*, which are *obvious* and *remarkable*[5]—The *Human Body* in all its *Appearances* (as Male, Female; Young, Old; Handsome, Ugly;) and in all its *Attitudes*, (as Laying, Sitting, Standing, & c.)—The *Natural Sounds peculiar* to the *Human* Species,

[3]A Figure painted, or a Composition of Musical Sounds have always a *natural Relation to that, of which they are intended to be the Resemblance*. But a Description in Words has rarely any such *natural Relation to the several Ideas, of which those Words are the Symbols. None* therefore understand the *Description*, but *those who speak the Language*. On the contrary, Musical and Picture-Imitations are *intelligible to all Men*.

Why it is said that Poetry is *not universally*, but *only for the greater part* artificial, see below, Chapter the Third, where what *Natural Force* it has, is examined and estimated.
[4]The Reason is, that *these* things are almost *wholly* known to us by their *Colour* and *Figure*. Besides, they are as *motionless*, for the most part, in *Nature*, as in the *Imitation*.
[5]Instances of this kind are the Flying of Birds, the Galloping of Horses, the Roaring of Lions, the Crowing of Cocks. And the Reason is, that though to paint Motion or Sound be *impossible*, yet the Motions and Sounds here mentioned having an *immediate and natural Connection with a certain visible* Configuration *of the Parts*, the Mind, from a Prospect of this *Configuration, conceives insensibly that which is concomitant*; and hence it is that, by a sort of *Fallacy*, the Sounds and Motions *appear to be painted also*. On the contrary, not so in *such* Motions, as the Swimming of many kinds of Fish; or in *such* Sounds, as the Purring of a Cat; because *here* is no such *special Configuration* to be perceived.

(such as Crying, Laughing, Hollowing, & c.)[6]—All *Energies, Passions,* and *Affections,* of the *Soul,* being in any degree *more intense* or *violent* than ordinary[7]—All *Actions and Events,* whose *Integrity* or *Wholeness* depends upon a *short and self-evident* Succession of Incidents[8]——Or if the Succession be extended, then *such Actions* at least, whose *Incidents are all along, during that Succession, similar*[9]——All *Actions* which being qualified as *above,* open themselves into a *large* Variety of Circumstances, *concurring all in the same Point of Time.*[10]——*All Actions* which are *known,* and known *universally,* rather than Actions *newly invented or known but to few.*[11]

[6]The Reason is of the *same* kind, as that given in the Note immediately preceding; and by the *same* Rule, the Observation must be confined to *natural Sounds only.* In *Language,* few of the Speakers know the *Configurations,* which attend it.

[7]The Reason is still of the *same* kind, *viz.* from their *Visible* Effects on the Body. They naturally produce either to the *Countenance* a particular *Redness* or *Paleness;* or a particular *Modification of its Muscles;* or else to the *Limbs,* a particular *Attitude.* Now all these Effects are *solely referable* to Colour and Figure, the two grand sensible Media, *peculiar* to Painting. See *Raphael's* Cartoons of St. *Paul* at *Athens,* and of his striking the Sorcerer *Elymas* blind: See also the Crucifixion of *Polycrates,* and the Sufferings of the Consul *Regulus,* both by *Salvator Rosa.*

[8]For of *necessity* every Picture is a *Punctum Temporis* or Instant.

[9]Such, for instance, as a Storm at Sea; whose *Incidents of Vision* may be nearly all included in foaming Waves, a dark Sky, Ships out of their erect Posture, and Men hanging upon the Ropes.——Or as a Battle; which from Beginning to End presents nothing else, than Blood, Fire, Smoak, and Disorder. Now *such Events* may be well imitated *all at once;* for how long soever they last, they are but *Repetitions of the same*——*Nicias,* the Painter, recommended much the same Subjects, *viz.* a Sea-fight or a Land-battle of Cavalry. His reasons too are much the same with those mentioned in Note 10: He concludes with a Maxim, (little regarded by his successors, however important,) that the Subject itself is as much a Part of the Painter's Art, as the Poet's Fable is a Part of Poetry.

[10]For Painting is not bounded in Extension, as it is in Duration. Besides, it seems true in *every Species of Composition,* that, as far as *Perplexity* and *Confusion* may be avoided, and the *Wholeness* of the Piece may be preserved *clear and intelligible;* the more ample the *Magnitude,* and the greater the *Variety,* the greater also, in proportion, the *Beauty* and *Perfection.*

[11]The Reason is, that a Picture being (as has been said) but a *Point* or *Instant,* in a Story *well known* the Spectator's Memory will supply the *previous* and the *subsequent.* But this cannot be done, *where such Knowledge is wanting.* And therefore it may be justly questioned, whether the most celebrated Subjects, borrowed by Painting from History, would have been any of them intelligible *thro' the Medium of Painting only,* supposing History to have been silent, and to have given *no additional Information.*

It may be here added, that *Horace,* conformably to this Reasoning, recommends even to *Poetic* Imitation a *known* Story, before an *unknown.*

——*Tuque*

Rectius Iliacum carmen *deducis in actus,*
Quam si proferres ignota, indictaque primus.

Art. Poet. v. 128.

And indeed as *the being understood to others,* either Hearers or Spectators, seems to be a *common Requisite* to *all Mimetic* Arts whatever; (for to those, who understand them not, they are in Fact no Mimetic Arts) it follows, that *Perspicuity* must be *Essential* to them *all;* and that no prudent Artist would neglect, if it were possible, any just Advantage to obtain this End. Now there can be no Advantage greater, than the *Notoriety of the Subject* imitated.

180

And thus much as to the Subjects of Painting.

§ 2. In Music, the fittest Subjects of Imitation are all such Things and Incidents, *as are most eminently characterised by* Motion *and* Sound.

Motion may be either *slow* or *swift, even* or *uneven, broken* or *continuous.——Sound may be either soft* or *loud, high* or *low.* Wherever therefore any of these Species of *Motion* or *Sound* may be found in an *eminent* (not a *moderate* or *mean*) *degree,* there will be room for Musical Imitation.

Thus, in the *Natural* or *Inanimate World,* Music may imitate the Glidings, Murmurings, Tossings, Roarings, and other *Accidents of Water,* as perceived in Fountains, Cataracts, Rivers, Seas, & *c.*—The same of Thunder—the same of Winds, as well the stormy as the gentle.——In the *Animal World,* It may imitate the *Voice* of some Animals, but *chiefly* that of singing Birds——It may also *faintly copy* some of their *Motions.*—In the *Human Kind,* it can also imitate some *Motions*[12] and *Sounds*[13]; and of Sounds those *most perfectly,* which are expressive of *Grief* and *Anguish.*[14]

And thus much as to the Subjects, which Music imitates.

§ 3. It remains then, that we *compare these two* Arts together. And here indeed, as to *Musical Imitation in general,* it must be confessed that—as it can, from its Genius, imitate *only* Sounds and Motions—as there are not *many* Motions either in the *Animal* or in the *Inanimate* World, which are *exclusively peculiar* even to any *Species* and scarcely any to an *Individual*——as there are no *Natural* Sounds, which characterise at least *lower than a Species* (for the *Natural* Sounds of *Individuals* are in every Species the *same*)——farther, as Music does but *imperfectly* imitate even these Sounds and Motions[15]——On the contrary, as Figures, Postures of Figures, and Colours characterise not only *every sensible Species,* but even *every Individual;* and for the most part also *the various Energies* and *Passions* of every Individual——and farther, as Painting is able, *with the highest Accuracy and Exactness,* to imitate all these Colours and Figures; and while Musical Imitation pretends *at most* to no more, than the raising of Ideas *similar,* itself aspires to raise Ideas *the very same*——in a word, as Painting in respect of *its Subjects,* is equal to the *noblest* Part of Imitation, *the imitating regular Actions consisting of a Whole and Parts;* and of *such* Imitation, Music is *utterly incapable*——from all this it must be

---

[12]As the *Walk* of the Giant *Polypheme,* in the Pastoral of *Acis* and *Galatea.*——*See what ample Strides he takes,* & c.

[13]As the *Shouts* of a Multitude, in the Coronation Anthem of, *God save the King,* & c.

[14]The Reason is, that *this Species* of Musical Imitation *most nearly* approaches Nature. For *Grief,* in most Animals, declares itself by *Sounds,* which are not unlike to *long Notes in the Chromatic System.* Of this kind is the Chorus of *Baal's* Priests in the Oratorio of *Deborah, Doleful Tidings, how ye wound,* & c.

[15]The Reason is from the *Dissimilitude* between the Sounds and motions of *Nature,* and those of *Music. Musical Sounds* are all produced from *Even* Vibration, most *Natural* from *Uneven; Musical Motions* are chiefly *Definite* in their Measure, most *Natural* are *Indefinite.*

confessed, that Musical Imitation is greatly below that of Painting, and that *at best* it is but an imperfect thing.

As to the *Efficacy* therefore of Music, it must be derived from *another* Source, which must be left for the present, to be considered of hereafter. There remains to be mentioned Imitation by Poetry.

CHAPTER SIX

On Music considered not as an Imitation, but as deriving its Efficacy from another *Source.——On its joint Operation by this means with Poetry.——An Objection to Music solved.—The Advantage arising to it, as well as to Poetry, from their being united.——Conclusion.*

In the above Discourse, Music has been mentioned as an *Ally* to Poetry. It has also been said to derive its *Efficacy* from *another Source*, than *Imitation*. It remains, therefore, that these things be explained.

Now, in order to this, it is first to be observed, that there are various *Affections*, which may be raised by the Power of *Music*. There are Sounds to make us *chearful*, or *sad; martial*, or *tender;* and so of almost every other Affection, which we feel.

It is also further observable, that there is a *reciprocal Operation* between our *Affections*, and our *Ideas;* so that, by a sort of *natural Sympathy*, certain *Ideas* necessarily tend to raise in us certain *Affections;* and those *Affections*, by a sort of Counter-Operation, to raise the *same Ideas*. Thus *Ideas* derived from Funerals, Tortures, Murders, and the like, naturally generate the Affection of *Melancholy*. And when, by any *Physical Causes*, that *Affection* happens to prevail, it as naturally generates the same *doleful Ideas*.

And hence it is, that *Ideas*, derived from *external* Causes, have at *different* times, upon the *same* Person, so *different* an Effect. If they happen to suit the Affections, which *prevail within*, then is their Impression *most sensible*, and their Effect *most lasting*. If the contrary be true, then is the Effect contrary. Thus, for instance, a Funeral will much more affect the same Man, if he see it when melancholy, than if he see it when chearful.

Now this being premised, it will follow, that whatever happens to be the *Affection* or *Disposition* of Mind, which ought naturally to result from the Genius of any *Poem*, the *same* probably it will be in the Power of some Species of *Music* to excite. But whenever the *proper Affection* prevails, it has been allowed that then *all kindred Ideas*, derived from external Causes, make the *most sensible Impression*. The Ideas therefore of Poetry must needs make the most sensible Impression, when the Affections,[16] peculiar to them, are

---

[16]Quintilian elegantly, and exactly apposite to this Reasoning, says of *Music——Namque & voce & modulatione grandia clatè, jucunda dulciter, moderata leniter canit, totâque arte* confentit cum eorum, quae dicuntur, Affectibus. *Infit. Orator.* I cap. 10.

already excited by the Music. For here a *double Force is made co-operate to one End*. A Poet, *thus assisted*, finds not an Audience in a Temper, averse to the Genius of his Poem, or perhaps at best under a cool *Indifference*; but by the Preludes, the Symphonies, and *concurrent Operation* of the Music in all its Parts, rouzed into *those very Affections*, which he would most desire.

An Audience, so disposed, not only embrace with Pleasure the Ideas of the Poet, when exhibited; but, in a manner, even *anticipate* them in their several Imaginations. The Superstitious have not a more previous Tendency to be frightened at the sight of Spectres, or a Lover to fall into Raptures at the sight of his Mistress; than a Mind, thus tempered by the Power of Music, to enjoy all Ideas, which are suitable to that Temper.

And hence the *genuine* Charm of Music, and the *Wonders* which it works, thro' its great Professors.[17] A Power, which consists not in Imitations, and the raising *Ideas*; but in the raising *Affections*, to which Ideas may correspond. There are few to be found so insensible, I may even say so inhumane, as when good Poetry is justly set to Music, not in some degree to feel the Force of so *amiable an Union*. But to the Muses Friends it is a Force *irresistible*, and penetrates into the deepest Recesses of the Soul.

——*Pectus inaniter angit,*
Irritat, mulcet, falsis terroribus implet.[18]

§ 2. Now this is *that Source*, from whence Music was said formerly *to derive its greatest Efficacy*. And here indeed, not in Imitation,[19] ought it to be chiefly cultivated. On this account also it has been called a *powerful Ally* to Poetry. And farther, it is by the help of this Reasoning, that the *Objection* is solved, which is raised against the *Singing of Poetry* (as in Opera's, Oratorio's, & c.) from the want of *Probability* and *Resemblance to Nature*. To one indeed, who has no musical Ear, this Objection may have Weight. It may even perplex a Lover of Music, if it happen to surprise him in his Hours of *Indifference*. But when he is feeling the Charm of Poetry *so accompanied*, let him be angry (if he can) with that which serves only to interest him *more feelingly* in the Subject, and support him in a *stronger* and *more earnest*

---

[17]Such, above all, is *George Frederick Handel;* whose Genius, having been cultivated by continued Exercise, and being itself far the sublimest and most universal now known, has justly placed him without an Equal, or a Second. This transient Testimony could not be denied so excellent an Artist, from whom this Treatise has borrowed such eminent Examples, to justify its Assertions in what it has offered concerning Music.
[18]" . . . with airy nothings wrings my heart, inflames, soothes, fills it with vain alarms . . . " *Horat. Epist.* II. I. vers. 211-212.
[19]For the *narrow* Extent and *little* Efficacy of Music, considered as a Mimetic or Imitative Art, see Ch. II § 3.

Attention; which enforces, by its Aid, the several Ideas of the Poem, and gives them to his Imagination with unusual Strength and Grandeur. He cannot surely but confess, that he is a *Gainer in the Exchange*, when he *barters* the want of a single Probability, that of *Pronunciation* (a thing merely arbitrary and every where different) for a *noble Heightening of Affections* which are suitable to the Occasion, and enable him to enter into the Subject with double *Energy* and *Enjoyment*.

§ 3. From what has been said it is evident, that these two Arts can never be so powerful *singly*, as when they are *properly united*. For *Poetry*, when alone, must be necessarily forced to *waste* many of its richest *Ideas*, in the mere raising of Affections, when, to have been properly relished, it should have *found* those Affections in their highest Energy. And *Music*, when alone, can only raise *Affections*, which soon *languish* and *decay*, if not maintained and fed by the nutritive Images of Poetry. Yet must it be remembered, in this Union, that *Poetry* ever have the *Precedence*; its *Utility*, as well as *Dignity*, being by far the more considerable.

§ 4. And thus much, for the present, as to Music, Painting, and Poetry, the Circumstances, in which they *agree*, and in which they *differ*; and the Preference, due to one of them above the other two.

CHAPTER NINE

CHARLES AVISON

An Essay on Musical Expression
(1752)

PART I.
SECTION I.

On the Force and Effects of Music.

As the public Inclination for Music seems every Day advancing, it may not be amiss, at this Time, to offer a few Observations on that delightful Art; such Observations, I mean, as may be chiefly applicable to the present Times; such as may tend to correct any Errors that have arisen, either in the Composition, or the Practice of Music.

If we view this Art in it's Foundations, we shall find, that by the Constitution of Man it is of mighty Efficacy in working both on his Imagination and his Passions. The Force of *Harmony*, or *Melody* alone, is wonderful on the Imagination. *A full Chord* struck, or a beautiful Succession of *single Sounds* produced, is no less ravishing to the Ear, than just Symmetry or exquisite Colours to the Eye.

The Capacity of receiving Pleasure from these musical Sounds, is, in Fact, a peculiar and internal Sense; but of a much more refined Nature than the external Senses: For in the Pleasures arising from our internal Sense of Harmony, there is no prior Uneasiness necessary, in order to our tasting them in their full Perfection; neither is the Enjoyment of them attended either with Languor or Disgust. It is their peculiar and essential Property, to divest the Soul of every unquiet Passion, to pour in upon the Mind, a silent and serene Joy, beyond the Power of Words to express, and to fix the Heart in a rational, benevolent, and happy Tranquillity.

But, though this be the natural Effect of *Melody* or *Harmony* on the Imagination, when simply considered; yet when to these is added the Force of *Musical Expression*, the Effect is greatly increased; for then they assume the Power of exciting all the most agreeable Passions of the Soul. The Force of Sound in alarming the Passions is prodigious. Thus, the Noise of Thunder, the Shouts of War, the Uproar of an enraged Ocean, strike us with Terror: So again, there are certain Sounds natural to Joy, others to Grief, or Despondency, others to Tenderness and Love; and by hearing *these*, we naturally sympathize with those who either *enjoy* or *suffer*. Thus Music, either by imitating these various Sounds in due Subordination to the Laws of *Air* and *Harmony*, or by any other Method of Association, bringing the Objects of our Passions before us (especially when those Objects are determined, and made as it were visibly, and intimately present to the Imagination by the Help of Words) does naturally raise a Variety of Passions in the human breast, similar to the Sounds which are expressed: And thus, by the Musician's Art, we are often carried into the Fury of Battle, or a Tempest, we are by turns elated with Joy, or sunk in pleasing Sorrow, roused to Courage, or quelled by grateful Terrors, melted into Pity, Tenderness, and Love, or transported to the Regions of Bliss, in an Extacy of divine Praise.

But beyond this, I think we may venture to assert, that it is the peculiar Quality of Music to raise the *sociable and happy Passions,* and to *subdue* the *contrary ones.* I know it has been generally believed and affirmed, that it's Power extends alike to every Affection of the Mind. But I would offer it to the Consideration of the Public, whether this is not a general and fundamental Error. I would appeal to any Man, whether ever he found himself urged to Acts of Selfishness, Cruelty, Treachery, Revenge, or Malevolence by the power of musical Sounds? Of if he ever found Jealousy, Suspicion, or Ingratitude engendered in his Breast, either from Harmony or Discord? I believe no Instance of this Nature can be alleged with Truth. It must be owned, indeed, that the Force of Music may urge the *Passions* to an excess, or it may fix them on false and improper Objects, and may thus be pernicious in it's Effects. But still the Passions which it raises, though they may be *misled* or *excessive*, are of the benevolent and social Kind, and in their Intent at least are disinterested and noble.[1]

---

[1]Lest the two Passions above-mentioned, of *Terror* and *Grief*, should be thought an Exception to this Rule, it may not be improper to remark as to the first, that the *Terror* raised by *Musical Expression*, is always of that grateful Kind, which arises from an Impression of something terrible to the Imagination, but which is immediately dissipated, by a subsequent Conviction, that the Danger is entirely imaginary: Of the same Kind is the Terror raised in us, when we stand near the Edge of a Precipice, or in Sight of a tempestuous Ocean, or, are present at a tragical Representation on the Stage: In all these Cases, as in that of musical Expression, the Sense of our *Security* mixes itself with the terrible Impressions, and melts them into a very sensible Delight. As to the second instance, that of Grief, it will be sufficient to observe, that as it always has something of the social Kind for it's Foundation, so it is often attended with a Kind of Sensation, which may with Truth be called *pleasing*.

As I take this to be the Truth of the Case, so it seems to me no difficult Matter to assign a sufficient reason for it: We have already seen that it is the natural Effect of Air or Harmony to throw the Mind into a pleasurable State: And when it hath obtained this State, it will of course exert those Powers, and be susceptible of those Passions which are the most natural and agreeable to it. Now these are altogether of the benevolent Species; inasmuch as we know that the contrary Affections, such as Anger, Revenge, Jealousy, and Hatred, are always attended with Anxiety and Pain: Whereas all the various Modifications of Love, whether human or divine, are but so many Kinds of immediate Happiness. From this View of Things therefore it necessarily follows, that every Species of musical Sound must tend to dispel the malevolent Passions, because they are *painful*; and nourish those which are benevolent, because they are *pleasing*.

. . . . .

SECTION II.

On the Analogies between Music *and* Painting.

From this short Theory we should now proceed to offer a few Observations relating to Composition.

But as musical Composition is known to very few besides the Professors and Composers of Music themselves, and as there are several Resemblances, or Analogies between this Art and that of *Painting*, which is an Art much more obvious in its Principles, and therefore more generally known; it may not be amiss to draw out some of the most striking of these Analogies; and by this Means, in some Degree at least, give the common Reader an Idea of musical Composition.

The chief Analogies or Resemblances that I have observed between these two noble Arts are as follow:

1st, They are both founded in Geometry, and have Proportion for their Subject. And though the Undulations of Air, which are the immediate Cause of Sound, be of so subtile a Nature, as to escape our Examination; yet the Vibrations of musical *Strings* or *Chords*, from whence these Undulations proceed, are as capable of Mensuration, as any of those visible Objects about which Painting is conversant.

2dly, As the Excellence of a Picture depends on three Circumstances, *Design, Colouring,* and *Expression*; so in Music, the Perfection of Composition arises from *Melody, Harmony,* and *Expression*. Melody, or Air, is the Work of Invention, and therefore the Foundation of the other two, and directly

187

analagous to *Design* in Painting. Harmony gives Beauty and Strength to the established Melodies, in the same Manner as Colouring adds Life to a just Design. And, in both Cases, the Expression arises from a Combination of the other two, and is no more than a strong and proper Application of them to the intended Subject.[2]

3*dly*, As the proper Mixture of Light and Shade (called by the *Italians Chiaro-Oscuro*) has a noble Effect in Painting, and is, indeed, essential to the Composition of a good Picture; so the judicious Mixture of Concords and Discords, resemble the soft Gradations from Light to Shade, or from Shade necessary to relieve the Eye, which is soon tired and digusted with a level Glare of Light; so Discords are necessary to relieve the Ear, which is otherwise immediately satiated with a continued, and unvaried Strain of Harmony. We may add (for the Sake of those who are in any Degree acquainted with the Theory of Music) that the *Preparations* and *Resolutions* of Discords, resemble the soft Gradations from Light to Shade, or from Shade to Light in Painting.

4*thly*, As in Painting there are three various Degrees of Distances established, *viz.* the *Fore-Ground*, the *intermediate Part*, and the *Off-Skip*; so in Music there are three different Parts strictly similar to these, *viz.* the Bass (or Fore-Ground), the Tenor (or intermediate), and the Treble (or Off-Skip). In Consequence of this, a musical Composition without its Bass, is like a Landscape without its Fore-Ground; without its Tenor it resembles a Landscape deprived of its intermediate Part; without its Treble, it is analogous to a Landscape deprived of its Distance, or Off-Skip. We know how imperfect a Picture is, when deprived of any of these Parts; and hence we may form a Judgment of those who determine on the Excellence of any musical Composition, without feeling or hearing it in all it's Parts, and understanding their Relation to each other.

5*thly*, As in Painting, especially in the nobler Branches of it, and particularly in History-Painting, there is a principal Figure which is most remarkable and conspicuous, and to which all the other Figures are referred and subordinate; so, in the greater Kinds of musical Composition, there is a

---

[2]*Melody* thus distinguished as the Foundation of a musical Composition, and compared to *Design* in Painting, hath been thought by some a vague and indeterminate Analogy; because *Harmony*, rather than *Melody*, ought to be esteemed the highest Excellence of every musical Work: Yet, though this be admitted, it may still justly be said, that *Melody* is, in Reality, the *Ground-Work*, as it is the *first Principle* which engages the Composer's Attention.

Thus, to strike out a *musical Subject*, and to carry it into *various Melodies*, may be compared to the *first Sketches*, or *Out-Lines* in a Picture; (*this, I conceive, is what the Painters call Design*) and thence these *leading Principles* may be called the *Foundation* of every finished Piece in either of the Arts.

Therefore, wherever I speak of Harmony, in the Course of this Essay, I do not consider it as the first, but most important Circumstance which adorns, and supports the whole Performance.

principal or leading *Subject*, or Succession of Notes, which ought to prevail, and be heard through the whole Composition; and to which, both the Air and Harmony of the other Parts ought to be in like Manner referred and subordinate.

6thly, So again, as in painting a Groupe of Figures, Care is to be had, that there be no Deficiency in it; but that a certain Fulness or Roundness be preserved, such as *Titian* beautifully compared to a Bunch of Grapes; so, in the nobler Kinds of musical Composition, there are several inferior Subjects, which depend on the Principal: And here the several Subjects (as in Painting the Figures do) are, as it were, to *sustain* and *support* each other: And it is certain, that if any one of these be taken away from a skillful Composition, there will be found a Deficiency highly disagreeable to an experienced Ear. Yet this does not hinder, but there may be perfect Composition in two, three, four, or more Parts, in the same Manner as a Groupe may be perfect, though consisting of a smaller, or greater number of Figures. In both Cases, the Painter or Musician varies his Disposition according to the Number of Parts or Figures, which he includes in his Plan.

7thly, As in viewing a Picture, you ought to be removed to a certain Distance, called the Point of Sight, at which all its Parts are seen in their just Proportions; so, in a Concert, there is a certain Distance, at which the Sounds are melted into each other, and the various Parts strike the Ear in their proper Strength and Symmetry. To stand close by a Bassoon, or Double-Bass, when you hear a Concert, is just as if you should plant your Eye close to the Fore-Ground when you view a Picture; or, as if in surveying a spacious Edifice, you should place yourself at the Foot of a Pillar that supports it.

Lastly, The various *Styles* in Painting—the grand—the terrible—the graceful—the tender—the passionate—the joyous—have all their respective Analogies in Music.—And we may add, in Consequence of this, that as the Manner of handling differs in Painting, according as the Subject varies; so, in Music, there are various Instruments suited to the different Kinds of musical Compositions, and particularly adapted to, and expressive of its several Varieties. Thus, as the rough handling is proper for Battles, Sieges, and whatever is great or terrible; and, on the contrary, the softer handling, and more finished Touches, are expressive of Love, Tenderness, or Beauty: So, in Music, the Trumpet, Horn, or Kettle-Drum, are most properly employed on the first of these Subjects, the Lute or Harp on the last. There is a short Story in the Tatler,[3] which illustrates this Analogy very prettily. Several eminent Painters are there represented in Picture as Musicians, with those

[3]No. 153.

Instruments in their Hands which most aptly represent their respective Manner in Painting.

PART TWO

ON MUSICAL COMPOSITION

SECTION III.

On Musical Expression, *so far as it relates to the* Composer.

So much concerning the two Branches of Music, *Air* and *Harmony:* Let us now consider the third Circumstance, which is *Expression.* This, as hath been already observed, "arises from a Combination of the other two; and is no other than a strong and proper Application of them to the intended Subject."

From this Definition it will plainly appear, that Air and Harmony, are never to be deserted for the Sake of Expression: Because Expression is founded on them. And if we should attempt any Thing in Defiance of these, it would cease to be *Musical Expression.* Still less can the horrid Dissonance of Cat-Calls deserve this Appellation, though the Expression or Imitation be ever so strong and natural.

And, as Dissonance and shocking Sounds cannot be called Musical Expression; so neither do I think, can mere Imitation of several other Things be entitled to this Name, which, however, among the Generality of Mankind hath often obtained it. Thus the gradual rising or falling of the Notes in a long Succession, is often used to denote Ascent or Descent, broken Intervals, to denote an interrupted Motion, a Number of quick Divisions, to describe Swiftness or Flying, Sounds resembling Laughter, to describe Laughter; with a Number of other Contrivances of a parallel Kind, which it is needless here to mention. Now all these I should chuse to stile Imitation, rather than Expression; because, it seems to me, that their Tendency is rather to fix the Hearers Attention on the Similitude between the Sounds and the Things which they describe, and thereby to excite a reflex Act of the Understanding, than to affect the Heart and raise the Passions of the Soul.

Here then we see a Defect or Impropriety, similar to those which have been above observed to arise from a too particular Attachment either to the *Modulation* or *Harmony*. For as in the first Case, the Master often attaches himself so strongly to the Beauty of *Air* or Modulation, as to neglect the *Harmony;* and in the second Case, pursues his Harmony or Fugues so as to destroy the Beauty of Modulation; so in this third Case, for the Sake of a forced, and (if I may so speak) an unmeaning Imitation, he neglects both Air and Harmony, on which alone true Musical Expression can be founded.

This Distinction seems more worthy our Notice at present, because some very eminent Composers have attached themselves chiefly to the Method here mentioned; and seem to think they have exhausted all the Depths of Expression, by a dextrous Imitation of the Meaning of a few particular Words, that occur in the Hymns or Songs which they set to Music. Thus, were one of these Gentlemen to express the following Words of *Milton,*

————Their Songs *Divide* the Night, and *lift* our Thoughts to Heav'n.

It is highly probable, that upon the Word *divide,* he would run a *Division* of half a Dozen Bars; and on the subsequent Part of the Sentence, he would not think he had done the Poet Justice, or *risen* to that *Height* of Sublimity which he ought to express, till he had climbed up to the very Top of his Instrument, or at least as far as a human Voice could follow him. And this would pass with a great Part of Mankind for Musical Expression, instead of that noble Mixture of solemn Airs and various Harmony, which *indeed* elevates our Thoughts, and gives that exquisite Pleasure, which none but true lovers of Harmony can feel.

Were it necessary, I might easily prove, upon general Principles, that what I now advance concerning Musical Imitation is strictly just; both, because Music as an imitative Art has *very confined Powers,* and because, when it is an Ally to Poetry (which it ought always to be when it exerts its mimetic Faculty) it obtains its End *by raising correspondent Affections* in the Soul with those which ought to result from the Genius of the Poem. But this has been already shewn, by a judicious Writer,[4] with the Precision and Accuracy which distinguishes his Writings. To his excellent Treatise I shall, therefore, refer my Reader, and content myself, in this Place, with adding two or three practical Observations by way of corollary to his Theory.

1*st,* As *Music* passing to the Mind through the Organ of the Ear, can imitate only *by Sounds and Motions,* it seems reasonable, that when *Sounds* only are the Objects of Imitation, the Composer ought to throw the mimetic Part entirely amongst the accompanying *Instruments;* because, it is probable, that the Imitation will be too powerful in the *Voice* which ought to be engaged in

[4]Vide three Treatises of *J[ames] H[arris]* the second concerning Poetry, Painting, and Music.

Expression alone; or, in other Words, in raising correspondent Affections with the Part.[5] Indeed, in some Cases, Expression will coincide with Imitation, and may then be admitted universally: As in such *Chromatic Strains* as are mimetic of the Grief and Anguish of the human Voice.[6] But to the Imitation of Sounds in the *natural* or *inanimate* World,[7] this, I believe, may be applied as a general Rule.

2dly, When Music imitates *Motions*, the Rythm, and Cast of the Air, will generally require, that both the vocal and instrumental Parts coincide in their Imitation. But then, be it observed, that the Composer ought always to be more cautious and reserved when he applies this Faculty of Music to *Motion*, than when he applies it to *Sound*, and the Reason is obvious; the Intervals in Music are not so strictly similar to animate or inanimate Motions, as its Tones are to animate or inanimate Sounds. Notes ascending or descending by large Intervals, are not so like the Stalking of a Giant,[8] as a Flow of even

[5]I cannot bring a finer illustration of my Meaning, than from the old Song in *Acis* and *Galatea*.
> Hush ye pretty warbling Quire,
> Your thrilling Strains
> Awake my Pains,
> And kindle soft Desire, & *c*.

Here the great Composer has very judiciously employed the vocal Part in the nobler Office of expressing, with Pathos, the plaintive Turn of the Words, while the symphony and Accompanyment very chearfully imitates the singing of *the warbling Quire*. But had Mr. Handel admitted this *Imitation of Sound* into the vocal Part, and made it imitate the *thrilling Strains of the Birds* by *warbling Divisions*, it is manifest the Expression would have been much injured, whereas, according to his Management of it, the *Imitation* greatly assists the Expression.

[6]As to take Mr *H*'s own Example, the Chorus of Baal's Priests in Deborah. *Doleful Tidings how ye wound.*

[7]Such as the Noise of Animals, the Roar of Thunder, Ocean, & *c*. The Murmur of Streams.

[8]Mr *H*. has himself quoted a Passage in *Acis* and *Galatea*, "*See what ample Strides he takes,*" as imitative of the *Walk of Polypheme*; but, I apprehend, the Majesty of that Air rather affected him by an *Association of Ideas*, than any great Similarity in the Imitation.

An Association of this Kind, seems to have struck the Author of the *Paralele des Italiens et des François en ce qui regarde la Musique* "Pour la Conformité (says he) de l'Air, avec le sens des paroles, je n'ay jamais rien entendu, en matiére de Symphonies, de comparable a celle qui fut exécutée à Rome, à l'Oratoire de S. Jerôme de la Charité, le jour de la Saint Martin de l'année 1697, sur ces deux mots, *mille saette, mille fléches*: c'etoit un Air dont les Notes etoient pointées à la maniére des Gigues; le caractére de cet Air imprimoit si vivement dans l'ame l'idee de fleche; et la force de cette idée seduisoit tellement l'Imagination, que chaque violon paroissoit être un arc; & tour les Archets, autant de fléches décochées, dont les pointes sembloient darder la Symphonie de toutes Parts; on ne sauroit entendre rien de plus ingenieux & de plus heureusement exprimé."

We may learn from this, how far *musical Imitation*, simply considered, may amuse the Fancy of many who are less susceptible of the more delicate and refined Beauties of *Expression*.—The particular Felicity of the *Frenchman*, in the musical Performance here described, seems to have depended on this Similitude, *viz*. that every *Violin* appeared as a *Bow*, and all the *Bows*, like so many *Arrows shot off*, the *Points* of which, seemed to *dart* the Symphony through all its Parts. Perhaps, so far as *Imitation* was necessary, his Observation might be just. But were this an Argument, that the Business of *Imitation* was superior to every other in musical Composition, it would reduce the noblest Species of it, still lower than the *Extravaganzi* of the instrumental Performances which we have noted in the Chapter on Modulation.

Notes are to the murmuring of a Stream;[9] and little jiggish Slurrs are less like the Nod of *Alexander*,[10] than certain Shakes and Trills are to the Voice of the Nightingale.[11]

3*dly*, As Music can only imitate Motions and Sounds, and the *Motions* only imperfectly; it will follow, that musical Imitation ought never to be employed in representing Objects, of which Motion or Sound are not the principle Constituents. Thus, to Light, or Lightning, we annex the Property of Celerity of Motions; yet, it will not follow from thence, that an extremely swift Progression of Notes will raise the Idea of either one or the other; because as we said, the Imitation must be, in these Cases, very partial.[12] Again, it is one Property of Frost to make Persons shake and tremble; yet, a tremulous Movement of Semitones, will never give the true Idea of Frost: though, perhaps, they may of a trembling Person.

---

[9]Here let me quote with Pleasure, the Air which Mr Handel has adapted to those charming Words of Milton.

> Hide me from Day's garish Eye,
> While the Bee, with honied Thigh,
> At her flow'ry Work does sing,
> And the Waters murmuring;
> With such Concert as they keep,
> Entice the dewy-feather'd Sleep.
> And let some strange mysterious Dream,
> Wave at his Wings in airy Stream
> Of lively Portraiture display'd,
> Softly on my Eyelids laid.
> Then, as I wake, sweet Music breath,
> Above, about, and underneath;
> Sent by some Spirit, to Mortals good,
> Or th' unseen Genius of the Wood.

Here the Air and the Symphony delightfully imitate the humming of the Bees, the murmuring of the Waters, and express the Ideas of Quiet and Slumber; but what, above all, demands this Eulogium, as the Master-Stroke of accompanying the Voice with Trebles and Tenors, only till he comes to these Words, "Then, as I wake, sweet Music breath," where *the Bass begins* with an Effect that can be felt only, and not expressed.

I have chosen to give all my Illustrations on this Matter from the Works of Mr Handel, because no one has exercised this Talent more universally, and because these Instances must also be most universally understood.

[10]With ravish'd Ears

> The Monarch hears,
> Assumes the God,
> Affects to nod,

And seems to shake the Spheres.

In which Air I am sorry to observe, that the *Affectation* of imitating this Nod, has reduced the Music as much below the Dignity of the Words, as *Alexander's* Nod was beneath that of *Homer's Jupiter*.

[11]Vide il Penseroso.

> Sweet Bird that shuns the Noise of Folly,
> Most musical, most melancholly.

[12]What shall we say to excuse this same great Composer, who, in his Oratorio of *Joshua*, condescended to amuse the vulgar Part of his Audience, by letting them *hear the Sun stand still.*

4*thly*, As the Aim of Music is to affect the Passions in a pleasing Manner, and as it uses Melody and Harmony to obtain that End, its Imitation must never be employed on *ungraceful Motions*, or *disagreeable Sounds*; because, in the one Case, it must injure the *Melody* of the Air, and in the other, the *Harmony* of the Accompanyment; and, in both Cases, must lose its Intent of affecting the Passions *pleasingly*.

5*thly*, As Imitation is only so far of Use in Music, as when it aids the Expression; as it is only analogous to poetic Imitation, *when Poetry imitates* through mere natural Media, so it should only be employed in the same Manner. To make the Sound eccho to the Sense in descriptive Lyric, and, perhaps, in the cooler Parts of Epic Poetry is often a great Beauty; but, should the tragic Poet labour at shewing this Art in his most distressful Speeches, I suppose he would rather flatten than inspirit his Drama: In like Manner, the musical Composer, who catches at every particular Epithet[13] or Metaphor that the Part affords him, to shew his imitative Power, will never fail to hurt the true Aim of his Composition, and will always prove the more difficient in Proportion as his Author is more pathetic or sublime.

What then is the Composer, who would aim at true musical Expression, to perform? I answer, he is to blend such an happy Mixture of Air and Harmony, as will affect us most strongly with the Passions or Affections which the Poet intends to raise: and that, on this Account, he is not principally to dwell on particular Words in the Way of Imitation, but to comprehend the Poet's general Drift or Intention, and on this to form his Airs and Harmony, either by Imitation (so far as Imitation may be proper to this End) or by any other Means. But this I must still add, that if he attempts to raise the Passions by Imitation, it must be such a temperate and chastised Imitation, as rather brings the Object before the Hearer, than such a one as induces him to form a Comparison between the Object and the Sound. For, in this last Case, his Attention will be turned entirely on the Composer's Art, which must effectually check the Passion. The Power of Music is, in this Respect, parallel to the Power of Eloquence: if it works at all, it must work in a secret and unsuspected Manner. In either Case, a pompous Display of Art will destroy its own Intentions: on which Account, one of the best general Rules, perhaps, that can be given for musical Expression, is that which gives Rise to the Pathetic in every other Art, *an unaffected Strain of Nature and Simplicity*.[14]

---

[13]To give but one Instance, how many Composers hath the single Epithet, warbling, misled from the true Road of Expression, like an *ignis fatuus*, and bemired them in a *Pun*?

[14]Whatever the State of Music may have been among the ancient *Greeks*, &c. or whether it was actually capable of producing those wonderful Effects related of it, we cannot absolutely determine; seeing all the Uses of their *Enharmonic Scale* are totally lost; and of their musical Characters, which should have conveyed to us their Art, slender Traces any where to be found. From the Structure of their Instruments, we cannot form any vast Ideas of their Powers: They

There is no Doubt but many Rules may be deduced, both from the Compositions of the best Masters, and from Experience, in observing the Effects which various Sounds have upon the Imagination and Affections. And I don't know, whether the same Propriety, in regard to the Part of Expression of *Poetry*, may not as well be applied to *Musical Expression*; since there are discordant and harmonious Inflections of musical Sounds when united, and various Modes, or Keys, (besides the various Instruments themselves) which, like particular Words, or Sentences in Writing, are very expressive of the different Passions, which are so powerfully excited by the Numbers of Poetry.[15]

seem to have been far inferior to those in Use at present: but which, indeed, being capable of as much Execution as Expression, are only rendered more liable to be abused. Thus, the too great Compass of our modern Instruments, tempting as well the Composer as Performer, to exceed the natural Bounds of Harmony, may be one Reason why some Authors have so warmly espoused the Cause of the ancient Music, and run down that of the modern.

I believe we may justly conclude, that the Force and Beauties of the ancient Music, did not consist so much in artful Compositions, or in any Superiority of Execution in the Performance: as in the pure Simplicity of its Melody; which being performed in Unisons, by their vast Chorusses of Voices and Instruments, no Wonder the most prodigious Effects were produced. Since the Time of Guido Aretino, the Laws and Principles of Harmony have been considerably enlarged, and by rendering this Art more intricate and complex, have deprived it of those plain, though striking Beauties, which, probably, almost every Hearer could distinguish and admire. And, I don't know whether this will not go some Way, towards determining the Dispute concerning the superior Excellency of ancient and modern Music. It is to be observed, that the Ancients, when they speak of its marvellous Effects, generally consider it as an Adjunct to Poetry. Now, an Art in its Progress to its own absolute Perfection, may arrive at some intermediate Point, which is its Point of Perfection, considered as an Art joined to another Art; but not to its own, when taken separately. If the Ancients, therefore, carried Melody to its highest Perfection, it is probable they pushed the musical Art as far as it would go, considered as an Adjunct to Poetry: but Harmony is the Perfection of Music, as a single Science. Hence then we may determine the specific Difference between the ancient and modern Compositions, and consequently their Excellency.

[15]"Soft is the Strain when *Zephyr* gently blows,
And the smooth Stream in smoother Number flow;
But when loud Surges lash the sounding Shore,
The hoarse, rough Verse should like the Torrent roar.
When *Ajax* strives some Rock's vast Weight to throw,
The line too labours, and the Words move slow;
Not so, when swift *Camilla* scours the Plain,
Flies o'er the unbending Corn, and skims along the Main.
Hear how *Timotheus* vary'd Lays surprise,
And bid alternate Passions fall and rise!
While, at each Change, the Son of *Libyan Jove*,Now burns with Glory, and then melts with Love:
Now his fierce Eyes with sparkling Fury glow,
Now Sighs steal out, and Tears begin to flow:
Persians and *Greeks* like Turns of nature sound,
And the World's Victor stood subdu'd by Sound!
The Power of Music all our Hearts allow;
And what *Timotheus* was, is *Dryden* now."

[Pope's] Essay on Criticism.

Perhaps, the Powers of Passion and Verse were never so happily exerted, for the purpose of Music, as in this Ode: and, as happily hath the *Genius* of the *Composer* been united with *That* of the *Poet*.

195

Thus the *sharp* or *flat Key*; slow or lively Movements; the *Staccato*; the *Sostenute*, or smooth-drawn Bow; the striking *Diesis*;[16] all the Variety of Intervals, from a Semitone to a Tenth, &c; the various Mixtures of Harmonies, the Preparation of Discords, and their Resolution into Concords, the sweet Succession of Melodies; and several other Circumstances besides these, do all tend to give that Variety of Expression which elevates the Soul to Joy or Courage, melts it into Tenderness or Pity, fixes it in a rational Serenity, or raises it to the Raptures of Devotion.

. . . . .

PART III.

On Musical Expression, *as it relates to the* Performer.

SECTION I.

On the expressive Performance of Music in general.

But as the Nature and Effects of *Musical Expression* do likewise relate to the *Performer*, and the different Instruments which are employed in the Practice of Music, so these in their Turn may be also considered.

For, as *Musical Expression* in the *Composer*, is succeeding in the Attempt to express some particular Passion;[17] so in the *Performer*, it is to do a *Composition* Justice, by playing it in a *Taste* and *Stile* so exactly corresponding with the Intention of the Composer, as to preserve and illustrate *all* the Beauties of his Work.

Again, as the *Composer* is culpable, who, for the Sake of some low and trifling *Imitation*, deserts the Beauties of *Expression*: So, that *Performer* is still more culpable, who is industrious to reduce a good Instrument to the State of a bad one, by endeavouring to make it subservient to a still more trifling *Mimickry*.

---

[16]Or *Quarter Tone*, or less, if performed by the Voice or Violin, being and Interval in the *Enharmonic Scale* of the Ancients, and amazingly powerful in rousing the Passions.

This interval is equally capable, in judicious Hands, of exciting Terror, Grief, Despondency, in this Case, is chiefly produced from their different Accompanyments, and the particular Modulations in which they are employed.

[17]The Word *Passion* is here taken in the most extensive Sense, as it may be applied to every Species of Excellence in musical Compositions; which, from the very Design of the Composer, demands an *energetic* Execution.

196

Such are all Imitations of *Flageolets, Horns, Bagpipes,* &c. on the Violin: a Kind of low Device, calculated merely to amaze, and which, even with the common Ear, cannot long prevail over the natural Love of Harmony.[18]

Even the Use of double Stops on this Instrument, may, in my Opinion, be considered as one of the Abuses of it; since, in the Hands of the greatest Masters, they only deaden the Tone, spoil the Expression, and obstruct the Execution. In a Word, they baffle the Performer's Art, and bring down *one good* Instrument to the State of *two indifferent ones.*

But surely it ought chiefly to be the Composer's Care, not to give the Performer any Opportunities whatever of disparaging his Art: And the more he avoids all such low Buffoonery, the more will this false Taste be discouraged: For whatever may be alledged against the Depravity of our Taste in the musical Science, it certainly can be fixed no where so properly, as on the Masters themselves; since, were they to persist with any Spirit or Resolution in the Exercise of their Genius in such Compositions only as are worthy of them, they would undoubtedly improve the public Ear, and acquire to themselves a Reputation and Character worth preserving.[19]

Let every Composer, whether for the Church, the Theatre, or Chamber, thoroughly consider the Nature and Compass of the Voices or Instruments, that are employed in his Work; and, by that Means, he will the more easily avoid the common Error of not sufficiently distinguishing what Stile or Manner is proper for Execution, and what for Expression.

[18]The singing of a *Cuckoo,* and the cackling of a Hen, have, in fact, been often introduced into musical Performances. Vivaldi, in his Seasons, or Concertos, so called, has imitated the barking of a Dog; besides many other strange Contrivances; attempting even to describe, as well as imitate, the various Changes of the Elements.

If those Composers, who take such Pleasure in their musical Imitations of the Noise of Animals, will shew their Ingenuity in that Way, I would advise them rather to follow the much more effectual Method of introducing the Creatures themselves. And, by way of Example, I shall given them the following Story, as it is related by Mr Bayle, in his Critical Dictionary under the Article of Lewis XI. "The Abbot de Baigne, a Man of great Wit, had invented many Things relating to musical Instruments; and, being in the Service of the King, was once commanded by him to procure him harmonious Sounds from the Cries of Hogs, imagining the Thing was absolutely impossible. The Abbot was not in the least perplexed at such a Command, but asked the King Money to perform it; which was immediately delivered to him, and he effected the most surprising and remarkable Thing that was ever heard. He got together a large Quantity of Hogs, all of different Ages, and put them into a Tent or Pavillion covered with Velvet, before which Tent there was a wooden Table all painted; and he made an organical Instrument with a certain Number of Stops so contrived, that when he hit upon those Stops, it answered to some Spikes, which pricking the Hogs that stood behind in a due Order, made them cry in such a harmonious Manner, that the King and all his Attendance were highly delighted with it."

[19]There is one Circumstance, that might tend greatly to the Repute and Utility of Music; which is, that the Professors themselves, would cultivate a sincere and friendly Commerce with each other, and cherish that benevolent Temper, which their daily Employ, one should think, ought naturally to inspire. In Truth, there is nothing enlarges the Mind to every social and laudable Purpose, so much as this delightful Intercourse with Harmony. They who feel not this divine Effect, are Strangers to its noblest Influence: For whatever Pretensions they may otherwise have to a Relish or Knowledge of its Laws, without this Criterion of the musical Soul, all other pretended Signatures of Genius we may look upon as counterfeit.

He should also minutely observe the different Qualities of the Instruments themselves. For, as vocal Music requires one kind of Expression, and instrumental another; so different Instruments have also a different Expression peculiar to them.

Thus, the *Hautboy* will best express the *Cantabile*, or singing Style, and may be used in all Movements whatever under this Denomination; especially those Movements which tend to the *Gay* and *Chearful*.

In Compositions for the *German* Flute, is required the same Method of proceeding by *conjoint Degrees*, or such other natural Intervals, as, with the Nature of its Tone, will best express the languishing, or melancholy Style. With both these Instruments, the running into *extreme Keys*, the Use of the *Staccato*, or distinct Separation of Notes; and all irregular Leaps, or broken and uneven Intervals must be avoided; for which Reason alone, these Instruments ought never to be employed in the *Repieno Parts* of Concertos for Violins, but in such Pieces only as are composed for them; and these, perhaps, would be most agreeably introduced as principal Instruments in some intervening Movements in the Concerto, which might not only give a pleasing Variety, but shew their different Expression to the greatest Advantage.

In continued Compositions, particularly for the *German* Flute, our Composers have been not a little unsuccessful; but whether this Failure may be imputed to the Deficiency of the Instrument, or their attempting to exceed its natural Expression, may, perhaps, be worth the Composer's while to consider.

The *Bassoon* should also have those gradual Movements which naturally glide in their Divisions, and have the easiest Transitions from one Key to another; and may be admitted as a *Principal* in the *Solo*, or *Rinforzo* in the *Chorus*, but never in the latter without a sufficient Number of other Basses to qualify and support it.[20]

The *Trumpet* and *French-Horn*, tho' equally limited in their *Scale*, yet have Pieces of very different Styles adapted to them. The one, perhaps, to animate and inspire Courage; the other to enliven and chear the Spirits; yet are not both to be alike discarded in the *figurate Descant*, or that Part of Composition where Discords are concerned. In this Species of Harmony I have known the French-Horn introduced with amazing Success; but it requires a very able Composer to manage it properly with such Accompanyments. Either of these Instruments, when fully accompanied, produce more wonderful Effects than when heard alone, because in all martial Compositions, their Airs and Expression are of so plain and unmixed a Nature, that their

---

[20]See the Sixth of Geminiani's Concertos, *Opera Settima*, where there is one Movement composed expressly for the Bassoon, the agreeable Effect of which, may be sufficient to evince how much better this Method is of introducing Wind-Instruments, than admitting them throughout the Concerto.

Harmony is more easily comprehended; and thence they strike the common Ear with a greater Degree of Pleasure and Admiration than any other Instrument whatever.

The organ and Harpsichord, though alike in so many Respects, that the same Performer may equally shew his Skill and Execution on both; yet are their respective Compositions, and Manner of Performance widely different: The former expressing the grand or solemn Stile, the latter, those lively or trickling Movements which thrill in the Ear.

Now, where any of the above Instruments over-rule in Concert, whether in the Chorus, or Solo; or are appointed to play such Airs or Movements, as they cannot easily express, we may then conclude, that the Composer hath unfortunately set out upon a wrong Principle, which capital Error will destroy every good Effect that might have been found in his Work, had he duly considered the distinct Limits and Properties of each Instrument.

In classing the different Instruments in Concert, we may consider them as the various Stops which complete a good Organ: And as the skillful Artist so contrives, that, when the full Organ is heard, no *Mixtures*, or *Furnitures*, &c. shall predominate, but that the *Diapasons*, with their *Octaves*[21] may unite and fill the whole; so we may rank the *Violins* with their *Basses* and *Double-Basses*, as the *Diapasons* and *Principals* of the Concert: For in Fact they may be said to contain the very Strength and Spirit of all Harmony; and have in them, not only the Expression of all the other Instruments, but contain a prodigious Variety of many other noble Properties peculiar to themselves, of which all the rest are utterly destitute. It is their remarkable Distinction, that no Concert can be formed without them, as they unite and agree as well with every Instrument, as with each other, and return every Advantage they receive. And, as the finest *instrumental Music* may be considered as an Imitation of the *vocal*; so do these Instruments, with their expressive Tone and the minutest Changes they are capable of in the Progression of Melody, shew their nearest Approaches to the Perfection of the human Voice.

Let the lover of Music call to Mind the delightful Effects they afford, when joined with the Organ to a Chorus of good Voices, particularly in Churches where the Expansion is large and ample, to soften every rough and grating Sound, and unite the Variety of Voices and other Instruments, that complete this grand and solemn Performance; he will, even in this Ideal Enjoyment of Music, with Pleasure own and prefer their harmonious Expression.

In fine, it is in those Productions only which include the Violin and its Species, where an extensive Genius may rove at large through all the various Kinds of Musical Expression; and may give the best Performers, though not in capricious and extravagant Flights, every desirable Opportunity of shewing their Skill.

. . . . .

[21]Principals and Flutes.

CHAPTER TEN

DANIEL WEBB

Observations on the Correspondence between Poetry and Music
(1769)

Though the influence of music over our passions is very generally felt and acknowledged; though its laws are universally the same, its effects in many instances constant and uniform; yet we find ourselves embarrassed in our attempts to reason on this subject, by the difficulty which attends the forming a clear idea of any natural relation between sound and sentiment.

Some have thought to elude this difficulty, by supposing, that the influence of sound on passion may arise from the habit of associating certain ideas with certain sounds. It cannot be necessary to enter into a formal examination of such a principle as this, since it must fall of course on the discovery of a better.

I have observed a child to cry violently on hearing the sound of a trumpet, who some minutes after, hath fallen asleep to the soft notes of a lute. Here we have evident marks of the spirits being thrown into opposite movements, independently of any possible association of ideas. This striking opposition in the effects of musical impressions seems to indicate the regular operation of a general and powerful principle.

All musical sounds are divided into acute and grave: the acute spring from strong, the grave from weaker vibrations. No sound, therefore, can act as a single impression, since we cannot have a feeling of it but in consequence of a succession of impressions: should it appear, that our passions act in like manner by successive impressions, or, that they affect us on a principle similar to that which is deduced from the analysis of sounds, we might then hope to become masters of the desired secret, and to discover, so far as such things are discoverable, the nature of the relation between sound and sentiment.

As we have no direct nor immediate knowledge of the mechanical operations of the passions, we endeavour to form some conception of them from the manner in which we find ourselves affected by them: thus we say, that love softens, melts, insinuates; anger quickens, stimulates, inflames; pride expands, exalts; sorrow dejects, relaxes: of all which ideas we are to observe, that they are different modifications of motion, so applied, as best to correspond with our feelings of each particular passion. From whence, as well as from their known and visible effects, there is just reason to presume, that the passions, according to their several natures, do produce certain proper and distinctive motions in the most refined and subtle parts of the human body.[1] What these parts are, where placed, or how fitted to receive and propagate these motions, are points which I shall not inquire into. It is sufficient for my purpose to have it admitted, that some such parts must exist in the human machine: however, as in our pursuits after knowledge, it is discouraging to be reminded every moment of our ignorance, I shall take advantage of the received opinion touching this matter, and assign the functions in question to the nerves and spirits. We are then to take it for granted, that the mind, under particular affections, excites certain vibrations in the nerves, and impresses certain movements on the animal spirits.

I shall suppose, that it is in the nature of music to excite similar vibrations, to communicate similar movements to the nerves and spirits. For, if music owes its being to motion, and, if passion cannot well be conceived to exist without it, we have a right to conclude, that the agreement of music with passion can have no other origin than a coincidence of movements.[2]

---

[1]Omnis enim motus animi suum quendam a natura habet vultum, et sonum, et gestum: et ejus omnis vultus, omnesque voces, ut nervi in fidibus, ita sonant, ut a motu animi quoque sunt pulsae.

                                                                    ˙ Cicero de Oratore

[III. lvii. 216. For every emotion has by nature its particular appearance and tone and gesture: and one's whole appearance and all his tones of voice, like strings in a lyre, sound according as they are struck by the emotions].

[2]Se quis igitur ita harmoniam accommodare posset, ut spiritus eodem prorsus motu, quo harmonici numeri, moveretur, is intentum effectum produceret haud dubiè, idem enim praeftaret quod in duobus polychordis exactissime concordatis fit; quorum alterutrum modulis harmonicis incitatum in altero etiam intacto eandem omnino harmoniam producit. Kirch. Musur. l. vii.

[If anyone can so adjust harmony that the spirit is wholly moved by the same motion as the harmonic rhythms, he will without doubt produce the actual effect, for the same thing will prevail that does in two polychords precisely tuned to one another, of which either, excited by harmonic rhythms, produces in the other, even if untouched, the very same harmony.]

When, therefore, musical sounds produce in us the same sensations which accompany the impressions of any one particular passion, then the music is said to be in unison with that passion; and the mind must, from a similtude in their effects, have a lively feeling of an affinity in their operations.

In my Remarks on the Beauties of Poetry, I have observed,

That, in music, we are *transported* by sudden transitions, by an impetuous reiteration of impressions.

That we are *delighted* by a placid succession of lengthened tones, which dwell on the sense and insinuate themselves into our inmost feelings.

That a growth or climax in sounds *exalts* and *dilates* the spirits, and is therefore a constant source of the *sublime*.

If an ascent of notes be in accord with the sublime, then their descent must be in unison with those passions which *depress* the spirits.

All musical impressions, which have any correspondence with the passions, may, I think, be reduced under one or other of these four classes.

If they agitate the nerves with violence, the spirits are hurried into the movements of anger, courage, indignation, and the like.

The more gentle and placid vibrations shall be in unison with love, friendship, and benevolence.

If the spirits are exalted or dilated, they rise into accord with pride, glory, and emulation.

If the nerves are relaxed, the spirits subside into the languid movements of sorrow.

From these observations it is evident, that music cannot, of itself, specify any particular passion, since the movements of every class must be in accord with all the passions of that class.—For instance, the tender and melting tones, which may be expressive of the passion of love, will be equally in unison with the collateral feelings of benevolence, friendship, and pity; and so on through the other classes.

On hearing an overture by Iomelli, or a concerto by Geminiani, we are, in turn, transported, exalted, delighted; the impetuous, the sublime, the tender, take possession of the sense at the will of the composer. In these moments, it must be confessed, we have no determinate idea of any agreement or imitation; and the reason of this is, that we have no fixed idea of the passion to which this agreement is to be referred. But, let eloquence co-operate with music, and specify the motive of each particular impression,

---

Whether we account for the imitations of music in this manner, or call them, after Aristotle, the homoiomata ton ethon kai pathon—simulacra morum et affectionum—we have alike in view a principle of assimilation; with this difference, that, by establishing a mode of operation, whether real or imaginary, we are enabled to convey our ideas with greater clearness touching the several modes of *imitation*.

while we feel an agreement in the sound and motion with the sentiment, song takes possession of the soul, and general impressions become specific indications of the manners and the passions.

It is imagined by some, that verse hath no other object than to please the ear. If by this they understand, that verse cannot excite or imitate passion, they would do well to reflect on the nature of pleasure: at least, through this medium, were there no other, verse must have an influence over all those passions which are founded in pleasure. But verse is motion, and verse produceth pleasure, which is likewise motion.[3]

How then? hath nature struck out a correspondence between external and mental motion in one instance, to the exclusion of all others: provident, industrious, in establishing laws for an inferior purpose, would she stop short at the first opening of advantage, and contract her system at the very point where it called for enlargement? I do not wish to set out upon better ground than in direct opposition to such ideas as these.

. . . . .

It has been supposed, that the correspondence of music with passion springs from a coincidence of movements; and that these movements are reducible to four classes, distinguished by their accords with the passions of pride, sorrow, anger, and love. Should these principles hold good in verse, which is the music of language, we shall have little reason to doubt of their extending to music in general.

If there are passions which come not within the reach of musical expression, they must be such as are totally painful. Painting and sculpture, on whatever subjects employed, act simply, as imitative arts; they have no other means of affecting us than by their imitations. But music acts in the double character of an art of impression as well as of imitation: and if its impressions are necessarily, and, in all cases pleasing, I do not see how they can, by any modification, be brought to unite with ideas of absolute pain. I am confirmed in this opinion by observing, that shame, which is a sorrowful reflection on our own unworthiness, and therefore intirely painful, hath no unisons in music. But pity, which is a sorrow flowing from sympathy, and tempered with love, hath a tincture of pleasure. Hence the poet:

Dimn sadness did not spare,
That time, celestial visages; yet, mix'd
With pity, violated not their bliss.[4]

[3]Let it be stated that pleasure is a certain motion of the soul. Aristotle, Rhetoric xi. l.

Hedone, voluptas—with this word everyone connects two things—unrestrained gladness of mind, and a delightful excitation of pleasure in the body. Cicero, de Finibus. ll. iv. 13.
[4]Paradise Lost.

Pity, therefore, hath its unisons in music; so hath emulation, which is noble and animating, to the exclusion of envy, which is base and tormenting. The same distinction must extend to anger and hatred; for anger hath a mixture of pleasure, in that it stimulates to revenge;[5] but hatred, having no such hope, works inward and preys upon itself.

The number of the passions thus excluded from becoming the subjects of musical expression will not be very considerable, since, on a strict inquiry into those passions which are generally esteemed painful, we shall find that this very often depends on their motives and degrees. Thus terror, though in reality it be founded in pain, is yet in several of its modes attended with pleasure, as is evident in every instance where the means employed to exite it, either by the idea or the movement, have any connexion with the sublime. But terror, like many other passions, though it be not absolutely painful in its nature, may become so from its excess; for horror, as I conceive, is nothing more than fear worked up to an extremity:

I could a tale unfold, whose lightest word
Would *harrow up* thy soul.[6]

It is on this same principle, that certain passions are found to add beauty or deformity to the countenance, according to the different degrees of force with which they act. A truth so well understood by capital painters, that they throw the extremes of passion into strong and charged features, while they reserve the finer expressions for the heightenings of beauty. Shakespear has touched on this last circumstance with his usual happiness:

O what a deal of scorn looks beautiful
In the contempt and anger of his lip.[7]

Mr. Locke, considering the passions as modes of pleasure or pain, divides them into such as are absolutely pleasing, or absolutely painful, to the entire exclusion of all mixed affections. This division is too vague and general; it may save us the trouble of a minute investigation, but it will never lead us into a knowledge of the human heart. Thus, desire, according to this philosopher, is founded in uneasiness; but Aristotle will have its foundation to be in pleasure: whereas, in truth, it is a compound of both: of uneasiness through the want of an absent good; of pleasure from the hope of obtaining that good. I am tempted to convey my idea of this subject by an illustration borrowed from painting. Let us suppose the painful passions to be *shades*, the pleasing *lights*; we shall then find that many of our passions are

---

[5]Arist. Rhet. l. II. c. ii. 2.
[6]Hamlet.
[7]Twelfth Night.

composed of mid-tints, running more or less into the light or shade, pleasure or pain, according to the nature, motive, or degree of the passion. For instance, if grief arises from the sufferings of others, it becomes pity, and is pleasing by its nature. If grief, proceeding from our own sufferings, be hopeless, and therefore excessive, it becomes misery or despair, and is painful from its degree.

Let grief be tempered with hope, it hath a tincture of pleasure

> All these and more came flocking, but with looks
> Down-cast and damp, yet such wherein appear'd
> Obscure, some glimpse of joy, t'have found their chief
> Not in despair.[8]

The remembrance of that which was dear to us, though it causes grief, yet it gives to our sorrow a cast of pleasure, as it produces in the soul the movements of love. It is in this situation, particularly, that we are said to *indulge* our grief:

> Ask the faithful youth,
> Why the cold urn of her whom long he lov'd
> So often fills his arms.[9]

If grief should spring from a consciousness of guilt, it is shame, and is painful from its motive; if attended with innocence, it may come within that beautiful description,

> She sat like patience on a monument
> Smiling at grief.[10]

In order to treat of the passions with precision, we should determine their several modes, and fix an unalienable sign on each particular feeling. To this end we should have a perfect intelligence of our own natures, and a consummate knowledge of every thing by which we can be affected: in short, we should have conceptions in all points adequate to their objects. Such knowledge would be intuitive. We should, in this case, want no comparisons of our ideas and sentiments; no illustration of one thing by its resemblance to another: thus every proposition would be reduced to a simple affirmation, the operations of the understanding would cease, and the beauties of the imagination could have no existence. Providence has judged better for us, and by limiting our powers has multiplied our enjoyments.

The wisdom so conspicuous in the abridgement of our perceptions,

---

[8]Paradise Lost.
[9]Akenside, Pleasures of Imagination.
[10]Twelfth Night.

appears with equal evidence in the bounds prescribed to those arts which were destined for our delight and improvement. It has been observed, that music can have no connexion with those passions which are painful by their nature; neither can it unite with our other passions when they become painful by their excess; so that the movements of music being in a continued opposition to all those impressions which tend either to disorder or disgrace our nature, may we not reasonably presume, that they were destined to act in aid of the moral sense, to regulate the measures and proportions of our affections; and, by counter-acting the passions in their extremes, to render them the instruments of virtue, and the embellishments of character.

I need not profess, that, in forming my ideas of the passions, I have trusted much more to poets than to philosophers: among the latter, there have been some who would by no means have admitted the distinction just now established between emulation and envy. Hobbes hath, after his manner, given us the portraits of these passions, but with such sister-like features, that it is no easy matter to distinguish the one from the other. He has, with equal industry, and for the same purpose, excluded from pity and the sympathetic affections every idea of benevolence or of natural beauty; conceiving them, contrary to all true feelings, to be nothing more than the different workings of one and the same narrow and selfish principle. It may be considered as a happiness in our subject, that it exempts us from a dependence on the systems of philosophers, or the refinements by which they are supported. The process in which we are engaged obliges us to trace the passions by their internal movements, or their external signs; in the first, we have the musician for our guide; in the second, the painter, and the poet in both: it is the province of music to catch the movements of passion as they spring from the soul; painting waits until they rise into action, or determine in character; but poetry, as she possesses the advantages of both, so she enters at will into the province of either, and her imitations embrace at once the movement and the effect. How delightful, in this point of view, to contemplate the imitative arts; those sister-graces, distinguished yet depending on a social influence; the inspirers of elegant manners and affections; the favourites of that Venus, or nature, whose beauties it is their office to cultivate, and on whose steps it is their joy to attend!

Among the opinions which have prevailed touching the union of music with passion, the most general seems to be this—That as melody is a thing pleasing in itself, it must naturally unite with those passions which are productive of pleasing sensations; in like manner as graceful action accords with a generous sentiment, or as a beautiful countenance gives advantage to an amiable idea. The proposition taken singly is vague and superficial; but the illustrations by which it is supported penetrate deeper, and give us an insight into the relation between the cause and the effect: for in what manner can action become the representative of sentiment, unless it strikes us as springing from some analogous movement in the soul? it is the same thing with regard to beauty, which can give no advantage to sentiment, without being thrown into motion; nor can this motion have any meaning or effect, unless it carries with it the idea of a corresponding agitation in the mind.

It was from a feeling of an imitative virtue in music, or of its aptness to excite pathetic motions, that Shakespear attributes to it the power of producing a kind of reverberation in the soul:

> *Duke.* How do'st thou like this tune?
> *Viola.* It gives a very echo to the seat
> Where love is throned.[11]

Let us apply this idea to the effects of the forté and piano in music. Loudness is an increased velocity in the vibration, or a greater vibration made in the same time.[12] Music therefore becomes imitative, when it so proportions the enforcement or diminution of sound to the force or weakness of the passion, that the soul answers, as in an echo, to the just measure of the impression. It is from a propensity in our nature to fall in with these reciprocal or responsive vibrations, that, in expressing our own sentiments, or in reciting those of others, the voice mechanically borrows its tone from the affection; thus it rises into vigor with the bold, and subsides into softenss with the gentler feelings. We may try the experiment on the following lines:

> Back from pursuit thy pow'rs with loud acclaim
> Thee only extoll'd, Son of thy Father's might,
> To execute fierce vengeance on his foes:
> Not so on man; "Him thro' their malice fall'n,
> Father of mercy and grace, thou did'st not doom
> So strictly, but much more to pity incline."[13]

This fall of notes, or weakness in the movement, is in the true spirit of musical imitation. The poet was so sensible of the happiness, that in the moment after he repeats the very same movement, and contracts it by measures the most lofty and sonorous:

[11]Twelfth Night.

[12]Hence it is, that those, who, through indelicacy of ear, are insensible to finer impressions, are observed to be affected by loud music; because the increase of the impression forces the dull and sluggish organ into responsive vibration.

If to loudness be united a greater intenseness or weight of sound, as when music acts in full chorus, the impression is still farther augmented; and the effects, though less exquisite, become more powerful.

But if the ear is so unhappily formed as that music can neither solicit nor compel the organ into unison, then the consequence will be, either that the impression shall produce weak and imperfect movements, and like a constant monotonous murmur lull the hearer asleep, or it will excite strong and irregular vibrations, in which case it acts like a repeated noise, sets the nerves on the fret, and throws the spirits into a painful disorder.

[13]Paradise Lost.

No sooner did thy dear and only son
Perceive thee purpos'd not to doom frail man
So strictly, but much more to pity inclin'd—
Hail, Son of God, Saviour of men! thy name
Shall be the copious matter of my song
Henceforth, and never shall my harp thy praise
Forget, nor from thy Father's praise disjoin.[14]

Somewhat different from the transition in this last example is an even and continued swell from the piano into the forté: this, in music, is attended with a high degree of pleasure: on repeating the following passage, we discover the source of this pleasure, and find that it proceeds from the spirits being thrown into the same movement as when they rise from sorrow into pride, or from an humble into a sublime affection:

If thou beest he: but O how fall'n, how chang'd
From him, who in the happy realms of light
Cloath'd with transcendent brightness didst outshine
Myriads, though bright.[15]

A descent of sound from the forté into the piano hath a no less pleasing effect, corresponding with the condition of the nerves, when from a state of exertion, which hath a mixture of pain, we feel the sweet relief of a gradual relaxation:

He stood
With Atlantean shoulders, fit to bear
The weight of mightiest monarchies; his look
Drew audience and attention still as night
Or summer's noon-tide air.[16]

From the tenor of these examples it appears, that pleasure is not, as some have imagined, the result of any fixed or permanent condition of the nerves and spirits, but springs from a succession of impressions, and is greatly augmented by sudden or gradual transitions from one kind or strain of vibrations to another. It appears further, that the correspondence between music and passion is most striking in those movements and transitions which in each are productive of the greatest pleasure; consequently the source of pleasure must be in both the same, and the foundation of their union can be no other than a common principle of motion.

. . . . .

[14]Paradise Lost.
[15]Paradise Lost.
[16]Paradise Lost.

Various have been the conjectures of learned and ingenious men touching the causes of the separation of Music from Poetry. The greatest difficulty with me is, to comprehend how their union could have subsisted after the institution of measures founded on artificial quantities. We must take this subject a little higher.

Musical pronunciation must depend on the laws of musical succession: accordingly, in the pronunciation of words of two syllables, music constantly throws its accent on the first: as in glóry, rúin; or on the second, as rejoíce, exúlt.[17] In words of three syllables, music takes no notice of quantities otherwise than by lengthening or shortening the duration of the middle syllable: as in émphasis, hármony, emphátic, harmónic. Words of four syllables are, in the language of music, nothing more than duplications of words of two; that is to say, they regularly fall, either into two iambics, as facílitáte, omnípoténce; or into two trochees, as únrelénting, únfrequénted. But this it appears, that the same principle, which throws our native monosyllables into measure, forms and directs the general pronunciation of our mixed language; with this difference, that, as the sense could have no part in determining the accents of polysyllables, the relative quantities of these syllables must have been decided intirely by the ear, and have fallen singly under the laws of musical accentuation: to which must be added, that these quantities are, by a regular and uniform pronunciation, become invariable; and so far partake of the advantage, while at the same time they point out the origin, of a fixed prosody.

The constancy with which we have adhered to these laws, hath preserved the native character of our verse through every stage of its improvement. By repeating the first stroke of the iambic, and the second of the trochee, the ancients formed their anapaest and dactyle. By reducing their polysyllables under the government of our musical accents, we have dispossessed them in some degree of their artificial advantages, and subdued them to the tenor of a monosyllabical rhythmus. The rhythmus of every language depends principally on the signs of simple ideas, as by these we more immediately express our feelings; these signs, in our language, are for the most part monosyllables. I need not repeat what hath been already observed concerning the construction of our language. How absurdly have our ancestors been charged with a dull neglect of classical advantages, and a perverse predilection for their own rude measures and barbarous articulation!

If from musical quantities we pass to the consideration of an artificial prosody, it will be difficult to conceive, that this change could have been made with a view, as some have imagined, to a more intimate and perfect

---

[17]A word, therefore, of two syllables hath no advantage, in point of movement, over two monosyllables thrown into the same measure. But eight verses out of ten, throughout our best poems, have no other advantage than what they derive from the use of dissyllables. What do we mean when we exclaim against a monosyllabical rhythmus?

210

union of Music with Poetry: since, should music observe the quantities by institution, she must abandon her own; should she neglect those quantities, the musical rhythmus would be at variance with the poetic.

The artifice of contracted measures, and the variety resulting from these contrasts, are most unfavorable to music, because they disturb her in the government of her accents, and thwart her in the exertion of her natural powers. It is for this reason, that, from our simple measures, music ever selects the most simple. But the ancient lyric poesy abounds with the most varied measures, and embraces every mode of versification: true; it abounds likewise with the most picturesque images, and the boldest metaphors: are we therefore to conclude that these are the true objects of musical imitation? How long are we to be amused with inferences drawn from an union which we do not comprehend, and from a practice of which we have not one decisive example?

Vossius[18] asserts with great confidence, that the music of the ancients derived its excellence from the force of their poetic rhythmus: this force he makes to consist in the power of conveying just and lively images of the things represented. It seems intirely to have escaped him, that these images are confined to objects of sound or motion; and that, in the imitation of such, music must, from its nature, be superior to verse; so that the more powerful imitation must have borrowed its advantages from the more imperfect. From this notable proposition he concludes, that modern language and poesy are totally unqualified to unite with music. And yet, where measure flows from the laws of musical pronunciation, Poetry and Music have one common rhythmus: and, if sentiment takes a part in determining the measure, their union becomes still more happy and intimate: for music hath no expression but in virtue of her accents; nor have her accents any imitative force but what they derive from sentiment. The truth is, music borrows sentiments from poetry, and lends her movements, and consequently must prefer that mode of verification which leaves her most at liberty to consult her own genius.

After what hath been already observed of the nature and origin of these sister-arts, it cannot be thought necessary, in this place, to prove, that a dramatic spirit must be the common principle of their union. This spirit is not confined to the regular drama; it inspires the lover's address, the conqueror's triumph, the captive's lamentation; in short, it may govern every mode of composition in which the poet assumes a character, and speaks and acts in consequence of that character.

To sentiments which spring from character and passion, the lyric poet should unite images productive of sentiment and passion. Objects in repose, or the beauties of still-life, fall not within the province of musical imitation, nor can music take a part in the colouring of language. Our modern lyric

---

[18]De Poematum Cantu et viribus Rhythmi [1673].

211

poesy is a school for painters, not for musicians. The form of invocation, the distinctions of the strophe, the antistrophe, and chorus, are mere pretensions. To what purpose do we solicit the genius of music, while we abandon, without reserve, the plectrum for the pencil, and cast aside the lyre, as a child doth its rattle, in the moment that we proclaim it to be the object of our preference?

But it is said, that music, by its impressions on one sense, may excite affections similar to those which take their rise from another: and it has been inferred from hence, that the musician can, by a kind of enchantment, *paint* visible objects. To paint by movements would be enchantment indeed; but the wonder ceases when we are made to understand, that music hath no other means of representing a visible object, than by producing in the soul the same movements which we should naturally feel were that object present.[19]

These observations lead us to the necessary distinction of the image from its effect; of its beauty as a visible object, from its energy as a source of pathetic emotions. Thus we draw the line between painting and music: nor does the occasion call for a master-stroke; their separation will be marked in the choice of their objects:

Long, pity, let the nations view
Thy sky-worn robes of tenderest blue,
   And eyes of dewy light![20]
Deserted at his utmost need
By those his former bounty fed,
On the bare earth expos'd he lies
With not a friend to close his eyes.[21]

If, instead of expressing our own, we describe the feelings of others, and so enter into their condition as to excite a lively sense of their several affections, we retain the spirit of the drama, tho' we abandon the form. The most perfect poem of this kind, in our language, is the Feast of Alexander, by Mr. Dryden. Here music unites with poetry in the character of a descriptive art; but then the objects of her descriptions are her own impressions.

It was objected by Aristotle to the poets of his time, that they were the principal speakers in their own poems; contrary to the practice of Homer, who well knew, that, while the poet speaks, the imitation or the drama ceases.[22] It is remarkable that this is the very area from which Plutarch dates the corruption of music. When the poet ceased to write from the movements of the heart, the musician began to sing from the caprice of the imagination.

[19]Dict. de Musique, Art. *Imitation.*
[20]Collins, Ode to Pity.
[21]Dryden, Alexander's Feast.
[22]De Poet. c. xxiv. 13-14.

In proportion as the spirit of expression declines, a taste for description will, of course, prevail; we *express* the agitations and affections of our minds; we *describe* the circumstances and qualities of external objects: the application of measure to either purpose depends on the nature of the subject, or the genius of the writer. A single instance may suffice to let this idea in the clearest light:

> When Ajax strives some rock's vast weight to throw,
> The line too labours, and the words move slow.[23]

So will they in the expression of a deep and heavy affliction:

> And in this harsh world draw thy breath in pain.[24]

Like parallels may be continued thro' all the examples which have been given of pathetic accords. Now, though the imitations of verse may be applied to the purposes either of expression or of description, it is not the same thing with regard to music, the effects of which are so exquisite, so fitted by nature to move the passions, that we feel; ourselves hurt and disappointed, when forced to reconcile our sensations to a simple and unaffecting coincidence of sound or motion.

Again, in descriptive poetry, the imitations often turn on the force of particular words, on the resemblance between the sign and the idea:

> *Jarring* sound
> Th' infernal doors, and on their hinges *grate*
> *Harsh* thunder.[25]

In this, and in every other instance where the resemblance is determined by sound, the characters of Poetry and Music are directly opposed; for, the nature of articulation strictly considered, it will appear, that in poetry, the imitations of harsh and rude sounds must be the most perfect; in music, it is just the reverse. It was for this reason, that our incomparable Milton, in his imitations of musical ideas, threw the force of the imitation, not on the sound, but on the movement:

> Save where silence yields
> To the night-warbling bird, that now awake
> Tunes sweetest his *love-labor'd* song.[26]

[23]Pope, Essay on Criticism.
[24]Hamlet.
[25]Paradise Lost.
[26]Paradise Lost.

Tasso was not so judicious, or trusted too much to the sweetness on his language:

Odi quello usignuolo,
Che vá di ramo in ramo
Cantando, Io amo, Io amo.[27]

Hear that sweet nightingale,
Who flies from grove to grove
His song—I love, I love.

These imitations of musical ideas by articulate sounds have much the same effect with the imitations of the force of particular words by musical sounds. Thus, Handel seldom fails to ascend with the word *rise*, and descend with the word *fall*. Purcell goes still farther, and accompanies every idea of *roundness* with an endless *rotation* of notes. But what shall we say to that musician, who disgraces the poet by realizing his metaphors, and, in downright earnest, makes the fields *laugh*, and the vallies *sing*. In music, it is better to have no ideas at all than to have false ones, and it will be safer to trust to the simple effects of impression than to the idle conceits of a forced imitation.

In our attempts to reduce music into an union with descriptive poetry, we should do well to consider, that music can no otherwise imitate any particular sound, than by becoming the thing it imitates: it hath an equal facility in conforming with simple ideas of motion. What effects can be expected from imitations, in which there is neither ingenuity in the execution nor importance in the object?

Verse on the other hand, considered as motion, falls far short of the promptness and facility of music; nor can it, with respect to sounds, rise above a distant and vague assimilation: its imitations, therefore, in either case, may be attended with some degree of surprise and pleasure. The misfortune is, that our poets dwell too much on this trifling advantage, and pursue it, to an almost total neglect of the nobler purposes of imitation.

. . . . .

[27]Aminta.

CHAPTER ELEVEN

JAMES BEATTIE

Essay on Poetry and Music as They Affect the Mind
(1776)
CHAPTER VI.
SECTION I.

Of Imitation. Is Music an Imitative Art?

Man from his birth is prone to imitation, and takes great pleasure in it. At a time when he is too young to understand or attend to rules, he learns, by imitating others, to speak, and walk, and do many other things equally requisite to life and happiness. Most of the sports of children are imitative, and many of them dramatical. Mimickry occasions laughter; and a just imitation of human life upon the stage is highly delightful to persons of all ranks, conditions, and capacities.

Our natural propensity to imitation may in part account for the pleasure it yields: for that is always pleasing which gratifies natural propensity; nay, to please, and to gratify, are almost synonymous terms. Yet the peculiar charm of imitation may also be accounted for upon other principles. To compare a copy with the original, and trace out the particulars wherein they differ and wherein they resemble, is in itself a pleasing exercise to the mind; and, when accompanied with admiration of the object imitated, and of the genius of the imitator, conveys a most intense delight; which may be rendered still more intense by the agreeable qualities of the *instrument* of imitation,—by the beauty of the colours in painting, by the harmony of the language in poetry;

and in music, by the sweetness, mellowness, pathos, and other pleasing varieties of vocal and instrumental sound. And if to all this there be added the merit of a moral design, Imitation will then shine forth in her most amiable form, and the enraptured heart acknowledge her powers of pleasing to be irresistible.

Such is the delight we have in imitation, that what would in itself give neither pleasure nor pain, may become agreeable when well imitated. We see without emotion many faces, and other familiar objects; but a good picture even of a stone, or common plant, is not beheld with indifference. No wonder, then, that what is agreeable in itself, should, when surveyed through the medium of skilful imitation, be highly agreeable. A good portrait of a grim countenance is pleasing; but a portrait equally good of a beautiful one is still more so. Nay, though a man in a violent passion, a monstrous wild beast, or a body agonized with pain, be a most unpleasing spectacle, a picture, or poetical description of it, may be contemplated with delight;[1] the pleasure we take in the artist's ingenuity, joined to our consciousness that the object before us is not real, being more than sufficient to counter-balance every disagreeable feeling occasioned by the deformity of the figure.[2] Even human vices, infirmities, and misfortunes, when well represented on the stage, form a most interesting amusement. So great is the charm of imitation.

That has been thought a very mysterious pleasure, which we take in witnessing tragical imitations of human action, even while they move us to pity and sorrow. Several causes seem to co-operate in producing it. 1. It gives an agreeable agitation to the mind, to be interested in any event, that is not attended with real harm to ourselves or others. Nay, certain events of the most substantial distress would seem to give a gloomy entertainment to some minds: else why should men run so eagerly to see shipwrecks, executions, riots, and even battles, and fields of slaughter? But the distress upon the stage neither is, nor is believed to be, real; and therefore the agreeable exercise it may give to the mind is not allayed by any bitter

---

[1]Aristor. Poet. sect. 4. Gerard on Taste, part I. sect. 4.

[2]Pictures, however, of great merit as imitations, and valuable for the morality of the design, may yet be too horrid to be contemplated with pleasure. A robber who had broke into a repository of the dead, in order to plunder a corpse of some rich ornaments, is said to have been so affected with the hideous spectacle of mortality which presented itself when he opened the coffin, that he slunk away, trembling and weeping, without being able to execute his purpose. I have met with an excellent print upon this subject; but was never able to look at it for half a minute together. Too many objects of the same character may be seen in Hogarth's *Progress of Cruelty.*— There is another class of shocking ideas, which poets have not always been sufficiently careful to avoid. Juvenal and Swift, and even Pope himself, have given us descriptions which it turns one's stomach to think of. And I must confess, that, notwithstanding the authority of Atterbury and Addison, and the general merit of the passage, I could never reconcile myself to some filthy ideas, which to the unspeakable satisfaction of Mr. Voltaire, Milton has unwarily introduced in the famous allegory of Sin and Death.

reflections, but is rather heightened by this consideration, that the whole is imaginary. To those who mistake it for real, as children are said to do sometimes, it gives pain, and no pleasure. 2. Throughout the performance, we admire the genius of the poet, as it appears in the language and sentiments, in the right conduct of the fable in diversifying and supporting the characters, and in devising incidents affecting in themselves, and conducive to the main design. 3. The ingenuity of the actors must be allowed to be a principal cause of the pleasure with which we witness either tragedy or comedy. A bad play well acted may please, and in fact often does; but a good play ill acted is intolerable. 4. We sympathise with the emotions of the audience, and this heightens our own. For I apprehend, that no person of sensibility would chuse to be the sole spectator of a play, if he had it in his power to see it in company with a multitude. When we have read by ourselves a pleasing narrative, till it has lost every charm that novelty can bestow, we may renew its relish by reading it in company, and perhaps be even more entertained than at the first perusal. 5. The ornaments of the theatre, the music, the scenery, the splendor of the company, nay the very dress of the players, must be allowed to contribute something to our amusement: else why do managers lay out so much money in decoration? And, lastly, let it be observed, that there is something very peculiar in the nature of pity. The pain, however exquisite, that accompanies this amiable affection, is such, that a man of a generous mind would not disqualify himself for it, even if he could: nor is the "luxury of woe," that we read of in poetry, a mere figure of speech, but a real sensation, wherewith every person of humanity is acquainted, by frequent experience. Pity produces a tenderness of heart very friendly to virtuous impressions. It inclines us to be circumspect and lowly, and sensible of the uncertainty of human things, and of our dependence upon the great Author of our being; while continued joy and prosperity harden the heart, and render men proud, irreligious, and inattentive: so that Solomon had good reason for affirming, that "by the sadness of the countenance the heart is made better." The exercise of pity, even towards imaginary sufferings, cannot fail to give pleasure, if attended, as it generally is, with the approbation of reason and conscience, declaring it to be a virtuous affection, productive of signal benefit to society, and peculiarly suitable to our condition, honourable to our nature, and amiable in the eyes of our fellow-creatures.[3]

Since Imitation is so plentiful a source of pleasure, we need not wonder, that the imitative arts of poetry and painting should have been greatly esteemed in every enlightened age. The imitation itself, which is the work of the artist, is agreeable; the thing imitated, which is nature, is also agreeable;

---

[3]Since these remarks were written, Dr. Campbell has published a very accurate and ingenious dissertation on this subject. See his *Philosophy of Rhetoric*, vol. i.

and is not the same thing true of the instrument of imitation? Or does any one doubt, whether harmonious language be pleasing to the ear, or certain arrangements of colour beautiful to the eye?

Shall I apply these, and the preceding reasonings, to the musical Art also, which I have elsewhere called, and which is generally understood to be, Imitative? Shall I say, that some melodies please, because they imitate nature, and that others, which do not imitate nature, are therefore unpleasing?—that an air expressive of devotion, for example, is agreeable, because it presents us with an imitation of those sounds by which devotion does naturally express itself?—Such an affirmation would hardly pass upon the reader; notwithstanding the plausibility it might seem to derive from that analogy which all the fine arts are supposed to bear to one another. He would ask, What is the natural sound of devotion? Where is it to be heard? When was it heard? What resemblance is there between Handel's *Te Deum*, and the tone of voice natural to a person expressing, by articulate sound, his veneration of the Divine Character and Providence?—In fact, I apprehend, that critics have erred a little in their determinations upon this subject, from an opinion, that Music, Painting, and Poetry, are all imitative arts. I hope at least I may say, without offence, that while this was my opinion, I was always conscious of some unaccountable confusion of thought, whenever I attempted to explain it in the way of detail to others.

But while I thus insinuate, that Music is not an imitative art, I mean no disrespect to Aristotle, who seems in the beginning of his Poetics to declare the contrary. It is not the whole, but *the greater part* of music, which that philosopher calls Imitative; and I agree with him so far as to allow this property to some music, though not to all. But he speaks of the ancient music, and I of the modern; and to one who considers how very little we know of the former, it will not appear a contradiction to say, that the one might have been imitative, though the other is not.

Nor do I mean any disrespect to music, when I would strike it off the list of imitative arts. I allow it to be a fine art, and to have great influence on the human soul: I grant, that, by its power of raising a variety of agreeable emotions in the hearer, it proves its relation to poetry, and that it never appears to the best advantage but with poetry for its interpreter: and I am satisfied, that though musical genius may subsist without poetical taste, and poetical genius without musical taste; yet these two talents united might accomplish nobler effects, than either could do singly. I acknowledge too, that the principles and essential rules of this art are as really founded in nature, as those of poetry and painting. But when I am asked, What part of nature is imitated in any good picture or poem, I find I can give a definite answer: whereas, when I am asked, What part of nature is imitated in Handel's *Water-music*, for instance, or in Corelli's *eighth concerto*, or in any particular English song or Scotch tune, I find I can give no definite answer:—

218

though no doubt I might say some plausible things; or perhaps, after much refinement, be able to show, that Music may, by one shift or other, be made an imitative art, provided you allow me to give any meaning I please to the word *imitative*.

Music is imitative, when it readily puts one in mind of the thing imitated. If an explanation be necessary; and if, after all, we find it difficult to recognise any exact similitude, I would not call such music an imitation of nature; but consider it as upon a footing, in point of likeness, with those pictures, wherein the action cannot be known but by a label proceeding from the mouth of the agent, nor the species of animal ascertained without a name written under it. But between imitation in music and imitation in painting, there is this one essential difference:—a bad picture is always a bad imitation of nature, and a good picture is necessarily a good imitation; but music may be exactly imitative, and yet intolerably bad; or not at all imitative, and yet perfectly good. I have heard, that the *Pastorale* in the eighth of Corelli's *Concertos* (which appears by the inscription to have been composed for the night of the Nativity) was intended for an imitation of the song of angels hovering above the fields of Bethlehem, and gradually soaring up to heaven. The music, however, is not such as would of itself convey this idea: and, even with the help of the commentary, it requires a lively fancy to connect the various movements and melodies of the piece with the motions and evolutions of the heavenly host; as sometimes flying off, and sometimes returning; singing sometimes in one quarter of the sky, and sometimes in another; now in one or two parts, and now in full chorus. It is not clear, that the author intended any imitation; and whether he did or not, is a matter of no consequence; for the music will continue to please, when the tradition is no more remembered. The harmonies of this *pastorale* are indeed so uncommon, and so ravishingly sweet, that it is almost impossible not to think of heaven when one hears them. I would not call them imitative; but I believe they are finer than any imitative music in the world.

Sounds in themselves can imitate nothing directly but sounds, nor in their motions any thing but motions. But the natural sounds and motions that music is allowed to imitate, are but few. For, first, they must all be consistent with the fundamental principles of the art, and not repugnant either to melody or to harmony. Now the foundation of all true music, and the most perfect of all musical instruments, is the human voice; which is therefore the prototype of the musical scale, and a standard of musical sound. Noises, therefore, and inharmonious notes of every kind, which a good voice cannot utter without straining, ought to be excluded from this pleasing art: for it is impossible, that those vocal sounds which require any unnatural efforts, either of the singer or speaker, should ever give permanent gratification to the hearer. I say, permanent gratification; for I deny not, that the preternatural screams of an Italian singer may occasion surprise, and momentary amusement: but those screams are not music; they are admired, not for their propriety or pathos, but, like rope-dancing, and the eating of fire, merely because they are uncommon and difficult.—Besides, the end of all genuine music is, to introduce into the human mind certain affections, or susceptibilities of affection. Now, all the affections, over which music has any power, are of the agreeable kind. And therefore, in this art, no imitations of natural sound or motion, but such as tend to inspire agreeable affections, ought ever to find a place. The song of certain birds, the murmur of a stream, the shouts of multitudes, the tumult of a storm, the roar of thunder, or a chime of bells, are sounds connected with agreeable or sublime affections, and reconcileable both with melody and with harmony; and may therefore be imitated, when the artist has occasion for them: but the crowing of cocks, the barking of dogs, the mewing of cats, the grunting of swine, the gabbling of geese, the cackling of a hen, the braying of an ass, the creaking of a saw, or the rumbling of a cart-wheel, would render the best music ridiculous. The movement of a dance may be imitated, or the stately pace of an embattled legion; but the hobble of a trotting horse would be intolerable.

There is another sort of imitation by sound, which ought never to be heard, or seen, in music. To express the local elevation of objects by what *we* call *high* notes, and their depression by *low* or *deep* notes, has no more propriety in it, than any other pun. *We* call notes *high* or *low*, in respect of their situation in the written scale. There would have been no absurdity in expressing the highest notes by characters placed at the bottom of the scale or musical line, and the lowest notes by characters placed at the top of it, if custom had so determined. And there is reason to think, that something like this actually obtained in the musical scale of the ancients. At least it is probable, that the deepest or gravest sound was called *Summa* by the Romans, and the shrillest or acutest *Ima*; which might be owing to the construction of their instruments; the string that sounded the former being perhaps highest in place, and that which sounded the latter lowest.—Yet some people would think a song faulty, if the word *heaven* was set to what we call a *low* note, or the word *hell* to what we call a *high* one.

All these sorts of illicit imitation have been practiced, and by those too from whom better things were expected. This abuse of a noble art did not escape the satire of Swift; who, though deaf to the charms of music, was not blind to the absurdity of musicians. He recommended it to Dr. Ecclin, an ingenious gentleman of Ireland, to compose a *Cantata* in ridicule of this puerile mimicry. Here we have *motions* imitated, which are the most inharmonious, and the least connected with human affections; as the *trotting, ambling,* and *galloping,* of Pegasus; and *sounds* the most unmusical, as *crackling* and *sniveling,* and *rough roystering rustic roaring strains*: the words *high* and *deep* have high and deep notes set to them; a series of short notes of equal

220

lengths are introduced, to imitate *shivering* and *shaking*; an irregular rant of quick sounds, to express *rambling*; a sudden rise of the voice, from a low to a high pitch, to denote *flying above the sky*; a ridiculous run of chromatic divisions on the words *Celia dies*; with other droll contrivances of a like nature. In a word, Swift's Cantata alone may convince any person, that music uniformly imitative would be ridiculous.—I just observe in passing, that the satire of this piece of levelled, not at absurd imitation only, but also at some other musical improprieties; such as the idle repetition of the same words, the running of long extravagant divisions upon one syllable, and the setting of words to music that have no meaning.

If I were entitled to suggest any rules in this art, I would humbly propose (and a great musician and ingenious writer seems to be of the same mind[4]), that no imitation should ever be introduced into music purely instrumental. Of vocal melody the expression is, or ought to be, ascertained by the poetry; but the expression of the best instrumental music is ambiguous. In this, therefore, there is nothing to lead the mind of the hearer to recognise the imitation, which, though both legitimate and accurate, would run the risk of being overlooked and lost. If, again, it were so very exact, as to lead our thoughts instantly to the thing imitated, we should be apt to attend to the imitation only, so as to remain insensible to the general effect of the piece. In a word, I am inclined to think, that imitation in an instrumental *concerto* would produce either no effect, or a bad one. The same reasons would exclude it from instrumental *solos*; provided they were such as deserve to be called music:—if they be contrived only to show the dexterity of the performer, imitations, and all possible varieties of sound, may be thrown in *ad libitum*; any thing will do, that can astonish the audience; but to such fiddling or fingering I would no more give the honourable name of Music, than I would apply that of Poetry to Pope's "Fluttering spready they purple pinions," or to Swift's *Ode on Ditton and Whiston*.

In vocal music, truly such, the words render the expression determinate, and fix the hearer's attention upon it. Here therefore legitimate imitations may be employed; both because the subject of the song will render them intelligible, and because the attention of the hearer is in no danger of being seduced from the principal air. Yet even here, these limitations must be laid upon the instrumental accompaniment, and by no means attempted by the singer, unless they are expressive, and musical, and may be easily managed by the voice. In the song, which is the principal part, expression should be predominant, and imitations never used at all, except to assist the expression. Besides, the tones of the human voice, though the most pathetic of all sounds, are not suited to the quirks of imitative melody, which will generally appear to best advantage on an instrument. In the first part of that excellent

[4]Avison on Musical Expression, Part II, Sect. III.

song, "Hide me from day's garish eye, / While the bee with honey'd thigh / At her flowery work does sing, / And the waters deep murmering, / With such concert as they keep, / Intice the dewy feathr'd sleep."—Handel imitates the murmur of groves and waters by the accompaniment of tenors: in another song of the same *Oratorio*," On a plat of rising ground, / I hear the far-off curfew sound, / Over some wide-water'd shore, / Swinging slow with sullen roar,"—he makes the bass imitate the evening-bell: in another fine song, "Hush, ye pretty warbling choir,"—he accompanies he voice with a flageolet that imitates the singing of birds: in the "Sweet bird that shun'st the noise of folly," the chief accompaniment is a German flute imitating occasionally the notes of the nightingale.—Sometimes, where expression and imitation happen to coincide, and the latter is easily managed by the voice, he makes the song itself imitative. Thus, in that song, "Let the merry bells ring round, / And the jocund rebecks sound, / To many a youth and many a maid, / Dancing in the chequer'd shade,"—he makes the voice in the beginning imitate the *sound* of a chime of bells, and in the end the *motion* and gaiety of a dance.

Of these imitations no body will question the propriety. But Handel, notwithstanding his inexhaustible invention, and wonderful talents in the sublime and pathetic, is subject to fits of trifling, and frequently errs in the application of his imitative contrivances. In that song, "What passion cannot music raise and quell," when he comes to the words, "His listening brethren stood around, / And wondering on their faces *fell*,"—the accompanying violoncello *falls* suddenly from a quick and *high* movement to a very *deep* and long note. In another song of the same piece[5], "Sharp violins proclaim / Their jealous pangs and desperation, / Fury, frantic "indignation, / *Depth* of pains and *height of passion*, / For the fair disdainful dame;"—the words "*Depth* of pains and *height* of passion," are thrice repeated to different keys; and the notes of the first clause are constantly *deep*, and those of the second as regularly *high*. The poet however is not less blameable than the musician.—And many other examples of the same kind might be produced from the works of this great artist.[6]

What has been said may serve to show both the extent, and the merit of Imitative Music.[7] It extends to those natural sounds and motions only, which are agreeable in themselves, consistent with melody and harmony, and associated with agreeable affections and sentiments. Its merit is so inconsider-

[5]Dryden's Ode on St. Cecilia's day.
[6]That pretty pastoral ode of Shakespeare, "When daisies pied and violets blue," has been set to music by Mr. Leveridge; who makes the finger imitate, not oly the note of the cuckoo (which may be allowed, because easily performed, and perfectly musical), but also the shriek of the owl.
[7]By Imitative Music I must always be understood to mean, that which imitates *natural* sounds and motions. Fugues, and other similar contrivances, which, like echoes, repeat or imitate particular portions of the melody, it belongs not to this place to consider.

able, that music purely instrumental is rather hurt than improved by it; and vocal music employs it only as a help to the expression, except in some rare cases, where the imitation is itself expressive as well as agreeable, and at the same time within the power of the human voice.

The best masters lay it down as a maxim, that melody and harmony are not to be deserted, even for the sake of expression itself.[8] Expression that is not consistent with these is not *musical* expression; and a composer who does not render them consistent, violates the essential rules of his art.[9] If we compare Imitation with Expression, the superiority of the latter will be evident. Imitation without Expression is nothing: Imitation detrimental to Expression is faulty: Imitation is never tolerable, at least in serious music, except it promote and be subservient to Expression. If then the highest excellence may be attained in instrumental music, without imitation; and if, even in vocal music, imitation have only a secondary merit; it must follow, that the imitation of nature is not essential to this art; though sometimes when judiciously employed it may be ornamental.

Different passions and sentiments do indeed give different tones and accents to the human voice. But can the tones of the most pathetic melody be said to bear a resemblance to the voice of a man or woman speaking from the impulse of passion?—The *flat key*, or *minor mode*, is found to be well adapted to a melancholy subject; and, if I were disposed to refine upon the imitative qualities of the art, I would give this for a reason, that melancholy, by depressing the spirits, weakens the voice, and makes it rise rather by *minor thirds*, which consist of but four semitones, than by *major thirds*, which consist of five. But is not this reason more subtle than solid? Are there not melancholy airs in the *sharp key*, and chearful ones in the *flat*? Nay, in the

---

[8]Avison on Musical expression, Part II, Sect. III.
[9]Harmony and Melody are as essential to genuine music, as perspective is to painting. However solicitous a painter may be to give expression to the figures on his back ground, he must not strengthen their colour, nor define their outlines, so as to hurt the perspective by bringing them too near. A musician must be equally careful not to violate the harmony of his piece, in order to heighten the pathos. There is likewise in poetry something analogous to this. In those poems that require a regular and uniform versification, a poet may perhaps, in some rare instances, be allowed to break through the rules of his verse, for the sake of rendering his numbers more emphatical. Milton at least is intitled to take such a liberty:
>   —Eternal wrath
>   Burn'd after them to the bottomless pit.   *Parad. Lost.*
But these licences must not be too glaring: And therefore I know not whether Dyer is not blameable for giving us, in order to render his numbers imitatitve, a Trochaic verse of four feet and a half, instead of an Iambic of five:

>   The pilgrim oft
> At dead of night, midst his oraison hears
> Aghast the voice of Time; disparting towers
> Tumbling all precipitate, down dash'd,
> Ratting around, & c.   *Ruins of Rome.*

same air, do we not often meet with a transition from the one key to the other, without any sensible change in the expression?

Courage is apt to vent itself in a strong tone of voice: but can no musical strains inspire fortitude, but such as are sonorous? The Lacedemonians did not think so; otherwise they would not have used the music of soft pipes when advancing to battle.[10] If it be objected, that the firm deliberate valour, which the Spartan music was intended to inspire, does not express itself in a blustering, rather in a gentle accent, resembling the music of soft pipes, I would recommend to the objector to chuse, from all the music he is acquainted with, such an air as he thinks would most effectually awaken his courage; and then consider, how far that animating strain can be said to resemble the accent of a commander complimenting his troops after a victory, or encouraging them before it. Shakespeare speaks of the "spirit-stirring drum;" and a most emphatical epithet it must be allowed to be. But why does the drum excite courage? Is it because the *sound* imitates the voice of a valiant man? or does the *motion* of the drumsticks bear any similitude to that of his legs or arms?

Many Christians (I wish I could say *all*) know to their happy experience, that the tones of the organ have a wonderful power in raising and animating devout affections. But will it be said, that there is any resemblance between the sound of that noble instrument, or the finest compositions that can be played on it, and the voice of a human creature employed in an act of worship?

One of the most affecting styles in music is the *Pastoral*. Some airs put us in mind of the country, of "rural sights and rural sounds," and dispose the heart to that chearful tranquillity, that pleasing melody, that "vernal delight," which groves and streams, flocks and herds, hills and vallies, inspire. But of what are these pastoral airs imitative? Is it of the murmur of waters, the warbling of groves, the lowing of herds, the bleating of flocks, or the echo of vales and mountains? Many airs are pastoral, which imitate none of these things. What then do they imitate?—the songs of ploughmen, milkmaids, and shepherds? Yes: they are such, as we think we have heard, or might have heard, sung by the inhabitants of the country. Then they must *resemble* country-songs; and if so, these songs must also be in the pastoral style. Of what then are these country-songs, the supposed archetypes of pastoral music, imitative? Is it of other country-songs? This shifts the difficulty a step backward, but does not take it away. Is it of rural sounds, proceeding from things animated, or from things inanimate? or of rural motions of men, beasts, or birds? of winds, woods, or waters?—In a word, an air may be pastoral, and in the highest degree pleasing, which imitates neither sound nor motion, nor any thing else whatever.

[10]Aulus Gellius, lib. I. cap. II.

After all, it must be acknowledged, that there is some relation at least, or analogy, if not similitude, between certain musical sounds, and mental affections. Soft music may be considered as analogous to gentle emotions; and loud music, if the tones are sweet and not too rapid, to sublime ones; and a quick succession of noisy notes, like those we hear from a drum, seems to have some relation to hurry and impetuosity of passion. Sometimes, too, there is from nature, and sometimes there comes to be from custom, a connection between certain musical instruments, and certain places and occasions. Thus a flute, hautboy, or bagpipe, is better adapted to the purposes of rural music, than a fiddle, organ, or harpsichord, because more portable, and less liable to injury from the weather: thus an organ, on account both of its size and loudness, requires to be placed in a church, or some large apartment: thus violins and violoncellos, to which any degree of damp may prove hurtful, are naturally adapted to domestic use; while drums and trumpets, fifes and french-horns, are better suited to the service of the field. Hence it happens, that particular tones and modes of music acquire such a connection with particular places, occasions, and sentiments, that by hearing the former we are put in mind of the latter, so as to be affected with them more or less, according to the circumstances. The sound of an organ, for example, puts one in mind of a church, and of the affections suitable to that place; military music, of military ideas; and flutes and hautboys, of the thoughts and images peculiar to rural life. This may serve in part to account for musical expressiveness or efficacy; that is, to explain how it comes to pass, that certain passions are raised, or certain ideas suggested, by certain kinds of music: but this does not prove music to be an imitative art, in the same sense in which painting and poetry are called imitative. For between a picture and its original; between the ideas suggested by a poetical description and the objects described, there is a strict similitude: but between soft music and a calm temper there is no strict similitude; and between the sound of a drum or of an organ and the affection of courage or of devotion, between a concert of violins and a chearful company, there is only an accidental connection, formed by custom, and founded rather on the nature of the instruments, than on that of the music.

It may perhaps be thought, that man learned to sing by imitating the birds; and therefore, as vocal music is allowed to have been the prototype of instrumental, that the whole art must have been essentially imitative. Granting the fact, this only we could infer from it, that the art was imitative at first: but that it continues to be so, does not follow; for it cannot be said, either that the style of our music resembles that of birds, or that our musical composers make the song of birds the model of their compositions. But it is vain to argue from hypothesis: and the fact before us, though taken for granted by some authors, is destitute of evidence, and plainly absurd. How can it be imagined, that mankind learned to sing by imitating the feathered

225

race? I would as soon suppose, that we learned to speak by imitating the neigh of a horse, or to walk by observing the motion of fishes in water; or that the political constitution of Great Britain was formed upon the plan of an ant-hillock. Every musician, who is but moderately instructed in the principles of his art, knows, and can prove, that, in the *sharp series* at least, the divisions of the diatonic scale, which is the standard of human music, are no artificial contrivance, but have a real foundation in nature: but the singing of birds, if we except the cuckoo and one or two more, is not reducible to that scale, nor to any other that was ever invented by man; for birds diversify their notes by intervals which the human organs cannot imitate without unnatural efforts, and which therefore it is not to be supposed that human art will ever attempt to express by written symbols. In a word, it is plain, that nature intended one kind of music for men, and another for birds: and we have no more reason to think, that the former was derived by imitation from the latter, than that the nests of a rookery were the prototype of the Gothic Architecture, or the combs in a bee-hive of the Grecian.

Music, therefore, is pleasing, not because it is imitative, but because certain melodies and harmonies have *an aptitude* to raise certain passions, affections, and sentiments in the soul. And, consequently, the pleasures we derive from melody and harmony are seldom or never resolvable into that delight which the human mind receives from the imitation of nature.

All this, it may be said, is but a dispute about a word. Be it so: but it is, notwithstanding, a dispute somewhat material both to art and to science. It is material, in science, that philosophers have a determined meaning to their words, and that things be referred to their proper classes, And it is of importance to every art, that its design and end be rightly understood, and that artists be not taught to believe that to be essential to it, which is only adventitious, often impertinent, for the most part unnecessary, and at best but ornamental.

SECTION II.

How are the pleasures we derive from Music to be accounted for?

It was said, that certain melodies and harmonies have *an aptitude* to raise certain passions, affections, and sentiments, in the human soul. Let us now enquire a little into the nature of this *aptitude*; by endeavouring, from acknowledged principles of the human constitution, to explain the cause of that pleasure which mankind derive from music. I am well aware of the delicacy of the argument, and of my inability to do it justice; and therefore I promise no complete investigation, nor indeed any thing more than a few cursory remarks. As I have no theory to support, and as this topic, though it may amuse, is not of any great utility, I shall be neither positive in my assertions, nor abstruse in my reasoning.

The vulgar distinguish between the sense of hearing, and that faculty by which we receive pleasure from music, and which is commonly called *a musical ear*. Every body knows, that to hear, and to have a relish for melody, are two different things; and that many persons have the first in perfection, who are destitute of the last. The last is indeed, like the first, a gift of nature; and may, like other natural gifts, languish if neglected, and improve exceedingly if exercised. And though every person who hears, might no doubt, by instruction and long experience, be made sensible of the musical properties of sound, so far as to be in some measure gratified with good music and disgusted with bad; yet both his pain and his pleasure would be very different in kind and degree, from that which is conveyed by a true musical ear.

I. Does not part of the pleasure, both of melody and of harmony, arise from the very nature of the notes that compose it? Certain inarticulate sounds, especially when continued, produce very pleasing effects on the mind. They seem to withdraw the attention from the more tumultuous concerns of life, and, without agitating the soul, to pour gradually upon it a train of softer ideas, that sometimes lull and soothe the faculties, and sometimes quicken sensibility, and stimulate the imagination. Nor is it absurd to suppose, that the human body may be mechanically affected by them. If in a church one feels the floor, and the pew, tremble to certain tones of the organ; if one string vibrates of its own accord when another is sounded near it of equal length, tension, and thickness; if a person who sneezes, or speaks loud, in the neighborhood of a harpsichord, often hears the strings of the instrument murmur in the same tone; we need not wonder, that some of the finer fibres of the human frame should be put in a tremulous motion, when they happen to be in unison with any notes proceeding from external objects. That certain bodily pains might be alleviated by certain sounds, was believed by the Greeks and Romans: and we have it on the best authority, that one species at least of madness was once curable by melody.[11] I have seen even instrumental music of little expression draw tears from those who had no knowledge of the art, nor any particular relish for it. Nay, a friend of mine, who is profoundly skilled in the theory of music, well acquainted with the animal economy, and singularly accurate in his inquiries into nature, assures me, that he has been once and again wrought into a feverish fit by the

[11]First book of Samuel, chap. xvi. vers. 23.

tones of an Eolian harp. These, and other similar facts that might be mentioned, are not easily accounted for, unless we suppose, that certain sounds may have a mechanical influence upon certain parts of the human body.—Be that however as it will, it admits of no doubt, that the mind may be agreeably affected by mere sound, in which there is neither meaning nor modulation; not only by the tones of the Eolian harp, and other musical instruments, but also by the murmur of winds, groves, and water-falls; nay by the shouts of multitudes, by the uproar of the ocean in a storm; and, when one can listen to it without fear, by that "deep and dreadful organ-pipe[12]," the thunder itself.

Nothing is more valued in a musical instrument or performer, than sweetness, fullness, and variety of tone. Sounds are disagreeable, which hurt the ear by their shrillness, or which cannot be heard without painful attention on account of their exility. But *loud* and *mellow* sounds, like those of thunder, of a storm, and of the full organ, elevate the mind through the ear; even as vast magnitude yields a pleasurable astonishment, when contemplated by the eye. By suggesting the idea of great power, and sometimes of great expansion too, they excite a pleasing admiration, and seem to accord with the lofty genius of that soul whose chief desire is for truth, virtue, and immortality, and the object of whose most delightful meditation is the greatest and best of Beings.[13] *Sweetness* of tone, and beauty of shape and colour, produce a placid acquiescence of mind, accompanied with some degree of joy, which plays in a gentle smile upon the countenance of the hearer and beholder. *Equable* sounds, like smooth and level surfaces, are in general more pleasing than such as are rough, uneven, or interrupted; yet, as the flowing curve, so essential to elegance of figure, and so conspicuous in the outlines of beautiful animals, is delightful to the eye; so notes *gradually swelling*, and *gradually decaying*, have an agreeable effect on the ear, and on the mind; the former tending to rouse the faculties, and the latter to compose them; the one promoting gentle exercise, and the other rest.

But of all sounds, that which makes its way most directly to the human heart, is the human voice: and those instruments that approach nearest to it are in expression the most pathetic, and in tone the most perfect. The notes of a man's voice, well tuned and well managed, have a mellowness, variety, and energy, beyond those of any instrument; and a fine female voice, modulated by sensibility, is beyond comparison the sweetest, and most melting sound, in art or nature. Is it not strange, that the most musical people upon earth, dissatisfied, as it would seem, with both these, should have incurred a dreadful reproach, in order to introduce a third species of vocal

[12]Shakespear's Tempest.
[13]See Longinus, sect. 34. Spectator, No. 413. Pleasures of Imagination [Akenside], book I. vers. 151. &c.

sound, that has not the perfection of either? For may it not be affirmed with truth, that no person of uncorrupted taste ever heard for the first time the music I allude to, without some degree of horror; proceeding not only from the disagreeable thoughts suggested by what was before his eyes, but also from the thrilling sharpness of tone that startled his ear? Let it not be said, that by this abominable expedient, choruses are rendered more complete, and melodies executed, which before were impracticable. Nothing that shocks humanity ought to have a place in human art; nor can a good ear be gratified with unnatural sound, or a good taste with too intricate composition. Surely, every lover of music, and of mankind, would wish to see a practice abolished which is in itself a disgrace to both; and, in its consequences, so far from being desirable, that it cannot truly be said to do any thing more than to debase a noble art into trick and grimace, and make the human breath a vehicle, not to human sentiments, but to mere empty screaming and squalling.

II. Some notes, when sounded together, have an agreeable, and others a disagreeable effect. The former are *concords*, the latter *discords*. When the fluctuations of air produced by two or more contemporary notes do mutually coincide, the effect is agreeable; when they mutually repel each other, the effect is disagreeable. These coincidences are not all equally perfect; nor these repulsions equally strong: and therefore all concords are not equally sweet, nor all discords equally harsh. A man unskilled in music might imagine, that the most agreeable harmony[14] must be made up of the sweetest concords, without any mixture of discord: and in like manner, a child might fancy, that a feast of sweet-meats would prove the most delicious banquet. But both would be mistaken. The same concord may be more or less pleasing, according to its position; and the sweeter concords often produce their best effect, when they are introduced by the harsher ones, or even by discords; for then they are most agreeable, because they give the greatest relief to the ear: even as health is doubly delightful after sickness, liberty after confinement, and a sweet taste when preceded by a bitter. Dissonance, therefore, is necessary to the perfection of harmony. But consonance predominates; and to such a degree, that, except on rare occasions, and by a nice ear, the discord in itself is hardly perceptible.

Musicians have taken pains to discover the principles on which concords and discords are to be so arranged as to produce the best effect; and have thus brought the whole art of harmony within the compass of a certain number of rules, some of which are more, and others less indispensable. These rules admit not of demonstrative proof: for though some of them may

[14]*Melody,* in the language of art, is the agreeable effect of a single series of musical tones: *Harmony* is the agreeable effect of two or more series of musical tones sounded at the same time.

be inferred by rational deduction from the very nature of sound; yet the supreme judge of their propriety is the human ear. They are, however, founded on observation so accurate and so just, that no artist ever thought of calling them in question. Rousseau indeed somewhere insinuates, that habit and education might give us an equal relish for a different system of harmony; a sentiment which I should not have expected from an author, who for the most part recommends an implicit confidence in our natural feelings, and who certainly understands human nature well, and music better than any other philosopher. That a bass of *sevenths*, or *fourths*, or even of *fifths*, should ever become so agreeable to any human ear, as one constructed according to the system, is to me as inconceivable, as that Virgil, turned in to rugged prose, would be read and admired as much as ever. Rousseau could not mean to extend this remark to the whole system, but only to some of its mechanical rules: and indeed it must be allowed, that in this, as well as in other arts, there are rules which have no better foundation than fashion, or the practice of some eminent composer.

Natural sensibility is not taste, though it be necessary to it. A painter discovers both blemishes and beauties in a picture, in which an ordinary eye can perceive neither. In poetical language, and in the arrangement and choice of words, there are many niceties, whereof they only are conscious who have practised versification, as well as studied the works of poets, and the rules of the art. In like manner, harmony must be studied a little in its principles by every person who would acquire a true relish for it; and nothing but practice will ever give that quickness to his ear which is necessary to enable him to enter with adequate satisfaction, or rational dislike, into the merit or demerits of a musical performance. When once he can attend to the progress, relations, and dependencies, of the several parts; and remember the past, and anticipate the future, at the same time he perceives the present; so as to be sensible of the skill of the composer, and dexterity of the performer;—a regular concerto, well executed, will yield him high entertainment, even though its regularity be its principal recommendation. The pleasure which an untutored hearer derives from it, is far inferior: and yet there is something in harmony that pleases, and in dissonance that offends, every ear; and were a piece to be played consisting wholly of discords, or put together without any regard to rule, I believe no person whatever would listen to it without great disgust.

After what has been briefly said of the agreeable qualities of musical notes, it will not seem strange, that a piece, either of melody or of harmony, of little or no expression, should, when elegantly performed, give some delight; not only to adepts, who can trace out the various contrivances of the composer, but even to those who have little or no skill in this art, and must therefore look upon the whole piece as nothing more than a combination of pleasing sounds.

III. But Pathos, or Expression, is the chief excellence of music. Without this, it may amuse the ear, it may give a little exercise to the mind of the hearer, it may for a moment withdraw the attention from the anxieties of life, it may show the performer's dexterity, the skill of the composer, or the merit of the instruments; and in all or any of these ways, it may afford a slight pleasure: but, without engaging the affections, it can never yield that permanent, useful, and heartfelt gratification, which legislators, civil, military, and ecclesiastical, have expected from it. Is it absurd to ascribe utility, and permanence, to the effects produced by this noble art? Let me expatiate a little in its praise.—Did not one of the wisest, and least voluptuous, of all ancient legislators, give great encouragement to music?[15] Does not a most judicious author ascribe the humanity of the Arcadians to the influence of this art, and the barbarity of their neighbours the Cynethians to their neglect of it?[16] Does not Montesquieu, one of the first names in modern philosophy, prefer it to all other amusements, as being that which least corrupts the soul?[17] Quintilian is very copious in the praise of music; and extols it as an incentive to valour, as an instrument of moral and intellectual discipline, as an auxiliary to science, as an object of attention to the wisest men, and a source of comfort and an assistant in labour, even to the meanest?[18] The heroes of ancient Greece were ambitious to excel in music; and it is recorded of Themistocles, as something extraordinary, that he was not. Socrates appears to have had checks of conscience for neglecting to accomplish himself in this art; for he tells Cebes, a little before he swallowed the deadly draught, that he had all his life been haunted with a dream, in which one seemed to say to him, "O Socrates, compose and practise music," in compliance with which admonition he amused himself while under sentence of death, with turning some of Aesop's fables into verse, and making a hymn in honour of Apollo,—the only sort of harmonious composition that was then in his power.[19] In armies, music has always been cultivated as a source of pleasure, a principle of regular motion, and an incentive to valour and enthusiasm. The Son of Sirach declares the ancient poets and musicians to be worthy of honour, and ranks them with the benefactors of mankind.[20] Nay, Jesus Christ and his apostles were pleased to introduce this art into the Christian worship; and the church has in every age followed the example.

Music, however, would not have recommended itself so effectually to general esteem, if it had always been merely instrumental. For, if I mistake

[15]Lycurgus. See Plutarch.
[16]Polybius. Hist. lib. 4.
[17]Esprit des loix, liv. 4. ch. 8.
[18]Inst. Orat. lib. i. cap. 8.
[19]Plat. Phaedon. sect. 4.
[20]Ecclesiasticus, xliv. 1.—8.

not, the expression of music without poetry is vague and ambiguous; and hence it is, that the same air may sometimes be repeated to every stanza of a long ode or ballad. The change of the poet's ideas, provided the subject continue nearly the same, does not always require a change of the music: and if critics have ever determined otherwise, they were led into the mistake, by supposing, what every musician knows to be absurd, that, in fitting verses to a tune, or a tune to verses, it is more necessary, that *particular words* should have *particular notes* adapted to them, than that the *general tenor* of the music should accord with the *general nature* of the sentiments.

It is true, that to a favourite air, even when unaccompanied with words, we do commonly annex certain ideas, which may have come to be related to it in consequence of some accidental associations: and sometimes we imagine a resemblance (which however is merely imaginary) between certain melodies and certain thoughts or objects. Thus a Scotchman may fancy, that there is some sort of likeness between that charming air which he calls *Tweedside*, and the scenery of a fine pastoral country: and to the same air, even when only played on an instrument, he may annex the ideas of romantic love and rural tranquility; because these form the subject of a prettily little ode, which he has often heard sung to that air. But all this is the effect of habit. A foreigner who hears that tune for the first time, entertains no such fancy. The utmost we can expect from him is, to acknowledge the air to be sweet and simple. He would smile, if we were to ask him, whether it bears any resemblance to the hills, groves, and meadows, adjoining to a beautiful river; nor would he perhaps think it more expressive of romantic love, than of conjugal, parental, or filial affection, tender melancholy, moderate joy, or any other gentle passion. Certain it is, that on any one of these topics an ode might be composed, which would suit the air most perfectly. So ambiguous is musical expression.

It is likewise true, that music merely instrumental does often derive significancy from external circumstances. When an army in battle-array is advancing to meet the enemy, words are not necessary to give meaning to the military music. And a solemn air on the organ, introducing or dividing the church-service, may not only elevate the mind, and banish impertinent thoughts, but also, deriving energy from the surrounding scene, may promote religious meditation.

Nor can it be denied, that instrumental music may both quicken our sensibility, and give a direction to it; that is, may both prepare the mind for being affected, and determine it to one set of affections rather than another;—to melancholy, for instance, rather than merriment, composure rather than agitation, devotion rather than levity, and contrariwise. Certain tunes, too, there are, which having been always connected with certain actions, do, merely from the power of habit, dispose men to those actions. Such are the tunes commonly used to regulate the motions of dancing.

232

Yet it is in general true, that poetry is the most immediate and most accurate interpreter of Music. Without this auxiliary, a piece of the best music, heard for the first time, might be said to mean something, but we should not be able to say what. It might incline the heart to sensibility: but poetry, or language, would be necessary to improve that sensibility into a real emotion, by fixing the mind upon some definite and affecting ideas. A fine instrumental symphony well performed, is like an oration delivered with propriety, but in an unknown tongue; it may affect us a little, but conveys no determinate feeling; we are alarmed, perhaps, or melted, or soothed, but it is very imperfectly, because we know not why:—the singer, by taking up the same air, and applying words to it, immediately translates the oration into our own language; then all uncertainty vanishes, the fancy is filled with determinate ideas, and determinate emotions take possession of the heart.

A great part of our fashionable music seems intended rather to tickle and astonish the hearers, than to inspire them with any permanent emotions. And if that be the end of the art, then, to be sure, this fashionable music is just what it should be, and the simpler strains of former ages are good for nothing. Nor am I now at leisure to inquire, whether it be better for an audience to be thus tickled and astonished, than to have their fancy impressed with beautiful images, and their hearts melted with tender passions, or elevated with sublime ones. But if you grant me this one point, that music is more or less perfect, in proportion as it has more or less power over the heart, it will follow, that all music merely instrumental, and which does not derive significancy from any of the associations, habits, or outward circumstances, above mentioned, is to a certain degree imperfect; and that, while the rules hinted at in the following queries are overlooked by composers and performers, vocal music, though it may astonish mankind, or afford them a slight gratification, will never be attended with those important effects that we know it produced of old in the days of simplicity and true taste.

1. Is not good music set to bad poetry as unexpressive, and therefore as absurd, as good poetry set to bad music, or as harmonious language without meaning? Yet the generality of musicians appear to be indifferent in regard to this matter. If the sound of the words be good, or the meaning of particular words agreeable; if there be a competency of hills and rills, doves and loves, fountains and mountains, with a tolerable collection of garlands and lambkins, nymphs and cupids, *bergères* and *tortorellas*, they are not solicitous about sense or elegance. In which they seem to me to consult their own honour as little as the rational entertainment of others. For what is there to elevate the mind of that composer, who condemns himself to set music to insipid doggerel? Handel's genius never soared to heaven, till it caught strength and fire from the strains of inspiration.—2. Should not the words

of every song be intelligible to those to whom it is addressed, and be distinctly articulated, so as to be heard as plainly as the notes? Or can the human mind be rationally gratified with that which it does not perceive, or which, if it did perceive, it would not understand? And therefore, is not the music of a song faulty, when it is so complex as to make the distinct articulation of the words impracticable?—3. If the singer's voice and words ought to be heard in every part of the song, can there be any propriety in noisy accompaniments? And as every performer in a numerous band is not perfectly discreet, and as some performers may be more careful to distinguish themselves than do justice to the song, will not an instrumental accompaniment be almost necessarily too noisy, if it is complex?—4. Does not the frequent repetition of the same words in a song, confound its meaning, and distract the attention of both the singer and the hearer? And are not long-winded divisions (or successions of notes warbled to one syllable) attended with a like inconvenience, and with this additional bad effect, that they disqualify the voice for expression, by exhausting it? Is not simplicity as great a perfection in music, as in painting and poetry? Or should we admire that orator who chose to express by five hundred words, a sentiment that might be more emphatically conveyed in five?—5. Ought not the singer to bear in mind, that he has sentiments to utter as well as sounds? And if so, should he not perfectly understand what he says, as well as what he sings; and not only modulate his notes with the art of a musician, but also pronounce his words with the propriety of a public speaker? If he is taught to do this, he does not learn of course to avoid all grimace and finical gesticulation? And will he not then acquit himself in singing like a rational creature, and a man of sense? Whereas, by pursuing a contrary conduct, is he not to be considered rather as a puppet or wind-instrument, than as an elegant artist?—6. Is not church-music more important than any other? and ought it not for that reason to be most intelligible and expressive? But will this be the case, if the notes are drawn out to such an immoderate length, that the words of the singer cannot be understood? Besides, does not excessive slowness, in singing or speaking, tend rather to wear out the spirits, than to elevate the fancy, or warm the heart? It would seem, then, that the vocal part of church-music should never be so slow as to fatigue those who sing, or to render the words of the song in any degree unintelligible to those who hear.—7. Do flourished cadences, whether by a voice or instrument, serve any other purpose, than to take off our attention from the subject, and set us a staring at the flexibility of the performer's voice, the swiftness of his fingers, or the sound of his fiddle? And if this be their only use, do they not counteract, instead of promoting, the chief end of music? What should we think, if a tragedian, at the conclusion of every scene, or of every speech, in Othello, were to strain his throat into a preternatural scream, make a hideous wry face, or cut a caper four feet high? We might wonder at the strength of his voice, the pliancy of his features, or the springiness of his limbs; but should hardly admire him as intelligent in his art, or respectful to his audience.

But is it not agreeable to hear a *florid song* by a fine performer, though now and then the voice should be drowned amidst the accompaniments, and though the words should not be understood by the hearers, or even by the singer? I answer, that nothing can be very agreeable, which brings disappointment. In the case supposed, the tones of the voice might no doubt give pleasure: but from instrumental music we expect something more, and from vocal music a great deal more, then mere sweetness of sound. From poetry and music united we have a right to expect pathos, sentiment, and melody, and in a word every gratification that the tuneful art can bestow. But in *sweetness* of tone the best singer is not superior, and scarcely equal, to an Eolus harp, to Vischer's hautboy, or to Giardini's violin. And can we without dissatisfaction see a human creature dwindle into mere wood and cat-gut? Can we be gratified with what only tickles the ear, when we had reason to hope, that a powerful address would have been made to the heart?—A handsome actress walking on the stage would no doubt be looked at with complacency for a minute or two, though she were not to speak a word. But surely we had a right to expect a different sort of entertainment; and were her silence to last a few minutes longer, I believe the politest audience in Europe would let her know that they were offended.—To conclude: A song, which we listen to without understanding the words, is like a picture seen at too great a distance. The former may be allowed to charm the ear with sweet sounds, in the same degree in which the latter pleases the eye with beautiful colours. But, till the design of the whole, and the meaning of each part, be made obvious to sense, it is impossible to derive any rational entertainment from either.

I hope I have given no offence to the connoisseur by these observations. They are dictated by a hearty zeal for the honour of an art, of which I have heard and seen enough to be satisfied, that it is capable of being improved into an instrument of virtue, as well as of pleasure. If I did not think so, I should hardly have taken the trouble to write these remarks, slight as they are, upon the philosophy of it. But to return:

Every thing in art, nature, or common life, must give delight, which communicates delightful passions to the human mind. And because all the passions that music can inspire are of the agreeable kind, it follows, that all pathetic or expressive music must be agreeable. Music may inspire devotion, fortitude, compassion, benevolence, tranquility; it may infuse a gentle sorrow that softens, without wounding, the heart, or a sublime horror that expands, and elevates, while it astonishes, the imagination: but music has no expression for impiety, cowardice, cruelty, hatred, or discontent. For every essential rule of the art tends to produce pleasing combinations of sound; and it is difficult to conceive, how from these any painful or criminal affections should arise. I believe, however, it might be practicable, by means of harsh tones, irregular rhythm, and continual dissonance, to work the mind into a disagreeable state, and to produce horrible thoughts, and criminal propensity, as well as painful sensations. But this would not be music; nor can it ever be for the interest of any society to put such a villanous art in practice.

Milton was so sensible of the moral tendency of musical expression, that he ascribes to it the power of raising some praise-worthy emotions even in the devils themselves.[21] Would Dryden, if he had been an adept in this art, as Milton was, have made the song of Timotheus inflame Alexander to revenge and cruelty?—At any rate, I am well pleased that Dryden fell into this mistake (if it be one), because it has produced some of the most animated lines that ever were written.[22] And I am also pleased to find, for the honour of music, and of this criticism, that history ascribes the burning of Persepolis, not to any of the tuneful tribe, but to the instigation of a drunken harlot.

IV. Is there not reason to think, that variety and simplicity of structure may contribute something to the agreeableness of music, as well as of poetry and prose. Variety, kept within due bounds, is pleasing, because it refreshes the mind with novelty; and is therefore studiously sought after in all the arts, and in none of them more than in music. To give this character to his compositions, the poet varies his phraseology and syntax; and the feet, the pauses, and the sound of contiguous verses, as much as the subject, the language, and the laws of versification will permit: and the prose-writer combines longer with shorter sentences in the same paragraph, longer with shorter clauses in the same sentence, and even longer with shorter words in the same clause; terminates contiguous clauses and sentences by a different cadence, and constructs them by a different syntax; and in general avoids all monotony and similar sounds, except where they are unavoidable, or where they may contribute (as indeed they often do) to energy or perspicuity. The musician diversifies his *melody*, by changing his keys; by deferring or interrupting his cadences; by a mixture of slower and quicker, higher and lower, softer and louder notes; and, in pieces of length, by altering the rhythm, the movement, and the air: and his *harmony* he varies, by varying his concords and discords, by a change of modulation, by contrasting the ascent or slower motion of one part to the descent or quicker motion of another, by assigning different harmonies to the same melody, or different melodies to the same harmony, and by many other contrivances.

Simplicity makes music, as well as language, intelligible and expressive. It is in every work of art a recommendatory quality. In music it is indispensable; for we are never pleased with that music which we cannot understand, or

[21]Paradise Lost, b. I. vers. 549.—562.
[22]Alexander's Feast, stanza 6.

which seems to have no meaning. Of the ancient music little more is known, than that it was very affecting and very simple. All popular and favourite airs; all that remains of the old national music in every country; all military marches, church-tunes, and other compositions that are more immediately addressed to the heart, and intended to please the general taste; all proverbial maxims of morality and prudence, and all those poetical phrases and lines, which every body remembers, and is occasionally repeating, are remarkable for simplicity. To which we may add, that language, while it improves in simplicity, grows more and more perfect: and that, as it loses this character, it declines in the same proportion from the standard of elegance, and draws nearer and nearer to utter depravation.[23] Without simplicity, the varieties of art, instead of pleasing, would only bewilder the attention, and confound the judgment.

Rhythm, or Number, is in music a copious source of both variety and uniformity. Not to enter into any nice speculation on the nature of rhythm, for which this is not a proper place, I shall only observe, that notes, as united in music, admit of the distinction of quick and slow, as well as of acute and grave; and that on the former distinction depends what is here called *Rhythm*. It is the only thing in a tune which the drum can imitate. And by that instrument, the rhythm of any tune may be imitated most perfectly, as well as by the sound of the feet in dancing:—only as the feet can hardly move so quick as the drumsticks, the dancer may be obliged to repeat his strokes at longer intervals, by supposing the music divided into larger portions; to give one stroke, for example, where the drummer might give two or three, or two where the other would give four or six. For every piece of regular music is supposed to be divided into small portions (separated in writing by a cross line called a *bar*) which, whether they contain more or fewer notes, are all equal in respect of time. In this way, the rhythm is a source of *uniformity*; which pleases by suggesting the agreeable ideas of regularity and skill, and, still more, by rendering the music intelligible. It also pleases, by raising and gratifying expectation: for if the movement of the piece were governed by no rule; if what one hears of it during the present moment were in all respects unlike and incommensurable to what one was to hear the next, and had heard the last, the whole would be a mass of confusion; and the ear would either be bewildered, having nothing to rest upon, and nothing to anticipate; or, if it should expect any stated *ratio* between the motion and the time, would be disappointed when it found that there was none.—That rhythm is a source of very great *variety*, every person must be sensible, who knows only the names of the musical notes, with such of their divisions and subdivisions as relate to time; or who has attended to the manifold varieties of quick and slow motion, which the drum is capable of producing.

[23]See *Le Vicende della Litteratura del. Sig. Carlo Denina.*

As order and proportion are always delightful, it is no wonder that mankind should be agreeably affected with the rhythm of music. That they are, the universal use of dancing, and of "the spirit-stirring drum," is a sufficient evidence. Nay, I have known a child imitate the rhythm of tunes before he could speak, and long before he could manage his voice so as to imitate their melody;—which is a proof, that human nature is susceptible of this delight previously to the acquirement of artificial habits.

V. I hinted at the power of accidental association in giving significancy to musical compositions. It may be remarked further, that association contributes greatly to heighten their agreeable effect. We have heard them performed, some time or other, in an agreeable place perhaps, or by an agreeable person, or accompanied with words that describe agreeable ideas: or we have heard them in our earlier years; a period of life, which we seldom look back upon without pleasure, and of which Bacon recommends the frequent recollection as an expedient to preserve health. Nor is it necessary, that such melodies or harmonies should have much intrinsic merit, or that they should call up any distinct remembrance of the agreeable ideas associated with them. There are reasons, at which we are gratified with very moderate excellence. In childhood, every tune is delightful to a musical ear; in our advanced years, an indifferent tune will please, when set off by the amiable qualities of the performer, or by any other agreeable circumstance.— During the last war, the *Belleisle march* was long a general favourite. It filled the minds of our people with magnificent ideas of armies, and conquest, and military splendor; for they believed it to be the tune that was played by the French garrison when it marched out with the honours of war, and surrendered that fortress to the British troops.—The flute of a shepherd heard at a distance, in a fine summer day, amidst a beautiful scene of groves, hills, and waters, will give rapture to the ear of the wanderer, though the tune, the instrument, and the musician, be such as he could not endure in any other place.—If a song, or piece of music, should call up only a faint remembrance, that we were happy the last time we heard it, nothing more would be needful to make us listen to it again with peculiar satisfaction.

It is an amiable prejudice that people generally entertain in favour of their national music. This lowest degree of patriotism is not without its merit: and that man must have a hard heart, or dull imagination, in whom, though endowed with musical sensibility, no sweet emotions would arise, on hearing, in his riper years, or in a foreign land, those strains that were the delight of his childhood. What though they be inferior to the Italian? What though they be even irregular and rude? It is not their merit, which in the case supposed would interest a native, but the charming ideas they would recall to his mind:—ideas of innocence, simplicity, and leisure, of romantic enterprise, and enthusiastic attachment; and of scenes, which, on recollection, we are inclined to think, that a brighter sun illuminated, a fresher verdure

238

crowned, and purer skies and happier climes conspired to beautify, than are now to be seen in the dreary paths of care and disappointment, into which men, yielding to the passions peculiar to more advanced years, are tempted to wander.—There are couplets in Ogilvie's Translation of Virgil, which I could never read without emotions far more ardent than the merit of the numbers would justify. But it was that book which first taught me "the tale of Troy divine,"[24] and first made me acquainted with poetical sentiments; and though I read it when almost an infant, it conveyed to my heart some pleasing impressions, that remain there unimpaired to this day.

There is a dance in Switzerland, which the young shepherds perform to a tune played on a bag-pipe. The tune is called *Rance des vaches*; it is wild and irregular, but has nothing in its composition that could recommend it to our notice. But the Swiss are so intoxicated with this tune, that if at any time they hear it, when abroad a foreign service, they burst into tears; and often fall sick, and even die, of a passionate desire to revisit their native country; for which reason, in some armies where they serve, the playing of this tune is prohibited.[25] This tune, having been the attendant of their childhood and early youth, recals to their memory those regions of wild beauty and rude magnificence, those days of liberty and peace, those nights of festivity, those happy assemblies, those tender passions, which formerly endeared to them their country, their homes, and their employments; and which, when compared with the scenes of uproar they are now engaged in, and the servitude they now undergo, awaken such regret as entirely overpowers them.

SECTION III.

Conjectures on some peculiarities of National Music.

There is a certain style of melody peculiar to each musical country, which the people of that country are apt to prefer to every other style. That they should prefer their own, is not surprising; and that the melody of one people should differ from that of another, is not more surprising, perhaps, than that the language of one people should differ from that of another. But there is something not unworthy of notice in the particular expression and style that characterise the music of one nation or province, and distinguish it from every other sort of music. Of this diversity Scotland supplies a striking example. The native melody of the highlands and western isles is as

[24]Milton's Penseroso.
[25]Rousseau. Dictionaire de Musique, art. *Rances des vaches.*

different from that of the southern part of the kingdom, as the Irish or Erse language is different from the English or Scotch. In the conclusion of a discourse on music as it relates to the mind, it will not perhaps be impertinent to offer a conjecture on the cause of these peculiarities; which, though it should not (and indeed I am satisfied that it will not) fully account for any one of them, may however incline the reader to think that they are not unaccountable, and may also throw some faint light on this part of philosophy.

Every thought that partakes of the nature of passion, has a correspondent expression in the look and gesture: and so strict is the union between the passion and its outward sign, that, where the former is not in some degree felt, the latter can never be perfectly natural, but, if assumed, becomes aukward mimickry, instead of that genuine imitation of nature, which draws forth the sympathy of the beholder. If, therefore, there be, in the circumstances of particular nations or persons, any thing that gives a peculiarity to their passions and thoughts, it seems reasonable to expect, that they will also have something peculiar in the expression of their countenance, and even in the form of their features. Caius Marius, Jugurtha, Tamerlane, and some other great warriors, are celebrated for a peculiar ferocity of aspect, which they had no doubt contracted from a perpetual and unrestrained exertion of fortitude, contempt, and other violent emotions. These produced in the face their correspondent expressions, which being often repeated, became at last as habitual to the features, as the sentiments they arose from were to the heart. Savages, whose thoughts are little inured to control, have more of this significancy of look, than those men, who, being born and bred in civilized nations, are accustomed from their childhood to suppress every emotion that tends to interrupt the peace of society. And while the bloom of youth lasts, and the smoothness of feature peculiar to that period, the human face is less marked with any strong character, than in old age:—a peevish or surly stripling may elude the eye of the physiognomist; but a wicked old man, whose visage does not betray the evil temperature of his heart, must have more cunning than it would be prudent for him to acknowledge. Even by the trade or profession the human countenance may be characterised. They who employ themselves in the nicer mechanic arts, that require the earnest attention of the artist, do generally contract a fixedness of feature suited to that one uniform sentiment which engrosses them while at work. Whereas, other artists, whose work requires less attention, and who may ply their trade and amuse themselves with conversation at the same time, have for the most part smoother and more unmeaning faces: their thoughts are more miscellaneous, and therefore their features are less fixed in one uniform configuration. A keen penetrating look indicates thoughtfulness and spirit: a dull torpid countenance is not often accompanied with great sagacity.

240

This, though there may be many an exception, is in general true of the visible signs of our passions; and it is no less true of the audible. A man habitually peevish, or passionate, or querulous, or imperious, may be known by the sound of his voice, as well as by his physiognomy. May we not go a step farther, and say, that if a man under the influence of any passion were to compose a discourse, or a poem, or a tune, his work would in some measure exhibit an image of his mind? I could not easily be persuaded, that Swift and Juvenal were men of sweet tempers; or that Thomson, Arbuthnot, and Prior were ill-natured. The airs of Felton are so uniformly mournful, that I cannot suppose him to have been a merry, or even a chearful man. If a musician, in deep affliction, were to attempt to compose a lively air, I believe he would not succeed: though I confess I do not well understand the nature of the connection that may take place between a mournful mind and a melancholy tune. It is easy to conceive, how a poet or an orator should transfuse his passions into his work: for every passion suggests ideas congenial to its own nature; and the composition of the poet, or of the orator, must necessarily consist of those ideas that occur at the time he is composing. But musical sounds are not the signs of ideas; rarely are they even the imitations of natural sounds: so that I am at a loss to conceive how it should happen, that a musician, overwhelmed with sorrow, for example, should put together a series of notes, whose expression is contrary to that of another series which he had put together when elevated with joy. But of the fact I am not doubtful; though I have not sagacity, or knowledge of music, enough to be able to explain it. And my opinion in this matter is warranted by that of a more competent judge; who says, speaking of church-voluntaries, that if the Organist "do not feel in himself the divine energy of devotion, he will labour in vain to raise it in others. Nor can he hope to throw out those happy instantaneous thoughts, which sometimes far exceed the best concerted compositions, and which the enraptured performer would gladly secure to his future use and pleasure, did they not as fleetly escape as they rise."[26] A man who has made music the study of his life, and is well acquainted with all the best examples of style and expression that are to be found in the works of former masters, may, by memory and such practice, attain a sort of mechanical dexterity in contriving music suitable to any given passion; but such music would, I presume, be vulgar and spiritless, compared to what an artist of genius throws out, when under the power of any ardent emotion. It is recorded of Lulli, that, once when his imagination was all on fire with some verses descriptive of terrible ideas, which he had been reading in a French tragedy, he ran to his harpsichord, and struck off such a combination of sounds, that the company felt their hair stand on end with horror.

[26]Avison on Musical Expression, pag. 88. 89. [The passage is not found in the sections chosen for this anthology.]

Let us therefore suppose it proved, or, if you please, take it for granted, that different sentiments in the mind of the musician will give different and peculiar expressions to his music;—and upon this principle, it will not perhaps be impossible to account for some of the phenomena of a national ear.

. . . . .

CHAPTER TWELVE

THOMAS TWINING

Two Dissertations on Poetical and Musical Imitation
(1789)
DISSERTATION II.

On the different senses of the word, imitative, as applied to music by the antients, and by the moderns.

The whole power of Music may be reduced, I think, to *three* distinct effects;— upon the *ear*, the *passions*, and the *imagination*: in other words, it may be considered as simply delighting the *sense*, as raising *emotions*, or, as raising *ideas*. The two last of these effects constitute the whole of what is called the *moral*,[1] or *expressive*, power of Music; and in these only we are to look for anything that can be called *imitation*. Music can be said to imitate, no farther than as it *expresses* something. As far as its effect is merely physical, and confined to the ear, it gives a simple, original pleasure; it expresses nothing, it *refers* to nothing; it is no more imitative than the smell of a rose, or the flavour of a pine-apple.

Music can raise ideas, *immediately*,[2] only by the actual resemblance of its

[1] *Moral*, merely as opposed to *physical*:—as affecting the *mind*; not as *Ethic*, or influencing the *manners*.

[2] Music *may* raise ideas *immediately*, by mere *association*; but I pass over the effects of this principle, (important and powerful as it is, in Music, as in everything else,) as having nothing to do with *imitation*. If, to raise an idea of any object by casual association, be to *imitate*, any one thing may imitate any other.

I inserted the word, *immediately*, because Music has also a power of raising ideas, to a certain degree, through the *medium* of *emotions*, which naturally suggest correspondent ideas; that is, *such* ideas as usually raise *such* emotions. (See Harris, *on Music*, &c. ch. vi. and below, note 4.)

243

sounds and *motions* to the sounds and motions of the thing suggested.[3] Such Music we call *imitative*, in the same sense in which we apply the word to a similar resemblance of sound and motion in poetry.[4] In both cases, the resemblance, though *immediate*, is so *imperfect*, that it cannot be seen till it is, in some sort, pointed out; and even when it *is* so, is not always very evident. Poetry, indeed, has here a great advantage; it carries with it, of necessity, its own explanation: for the same word that imitates by its *sound*, points out, or hints, at least, the imitation, by its *meaning*. With Music it is not so. It must call in the assistance of language or something equivalent to language, for its interpreter.[5]

Of all the powers of Music, this of raising ideas by direct resemblance is confessed to be the weakest, and the least important. It is, indeed, so far from being essential to the pleasure of the art, that unless used with great caution, judgment, and delicacy, it will destroy that pleasure, by becoming to every competent judge, offensive, or ridiculous. It is, however, to Music of *this* kind only that Mr. Harris, and most other modern writers, allow the word *imitative* to be applied.[6] The highest power of Music, and that from which "it derives its greatest efficacy," is, undoubtedly, its power of raising *emotions*. But this is so far from being regarded by them as *imitation*, that it is expressly *opposed* to it.[7]

The ideas, and the language, of the antients, on this subject, were different. When *they* speak of Music as imitation, they appear to have solely, or chiefly, in view, its power over the *affections*. By *imitation*, they mean, in short, what *we* commonly distinguish from imitation, and oppose to it, under the general term of *expression*.[8] With respect to Aristotle, in particular, this will clearly appear from a few passages which I shall produce from another of his writings; and, at the same time, the expressions made use of in these

---

[3]See *Harris, ibid. ch.* ii. where this subject is treated with the author's usual accuracy and clearness.

[4]See *Dissert.* I.

[5]When the idea to be raised is that of a visible object, the imitation of that object by painting, machinery, or other visible representation, may answer the same end.—A visible object strongly characterized by motion, *may* be suggested by such *musical* motion as is analogous to it. Thus, a rapid elevation of sounds, bears, or at least is *conceived* to bear, some analogy to the motion of flame;—but this analogy must be pointed out—"Il faut que l'auditeur soit averti, ou par les *paroles*, ou par le *spectacle*, ou par quelque chose d'equivalent, qu'il doit substituer l'idée du *feu* à celle du *son.*" See M. Dalembert's *Melanges de Literature, vol.* v. *p.* 158,—where the philosophical reader will, perhaps, be pleased with some very ingenious and uncommon observations, on the manner in which the imitative expression even of *Music without words*, may be influenced by the phraseology of the language in which the hearer *thinks.*

[6]Dr. Beattie, *On Poetry and Music,* p. 138, & *passim.*—Lord Kaims, *El. of Crit. vol.* ii. *p.* 1. Avison, &c.—There is but *one* branch of this imitation of *sound* by *sound,* that is really important; and *that* has been generally overlooked. I mean, the imitation of the *tones* of *speech.*—Of this, presently.

[7]Harris, *On Music,* &c. Ch. II, §3; Ch VI, §1-2.

[8]"If we compare *imitation* with *expression,* the superiority of the latter will be evident."—Dr. Beattie, *On Poetry and Music,* Ch. VI, Section II.—Avison, *on Mus. Expression, Part* II. §3.

passages, will help us to *account* for a mode of speaking so different from that of modern writers on the subject.

What Aristotle, in the beginning of his treatise on Poetry, calls MIMESIS—*imitation*—he elsewhere,[9] in the same application of it, to *Music*, calls HOMOIOMA—*resemblance*. And he, also, clears up his meaning farther, by adding the *thing resembled* or *imitated*:—homoioma TOIS ETHESI—homoiomata TON ETHON[10]—"resemblance to human *manners*," i.e. *dispositions*, or *tempers*; for what he means by these *ethe*, he has, likewise, clearly explained by these expressions—homoiomata ORGES kai PRAOTETOS, eti d'ANDRIAS kai SOPHROSYNES, etc. "resemblances of the *irascible* and the *gentle* disposition—of *fortitude* and *temperance*, etc."[11] This resemblance, he expressly tells us, is "in the *rhythm* and the melody:"—homoiomata—en tois RHYTHMOIS kai tois MELESIN, orges kai praotetos.[12] In these passages, Aristotle differs only in the *mode* of expression from Mr. Harris, when *he* affirms that "there are sounds to *make us chearful* or *sad, martial* or *tender,*" &c.[13]:—from Dr. Beattie, when he says, "Music may *inspire devotion; fortitude, compassion;*—may *infuse* a *sorrow,*" &c.[14]

It appears then, in the *first* place, that Music, considered as affecting, or raising *emotions*, was called imitation by the antients, *because* they perceived in it that which is essential to all imitation, and is, indeed, often spoken of as the same thing—*resemblance*.[15] This resemblance, however, as *here* stated by Aristotle, cannot be *immediate*;[16] for between *sounds themselves*, and *mental affections*, there can be no resemblance. The resemblance can only be a resemblance of *effect*:—the *general emotions, tempers,* or *feelings* produced in us by certain sounds, are *like* those that accompany actual grief, joy, anger, &c.—And this, as far, at least, as can be collected from the passage in question, appears to be all that Aristotle meant.

---

[9]Politics viii, 1340[a], 14, 19, 20.

[10]In the same passage he uses the word *mimema*, as synonymous with *homoioma*. Plato uses mimemata TROPON in the same sense. Laws ii, 668.

[11]The word *ethe*, taken in its utmost extent, includes *everything* that is *habitual* and *characteristic*; but it is often used in a limited sense, for the *habitual temper*, or *disposition*. That it is here used in that sense appears from Aristotle's own explanation. I therefore thought it necessary to fix the sense of the word *manners*, which has the same *generality* as *ethe*, and is its usual translation, by adding the words "*dispositions* or *tempers*."

[12]The same expressions occur in the [pseudo-Aristotle] *Problems*, Sect. xix., Prob. 29 and 27.

[13]Chap. vi.

[14]*On Poet. and Mus.* Ch. VI, Sect. II: iii. 7.—In another place Dr. Beattie approaches very near indeed to the language of Aristotle; he says, "After all, it must be acknowledged, that there is some *relation*, at least, or *analogy, if not* similitude, between certain musical *sounds*, and mental *affections*, &c." (Ch. VI, Sect. I.)

[15]"Imitations, *or* resemblances, of something else." (Hutcheson's *Inquiry into the Orig.* of *our Ideas* of *Beauty*, &c. p. 15.) "Taking *imitation* in its *proper sense*, as importing a *resemblance* between two objects." (Lord Kaims, *El.* of *Crit.* ch. xviii. § 3.) Imitation, indeed, necessarily implies resemblance; but the converse is not true.

[16]See *Dissert.* I. first pages.

But, *secondly;*—the *expressions* of Music considered in itself, and *without words*, are, (within certain limits,) vague, general, and equivocal. What is usually called its power over the *passions*, is, in fact, no more than a power of raising a *general emotion, temper*, or *disposition*, common to several different, though *related*, passions; as pity, love—anger, courage, &c.[17] The effect of *words*, is, to strengthen the expression of Music, by confining it—by giving it a precise direction, supplying it with ideas, circumstances, and an *object*, and, by this means, raising it from a calm and *general* disposition, or emotion, into something approaching, at least, to the stronger feeling of a particular and determinate *passion*. Now, among the antients, Music, it is well known, was scarce ever heard *without* this assistance. Poetry and Music were then far from having reached that state of mutual independence, and separate improvement, in which they have now been long established. When an ancient writer speaks of Music, he is, almost always, to be understood to mean *vocal* Music—Music and Poetry united. This helps greatly to account for the application of the term *imitative*, by Aristotle, Plato, and other Greek writers, to musical *expression*, which modern writers *oppose* to musical *imitation*. That emotions *are* raised by Music, independently of words, is certain;[18] and it is as certain that these emotions resemble those of actual passion, temper, &c.—But, in the vague and indeterminate assimilations of Music purely instrumental, though the effect is felt, and the emotion raised, the idea of *resemblance* is far from being necessarily suggested; much less is it likely, that such resemblance, if it did occur, having no *precise* direction, should be considered as *imitation*.[19] Add *words* to this Music, and the case will be very different. There is now a precise object of *comparison* presented to the mind; the *resemblance* is pointed out; the thing *imitated* is before us. Farther, one principal use of Music in the time of Aristotle, was to accompany *dramatic* Poetry—*that* Poetry which is most peculiarly and strictly *imitative*, and where *manners* and *passions* (ethe kai pathe) are peculiarly the *objects* of imitation.

---

[17]The expression of Aristotle seems therefore accurate and philosophical. It is everywhere—homoioma ETHON,—not PATHON—a resemblance "to *manners*, or *tempers*, "not" to *passions*.
[18]This is expressly allowed by [pseudo-] Aristotle in the Problem which will presently be produced.
[19]I observed that Music is capable of raising *ideas*, to a certain degree, through the medium of those *emotions* which it raises immediately. But this is an effect so delicate and uncertain—so dependent on the fancy, the sensibility, the musical experience, and even the temporary disposition, of the *hearer*, that to call it *imitation*, is surely going beyond the bounds of all reasonable analogy. Music, here, is not *imitative*, but if I may hazard the expression, merely *suggestive*. But, whatever we may call it, this I will venture to say,—that in the *best* instrumental Music, expressively *performed*, the very indecision itself of the expression, leaving the hearer to the free operation of his *emotion* upon his *fancy*, and, as it were, to the free *choice* of such ideas as are, *to him*, most adapted to react upon and heighten the emotion which occasioned them, produces a pleasure, which nobody, I believe, who is able to feel it, will deny to be one of the most delicious that Music is capable of affording. But far the greater part even of those who have

It is, then, no wonder, that the Antients, accustomed to hear the expressions of Music thus constantly *specified*, determined, and referred to a precise object by the ideas of Poetry, should view them in the light of *imitations*; and that even in speaking of *Music, properly* so called, as Aristotle does, they should be led by this association to speak of it in the same terms, and to attribute to it powers, which, in its separate state, do not, in strictness, belong to it. With respect, however, even to the *instrumental* Music of those times, it should be remembered, that we cannot properly judge of it by our *own*, nor suppose it to have been, in that simple state of the art, what it is now, in its state of separate improvement and refinement. It seems highly probable that the Music of the antients, even in performances merely instrumental, retained much of its vocal style and character, and would therefore appear more *imitative* than *our* instrumental Music: and perhaps, after all, a Greek Solo on the flute, or the cithara, was not *much* more than a song without the words, embellished here and there with a little embroidery, or a few sprinklings of simple *arpeggio*, such as the fancy, and the fingers, of the player could supply.

But there is another circumstance that deserves to be considered. *Dramatic* Music is, often, *strictly imitative*. It imitates, not only the *effect* of the words, by exciting correspondent *emotions*, but also the *words* themselves *immediately*, by tones, accents, inflexions, intervals, and rhythmical movements, *similar* to those of speech. That this was peculiarly the character of the *dramatic* Music of the antients, seems highly probable, not only from what is said of it by antient authors, but from what we know of their Music *in general*; of their scales, their *genera*, their fondness for *chromatic* and *enharmonic* intervals, which approach so nearly to those sliding and unassignable inflexions, (if I may so speak,) that characterize the melody of *speech*.

I am, indeed, persuaded, that the analogy between the melody and rhythm of *Music*, and the melody and rhythm of *speech*, is a principle of greater extent and importance than is commonly imagined. Some writers

---

an ear for Music, have *only* an *ear*; and to *them* this pleasure is unknown.—The complaint, so common, of the separation of Poetry and Music, and of the total want of meaning and expression in *instrumental* Music, was never, I believe, the complaint of a man of true musical feeling: and it might, perhaps, be not unfairly concluded, that [pseudo-] Aristotle, who expressly allows that "Music, even *without words, has expression*," (See the Problem below) was more of a musician than his master Plato, who is fond of railing at instrumental Music, and asks with Fontenelle,—"Sonate, que me *veux* tu?" (The story of Fontenelle is well known.—"Je n'oublierai jamais," says Rousseau, "la saillie du celebre Fontenelle, qui se trouvant excedé de ces eternelles symphonies, s'ecria tout haut dans un transport d'impatience: *Sonate, que me veux tu?" Dict. de Mus.*—Sonate.) I would by no means be understood to deny, that there is now, and has been at all times, much unmeaning trash composed for instruments, that would justly provoke such a question. I mean only to say, what has been said for me by a superior judge and master of the art:—"There is *some* kind, even of instrumental music, so divinely composed, and so expressively performed, that it wants no *words* to explain its meaning."—Dr. Burney's *Hist. of Music*, vol. i. p. 85.

have extended it so far as to resolve into it the whole power of Music over the affections. Such appears to have been the idea of Rousseau. He divides all Music into *natural* and *imitative*; including, under the latter denomination, all Music that goes beyond the mere pleasure of the sense, and raises any kind or degree of emotion; an effect which he conceives to be wholly owing to an imitation, more or less perceptible, of the accents and inflexions of the voice in animated or passionate speech.[20] Professor Hutcheson was of the same opinion. In his *Inquiry concerning Beauty*, &c. he says—"There is also another charm in Music to various persons, which is distinct from the *harmony*, and is occasioned by its *raising agreeable passions*. The *human voice* is obviously varied by all the stronger passions;[21] now when our *ear* discerns any *resemblance* between the air of a tune, whether sung, or played upon an instrument, either in its *time* or *modulation*, or any other circumstance, to the *sound of the human voice in any passion*, we shall be touched by it in a very sensible manner, and have *melancholy, joy, gravity, thoughtfulness*, excited in us by a sort of *sympathy* or *contagion*." [Sect. 6. p. 83.] This ingenious and amiable writer seems to have adopted this opinion from Plato, to whom, indeed, in a similar passage in his System of Moral Philosophy,[22] he refers, and who, in the *third* book of his Republic, speaks of a *warlike* melody, inspiring *courage* as "*imitating* the *sound* and *accents* of the courageous man;" and, of a *calm* and *sedate* melody, as *imitating* the *sounds* of a man of *such* a character.

With respect to Aristotle—whether this was *his* opinion, or not, cannot, I think, be determined from anything he has *expressly* said upon the subject. In the passage above produced, where so much is said of the resemblance of melody and rhythm to manners, or tempers, not a word is said from which it can be inferred, that he meant a resemblance to the tones and accents by which those manners are *expressed* in speech. On the contrary, the expressions there made use of are such as lead us naturally to conclude, that he meant no more than I have above supposed him to mean; *i.e.* that the Music produces in us, immediately, feelings resembling those of real passion, &c.—For, after having asserted, that there is "a resemblance in rhythms and melodies to the irascible and the gentle disposition," he adds,—"This is evident from the manner in which we find ourselves affected

---

[20]Dict. de Mus. Art. *Musique—Melodie*, etc.
[21]Thus Theophrastus, in a curious passage cited by Plutarch in his *Symposiacs*, p. 623, *Ed. Xyl.*— "There are *three principles* of Music, *grief, pleasure,* and *enthusiasm*; for each of these passions *turns the voice* from *its usual course*, and gives it inflexions different from those of ordinary speech."—"Il n'y a qui les *passions* qui *chantent*," says Rousseau; l'entendement ne fait que *parler*."——This passage of Theophrastus is introduced to resolve the question—In what sense *love* is said to *teach Music*?—"No wonder," says the resolver, "if love, having in itself all these three *principles* of Music, *grief, pleasure,* and *enthusiasm,* should be more prone to vent itself in Music and Poetry than any other passion."
[22]Vol. i. p. 16.

by the *performance* of such Music; for we perceive *a change produced in the soul* while we listen to it." And again—"In melody itself there are *imitations* of human *manners*: this is manifest, from the melodies or modes, which have, evidently, their distinct nature and character; so that, when we hear them, we *feel ourselves affected* by each of them in a different manner, &c."[23]—But the passage furnishes, I think, a more decisive proof that the resemblance here meant, was not a resemblance to *speech*. Aristotle asserts here, as in the *problem* of which I shall presently speak, that, of all that affects the *senses*, Music alone possesses this property of resemblance to human manners. In comparing it with painting, he observes, that *this* art can imitate, immediately, only *figures* and *colours;* which are not *resemblances* (homoiomata) of manners and passions, but only *signs* and *indications* of them (semeia) in the human body: whereas, in Music, the resemblance to manners "*is in the melody itself.*" Now, whatever may be the meaning of this last assertion—for it seems not quite philosophical to talk of *such* a resemblance as being *in the sounds themselves*—whatever may be its meaning, it cannot well be, that the melody resembles manners *as expressed by speech*; because this would destroy the distinction between Music and Painting: for *words* are exactly in the same case with *colours* and *figures;* they are not *resemblances* of manners, or passions, but *indications* only. We must then, I fear, be contented to take what Aristotle says as a popular and unphilosophical way of expressing a mere resemblance of *effect*.

In one of his *Musical Problems*, indeed, he advances a step farther, and inquires into the *cause* of this effect of Music upon the mind. The text of these problems is, in general, very incorrect, and often absolutely unintelligible; *this* problem, however, seems not beyond the reach of secure emendation, though it may, possibly, be beyond that of secure *explanation*. As it has not, that I know of, been noticed by any writer on the subject, and may be regarded at least as a curiosity not uninteresting to the musical and

---

[23]The Harmoniai, i.e. *melodies*, (or, more properly perhaps, *enharmonic melodies*) here spoken of, must not be confounded with what are usually called the *modes*, and described by the writers on antient music, under the denomination of *tonoi*, i.e. *pitches*, or *keys*:—these were mere transpositions of the *same* scale, or system; the Harmoniai appear to have been, as the name implies, different *melodies*—scales, in which the arrangement of intervals, and the divisions of the tetrachord (or *genera*) were different. Aristides Quintilianus is the only Greek writer who has given any account of these harmoniai. (p. 21. Ed. Meib.) He asserts, that it is of *these*, not of the *tonoi*, that Plato speaks in the famous passage of his *Republic, lib.* iii. where he rejects some of them, and retains others. *This*, at least, is clear, that whatever the harmoniai of Plato were, Aristotle here speaks of the same. See his *Politics* viii, 1340.—Their distinctive names, Lydian, Dorian, &c. were the same with those of the tonoi, that of *syntono-Lydian* excepted, which, I think, is peculiar to the harmoniai. This coincidence of names seems to have been the chief cause of the confusion we find in the *modern* writers on this subject. The distinction has been pointed out in Dr. Burney's *Hist.* of *Mus.* vol. i. p. 32.—See also Rousseau's Dict. art. Syntono-Lydien, & Genre.

philosophical reader, I shall venture to give the entire problem, as I think it *should* be read.

Problem xxvii, Sec. 19

"Why, of all that affects the senses, the audible only has any *expression* of the manners; (for melody, even *without words*, has this effect—) but colours, smells, and tastes, have no such property?——Is it because the audible alone affects us by *motion?*—I do not mean *that* motion by which as mere *sound* it acts upon the *ear;* for *such* motion belongs equally to the objects of our *other* senses;—thus, colour acts by motion upon the organs of sight, &c.—But I mean *another motion* which we perceive *subsequent* to that; and *this* motion bears a resemblance to human manners, *both* in the *rhythm*, and in the *arrangement* of *sounds* acute and grave:—not in their *mixture;* for harmony *has no expression.*[24] With the objects of our other senses this is not the case.——Now these motions are analogous to the motion of human *actions;* and those *actions* are the index of the *manners.*"

[24]This passage is remarkable. It is exactly the *language of* Rousseau—"il n'y a aucun rapport entre des *accords,* & les objets qu'on veut peindre, ou *les passions qu'on veut exprimer.*" (*Dict. de Mus.* art. Imitation: see also the last paragraph of art. Harmonie.) Thus, too, Lord Kaims:—"Harmony, properly so called, though delightful when in perfection, *hath* no relation *to sentiment.*" (*El. of Crit.* i. 128.) But how is this? The *same* intervals are the materials both of melody and of harmony. These intervals have, each of them, their peculiar effect and character, and it is by the proper choice of them in *succession,* and by that only, that *melody,* considered abstractedly from rhythm or measure, becomes *expressive,* or has *any* "relation to sentiment." Do these intervals, then, lose at once, as by magic, all their variety and striking difference of character, as soon as they are heard in the simultaneous combinations of harmony? If this be the case, the vocal composer is at once relieved from all care of adapting the harmonies of his accompaniment to the expression of the sentiments conveyed in the words; and it must be matter of perfect indifference whether, for example, he uses the major or minor *third*—the perfect, or the false, *fifth*—the common chord, or the chord of the diminished *seventh,* &c.——With respect to Rousseau, it is not easy to see how this assertion of his can be reconciled with what he has elsewhere said. In his letter *Sur la Musique Françoise,* he expressly allows that every interval, consonant or dissonant, "a son caractere particulier, c'est à dire, une maniere d' *affecter l'ame* qui lui est propre."—And upon this depend entirely all the admirable observations he has there made, concerning the ill effects which a crowded harmony, and the *"remplissage"* of chords, have upon musical expression.—In another article (Accord) of his dictionary, this inconsistence is still more striking. One would not think it possible for the same writer, who in *one* place talks of intervals, "propres, par leur dureté, à *exprimer l'emportement, la colere,* et les passions aigues"—and, of—"une *harmonie plaintive* qui attendrit le coeur"——to assert in another part of the same work; that *"il n'y a aucun rapport entre des accords,* et les passions qu'on veut *exprimer.*"

Had these writers contented themselves with saying, that harmony has much *less relation* to sentiment than melody, they would not have gone beyond the truth. And the reason of this difference in the effect of the *same* intervals, in melody, and in harmony, seems, plainly, this—that in melody, these intervals being formed by *successive sounds,* have, of course, a much closer, and more obvious *relation* to the tones and inflexions by which sentiments are expressed in *speech,* than they *can* have in harmony, where they are formed by sounds *heard together.*

As to the assertion of [pseudo-] Aristotle, it seems only to furnish an additional proof that the antients did not practise anything like our counterpart, or *continued harmony in different parts.* Where the utmost use of harmony seems to have been confined to unisons, octaves, fourths, and fifths—where at least no discords, (the most expressive materials of modern harmony,) were allowed—we cannot wonder that the *"mixture"* of sounds in consonance should be thought to have *no relation* to *sentiment,* and that all the power of Music over the passions, should be confined to melodious and rhythmical *succession.*

In this problem, the philosopher plainly attributes the *expressive* power of musical sounds to their *succession*—to their *motion* in *measured melody*. He also distinguishes the *rhythmical*, from the *melodious*, succession; for he says expressly, that this motion is *"both* in the *rhythm* (or *measure*,) *and* in the *order* or *arrangement* of *sounds acute* and *grave."*—But *whence* the effect of these motions? He answers, from their analogy to the motions of human *actions*, by which the manners and tempers of men are expressed in common life. With respect to the analogy of *rhythmic* movement to the various motions of men in action, this, indeed, is sufficiently obvious. But Aristotle goes farther, and supposes that there is also such analogy in the motion of melody considered *merely* as a succession of different *tones*, without any regard to *time*. He plainly asserts, that this succession of *tones*, also is analogous to the motion of human *actions*. Now it seems impossible to assign any human action to which a succession of *sounds* and *intervals*, merely as such, has, or *can* have, any relation or similitude, except the *action* (if the expression is allowable,) of *speaking*, which *is* such a succession. *If* this be Aristotle's meaning—and I confess myself unable to discover any other—I do not see how we can avoid concluding, that he agreed *so* far with Plato, as to attribute *part*, or at least, of the effect of Music upon the affections to the analogy between melody and speech.

This analogy is, indeed, a curious subject, and deserves, perhaps, a more thorough examination and development than it has yet received.[25] But I shall not trust myself farther with a speculation so likely to draw me wide from the proper business of this dissertation, than just to observe, that the writers above-mentioned, who resolve *all* the pathetic expression of Music into this principle, though they assert more than it seems possible to prove, are yet much *nearer* to the truth than those, who altogether overlook, or reject, that principle;[26] a principle, of which, instances so frequent and so palpable are to be traced in the works of the best masters of vocal

[25]Much light has been flung upon this subject, as far as relates to speech, by Mr. Steele, in his curious and ingenious essay *On the Melody and Measure of Speech*. But the object of *his* enquiry was *Speech*, not *Music*. His purpose in tracing the resemblance between them, was only to shew that speech is capable of *notation*; not to examine how far the effect of *Music* on the passions depends on that resemblance.—His *notation* is extremely ingenious; but with respect to his project of accompanying the declamation of Tragedy by a drone bass, I must confess that, for my own part, I cannot reflect without some comfort upon the improbability that it will ever be attempted.

[26]After allowing that "different passions and sentiments do indeed *give different tones* and *accents* to the human voice," Dr. Beattie asks—"but can the tones of the most pathetic melody be said to bear a resemblance to the voice of a man or woman speaking from the impulse of passion?" I can only answer, that to *my* ear, such a resemblance, in the *"most pathetic melody,"* is, *often,* even striking: and I have no doubt that in *many* passages we are affected from a more delicate and latent degree of that resemblance, sufficient to be *felt*, in its effect, though not to be *perceived*.— Dr. Beattie also asks—"if there are not melancholy airs in the *sharp key*, and chearful ones in the *flat*?"—Undoubtedly, the peculiar and opposite characters of these keys, may be variously *modified* and *tempered* by the movement, the accent, and the *manner* of *performance*, in general: but they can never be *destroyed*; much less can they be changed, as Dr. Beattie supposes, to their

composition—in those of Purcell, for example, of Handel, and above all, of Pergolesi—that I have often wondered it should have been neglected by so exact a writer as Mr. Harris, though it lay directly in his way, and, in one place, he actually touched it as he passed.[27] He seems, here, to have deserted those antients whom, in general, he most delighted to follow.

But to return to *Aristotle*, and his treatise on Poetry:—the reader will observe that he does not there assert in general terms, that *"Music is an Imitative Art,"* but only, that the Music *"of the flute and the lyre"* is imitative; and even that, not always, but *"for the most part."* I just mention this, because I have observed in many of the commentators, as well as in other writers, a disposition to extend and generalize his assertions, by which they have sometimes involved the subject and themselves in unnecessary difficulties.

With respect to *modern* writers, at least, there seems to be a manifest impropriety in denominating Music *an Imitative Art*, while they confine the application of the term *Imitative* to what they confess to be the slightest and least important of all its powers. In this view, consistence and propriety are, certainly, on the side of Dr. Beattie, when he would "strike Music off the list of *Imitative Arts.*"[28] But perhaps even a farther reform may justly be considered as wanting, in our language upon this subject. With whatever propriety, and however naturally and obviously, the arts both of *Music*, and of Poetry, may be, separately, and occasionally, regarded and spoken of as *imitative*, yet, when we arrange and *class* the arts, it seems desirable that a

---

very *opposites*. A *chearful* air in a *flat* key, I confess, I never heard. If Dr. Beattie thinks the jig in the fifth solo of Corelli *chearful*, because the *movement* is *allegro*, I would beg of him to try an experiment: let him only play the first bar of that jig, (with the bass,) upon a harpsichord, &c. in g *major*: and when he has attended to the effect of that, let him return to the *minor* key, and hear the difference.—As to *"melancholy* airs in a *sharp* key," the word *melancholy* is, I think, used with considerable latitude, and comprehends different *shades*. In the *lightest* of these shades, it may perhaps be applied to some airs in a major key: that key may, by slowness of movement, softness and smoothness of tone, &c. become solemn, tender, touching, &c.—but I cannot say I recollect any air in that key which makes an impression that can *properly* be called *melancholy*. But we must be careful in this matter to allow for the magic of *association*, which no one better understands, or has described with more feeling and fancy, than Dr. Beattie himself.——With respect to "a transition from the one key to the other" (from major to minor, &c.) "in the *same air, without any sensible change* in the expression," I must also confess that it is to me, totally unknown.—One word more:—Dr. Beattie is "at a loss to conceive how it should happen, that a musician overwhelmed with sorrow, for example, should put together a series of notes, whose expression is contrary to that of another series which he had put together when elevated with joy."—But is not Dr. Beattie equally at a loss to conceive how it should happen that any man overwhelmed with *sorrow*, should put together, in *speaking*, (as he certainly does) a series of *tones*, whose expression is contrary to that of *another* series which he had put together when elevated with *joy*?—The two *facts* are equally certain, and, even at the first view, so nearly allied, that whoever can account for the one, need not, I am persuaded, be at the trouble of trying to account separately for the other. [The references are to Beattie's Ch. VI: to Sect. I (towards the end); Sect. II, Par. V; and Sect. III (near the beginning).]

[27]Ch. ii. Par. 2.—particularly note 14.

[28]Near the beginning of Ch. VI.

clearer language were adopted. The notion, that Painting, Poetry and Music[29] are all *Arts of Imitation*, certainly tends to produce, and has produced, much confusion. That they all, in *some* sense of the word, *or other*, imitate, cannot be denied; but the senses of the word when applied to Poetry, or Music, are so different both from each other, and from that in which it is applied to Painting, Sculpture, and the arts of design in general—the only arts that are *obviously* and *essentially* imitative—that when we include them all, without distinction, under the same general denomination of *Imitative Arts*, we seem to defeat the only useful purpose of all classing and arrangement; and, instead of producing order and method in our ideas, produce only embarassment and confusion.

Additional Reading

Avison, Charles. *An Essay on Musical Expression.* London, 1752.

Beattie, James. *Essays.* 3rd ed. London, 1779.

Brown, John. *A Dissertation on the Rise, Union and Power . . . of Poetry and Music.* Dublin, 1763.

Darenberg, Karlheinz. *Studien zur englischen Musikästhetik des 18. Jahrhunderts.* Hamburg, 1960.

Deditius, Annemarie. *Theorien über die Verbindung von Poesie und Musik: Moses Mendelssohn, Lessing.* Liegnitz, 1918.

Harris, James. *Three Treatises.* 4th ed. London, 1783.

Hecht, H. *Daniel Webb.* Hamburg, 1920.

Jones, William. *Poems . . . with two Essays, on the Poetry of the Eastern Nations and on the Arts called Imitative.* Oxford, 1772.

Kristeller, Paul Oskar. "The Modern System of the Arts: A Study in the History of Aesthetics." *Journal of the History of Ideas* 12-13, 1951-1952.

Rogerson, Brewster. *Ut musica poesis: The Parallel of Music and Poetry in Eighteenth-Century Criticism.* Princeton, 1945. (dissertation)

---

[29]What shall we say to those who add Architecture to the list of *Imitative Arts?*—One would not expect to find so absurd a notion adopted by so clear and philosophical a writer as M. d'Alembert. Yet in his *Discours Prel. de l'Enclyclop.* he not only makes Architecture an imitative art, but even classes it with *painting* and *sculpture.* He allows, indeed, that the imitation *"de la belle nature*, y est *moins frappante* & *plus resserrée* que dans les deux autres arts:"—but how is it any imitation at all?—only because it imitates *"par l'assemblage et l'union des differens corps qu'elle emploie"*—what?—*"l'arrangement symmetrique* que *la nature* observe plus ou moins sensiblement dans chaque individu, &c." [*Mel. de lit.* i. 63.] I can only say, that, upon this principle, the joiner, the smith, and the mechanic of almost every kind, have a fair claim to be elevated to the rank of *Imitative Artists*: for if a *regular building* be an imitation of *"la belle nature,"* so is a chair, a table, or a pair of fire-tongs.

Schueller, Herbert M. "Correspondences between Music and the Sister Arts according to 18th-Century Aesthetic Theory." *Journal of Aesthetics* 11, 1953.

Serauky, Walter. *Die musikalische Nachahmungsästhetik im Zeitraum von 1700 bis 1850.* Münster, 1929.

Smith, Adam. *Essays on Philosophical Subjects.* London, 1795.

Twining, Thomas. *Aristotle's Treatise on Poetry, and Two Dissertations, on Poetical, and Musical, Imitation.* 2nd ed. 2 vols. London, 1812.

Webb, Daniel. *Observations on the Correspondence between Poetry and Music.* London, 1769.

PART SEVEN

The French Polemic Against Imitation

The major concerns of French musical aesthetics in the eighteenth century are the question of imitation, the controversy over the priority of melody and harmony, the nature of opera, and the comparison of French and Italian opera, which became the focal point of the problem of stylistic diversity and conflicting taste. Musical writings, like those in England and Germany, now gave little attention to the traditional subject of beauty, with its metaphysical and religious values and its mathematical and formal properties of unity, order, symmetry, and so on—a tradition we encountered in Augustine and Mersenne. In general aesthetics, on the other hand, which is based primarily on visual art and literature, beauty and its moral significance continue to be the chief matter of interest, from the writings of Du Bos and Hutcheson to those of Schiller and Kant. But music plays no significant part either in the work of Baumgarten, who gave aesthetics its name in 1750, or in that of Kant, who gave it its philosophic autonomy in 1790. As for imitation, it is routinely acknowledged as an essential characteristic of art in the early decades of the century, but does not become the central issue of aesthetic discussion until Batteux.

French tracts on musical imitation are quite similar to those in England. Many of the same considerations are involved and there is an equivalent clarity of thought, although with wit and greater brilliance of style in addition. The French arguments also contain a greater range of ideas and especially a greater understanding of the nature of musical expression, which, as in England, is conceived without any appeal to the elaborate model of rhetoric that is so central in German musical poetics. Indeed, the French writings concern themselves with specifically musical expressiveness as well as with the arousal of emotions otherwise known, and the pleasure and emotions due to music are distinguished from and also related to those connected with other experience.

Imitation has its most impressive proponent in Rousseau (See the extract, in Section VIII, of his *Essai sur l'origine des langues* of 1753), whose view, in comparison with that of Batteux (1743 and especially 1747, in the *Cours des belles-lettres*), was uncompromising. But still in 1771, Morellet presents an impressive justification of music as an art of imitation. By the end of the 1770's, however, imitation is definitely discarded as the basis of musical aesthetics. Boyé and Chabanon take a position that is sharply opposed to the previously definitive thesis represented by Batteux and Rousseau. They both provide answers to Fontenelle's difficult and characteristically French question, "Sonate, que me veux-tu?" The issue that appears with the discard of imitation is of course the one presented in its most striking form by the increasingly prominent art of instrumental music. In France, however, this new art was restricted for the most part to overtures and dances, in which the nature of specifically musical expressiveness was well defined at least in general terms. It is understandable, then, that the most numerous, imaginative, and adequate solutions of this major aesthetic riddle were offered in the next decades by German writers, although the problem persisted, of course, into the twentieth century.

CHAPTER THIRTEEN

CHARLES BATTEAUX

Les Beaux arts réduits à un même principe (1743)

Part III

In which the principle of imitation is verified by its application to the different arts.

SECTION III.

On music and on dance.

Music formerly had a much greater scope than it has today. It lent the graces of art to every species of sound and gesture: it comprised song, dance, versification, and declamation: *Ars decoris in vocibus et motibus* [The art of decorum in voices and motions]. Today, when versification and dance have formed two separate arts, and when declamation, abandoned[1] to itself, no

---

[1]We have abandoned the art of declamation. Would this be because we have believed ourselves to be sufficiently rich in respect of language? If that were so, the Greeks and the Romans would have had greater cause to neglect it. However gesture alone could make up a connected discourse for them. We know the history of pantomime. When we lament the feebleness of our eloquence, we sometimes lay the blame on the form of our governments. But if the affairs of state are no longer treated by our orators today, do they not indeed have those of religion? Did Bourdaloue have less advantage in respect of material than Demosthenes? Is the fear of a

longer constitutes an art, music properly speaking is reduced to melody alone; it is *the science of tones*.

But as the separation was rather of the artists than of the arts themselves, which have always remained intimately connected among themselves, we shall treat music and dance here without separating them. The reciprocal comparison that will be made of the one with the other will help to make them better known: they will furnish light in this work, just as they furnish embellishment on the stage.

CHAPTER I

One must recognize the nature of music and dance by that of tones and of gestures.

Men have three means of expressing their ideas and their feelings: speech, the tone of the voice, and gesture. We understand by gesture exterior movements, and attitudes of the body: *Gestus*, says Cicero, *est conformatio quadam et figura totius oris et corporis* [Gesture is a certain conformation and figure of the whole countenance and body].

I mentioned speech first, because it is in possession of the first rank, and because men ordinarily pay it the most attention. But the tones of the voice and gestures have several advantages over it: they are of a more natural usage, we have recourse to them when words fail us: more widespread, they are a universal interpreter that accompanies us to the extremities of the world, that makes us intelligible to the most barbarous nations, and even to animals. Finally they are dedicated in a special way to feeling. Speech instructs us, convinces us, it is the instrument of reason: but tone and gesture are the instruments of the heart: they move us, win us over, persuade us. Speech expresses passion only by means of the ideas to which the feelings

---

miserable eternity less vivid than that of a tyrant? Do our orators indeed have no Milos to defend from time to time, no Verrès to attack, no Caesars to praise? Have we no discourses the reading of which gives us as much pleasure as the reading of some of the ancients? But we believe those of the ancients to have been superior to all those that we have. They were so perhaps only through the declamation, which alone contained almost two-thirds of the expression. I mean tone and gesture. Demosthenes even reduced the whole art of oratory to this, and he spoke on the basis of his own experience. One asks where the place is in the oration for Ligarius which brought about the arrest of Caesar's hand. One would not ask if the tones and the gestures could have been transmitted to us as well as the words. But we have only the body of this discourse, the soul is no longer there, and we judge of what it could have been only through our experience and our weakness. What confidence is that of a young orator, who appearing in public with prepared words and phrases, fancies that the tones and the gestures which should accompany and animate those phrases will be stored away perfectly ready for him, with the exquisite degree of force and of grace that each thought demands! Everything that may be sometimes good, sometimes bad, has need of rules, and however fortunate one supposes nature to be, it always requires the help of art to be perfect: *nihil credimus esse perfectum, nisi ubi natura cura juvetur.*

are tied, and as though by reflection.[2] Tone and gesture reach the heart directly and without any detour. In a word, speech is a language of institution, which men have formed for communicating their ideas more distinctly: gestures and tones are like the dictionary of plain nature; they contain a language that we all know upon being born and of which we make use to announce everything that is related to our needs and to the conservation of our being: also they are vivid, short, energetic. What better basis for the arts whose object is to move the soul, than a language all of whose expressions are rather those of humanity itself than those of men!

Speech, gesture, and tone of voice have degrees in which they correspond to the three species of arts that we have indicated.[3] In the first degree they express simple nature, for need alone: this is the naive portrait of our thoughts and of our feelings: such is, or should be, conversation. In the second degree it is nature polished by the help of art; to add embellishment to utility, one chooses with some care, but still with reserve and modesty, the words, the tones, and the gestures most proper and most pleasing: this is oration and sustained recitation. In the third, one has in view only pleasure: these three expressions have not only all the graces and all the natural force here, but also all the perfection that art can add to them; I mean measure, movement, modulation, and harmony, and this is versification, music, and dance, which are the greatest perfection possible of words, of tones of the voice, and of gesture.[4]

From which I conclude first: That the principal object of music and of dance should be the imitation of feeling or of passions: instead of which that

[2]Words may express the passions in naming them: one says: "I love you, I hate you"; but if one does not join to them either tone or gesture, one expresses an idea rather than a feeling. Whereas a movement, a glance, displays the passion itself openly. Let one read coldly the imprecation of Camille, without any inflection of the voice, and without any gesture; the heart will remain cold, or if it warms, this will be only because one imagines the tones and the gestures that should accompany these words in a furious person. *Affectus lanquescant necesse, nisi voce, vultu, totius propè habitu corporis inardescant.*

[3]In Chapter I of the first Part.

[4]It follows from this principle that in the arts that are made for pleasure, everything having to be in its greatest possible perfection, the tones and the gestures of theatrical declamation should be measured, just like the word, and notated by a composer. The ancients had arrived at this very consequence, and they had made a rule of it in practice. See the learned dissertation of Father Varry on this matter in Tome 8 of the *Mémoires de l'Académie des Inscriptions.* But among us, habit and prejudice are opposed to it. I say prejudice, for the verisimilitude would lose nothing thereby, because on the one hand, beautiful nature demands not only a perfect action, but also a language and a pronunciation that have all their possible beauty, consideration taken of the condition of the actors and of their situation; and because on the other hand, *declamatory* dance and music derive their very character and their expression from natural declamation. Measure destroys nothing, it does nothing but regulate that which was not in this state, while leaving it such as it was beforehand. Our most beautiful recitations in music have for the basis and for the foundation of their song only natural declamation. When Lully composed his, he sometimes asked Chammelé to declaim their words to him: he rapidly took down their tones; and afterwards he reduced them to the rules of art.

of poetry is principally the imitation of actions. But as passions and actions are almost always united in nature, and as they should also be together in the arts, there will be this difference of poetry from music and dance: that in the first the passions will be employed as means or motives that prepare the action and produce it; and in music and dance the actions will be only a sort of canvas destined to carry, sustain, conduct, and connect the different passions that the artist wishes to express.

I conclude secondly: That if tone of voice and gesture had a signification before being measured, they must conserve it in music and in dance, just as words conserve theirs in versification, and in consequence, that all music and all dance must have sense.

Thirdly: That all that art adds to tones of the voice and to gesture must contribute to augment this sense, and to render their expression more energetic. We are going to develop these three consequences in the chapters that follow.

CHAPTER II

The passions are the principal object of music and of dance.

Actions and passions are nearly always united and mixed together in everything men do. They are produced and announced reciprocally. They should therefore nearly always be together in the arts. When artists present an action, it should be animated by some passion; similarly when they present passions, they should be sustained by an action. That does not need to be verified by examples. But as the arts, considering the means they employ to express, may be appropriate to express one part of nature rather than another, it follows that the part that should dominate in them is that which is related most to this means of expression.

Thus poetry having chosen speech, which is most particularly the language of the mind, and music and dance having taken for themselves, the one the tones of the voice, and the other the movements of the body, and these two sorts of expressions being dedicated above all to feeling, true poets have had to attach themselves above all to actions and to discourse, and true musicians to feelings and to passions: and if these two parts are inseparable from one another, they have had to join them together in such a way that the passions were subordinated to the actions or the actions to the passions, in accordance with the means of expression that dominate in the genre in which the artist works.

Also one sees that in the majority of tragedies made to be set to music what interests us most is not the actual basis of the action, but the feelings that proceed from the situations introduced by the action. Instead of which, in other tragedies it is the actual enterprise of the heros that strikes us: the traits that are strewn about in them, if they have no relation at all to this enterprise, are only hors d'oeuvres, misplaced beauties.

From this it follows that everything which is no more than simply action, no more than idea or image, is little appropriate to music. It is for that reason that lengthy recitations, expositions of the subject, transitions, metaphors, plays of wit, in a word, all that proceeds from memory or from reflection, resists music so strongly.

In contrast, that which is an expression of feeling seems to be disposed to it of itself. Tones are half-formed in words; it demands only a little art to draw them out, particularly when the feeling is naive, simple, when it emanates from the abundance of the heart. For the heart also has its metaphysic. If the feeling is refined, subtilized, music no longer renders it, or, rendering it only in part, it becomes obscure in sense, equivocal, its expression is feeble or inappropriate, or distorted, and consequently incapable of producing that pleasing impression that the savants and the ignorant experience and should experience equally, when one speaks to them frankly the language of nature.

It is with dance as with music. Declamation necessarily languishes when the soul is not moved, and when there is a question only of instructing: because then all the movements of the body signifying almost nothing, they give no pleasure to those who see them. A gesture is beautiful only when it portrays grief, tenderness, pride; the soul, in a word: if we are dealing with a logical argument, it is ridiculous of itself, because it is useless to the thing one is saying: one reasons in cold blood: and if in quiet reasoning there is a small gesture and a certain natural tone that accompany it, this is to make visible that the soul of the one who is reasoning desires that the truth he is teaching persuade the heart while he is trying to convince the mind of it. Thus it is always feeling which produces that expression.

If one now joins what we have said touching the lyric spectacle in Chapter V of this third Part, and touching the nature and the object of that same poetry in Chapter X, with what we have just said on the natural object of music and on dance, it will not be difficult to draw from it a just idea of what a lyric spectacle should be.

One will see on the one hand the gods who act: and on the other the passions expressed: the action of the gods, which bestows on the spectacle the marvellous, which strikes the eyes and occupies the imagination: the expression of the passions, which produces emotion in the heart, which inflames it and troubles it.

Accordingly, to unite these two parts in a work of art it is necessary first to select actors who may be either gods or demigods or at the least men in whom there is something which is supernatural and which gives them some

263

association of importance with the gods. Then one will place these actors in situations in which they will experience vivid passion: there is the basis of the lyrical spectacle. And the reciprocal relation of gods and men once granted according to the fabulous system, that spectacle is not, in itself, more monstrous than the recitation of a muse in the epic. It is the same thing precisely. Just as the epic in its genre is only an imitation of a heroic action and of its causes, natural or supernatural, true or probable, the lyrical spectacle in its own is only an imitation of heroic passions and their effects, natural or supernatural, true or probable. In the one and in the other it is gods who act like gods, and men like heroes protected or persecuted by gods. The only difference is that the epic is a narrative of action and the other a spectacle of passions. And if one examines the defects of *tragédies lyriques*, one will see that they all proceed either from the fact that the marvellous is poorly placed, that is to say, in actors who do not have all that is necessary to produce it, or from the fact that the words are not at all susceptible of a true music, that is to say, that they do not at all express the passions sufficiently and that they are rather the language of the mind than that of the heart.

CHAPTER III

All music and all dance must have a signification, a sense.

We shall not repeat here at all that the melodies of music and the movements of dance are only imitations, only an artificial tissue of tones and of poetic gestures, which possess only likelihood. The passions here are as fictitious as the actions in poetry: they are comparably the sole creation of genius and of taste: nothing in them is true, all is artifice. And if sometimes it happens that the musician or the dancer may actually be feeling what he expresses, that is an accidental circumstance which is not at all the intention of the art: it is a painting which is on a living skin and which should be only on canvas. Art is made only to deceive, as we believe we have said often enough. We shall speak here only of expression.

Expressions, in general, are not in themselves either natural or artificial: they are only signs. Whether art employs them, or nature, whether they are tied to reality, or to fiction, to truth, or to lie, they change quality, but without changing their nature or their status. Words are the same in conversation and in poetry; traits and colors in natural objects and in pictures, and consequently, tones and gestures should be the same in the passions, whether real or fictitious. Art does not create expressions or destroy them: it only orders them, strengthens them, polishes them. And just as it cannot depart from nature to create things, it can just as little depart from it to express them: that is a principle.

264

If I said that I cannot enjoy a discourse that I do not understand, my acknowledgment would not have anything singular about it. But if I dare to say the same thing of a piece of music, some one will say to me, do you believe yourself sufficiently a connoisseur to hear the merit of fine music wrought with care? I dare to respond: yes, for it is a matter of hearing. I do not claim at all to calculate the tones, or the relationships, whether between themselves or with our organ of hearing: I am speaking here neither of vibrations of strings or of mathematical proportions. I abandon to the learned theorists these speculations, which are only like the grammatical design or the dialectic of a discourse, of which I can hear the merit without entering into this detail. Music speaks to me through tones: that language is natural to me: if I do not understand it at all, art has corrupted nature rather than perfected it. One should judge a piece of music like a picture. I see in the latter features and colors of which I understand the sense; it pleases me, it touches me. What would one say of a painter who contented himself with throwing onto the canvas bold features and the most vivid masses of colors without any resemblance to some known object? The application is made of itself to music. There is no disparity at all, and if there is one, it strengthens my proof. The ear, one will say, is much more subtle than the eye. Then I am more capable of judging a piece of music than a picture.

I summon the composer himself: which are the places that he approves most, that he cherishes by preference, to which he returns unceasingly with a secret satisfaction? Are they not those in which his music is, so to say, speaking, in which it has a clear sense, without obscurity, without equivocation? Why does one choose certain objects, certain passions, rather than others? It is not because they are easier to express, and because the spectators grasp their expression with greater facility?

Accordingly, let the profound musician be applauded, if he wishes it, for having conciliated, by a mathematical harmony, tones that appear never to have to encounter one another; if they signify nothing, I shall compare them to those gestures of orators which are only signs of life, or to those artificial verses which are only measured noise, or to those traits of writers which are only a frivolous ornament. The worst of all pieces of music is the one that has no character at all. There is not a sound of art which does not have its model in nature, and which does not have to be, at the least, a commencement of expression, like a letter or a syllable is in speech.[5]

[5]That is equally true both of simple song and of harmonic song: both the one and the other should have a sense, a signification: but with this difference, that the simple song is like a discourse which is addressed to the people, and which in no way supposes study to be understood: whereas harmonic song demands a sort of musical erudition, of ears instructed and exercised. It is almost a discourse made for scholars; it supposes in the auditors a certain acquired knowledge without which they would not be at all in a condition to judge of its merit. There remains to know whether a discourse that is only for scholars may be truly eloquent.

There are two sorts of music: one which imitates only non-impassioned sounds and noises: it corresponds to the landscape in painting: another which expresses animate sounds, and which adheres to the feelings: this is the portrait.

The musician is not freer than the painter: he is everywhere and constantly subject to the comparison that one makes of him with nature. If he paints a storm, a brook, a zephyr, his tones are in nature, he can take them only from there. If he paints an ideal object, which has never had reality, like the bellowing of the earth would be, the quivering of a shade who would be issuing from the tomb, let him do as the poet:

Aut famam sequere, aut sibi convenientia finge. [Either follow tradition or invent what is self-consistent. Horace. *Ars poetica*, v. 119.]

There are sounds in nature that correspond to his idea, if it is a musical one, and when the composer has found them, he will recognize them at once: it is a truth: as soon as one discovers it, it seems that one recognizes it, although one may never have seen it. And however rich nature may be for musicians, if we could not comprehend the sense of the expressions it contains, it would no longer be riches for us. It would be an unknown idiom, and consequently useless.

Music being significative in the symphony, where it *has only a demi-life, only half of its being,* what will it be in song, where it becomes the picture of the heart? All feeling, says Cicero, has a tone, a proper gesture that announces it; this is like the word attached to the idea: *Omnis motus animi suum quemdam à natura habet vultum et sonum et gestum.* Thus their continuity should form a species of coherent discourse: and if there are expressions that embarrass me, in default of being prepared or explained by those that precede or that follow, if there are some that deter me, that are inconsistent, I cannot be satisfied.

It is true, one will say, that there are passions that one recognizes in singing, for example, love, joy, sadness: but for a few marked expressions there are a thousand others of which one cannot name the object.

One could not name it, I admit it; but does it follow that there is none at all? It suffices that one sense it, it is not necessary to name it. The heart has its intelligence independent of words, and when it is touched it has understood everything. Besides, just as there are great things to which words cannot attain, there are also fine ones on which they have no grip at all: and it is above all in the feelings that these occur.

Let us conclude then that the music the best calculated in all its tones, the most geometric in its harmonies, if it happened that with these qualities it had not a single signification, it could be compared only to a prism, which presents the most beautiful colors and forms no picture at all. It would be a species of chromatic clavecin, which would present colors and transitions, perhaps to amuse the eyes, and certainly to bore the mind.

CHAPTER FOURTEEN

ANDRÉ MORELLET

De l'Expression en musique et de l'imitation dans les arts
(1771)

Etiam quaedam nunc artes expoliuntur,
  nunc etiam augescunt. Lucret. lib. v.
[Even now some arts are being perfected, some are developing.]

Music has its poetics which without doubt deserves to be investigated. It is well to be acquainted with all the sources of our pleasures; we shall succeed perhaps in rendering them more abundant, or at least more pure, by perfecting that taste which is only the clarified feeling for the fine arts.

The path is too long for me to propose to traverse it in its entirety; I will try simply to take a few steps. I wish to treat here only of the expression that is attributed to music.

Music is a succession or a simultaneity of tones of measured duration; a succession in simple melody, a simultaneity in harmony.

I regard as synonymous, at least in the present question, the terms *express* and *depict* (which perhaps are always so); and as all depiction is an imitation, to ask if music has expression, and in what the expression consists, is to ask if music imitates, and how.

One can distinguish two kinds of objects that music undertakes to depict and to express, physical objects, with their diverse actions, their movements, and their effects, and the passions, or more generally, all the affections of the human heart.

Let us investigate the means that it has for these two species of imitation, beginning with the first.

269

Being executed by the same organ as spoken language, and affecting the same sense, music itself becomes a language. Thus it may be useful first of all to investigate whether languages express and imitate physical objects, and by what means they carry out that imitation.

The imitation of physical objects by the organ of speech appears to have guided men in the formation of all languages. Nearly all the words that signify perceptible objects and their diverse actions depict them at the same time, in imitating the sound that they make audible, or the movement that they have, or the shape that they assume, or the effects that they produce, etc.; such are the names given to objects that make noise or that have movement: to thunder, to wind, to rivers, to animals, to the actions of *pricking*, of *piercing*, of *scooping*, of *soaring*, of *glissading*, of *bruising*, etc. The terms that express these ideas are imitative in all the languages of the world, and this imitation is recognized through all the changes that the languages have suffered in the progress of societies.

This truth is too well known for us to be obliged to prove it by examples, which appear of themselves; but what is important to remark here is the force of the analogies and relationships which have led to that imitation. One may believe them weak at first glance; but one sees that their influence on the formation of languages has been extremely powerful, since they have guided at the same time and along the same route all the peoples of all nations. There is, if you wish, a very slight resemblance of the world *fragor* (to crash) to the noise of a tree that splits into pieces; of the names of thunder (*tonnere*), lightning (*foudre*), and wind (*vent*) with these diverse physical objects; of the words *akmē* (point), *acuere* (to sharpen), *aiguille* (needle), *hache* (axe), etc., and generally of the syllable *ac*, to the actions of piercing, of pricking, of cutting etc.; of the words *fleuve* (river), *flatus* (breath), *souffle* (sigh), etc., in which the articulation *fl* expresses fluidity, with the running of a fluid, etc.; but that resemblance, or if you wish, that analogy, is real and authentic. It recalls the idea of the object; it retraces, at least in part, the sensations that its presence has caused; it therefore furnishes to languages a first means of imitation that adheres, so to speak, to the words, even isolated from one another, and before we unite them to form phrases and discourse of them.

But soon there is opened up another source infinitely more abundant from which imitation can draw; this is the assemblage, the combination of these same sounds in the sentence and in discourse. There those first weak analogies, at least in appearance, between words and things, are gathered together, and mutually lend one another a new force. The imitation becomes truer in offering us more features at the same time. It is certain that this part of a sentence: *le murmure d'un ruisseau qui roule ses flots argentés*, etc., forms an imitation whose truth can not be misconceived; the resemblance of the description increases even in a much greater ratio than the number of features included in it; just as, when I sketch a face, if one or two strokes of the pencil, although faithful, are still equivocal, three or four no longer are.

In this imitation of objects by sentences and discourse, movement is already perceptible; the movement whose employment is the great wealth and the great power of the arts; but it is in poetry that it begins to produce powerful effects. Number and measure here come to the aid of the imitation, and give it a totally different energy.

Taenarias etiam fauces, alta ostia, ditis,
Et caligantem nigra formidi ne lucum, etc.

Chiama gli abitator dell'ombre eterne
Il rauco suon della tartarea tromba, etc.

Dans le sein de la mort, ses noir enchantemens, etc.

Vade, age, nate; voca zephyros et labere pennis.

While one may protest that each word of these admirable verses imitates and paints nothing in considering it as isolated, who can refuse to feel with what truth their assemblage, their movement, their meter, paints and imitates the somber horrors of the realm of Pluto, the rapid and light flight of Mercury and of the Zephyrs, etc.?

Now it is easy to see that the means of imitation that the vocal organ possesses to paint physical objects, their action, their movements, etc., music can make use of and employ with much more advantage to carry out the imitation on which it is working.

Like languages, like poetry, it will choose, in perceptible objects, the sounds, the actions, the movements, the effects, and in general the circumstances that can be imitated by the sounds and the movement of the voice and of the different species of instruments; it will paint noises and sounds by the most analogous sounds; movement by movements; the height of an object by high sounds, and its depth by low sounds; distance by the opposition of these two sorts of sound, flight by sustained sounds that all fade away by degrees, like the impressions made on our senses by an object that withdraws and flees; the approach of an object by a contrary progression; the violence of a torrent that carries everything away in its passage, by a rapid succession of sounds strongly articulated and bound together, which represent the movement of that mass of water acting like a solid body; a floating cloud that rises, by a melody promenaded on a base of smooth harmony; the agitated sea by a rapid movement of sounds tied together, like the waves that push forward and succeed one another; the noise of rolling thunder by a diatonic succession of detached sounds running from high to low and from low to high; brilliant lightning by high and light flashes of melody, and claps of thunder by lower and more forcible sounds, both bursting forth suddenly from a full and sustained harmony; rain by detached sounds descending from high to low by quite narrow intervals, the movement of which will paint what the Romans call *stillicidium* [dripping], a name assuredly imitative; the peaceful course of a brook by the repetition of a short diatonic phrase entrusted to the gentlest instruments and sustained by a continuous and very simple bass; a river whose waters roll along with more rapidity and majesty by an imitation quite similar, but with lower sounds, louder and fuller instruments, and a more elaborated bass; the break of day by a twittering of high instruments, comparable to the song of birds; the freshness of morning by nimble movements and delicate sounds, and by a simple and facile harmony which will be grasped without effort and which will put the soul into that state of gentle emotion that is caused by the spectacle of the awakening of nature; the phenomenon of the gradual growth of light can be imitated by the gradual growth in the force of the harmony; the brightness of day by the brightness of sounds; the majestic slowness of the sun by the gravity of movement; and the power of its rays by a full and powerful harmony; its setting by the gradations and gradual weakening of the sounds; the return of the flocks by songs imitative of those of the shepherds that have a character of gentleness and of simplicity; the silence of night by the playing of soft and muted instruments, by sounds that are veiled as nature is; the uncertainty and the groping of a man in the shadows by broken and vague sounds; a combat by bold and rapid movements, by the use of all the warlike instruments, by brusque changes in modulation, by many dissonances, by chromatic melodies expressing the doleful cries of the wounded and dying; the victory by heroic and brilliant melodies, by strong and virile voices, etc.

I will not further press this enumeration, which is only very incomplete, but which nevertheless can give some idea of the resources that music possesses for imitating perceptible objects.

It will be said that this pretended imitation is absolutely arbitrary, and the work of an imagination which creates agreeable fictions for itself, which sees relationships and resemblances where there are none of them at all. What resemblance can there be between the rising of the sun, the freshness of morning, and all the means of music?

Without doubt the imitation that we attribute here to music supposes resemblances, or rather analogies (which are weaker and more removed resemblances), between the means of imitation and the object imitated. But these analogies can not be contested. The use that is made of them alone proves their reality. One well knows that music cannot be *fresh* like the morning air, nor *sweet* like the aroma that the earth, moistened by the dew, exhales at sunrise. But there must indeed be something in common between the impressions that a beautiful sunrise makes us experience and the feeling we receive from a certain employment of tones for people to have conceived of painting, by means of music, both the sunrise and the morning freshness.

This analogy can also be substantiated by the metaphors employed in all languages to describe the phenomena and the effects of music.

What is a metaphor? It is the use of an expression employed to render the impressions made on one of our organs to describe impressions belonging to another organ. When we say a *cold* and *brilliant* voice, we borrow these expressions from the senses of touch and vision; for there is no *cold*, rigorously speaking, except what one touches, and no *brilliant* except what one sees. Yet these expressions are accepted in all languages, and are not equivocal in any. How can this be? It is because there is an analogy, a resemblance, a relationship between the three kinds of impressions received through touch, of a *cold* object, through vision, of a *brilliant* object, and through hearing, of the voice that we call *cold* and *brilliant*. To what is this analogy due? Might it be that, in the most sensitive part of ourselves, the fibers which receive the three kinds of impressions are adjacent to one another, reciprocally communicate their agitations, lead to a common center, etc.? One may exhaust oneself in metaphysical conjectures on this subtle subject, without finding anything satisfying; but the facts cannot be denied; the facts: that is to say, the employment of this kind of metaphor in all languages, and the reality of the analogy that this employment supposes.

It is, to say it in passing (for this is perhaps not the place for that reflection), it is, I say, that same correspondence of different organs that authorizes music to depict, by means of sounds that seem to affect only hearing, the impressions made on other senses. In this way, music is in large part a metaphorical language. To describe objects, it leans like languages on the analogy that the impressions made on different organs have among themselves.

Sound and movement, for example, the one perceptible to the eye, the other perceptible to hearing, correspond reciprocally and exist together in the physical object. Music profits from that association; and if it cannot depict an object by the inflections of the voice, it imitates it by movement, or rather it most often unites these two means of imitation and of expression which lend one another mutual aid.

The example of those obscure analogies that have directed men in the formation of language thus makes us comprehend how music may avail itself of the ones we have indicated; for why in music, which is a language, would men have been more particular? May one not say: precisely because music is, more than spoken language, a work of art, because it is more a language of convention, it has had to content itself more willingly with the slightest resemblances? Weaker than nature, it has had to seize upon all the supports it encountered on its path.

We must also take into account the facility with which small reasons make a determination when there are no stronger ones.

Observe a path traced out in a prairie; all the sinuosities that you remark in it may appear to be the effect of chance, and yet there is not one of them that has not been determined by causes. A little knoll, a clump of grass that one mechanically wanted to avoid, a distant object towards which one guided oneself without thinking about it, have turned the first steps in one direction rather than another. That first track, often imperceptible, has been followed, and the path has formed.

It is thus that distant relationships, weak analogies, have insensibly directed the steps of man in the efforts he has made to depict nature through music as well as through language.

If it is permitted to me to give also a more metaphysical explication of the phenomenon I shall say that it is connected with the facility with which ideas and expressions connect themselves as much with one another as with the slightest circumstances. A striking example of this facility is the one offered to us by the association of ideas with words, even when the words have none of those relationships with the objects of the ideas on which we said above that languages could establish a sort of imitation. One sees extremely long chains of impressions and ideas attached by an imperceptible thread to a small number of syllables and reproducing themselves instantly when these syllables are pronounced. It suffices to have heard a word at the same moment in which one acquired an idea, in which one experienced an impression, for there to be established between the word and the idea or the impression an association that will never be broken. The word *laideur* [ugliness] will always awaken in me the idea of a disagreeable thing because the syllables that compose it were pronounced in my presence while I was shown a disagreeable object.

Now this same facility with which ideas and impressions are awakened serves music admirably. It makes it sufficient for it to let us hear one of the noises produced by the physical object, or to represent its movement to us or in general one of the circumstances that would accompany it, in order to awaken all at once the impression that its presence had made on our senses and on our imagination, and to make us experience all the effects of the expression that we attribute to music. One sees that it would be simple for us to explain these by more than one example; but our readers will easily supply them.

Finally, I will conclude what I had to say of these analogies by calling to attention that the works of estimable masters will demonstrate their reality to those who want to adopt a means that I have sometimes employed myself. One has only to take note in Pergolesi, Terradellas, Galuppi, Jomelli, Hasse, and so on, of the pieces in which they have wished to paint the same physical object; one will find that always, or nearly always, they have a similar conduct and something in common, either in the movement, or in the rhythm, or in the intervals, or in the mode. All the *dal torrente che rovina*, etc.,

274

all the *destrier che all'armi usato*, etc., all the *fiumicel che s'ode a pena*, etc., all the *vo solcando un mar crudele*, etc. of the various composers have striking resemblances, without being copied, because of that, from one another. Now how would all the composers have taken the same path, or at least such adjacent paths, if they had not been led there by those very analogies, those relationships whose reality we wish to establish?

Let us pass now to the expression of the passions and the diverse affections of the human heart, and let us see what means music possesses for imitating them.

All the passions and all the sentiments of the human heart have their natural declamation; I understand by natural declamation: 1. the accents of strong emotions when they are produced outwardly by inarticulate vocalizations, such as cries, sighs, or sobs, or when they are expressed by words that do not form connected discourse at all, such as interjections; 2. the vocal inflections taken on by connected discourse that is employed to express those same passions and the other feelings of the human heart.

I call this declamation *natural* to distinguish it from oratorical and theatrical declamation, which itself is founded on the accents of strong emotions and on those which the usage of spoken language attaches to the words and to the phrases of connected discourse. Now I maintain that this natural declamation is the model that musical imitation copies.

The organ of speech being one of the most powerful means that nature has given to man to express and depict his ideas and his feelings, it is very natural that music makes use of it and that it borrows its expression from it. It will choose, then, in natural declamation the most marked accents; it will dispose them with more art; it will prepare them to augment their effect; it will render them more perceptible by opposing contrasts to them (one of the most powerful means of the arts); it will recall them more often; it will pronounce them more strongly; it will occupy us with them for a longer time; in a word, it will produce by means of them those strong and profound impressions which all sensitive souls have experienced, and which those alone will be able to mistake who are not worthy of feeling them.

It is above all in the imitation of the accents of the great passions that music will triumph. It is there that one will not be able to contest its faculty of expressing and of depicting. It will become an energetic declamation and something intermediate between the sustained sounds of the fully deployed voice and the cries, at times muffled and at times violent, of the passions. The composer will seize upon the cries of nature like the declamatory speaker, but he will pronounce them with much more force. The intelligent actor will reinforce them still beyond what the composer conceived. He will sacrifice as a matter of course the beauty of his vocal organ to the truth of the expression: the freshest and most brilliant voice will take on a somber and gentle tint, and by means of a magic which that charming art alone can employ, we shall hear lamenting and tender moans penetrate and appear through melodious song.

We need not confine the faculty of thus imitating the accents of the passions to the vocal organ alone; instruments also have that aptitude, and some of them to a very high degree, especially in the hands of a sensitive artist. For the same reason, a multitude of instruments, each of which has its voice and an accent that is proper to it, employed in turn and appropriately, combined together and lending mutual aid to one another, will be able to express the feelings and the passions in a manner sufficiently true to make us recognize them, and at the same time sufficiently delicate to allow us the attainment and the pleasure of divining them. Instrumental music entirely alone will be at least a language that is written without vowels, like some oriental languages; and if it accompanies sung words, the vowels are put in.

This union of natural declamation and singing can not be explained by words; the composer, even the actor, would not know how to define in what it consists. A secure feeling, but a hidden one, guides them, the one in choosing melodies which have that resemblance to the accents of the passions, the other in rendering them with sensitivity. But it is impossible to trace out for them the route they should follow, and perhaps even to recognize it after they have traveled it. It is the art of those men fortunately born, if not for themselves, at least for us, who have a goodly portion of that sensitivity that is lacking in so many beings poorly constructed; it is the art of the great masters and of the great actors.

Besides the large movements of the passions, music will also express, by means of imitation of natural declamation, certain sentiments of the human heart that are not produced outwardly by articulations so strong and so well determined, such as melancholy, desire, hope, love, hate, contempt, irony, etc. And its expression will consist again in imitating the natural declamation that the words by which feelings are expressed receive in each language; it will imitate the vocal accents of hate, of contempt, of tenderness, as well as those of grief; and the vocal inflections of irony as well as the cries of despair; it will paint the uneasiness of the miser, his suspicious and slow walk; the grumbling disposition of the disagreeable old man; the petulance and the outbursts of the young man; the naivety of the girl; the reproaches of the jealous lover; the feigned coldness of the sweetheart; the sulkiness that allows feeling to break through; the more tender caresses of reconciliation, etc; in a word, it will be comic with as much success and truth as we have seen it tragic, and perhaps this new field will be more vast and more fecund for it than that of the great emotions and the great passions.

In thus basing the expression of the passions by music on the imitation of natural declamation, we must resolve an objection that presents itself. If declamation is arbitrary, one will say to us, if such and such a local inflection, if such and such an intonation today devoted to the expression of a feeling was able in one nation, or at least in different nations, to be employed to express a contrary or at least a dissimilar feeling, what will be the expression of the music based wholly on the imitation of natural declamation and of the accent of spoken language?

1. I shall say that, while supposing declamation to be arbitrary in its origin, it is so established and consecrated by the usage of all languages and among all nations, that music may take it as a model. That it could have been entirely different is something about which the composer should not trouble himself. When he imitates the accents of spoken language, his expression is true, since it has a constant model with which it may be compared: it is true, just as every day we reason logically according to a supposition that is not a fact.

While the difference in the declamation of a single passion among different nations may be larger than it is in effect within each one, music copying the national declamation would have a very true expression, since it would awaken all the ideas and all the feelings that are expressed and awakened in each country by the words and the accentuated discourse to which such feelings and such ideas are attached.

2. It is false that the declamation we have called natural is arbitrary: it depends certainly on physical causes whose effects are determined, at least up to a certain point. The passions are the same in all men, and to exhibit themselves externally, they can make use only of similar organs, such as the voice, gesture, etc. That organ itself the passion which uses it modifies in the same manner, or at least in a manner very little different, in all men and in all nations.

The modification that the organ assumes being itself the work of the passion, it is unable not to be analogous to it. There is a relationship between grief and the voice of grief that is just as little arbitrary as the one which exists between the threat and the threatening gesture, between the supplication and the supplicating posture.

Without doubt Chinese declamation and, without going too far from home, English declamation are not the same as ours; but the difference is slight: neither the Chinaman nor the Englishman expresses somber grief by piercing cries; their voice does not rise to paint sadness, and their declamation is not subdued and dragging to express the movement of joy. One can observe the same resemblance between the declamation employed in all languages to render those of our sentiments that do not have accents as marked as grief or despair, etc., like tenderness, contempt, or irony. Finally, the declamation of a single feeling is comprised everywhere within a certain latitude which it does not exceed at all, and the accents and the sounds and the diverse combinations of the one and the other, contained between these limits, are the models that the musical imitation copies.

3. But I will go further, and I say that the employment and the truth of that type of expression which has for its object the passions and the feelings of the human heart are based, like the imitation of physical objects, on certain relationships and certain analogies which such and such combinations of sounds and of movements have with the feelings that music undertakes to depict.

The analogies that we have noted above, between physical objects and the means which music employs, can help us to conceive those that are in question here.

It is quite difficult to explain with precision in what they consist; but it is sufficient that they are real, and that one may recognize them in the effects which music produces. I shall indicate some of them here that will warrant us in supposing many others which we are not in a position to indicate.

There is a relationship between smothered sounds and the oppression of the heart that the sorrows of the soul or the feeling of fear make us experience.

There is a relationship between certain movements in music and the inner agitation that the passions cause; between slow movements and despondency.

There is a relationship between a moderate and yet *andante* movement, and serenity of mind; between a lively movement and gaiety; and, for the opposite reason, between slowness of melody and sadness.

There is a relationship between the movement of a melody that proceeds chromatically, and the feeling of grief, even when this is mute.

There is a relationship between the minor mode and melancholy, and between the major mode and gaiety.

There is a relationship between certain intervals, such as the minor third, the ascending minor sixth, the descending fourth and diminished fifth, etc., and gentle feelings; and between the intervals of the major third, the fifth, the ascending major sixth, and more resolute and more definite feelings.

When the sounds forming these same intervals are combined, they form harmonies that have relationships and analogies of the same kind, or at least characters that are very different in accordance with the nature of the intervals, etc.

I cannot repeat too often that these observations are very incomplete; that some may lack justice, or demand restrictions and modifications; it is for the artists to confirm them or to take issue with them; but it suffices that they have a basis in truth: now this is what I do not believe may be contested. I am persuaded that all composers are guided, perhaps without perceiving it themselves, by relationships of this kind; which suffices to establish the truth of the general observation, whatever judgment one might pass on each in particular.

We may conclude that music is able to imitate and depict physical objects and their diverse actions, the passions, and even as much as certain sentiments of the soul that seem still more to elude imitation.

It remains for me to respond to a general objection which tends to overturn the principles I have just set forth, and which, once resolved in a satisfactory manner, leaves them more solidly established.

The imitation to which music applies itself when it undertakes to paint either physical objects or sentiments of the human heart is without doubt very imperfect; the noises that physical objects render, their movements and their effects, even the cries of the passions and the accents of spoken language, all these things are imitated by music so vaguely, so slightly, that one is not able to regard its depiction as a likeness. The melody of a voice or of a violin, however delicate it may be, does not resemble at all that of a nightingale, nor the noisiest music a battle, or a tempest, or a torrent. Even the accents of the powerful passions, and with still more reason, natural declamation and all the other feelings, are not faithfully rendered by the intervals of music. The accents of spoken language are neither appreciable to the ear of the composer, nor can they be executed by the singing voice or by instruments; they are not submitted to any measure nor to any period; measure and period cannot be reconciled, in any case, with the agitation and the disorder of the passions, or with the vagueness and the liberty of the diverse affections of the human heart: with so many differences from the original of the supposed depiction, what becomes of imitation, of expression in music?

This difficulty is founded merely on a false idea that people form of what imitation in the arts should be: they demand here too much exactitude.

One would admit more readily that music expresses and imitates physical objects and passions of the human heart if one persuaded oneself that its imitation has no need to be either complete, nor exact, nor rigorous; that it should even be imperfect, and different from nature in some aspect, under pain of losing a part of its rights over our soul, and the power to produce in us the impressions it desires to obtain.

This is what I am going to attempt to explain; and I hope that what I shall say will serve not only to resolve the objection offered, but even to decide many other questions debated for a long time in the theory of the fine arts.

Imitation in all the arts should embellish nature, that is to say, give the soul more pleasure than the truth itself. It is not the truth, but an embellished resemblance that we demand from the arts; it is to give us more than nature that art engages in imitating.

All the arts make a kind of pact with the soul and the senses that they affect. That pact consists in demanding licenses and in promoting pleasures which they would not bestow without these fortunate licenses.

Poetry demands to speak in verse, in images, and in a tone more elevated than nature.

Painting demands to enhance the tone of color, to correct its models, to give its imitations nobility, grace, elegance, freshness, in a word, beauties that the objects themselves do not possess. The art of writing itself is acquainted with and knows how to employ this type of liberty; it deviates sometimes from exactitude and from rigorous truth; it sacrifices precision and accuracy to images and to harmony in order to provide greater pleasures.

Music takes similar licenses; it demands to cadence its course, to round its periods, to sustain, to fortify the voice with the accompaniment, which is certainly not in nature. That, without doubt, alters the truth of the imitation, but at the same time augments its beauty, and gives to the copy a charm that nature has refused to the original.

Homer, Guido, Pergolesi, make the soul experience delightful sentiments to which nature alone would never have given rise; they are, however, models of art: art accordingly consists in giving us more than nature.

One does not find in nature measured airs, connected and periodic melodies, accompaniments subordinated to these melodies; but no more does one find there the verses of Vergil, nor the Belvedere Apollo: art may thus alter nature, or at least dress it out in order to embellish it.

Nothing resembles the song of the nightingale so much as the sounds of that little pipe which children fill with water, and which their breath makes warble; what pleasure does that imitation give us? None, or at most one of surprise; but when we hear a flexible voice and an agreeable symphony that express (less faithfully without doubt) the song of the same nightingale, the ear and the soul are in rapture: this is because the arts are something more than the exact imitation of nature.

But why should I content myself here with comparing music that imitates the song of the nightingale to another imitation, although truer than that of music? I will dare to say that it outweighs also the model of nature itself, and that we take a much greater pleasure in hearing *Se perde l'ussignuolo, il caro amato bene*, etc., set to a delightful melody sung by a sweet and flexible voice, than in hearing all the nightingales of a grove. I well know that if a sensitive soul, amorous above all, hears the nightingale on a lovely night, in the peaceful contemplation that the integrity of solitude brings, in the silence of nature and with the removal of all other impressions, it will be able to experience emotions stronger and more profound than those which the most pleasing music would give to it; but this is because then a crowd of other feelings and circumstances will unite to produce effects that one will no longer be able to attribute to the song of the nightingale alone.

If one now asks what means art employs to thus embellish nature, in falling away from the rigor and from the exactitude of imitation, I find several that deserve to be remarked.

The first is the choice of traits. There are moments when nature in its entire simplicity has all the charm that its imitation may possess: then what the latter can best do is to be faithful; but these moments are rare and short: such a mother or such a lover complains naturally with tones of voice so .

280

tender that music could be touching by contenting itself with taking up and repeating her complaints; but nature is not beautiful in all mothers, and even when it is beautiful, it does not sustain itself; its beauty sometimes knows only an instant. The true Bérénice must have allowed cries to escape and given herself up to movements disagreeable to the ear and to the eyes. Music, in choosing the most beautiful expressions of grief and in discarding all those which could wound the sense organs, will thus embellish nature and will give us greater pleasures.

The second means that art employs to procure us more pleasure than nature in deviating from the truth of imitation is the right that it assumes to present simultaneously, in a single object, a multitude of pleasing traits, of dispersed beauties that have never been assembled. Each one of the traits of the Venus of the Medicis has existed separately in nature; the whole has never existed: in the same way, a beautiful pathetic air is the collection of a multitude of accents that have escaped from sensitive souls. The sculptor and the musician unite these dispersed features and give us pleasures which nature and truth would never have given us.

3. But the greatest of the pleasures which imitation less rigorous than the truth produces is that of reflection on the ingenious artifice which has been made use of to seduce us; a confused but very ardent pleasure, without which the greatest charm of the imitation is destroyed, and which disappears as soon as the imitation is taken for the truth itself, and the illusion is entire and complete.

Let us imagine the Venus of the Medicis painted and colored, and let the colors be so alive that the illusion becomes insurmountable; this beautiful figure will no longer give the same visual pleasure as a work of art: I say *as a work of art*, for I do not doubt that we should experience a very vivid pleasure, but it would be of a different type that we are not discussing here at all.

The Capuchins of Bologna, opposite Saint Michael of the Wood, have a Saint Francis of a renowned artist which is a very beautiful piece of sculpture colored perfectly; we think we are encountering a Capuchin, and we are not very thankful to the artist for the illusion. That statue does not give as much visual pleasure as a picture without relief or a statue that lacks color.

When two arts, like sculpture and painting, are combined, and each employs its means of imitating nature, that is to say, a solid body and colors to imitate a solid and colored body, the merit of the art diminishes because it has employed too many means, and means that are too powerful when they are combined; and we no longer see the imitation, for the very reason that it is too perfect.

It is necessary, in the statue, for the beauty and the truth of the attitude, of the contours, of the draperies, of the whole expression, to combat, so to speak, the dead color of the marble and of the stone, for us to be thankful to the artist for not having wanted to deceive us entirely, and for having succeeded nevertheless in creating an illusion for us up to a certain point in spite of the difference he has allowed to remain between his work and that of nature.

When I say that the illusion should not be complete, that calls for an explanation; for it appears that when we have a beautiful work of art before our eyes, the moment at which we experience the greatest pleasure is that at which the illusion is the strongest. Mérope never moves us more than when we believe we see a genuine mother ready to stab her son, and we are never more touched by the beauties of Zaïre than when that interesting fiction assumes for our eyes an entire air of truth.

I believe one may explain this apparent contradiction by distinguishing two phases in the impression that works of art make on us: there must be a moment at which we are ignorant that we are being deceived, and a moment at which we know that we have been deceived; a moment at which we believe we see nature, and another at which we perceive the art which is fleeing and concealing itself, but which, like the shepherd in Vergil, *Se cupit antè videri* [Wants himself first to be seen]. These moments must succeed one another alternately and at short intervals; for if after having caused me to see an imitation which I have taken for a reality and having left me in that illusion for some hours, one apprizes me that this is only an illusion, it is too late an admonishment, and I have been deceived for too long a time. It is perhaps to this unceasing alternation of illusions and *disabusements* (I beg to be pardoned this word, which is the most appropriate that can be employed) that we are indebted for the greatest pleasures the arts afford us; it deploys two of the greatest resources of the soul, sensitivity and sagacity, and what is most interesting to remark, it compresses them alternately, from which there result variety and contrast, the fecund source of our pleasures.

And we must not think that the illusion, thus interrupted, will be less strong and less vivid in the moment in which it is exercised. I am persuaded, on the contrary, that in this struggle of truth against it, it gains new forces to subjugate our senses and our imagination. When it returns victorious, we are in collusion with it, and we anticipate its yoke. We lend ourselves to all the suppositions, we set aside everything that could undeceive us and make us forget the errors that are dear to us; and what is easier for art than to deceive us when we make ourselves its accomplices? Our awakened sensitivity, our imagination exalted by the beauties, the riches of this luxurious type of art, dispose us to an illusion, which, although of short duration, makes stronger impressions on us than a more exact imitation with which the illusion would sustain itself for a longer time.

Plutarch, in the fifth book of his *Symposiaca*, develops these same principles in a manner so true that I cannot refrain from citing him, and I will transcribe that passage of the translation of Amyot, even though it may be only to refresh myself from what I am writing.

He asks *why we hear and see with pleasure those who act the part of enraged and disagreeable people but not those who in truth are so.* "It is," he says, "because we love ingenious and artificial things; if one is about to give some bread to a little child," he adds, "either a little dog or a little ox made of dough, you will see that he will come running to what is represented. Likewise also, if one offers him a lump of silver, and another little animal of some kind formed of silver, he will much rather take that in which he sees there has been the spirit of artifice intermingled. . . . He who becomes angry in fact, displays only common and ordinary passions; but to represent and counterfeit them, he who knows how to do it well has dexterity and subtlety of spirit; it is for that reason that we take pleasure in seeing the one, and displeasure in viewing the other. We observe with boredom and sadness those who are dying or who are ill, and in contrast we take pleasure in seeing and admire a Philoctetus painted in a scene, and a Jocasta of cast bronze, etc. . . : in the pastime of seeing and hearing, the pleasure is neither in the sight nor in the hearing, but in the understanding. . . . ; for our understanding delights in imitation as in a thing which is proper to it, etc."

I have said that this principle (that the imitation should not be entire and perfect) is common to all the fine arts, and that one may conveniently make use of it to decide many questions disputed for a long time in dramatic art, poetry, oratory, etc. I will permit myself to apply it here to dramatic art alone.

It is disputed whether dramatic works should be in verse or in prose; whether the tragedy should be written in the style that is called natural; whether the beauty even of the verse of Racine is not a hindrance to its verisimilitude; whether the occurrences should be conveyed exactly as they happen in nature; whether one may set aside the three unities; whether the declamation should be elevated and sustained, or familiar, etc.

It seems to us that those who desire absolutely that Caesar and Agamemnon speak in prose, that they speak in the same style that a Greek or a Roman would speak to his friend or to his wife in his home; that those who find that Athalie and Clytemnestra should declaim like a bourgeois, or if you wish, like a queen was able to speak to her daughter or to her husband in her bedroom; that all those, in a word, who do not recognize a theatrical verisimilitude totally distinct from actual physical verisimilitude, from that of the events, err in desiring that the imitation be too perfect, and such that it is incompatible with the genius and the riches of the fine arts.

Basically, why is it necessary that the imitation be so exact, if art itself is able to render us more indulgent toward verisimilitude? Now that is in effect what happens; those accessories that we regard as separating us from nature, the harmony and the beauty of the verses, the nobility (I do not say

283

the emphasis) of the declamation, in making vivid impressions on us, dispose us sufficiently strongly to illusion to render useless a more meticulous imitation, at the same time as they give us pleasures that exact imitation would not give us.

Comedies were performed for a long time in Naples in which nature was copied exactly; the setting was not, as in our theaters, a painted decoration, but one or two actual houses, a garden, a street. In one of these houses of which the interior is seen, a lover and his mistress, a husband and his wife, are engaged in conversation; a man is sick in his bed, while his daughter, at a balcony, makes signs to her *cicisbeo*; ten or twelve persons, and sometimes thirty or forty, are on the scene at once; some play, the rest talk; one sees here all the fuss of a household: lackeys who come and go, a master who issues his orders, an expected person who arrives in a carriage with all his retinue; people eat, people drink, etc. In a word, it is not a representation at all, but the thing itself. I know that, on the strength of this account, some of my readers, and perhaps more than one man of letters, will be able to lament this type of spectacle. People will be able to cite against me the very passion that the Neapolitans have shown for this comedy; but I shall always say that this is the spectacle of a people still in the childhood of the fine arts, of a nation which has forgotten Menander and Terence, and which has never known Racine and Molière. They are the ancient Attalids; and to re-introduce them among us would be to reduce people accustomed to good living to the viands of the golden age.

How have we been able to believe that art gained something in thus confounding itself with nature, and in copying it servilely? This was to annihilate it in wanting to perfect it. If I want to see only what takes place in the street and in my house I have no need to go to the theater. People tell me that the spectacle is such a likeness that it is the thing itself; but it is in this that it is vicious, for it is not the thing itself that I wish to see; it is its imitation.

Let us return to music, from which this digression has not really removed us, and let us conclude that, like the other fine arts, it may content itself with a slight imitation; that this will not be a weakness in it, but a delicacy of expression; that slight analogies will be means of imitation for it; that its imitation will not for this reason be less true, and that its portraits will be likenesses, if not through the exactitude of each feature, at least through the number of the similitudes that it will have been able to gather together; and finally that *imitation* and *expression* belong to it perhaps in an equally high degree as to the other arts that have so great a dominion over us, and that cast our senses and our imagination into such pleasant illusions.

CHAPTER FIFTEEN

BOYÉ

L'Expression musicale, mise au rang des chimères
(1779)

Lorsque ton ame éprouve un mouvement tragique, Es-tu jamais tenté de le dire en Musique? [When your soul feels a tragic emotion, Are you ever tempted to utter it in music?]

Can music express the passions? The question will be decided if one refers it to the opinions already pronounced; for it does not appear to be doubted that that art has the gift of painting all the modifications of our soul: those who have written about it have never omitted trying to persuade us that a musician may subject to its genius the accents of love and of hate, the transports of pleasure, the cries of grief, the charms of voluptuousness, and the horrors of despair, etc. etc. It has sometimes been said, however, that it is not natural to cry in song; but so feebly, that the error has always triumphed.

Before attacking the prejudices that we wish to combat, let us recall that essential truth, that the soul being inaccessible to our senses, it can manifest the affections it feels only by external signs, that is to say, by alteration of the features, by attitudes, gestures, inflections of the voice, exclamations, sighs, sobs, finally by words and the manner of articulating them, etc. etc.

Now although expression in the arts is occupied only with movements of the soul, it is not less true that it consists absolutely in the imitation of those external signs of which we have just spoken. This being granted, when some one says to me that an art is capable of expression, I have no means more certain to convince myself of this than to compare the objects it expresses with their models, which models must be laid hold of in nature.

It is with such a guide that, having contemplated engraving, painting, sculpture, pantomime, and poetry with an attentive eye, I have not been able to deny to each of these arts the advantage of expressing in a very sensitive manner the passions that they have desired to imitate.

But having examined the productions of music with the same scrupulousness, it has always appeared to me to be at a prodigious distance from its pretentions: and that must be the case; for in considering always what has a relationship to the passions, if features are imitated by features, colors by colors, as in painting; gestures by gestures, as in pantomime; and phrases by phrases, as in poetry; it follows that music would have to imitate the accents of song by the accents of song, if it was true that the passions naturally employed such a language. But as the passions never manifest themselves in song, but are expressed only by the inflections of the speaking voice, it is also only the inflections of the speaking voice that are able to imitate them, as in declamation.

It seems to me I hear a logician assure me that he is going to confound me in two words. What? he will say to me, when I speak, does my voice not make sounds audible? Do not these sounds naturally constitute musical notes? Let us say that I show joy or anger, that I laugh, that I sigh or that I weep, is it not through *do*'s, through *re*'s, through *mi*'s? etc. If that is the case, as I do not doubt, the musician can then reduce the natural inflections of my voice to notes: he can thus express, and there you are confounded.

Ah, no! monsieur, there is nothing of all that: your voice makes heard neither *do*, nor *re*, nor *mi*, etc., when you say to the object of your endearment: "Dear soul of my life, my being breathes only for you: I exist only to adore you: what! you deign to listen to my vows; oh! inexpressible felicity: oh! delirium of delight."

I protest, monsieur, that there is no musician who can notate the tone which you will sound in pronouncing these words. He will not be more fortunate when a wife says tenderly to her husband: "Look at you, then, abominable crocodile, have you just stirred up my rage again? How has the earth been able to produce a monster as horrible as you?"

In short, the whole possible art of music would be able to notate neither cries, nor moans, nor sighs, nor exclamations, nor sobs, nor laughter, nor laments: it is an incontestable fact.

I expect that I am going to be pressed for the reason why: but before responding I foresee the frivolity of letting the demon out of the bottle: the details into which I am going to enter may produce some fumes: there is no question here of an Oriental fairy tale.

In music, when any *note* is sounded, that *note* is fixed and constantly the same from the instant it begins to the one that terminates it. For example, if one sings a *sol*, the voice will remain on the same *tone* during the whole duration of this *sol*.

286

It is not thus with ordinary language, in which the *sounds* one articulates are indeterminate. For example, when you say a yes or a no, your voice escapes rapidly from the point from which it has departed, to terminate this yes or this no, sometimes *louder*, sometimes more *subdued*, in accordance with the purpose that motivates you. It is the same with other syllables, as anyone may easily convince himself. The difference between the musical *sound* and the *sound* of speech accordingly consists in the fact that the first is fixed and the second indeterminate. How can one imagine now that the latter may be imitated by the former? That is obviously impossible: I would rather be persuaded to believe that a draughtsman can imitate curved forms with straight lines.

A remark not less essential than the preceding is that the smallest musical interval is a semitone: thus one may regard semitones as the elements that serve to form all the intervals practicable in music; and the ordinary compass of the voice, which is about two octaves, contains in consequence about twenty-four of these semitones.

Let us also consider attentively the elements of the speaking voice, and we shall see that they are much smaller than the first: for in conversation one makes fourth, eighth, sixteenth, and twentieth parts of tones, etc. Confining ourselves even to this last division, it turns out that the compass of the voice contains two hundred of these elements. The number of means of the speaking voice is thus at least ten times as large as that of the singing voice. Do not all these reasons constitute the most complete demonstration of the impotence of music in respect of imitation?

A composer who claims to copy the impassioned accents of nature is thus as ridiculous as some one who desires to form all imaginable words with three letters of the alphabet.

If a man said to you, I am going to take several small stones, of which the smallest will be as large as a fist, and gluing them together, I shall make you a Venus as perfect as that of Versailles; would you not treat it as insane? Would you not tell him that his small elementary and formative stones are too coarse for features so delicate? Well! the semitones in music are like coarse small stones with which the composer claims to imitate the subtle features of speech.

Let us now be honest, and let us regard all operas as so many pictures of those clumsy old painters, who were obliged to write over each head what the personage signified: for if one detaches the poem from an opera, each phrase of melody will become as a result an inexplicable hieroglyph.

One of my dear colleagues, irritated that I was going to divulge the secrets of the school, said to me the other day that I would at least be forced to accord to the musical art the advantage of expressing joy. You are mistaken, my friend, I responded to him: observe your intonations when you rediscover a friend whom you had lost a long time ago, or when it has just been announced to you that you are going to possess that which you desire; and recall to yourself what the expression is.—But if a composer can not render those great excesses of joy, he will at least be able to imitate a musical gaiety; for often I sing when I am content.—Why, of course! that is well worth announcing so loudly; does it mean anything? Except that music can imitate music? Is this not a consideration of great weight, that lays claim to competition with the paint brush of the Raphaels and the Michelangelos?

Here I am, then, armored now against all the objections that are going to swoop down on me: it will not be difficult for me to forestall them; for I can say of my adversaries, to whom I have communicated my ideas, what the ladies say of their lovers: they all make the same professions.

I perceive a pedant, who in a tone of confidence presents to me this frightening argument:

The functions of the arts being to please us, they should not always imitate nature such as it is; for one often finds it hideous and disgusting: it conceals in its bosom beings that would frighten us, if they were copied with too much resemblance. Besides, if there is a reason to exclude music from imitation, because one does not sing when speaking, why treat poetry with less rigor? Does one speak in verse? Which of us would be able to say naturally:

L'honneur est comme une isle escarpée et sans bords;
On n'y rentre jamais lorsqu'on en est dehors.

Have you finished, Monsieur Observer? I know as well as you that an artist must not indiscriminately take hold of all the traits he comes upon: on the contrary, he rejects the greater number of them: it is up to him to know how to make a choice of the objects most suitable to the purpose he has in view: taste makes him assemble parts that he has found only very far apart; and from that assemblage there results a whole often more pleasing than the beings which surround us: but the parts of this whole must be taken from nature.

When Zeuxis desired to paint a perfect beauty, he gathered together the features of several existing beauties, and his painting surpassed everything most faultless that the universe is able to offer.

The parts of this same painting were therefore taken from nature.

The same response is applicable of itself to your remark on poetry: for a drama, a dramatic scene, an ode, a madrigal, a verse, etc. are so many wholes, of which the ideas, the meanings, the phrases, and the words are the parts; now there is no need to tell you that these parts are again taken from nature.

Certainly it is not this way in music: for an opera, an air, an ariette, a monologue, a recitative, etc. are so many wholes. What are the parts? Fixed and determined tones, cadences, portamentos, trills, roulades, etc. etc. Now recall what we observed previously, and I defy you to say that anything of all that is taken from nature.

In truth, seeing that Cicero could not comprehend how two soothsayers could meet without laughing, I believe that we can say as much of two composers.

Oh! Oh! here is Madame Gertrude, who is arriving all in tears: what is the matter, then, Madame, has your dressmaker broken her promise?—Ah! Monsieur, I have just heard the opera *Armide*; I am still overcome by it; feel how my heart beats; I am afraid I'll be ill over it; how this Gluck can depict the passions; how he can make himself the master of all the parts of the soul; what truth in his expressions! Do you still maintain your system? Whence come the tears that I have shed, if not from the manner in which the music expresses the words?—What a tender heart you have, Madame; your extreme sensitivity makes me fear for your health: there, I shall not even ask you why you go to cry at the Opéra, while you play the devil at home? I will say to you only that even though indeed your eyes may gush like two fountains, you should ascribe the cause of it only to the interest of the poem and to the feeling of the actor.

The first part of this solution does not call for comment: let us give more space to the second.

A true actor who must fill a musical role does not fail to perceive that if he sang exactly only what is marked on the paper, the auditors would hardly be satisfied with a manner so puerile and so removed from the sense of the words: he sees that each phrase of song, each intonation, each note, is as much as a shackle for him.

Fortunately all resources have not been taken away from him: he can in spite of that modify the tone color of his voice, he makes audible tones more or less doleful, more or less sparkling: he veils them, he expands them: sometimes he expels them with force, sometimes he enfeebles them languorously. Finally, he presents virile and assured tones, troubled and broken tones. He knows how to turn to account all the means of pronunciation: he interests himself above all in the articulation of the consonants: he more or less doubles one, while he lays very little stress on the other, all according to the type and degree of the passions that animate him.

It is, I say, through the conjunction of all these things that a lyric actor succeeds in interesting those who hear him: that he shares the glory of the composer, that often he takes it away from him entirely.

He shares it when the melody agrees with the words, with as much suitability as the limits of the art may be able to allow: such as in this passage of Monsieur Grétry, in *Zémire et Azor: "Ah! laissez-moi, laisser-moi donc pleurer!"*

He takes it away when that suitability is entirely neglected, such as in the first reprise of this air of Monsieur Gluck:

J'ai perdu mon Euridice,
Rien n'égale mon malheur,
Sort cruel, quelle rigueur?
Rien n'égale mon malheur.   *(bis)*

The style of the song has been found so gay, that a very jolly contredance has been made of it: in effect, the words that follow would be much more appropriate:

J'ai trouvé mon Euridice,
Rien n'égale mon bonheur;
   Quels momens!
   Quels transports!
Rein n'égale mon bonheur.   *(bis)*

However, when Monsieur le Gros performs this piece the way it stands in the opera, that is to say, with the words "J'ai perdu mon Euridice," he has the ability to correct its defects by tones so pathetic, that the tears flow, that hearts melt at the terrible situation which he feigns to experience.

One is now reduced to asking me if musical art is not susceptible of various characteristic qualities? I answer yes; and it is precisely this which has misled us up to the present: we have confounded the frame with the picture, and the appearance of the physiognomy with the affections of the soul. Music has several characteristic qualities, without doubt; it is naive in romances, gay in allemandes, virile and majestic in *marches militaires*; it is sometimes languorous, such as in adagios and *cantabiles*: one knows that the sonatas of the celebrated Giardino are sprightly and gracious; that the quartets of Boccherini have an indefinable melancholy that has made them comparable to the *Nights* of Young.

These things are entirely only modifications of musical style; but I repeat it again, there is no music at all either for hate, nor for friendship, nor for disdain, nor for a fit of rage, nor for anger, nor for transport, nor for despair, etc. Besides, why attach more importance to the qualities themselves than to those that one remarks in the façade of an edifice, in the decorations of a public promenade, in the designs of a flower-bed, and in the general effect of a face? Because the exterior of a prison bears a sombre and sad character, has the architect ever been sufficiently foolish to conclude from it that that expresses the regret of those who are within?

If it was permitted to thus confound characteristic qualities with the passions, although the one are to the other approximately what rest is to movement, my dressing gown would then have expression, for my cook told me the other day that the design is melancholy.

290

It is at the Théâtre du Louvre that I perceive the true expression of impassioned accents: it is there that the imitator may unceasingly be compared with nature, that the copy bears the imprint of its model: it is there that one recognizes in the actor the hero that he represents: it is there, I say, that I learn to detect better the ridiculosities of the musician. Let us cease finally to share them; let us laugh at his reveries; may he retain them as long as they are dear to him; but as for us, let us accord to music only characteristic qualities, and let us leave to declamatory art the vast empire of expression.

That is not all; musicians claim also that the orchestra should have its particular expression; that the accompaniments should depict all the situations of the singers; that it is by the conjunction of the means of the instruments and those of the voice that there result perfect imitations and tableaux of the greatest force.

Well! Messieurs, should you not feel now that if the inflections of the singing voice succeed poorly in seconding your intentions, all the violins and all the basses possible will succeed in this still less. Moreover, does anyone who is affected look for accompanists? Or indeed does he have an orchestra in his chest? Is the voice double, triple, or quadruple? Does one produce chords when one speaks?

Let us attack in our turn: I am going to prove a fact on which one hardly counts; it is that the music that most approaches expression is the most boring; there is only the question of recognizing this. Let us not search elsewhere than in recitatives, since it is true that this genre is freed from all the ornaments of song, that it copies as much as the art can permit it the intonations of conversation, that measure almost does not reveal itself there, that the long and the short syllables are less unheeded there than elsewhere. Well! what sensations follow from all that? Will I be told that a recitative procures a quite delicious pleasure? No, without doubt: one does no more than tolerate those that are best made for ten minutes at the very most; but if some one was regaled for three hours by such pieces, he would have migraine for three days.

Why have the operas of Monsieur Gluck had so much difficulty in finding favor, in spite of the reputation that had preceded this great man in our capitol, in spite of the powerful patrons that he had, and in spite of the avidity that we show, we other Frenchmen, for all that comes from abroad? It is that the productions of this celebrated man are too overloaded with recitatives, that the usual effect of this genre is to be cold, boring, and distasteful.

I do not fear that ill-disposed people will impute to me the desire to diminish the merit of this great artist, I do myself glory in the contrary to render hommage to his rare genius, I attack only the system and in no way the talent.

291

Let us also remark that other superiority of melodious airs over recitatives, that the first have the gift of charming the ear, even when one does not comprehend the words. I say that the airs: *"Ah! quel torment d'être sensible!"* ... *"Ne crois pas qu'un bon ménage. ... "* *"Qu'il est doux de dire en aimant. ..,"* will please a Spaniard, a Russian, a Chinaman; say as much, if you dare, of a French recitative; I will assert more, these same airs will still be able to inspire interest even though they be performed on instruments, while if anyone ventured to play a recitative on the flute, that would be something to make an audience walk out.

If one does not find oneself sufficiently convinced, let him betake himself to the opera houses of Italy; he will see that the spectators are talking, gaming, drinking, and eating during the recitatives, and that they reserve their attention for what one calls the *bravura* arias, pieces which, in truth, are very seductive and procure us very great pleasure, although these objects are the least expressive things in the world. Now if my opinion accords with Italian ears, the most delicate and the most musical ears in the universe, let the reader deliver his verdict.

It will not be difficult to prove that there can be no *musique pittoresque* in this question; I am talking about music in which one claims to imitate the warbling of birds, the cries of animals, and the sounds of inanimate objects. I have traveled through forests, orchards, and groves, and among birds I have been able to distinguish only a single one whose song could be notated: it is the bird of bad omen for husbands; yes, the cuckoo very distinctly sounds two tones perceptible to the ear of the musician; which tones form between them the interval of a major third: also, has one not gone wrong in making of it the subject of a sonata for violin, entitled *Le Coucou*: there is no performer who does not know it. But although Senaillé, the composer of that piece, takes his cuckoo out for an airing through numerous modulations, I defy the listener to surmise the intention if he is not taken into confidence: for in order that the imitation be perceived, it is not sufficient to have translated the language of the cuckoo musically; an instrument would be necessary of which the quality of the tones was similar to the voice of that bird; now the tone color of the violin possesses nothing less than that: also, the cuckoos of certain wooden clocks that are sold along the streets set at defiance the *Coucou* of Senaillé.

As to the other birds, crows, warblers, owls, and nightingales, let us say; or pigeons, turtle-doves, hens, turkey-cocks, ducks, and all the winged species you please, it is absolutely impossible to notate any of their twittering; and that is so because their sounds are as indeterminate as those of the speaking voice. It is the same with the cries of all the animals: dog, cat, horse, donkey, calf, mule, pig, etc.; all those good servants offer no more hold to musical art than the birds.

Let us examine now whether music can imitate the sounds of inanimate objects, such as the rippling of streams, the rustling of leaves, waterfalls, tempests, etc., and we shall see immediately that it is the height of absurdity to claim so. At least the sounds of the speaking voice, like those of the language of animals, need only to be fixed to become musical lines: that is what happens in effect when one sings, or when a canary repeats an air it has been taught: but as for noise, arrange it as you like, it will always be noise, and in consequence without the least relationship to music.

However the composers do not acknowledge that; one can not drive out of their heads the belief that their art embraces all objects the nature of which strikes our ear: what! Messieurs, because you sound many notes on your instruments, I must take that for battles, or for the impetuosity of the winds; because you sound several amphigories on the flute, I must think I hear a winding stream, or indeed the sigh of the zephyr; and you will demand that I confound the farting of the bassoon with claps of thunder or the sound of cannon; but do you really declare the resemblances to be very perfect?

Go to the marionettes, and you will hear there the noise of thunder one hundred times better imitated than by all the fracas of your orchestra. Take yourself to the representation of *Adelaïde du Guesclin*, and you will see what it is to imitate the sound of cannon.

Do you recall the Cabinet of Annette and Lubin? Is it not there that one can recognize the chirping of birds? If the Tempest of Roi and Le Fermier produces the illusion of a heavy rain, is it not the machine that is moved behind the scenes which produces the whole effect? Listen to the way hunters can imitate the quail, the lark, the partridge, the screech-owl, etc., and this so perfectly that the birds are fooled by it themselves: there is what I call imitation. Avow now that if you compare all these things with the feebleness of your means, it will not be possible to believe that music is an imitative art.

A modern author believes he has removed all these difficulties in saying that music imitates in its fashion. . . . A pleasant imitation, that of not imitating at all.

The musicians do not stop there: they wish absolutely to persuade us that they can imitate effects that have struck only their eyes, such as flashes of lightning, the rays of the sun, the progress of clouds, the course of the planets, etc. I think that it would be to lower oneself to the level of these pieces of childishness to pay serious attention to them. Let us content ourselves with laughing at them.

One thing that surprises me is not simply to see the ridiculous carried to the point of placing sleep, the peace of night, solitude, and silence among the models of the pretended musical imitation, but to see the pains that J.J. Rousseau takes to justify such chimeras. Here is how he explains himself in the article "Opéra" of his *Dictionnaire*:

> When all of nature has fallen asleep, the one who contemplates it does not sleep, and the art of the musician consists in substituting for the insensible

image of the object that of the movements which its presence excites in the mind of the spectator: he does not represent distinctly the thing; but he awakens in our soul the same sentiment that one experiences in seeing it.

First of all, it suffices to interrogate composers to convince oneself that they have never had the intention that J.J. Rousseau supposes of them. Secondly, if that were so, it would remain to be proven that the spectator of nature asleep sings or plays the violin. Is it not easier to imagine that when J.J. Rousseau wrote his remark, he was asleep himself?

After having said what music is not, it is time to examine what it is. It would be superfluous, without doubt, to remark its deficiencies, if one did not pay attention to the effects that determine its essence.

The principal object of music is to please us physically, without the mind putting itself to the trouble of searching for useless comparisons to it. One should regard it entirely as a pleasure of the senses and not of the intelligence. As much as one strives to attribute the cause of the impressions that it makes us experience to a moral principle, one will only be losing one's way in a labyrinth of extravagances: in vain will one search for music there; it will steal away ceaselessly from the efforts of our reason; but when one acknowledges that a concert is to the hearing what a banquet is to the sense of taste, what perfumes are to the sense of smell, and what fireworks are to the eyes; then one will be able to flatter oneself with having adopted the system of truth, and consequently the only one that is in accord with the principle of musical sensations.

. . . . .

CHAPTER SIXTEEN

MICHEL PAUL GUI DE CHABANON

Observations sur la musique
(1779)

CHAPTER II

IS MUSIC AN ART OF IMITATION?
IS ITS PRINCIPAL OBJECT TO IMITATE?

All the arts are an imitation of nature. This principle, accepted from earliest Antiquity, has been transmitted to the moderns with the weight of an authority that is nearly absolute: we almost regard it as an axiom. I am not at all surprised by this; it has a kind of obvious truth, and its simplicity recommends it above all. But this very simplicity that makes it accepted indiscriminately for all the arts in order to submit them to a common principle, perhaps constitutes a defect of this axiom when it is applied too generally. To judge if it is suitable to music as well as to the other arts let us seek to know music well, and to do so let us go back to the simplest idea of it that we may obtain. It is in this way that chemistry proceeds in respect of matter and metaphysics in respect of ideas; both decompose the object of their research through the route of analysis, and know it that much better for having reduced it to its simplest elements.

What is music? *The art of making tones succeed one another in conformity with regulated movements and in accordance with appreciable degrees of intonation that render the connection of these tones agreeable to the ear.* In this definition we do not include harmony at all, because we do not judge it to be essentially connected with the foundation of the art. Centuries passed without men being acquainted with it, and even now ordinary people, like many foreign and savage nations, have not learned to employ it at all.

The whole essence of music is thus comprised in the single word *song* or *melody*. The principle of the art being thus recognized, nothing remains but to confront it with all the accessories one might wish to join to it: those which may be of such a nature as to contradict the constitutive principle will be of such a nature as to be rejected. Finally, since what is proper to music is singing, to demand of it what it cannot do by singing is to inflict absurd laws upon it, and to subject it to this is to pervert it and denature it.

Everyone will readily avow that music should sing, that it is only by singing that it can please. How, in agreeing on that truth, do we agree so little about good or bad music? There are words in the language that everyone believes they understand and no one understands precisely; such is the word *genius*. Its use is familiar, its application difficult. What disputes to determine whether La Fontaine and Racine are geniuses! It is thus that the word *song*, employed by persons whose taste differs, does not have in their mouth the same meaning. What is songlike and agreeable for ears experienced in music is not so for those that have heard it rarely. "How much escapes us in song," said Cicero, "and how the practice of the art teaches us to hear"![1] There is not a single opera of Rameau, beginning with *Castor*, which did not at first endure as many outrages as it later received eulogies. "Lulli, whom we judge so simple and so natural, appeared excessive in his time. It was said that he corrupted the taste of dance, that he caused it to degenerate into badinage, because he accelerated the movements of the music."[2] Thus Lulli himself received the reproaches that he passed on to his successors: thus a man of genius bequeaths to the genius who replaces him, like a heritage of property, the abuse that oppressed him in its error and prejudice; and the larger part of the public finishing always by being of the opinion of the one who is right, finds itself to have defamed itself in defaming the new talent that enlightened it.

Let us return to the question that occupies us: should music according to its essence imitate?

I observe first of all that the charm of this art does not exist only for beings endowed with understanding and speech, such as man. Animals are responsive to it. This musical instinct is sufficiently recognized in the cat and in the spider. "Deer," says Plutarch, "are moved by the sound of the flute. To excite the stallion close to the mare, one plays a melody to him. Dolphins at the sound of instruments raise their heads above the water and perform different bodily movements almost like actors."[3] To this authority let us join that of Buffon: it is he who speaks as follows:

[1] *Cicer. acad. quest.*
[2] *Essai sur l'Orig. des Connoissances Humaines & Réfl. critiques sur la Poésie & la Peinture.*
[3] *Plut. sympos.*

The elephant has an excellent sense of hearing; he delights in the sound of instruments, and appears to love music: he easily learns to mark the measures and to move in cadence, even to join in on the occasion of certain accents with the beat of the drums and the sound of the trumpets. I have seen several dogs that have a marked taste for music, and that have made their way to a concert from the poultry-yard or from the kitchen, remained there throughout the time it lasted, and then returned to their usual domicile. I have seen others quite exactly sound the unison of a high tone that some one close by made them hear by crying out into their ear: but that sort of instinct or faculty among dogs is possessed by only a few individuals. A driver sings or whistles almost continuously at oxen to keep them moving in their most laborious tasks, and they stop and appear discouraged when their driver stops whistling or singing. We know how horses become animated at the sound of the trumpet, and dogs at the sound of the horn. It is claimed that porpoises, seals, and dolphins approach ships when during a calm interval they are allowed to hear loud music: but this fact has not been reported by any serious author.[4]

Several species of bird, such as canaries, linnets, goldfinches, bullfinches, and siskins, are very susceptible to musical impressions, since they learn rather lengthy melodies. Nearly all other birds are also affected by sounds: we are familiar with the contests of the nightingale with the human voice or with some instrument. There are a thousand particular examples of the musical instinct of birds. The fact of the spiders who descend from their work and keep themselves suspended while an instrument continues playing, and who then reascend to their usual place, has been attested to me by so large a number of eye witnesses that it can scarcely be called into doubt.

I have myself observed more than once this fact concerning the spider: it is above all slow and harmonious music that seems to please this insect and to attract it. I have also seen little fish that were kept in a tank of which the upper part was uncovered, search for the sound of a violin, rise to the surface of the water to hear it, raise their heads, and remain motionless in that position: if I approached them without playing the instrument, they seemed frightened, and dived to the bottom of the tank. I have repeated this experiment twenty times.

The musical instinct recognized in animals is still more perceptible in the babe in arms. This weak creature, whose reason is, so to speak, like its limbs, enveloped in the swaddling clothes of infancy, enjoys tones before having a single distinct and precise idea. The song of a nurse soothes his woes, calms his impatience, and brings him a happiness attested to by his innocent smile.[5]

Let us transport ourselves into the forests inhabited by fierce and undisciplined peoples. There we shall see music, the inseparable companion

[4]Monsieur de Buffon does not recall that it was by Plutarch.
[5]It is an established fact that, in infancy, we have sensations a long time before knowing how to extract ideas from them. *Essai sur l'Origine des Connoissances humaines.*

297

of man, and like him reduced to the most savage instinct. Music taken thus in its infancy, should preserve all the characteristics of its natural constitution, and all its original qualifications which no convention has falsified. Let us see if in that state it seeks to imitate.

The savages employ music in their festivals, which are military or funereal; and their songs, in the fashion they name them themselves, are songs of war or of death. What idea is there of the modulated accents by which fierce people rejoice in a barbaric victory or prepare for a bloody execution? If ever music should paint or express it is in this circumstance. Yet the songs of savages have none of the characteristics of which our imagination judges them to be susceptible. Their melody is gentle and gay rather than terrifying, and (as we must take note) the song of war which should be vigorous and noisy does not differ from the song of death: this is neither sad nor slow.[6] The same incoherence of song and speech makes itself felt in the songs of the negroes who people our colonies. They set into song all the events they witness; but whether the event be happy or disastrous, the melody has nevertheless the same character.

Sailors, and in general all common people and peasants, put into their song that indefinable drawling inflection that gives it a character of sadness: but they are happy at the same moment at which they sing sadly. Thus music for them is not a language or expression: it is not an art that imitates, or that even seeks to imitate.

CHAPTER III

CONTINUATION OF THE SAME INQUIRY.

Let us give to the principle we have just established all the extension of which it is susceptible; let us carry it to the point of exaggeration: all the steps that we shall take beyond the truth will not be unfruitful for our investigation. To exceed our limits in this way is to be familiar with the approaches to the place in which we seek to render ourselves impervious to attack.

To take the words in their strict meaning, song can imitate only that which sings; what am I saying? Its power does not extend to that point. The singing of birds could never be rendered well by our music because it obeys laws, harmonic relationships; while birds, inaccurate melodists, connect their tones following an order that harmony does not acknowledge. Also, since

[6]These songs will be found notated in an appendix.

the time when lyric poets summoned the birds to the aid of the art they befriended, that art, ineffectual in its means, has not reproached itself again with the truth of that imitation. A strange art of imitation, if it renders the things that are most analogous to it in such a fashion that the copy never resembles the model!

I should not keep secret the responses the Abbé Morellet made to this difficulty which he proposed to himself: the more ingenious it is, the more we have a duty to cite it.[7]

> Musical imitation does not need to be complete, or exact, or rigorous: it should in fact be imperfect, and different from nature in some respect.
>
> All the arts make a kind of pact with the soul and the senses that they affect: this pact consists of demanding licenses, and of promoting pleasures that they would not give without these licenses. . . . Music takes parallel licenses. It demands to cadence its progress, to round its periods, to support and to reinforce the voice by the accompaniment, which certainly is not found in nature. That without doubt alters the truth of the imitation, but at the same time augments its beauty and gives to the copy a charm that nature has refused to the original.
>
> Nothing so much resembles the song of the nightingale as the sounds of the little pipe that children fill with water and that their breath makes warble. What pleasure does this imitation give us? None at all. But let one hear a light voice, an agreeable symphony that expresses (less faithfully without doubt) the song of the same nightingale; the ear and the soul are in raptures: the arts are something more than the exact imitation of nature.

I am aware of all the ingenuity and truth that are contained in this response: but let me be permitted to ask Abbé Morellet why poetry, painting, and sculpture are confined to giving us images of the objects they imitate that are faithful, true, and similar, while music is exempt from this? Is it not because this art is less an art of imitation than the others? The children's pipe, although it imitates with the greatest perfection an effect agreeable in itself (the warbling of the nightingale), gives us no pleasure: on the contrary, a light symphony which has only a very slight resemblance to that warbling but whose song is melodious—this symphony, I say, flatters and rejoices our ear; do not these two facts brought together unite to prove that imitation has little part in the agreeable effects of music, and that the charm of melody constitutes nearly all of them?

But, you will say, if music is not an imitation of nature, what then is it? Strange need of the human spirit to torment itself with difficulties that it forges itself, and to detain itself with the meaning of captious words which when thoroughly examined have none! Music is for hearing what the

---

[7]The little tract in which Abbé Morellet discusses musical expression is full of perceptive and accurate views: I do not know if anything finer has been written concerning music.

objects that affect them the most delightfully are for each one of our senses. And what indeed, when a lovely face attracts your glances and fixes them through an irresistible charm, does imitation have in common with the pleasure you feel? It is entirely foreign to this. Why then do you not wish the ear to have, like the eyes, the sense of smell, and the sense of touch, its voluptuous sensations and its immediate pleasures? Are there others such for it than those that result from tones harmoniously combined? Is it because it has pleased you to call music an art that you intend to subject it to the common definition of the arts? We shall see in what follows the extent to which this denomination is suited to it: let us accomplish the proof that it pleases independently of all imitation.

CHAPTER IV

MUSIC PLEASES INDEPENDENTLY OF IMITATION.

Animals are susceptible to music; therefore it does not need to imitate to please; for the most perfect imitation is nothing to an animal. Present its image to it sketched on a canvas, it is neither affected by it nor surprised. One enjoys imitation only to the extent that one comprehends its difficulty: now that comprehension surpasses the intelligence of animals.

The baby who is pleased at the songs of his nurse seeks in them nothing imitative: he enjoys them like he enjoys the milk on which he is nurtured.

The savage, the negro, the sailor, and the common man repeat the artless songs that amuse them without even bringing their character into agreement with the actual disposition of their soul.

A skillful hand that preludes on the harp or on the clavecin engages the most learned ears. But imitation in no way presides over the formation of a prelude, which only runs successively through various chords.

Music has comforted, even cured people who were ill. That fact is attested to by the *Mémoires* of the Academy of Sciences, and I have seen the proof of it. A young person bled six times for acute pain of the eye forgot his suffering for two hours in listening to clavecin playing. Is it by virtue of imitation that such a spell operates? Is a spirit overwhelmed by suffering in a state to enjoy a pleasure that demands reflection?

Music therefore acts immediately on our feelings. But the human spirit, that swift, active, curious, and reflective intelligence, enters into the pleasure

300

of the senses. It is not able to be a dormant and indifferent spectator of it. What part can it play in sounds, which having in themselves no determinate signification, never present clear and precise ideas? It searches in them for relationships, analogies with various objects or various effects of nature. What does it achieve? Among the nations whose intelligence is perfected, music, jealous in some way of obtaining the approbation of the spirit, strives to present to it those relationships, those analogies, which please it. Music imitates to the extent that it can and by the express command of the spirit, which, drawing it beyond its direct purpose, proposes imitation to it as a secondary purpose. But the spirit in its aspect that evaluates the weakness of the means that music employs to arrive at imitation, gives itself little difficulty on this point. The slightest analogies, the faintest relationships are sufficient for it: it calls this art *imitative* when it hardly imitates: it is grateful to it for the efforts it has made to please it, and is content with the part assigned to it in the pleasures that would seem to be made uniquely for the ear.

When one is not in any way blinded by the systematic spirit, and does not seek to impose it either on oneself or on one's readers, one should certainly not pass over in silence the most contrary objections to the sentiments one is professing. Here is one of this nature, which at first intimidated me in my opinion. "If the pleasure of music is for the ear what a beautiful face is for the sense of sight, why do we feel more impelled to make one of these sensations imitative than the other?" Aristotle in his *Problems*[a] proposed to himself in other terms the same difficulty that we propose to ourselves here; the solution he gave to it is the one to be read now: All sensation produced by an object without movement can hardly be imitative, it can have no conformity with our actions, our morality, and our character. Let only one tone be heard by the ear and prolong its duration; this dead and inactive sensation will never be able to depict the spirit. By way of contrast, let several tones succeed one another as music does; their slow or rapid progression, uniform or differentiated, will give them a character and render them susceptible to being assimilated to other objects. Let us observe that this is proper only to music. Indeed if one affects successively the sense of touch, the sense of smell, and even the sense of sight through the presence of several objects that replace one another, one will never arrive at that effect that the succession of musical tones produces. Each of the impressions that the other senses receive is isolated, and quite independent of those that follow it and those that precede it: that is so much the case that one can look at or smell a rose after such and such other flower without the coloring and the perfume of the rose being modified by it. It is quite another thing in music: each tone that sounds depends on the one that has preceded it; and according to the relationships of tones that succeed one another, they

[a]The Pseudo-Aristotle *Problems*, compiled about 100 A.D.

301

assume a character of gentleness or asperity, of languor or vivacity. Let us learn accordingly not to judge one of our diverse sensations by the other at all; and let us not apply indistinctly to music everything that may be true of the other arts.

CHAPTER V

IN WHAT MANNER MUSIC PRODUCES ITS IMITATIONS[8]

Here we are, already far from the paradox that at first we had appeared to support, that music lacks proper means of imitation: in departing from that exaggerated assertion we find ourselves brought back to the examination of the means by which music imitates. It assimilates (as far as it is able to) its sounds to other sounds, its movements to other movements, and more than all of that, its sensations to our feelings. This last manner of imitating will be the subject of a separate chapter.

Musical imitation is obviously genuine only when it has songs for its object; I will explain. In music, one imitates with veracity military fanfares, hunting calls, rural songs, and so on because it is a matter then of giving to one melody the character of another melody: with song one imitates song, the art in that suffers no violence. But in going beyond that, imitation wanes and is weakened by reason of the insufficiency of the means that music employs.

Is it a matter of depicting a brook? The weak and continued fluctuation of two notes adjacent to one another makes the melody undulate nearly like water that flows along. This relationship that presents itself first to the mind is the sole one that the art has seized upon up to the present, and I doubt that a more striking one will ever be discovered. The intention of depicting a brook will thus bring all the musicians who have it together in a melodic form already known and almost worn out. The disposition of the notes is as though foreseen and given in advance: the melody, a slave of that constraint, will have little grace and novelty. According to this calculation, the ear loses in that depiction nearly all that the mind gains.

---

[8]This chapter is one of those in which our ideas are conformable to those of the Abbé Morellet.

Let one join to the depiction of brooks the warbling of birds; in this case the imitative musician has long cadences sustained by the voice and by the instruments; he mixes in roulades, although there is not a single bird that has ever sung roulades. This imitation has the double disadvantage of being, for one thing, very imperfect, and for another, of subjecting the musician again to forms often employed. Abbé Morellet is full of praise for the Italian aria of which the words are: *Se perde l'ussignuolo*, etc. Without recalling this aria distinctly, I would dare the guaranty that the section of it which is the most pleasing is not that which endeavors to imitate the song of the nightingale.

I will make the supposition of a skillful composer, necessitated by the words to depict a bubbling wave and a warbling bird; would we dare to blame him if he reasoned as follows? "My art can not render truthfully the effects that my poet expects of it: in striving to attain them I run the risk of resembling all those who have essayed the same tableau. The painting of streams, flowers, gentle breezes, and foliage is judged so lyrical only because the sight of a pleasant and sylvan landscape produces on our senses a gentle impression, and disposes our soul to a blissful peace: if accordingly, abstaining from the imitation of what I am not able to render, I imagined only a gracious and tranquil melody such as one would desire to hear when one rests in the cool shade with a view of the most beautiful countryside, would I fail my poet and my art?" If this reasoning artist was a man of talent in the least, if he knew how to execute such a plan ever so little, I do not know what the partisans of imitation would have to reproach him with.

The sky is covered with clouds, the wind whistles, the thunder extends its long reverberations from one end of the horizon to the other. . . . How weak music is in portraying such effects, above all if the musician interests himself in detailing them; if he wants a rising or falling volley of notes here to express lightning, or the force of the wind, or the crash of thunder; for he has the choice; he can give to this picturesque feature one denomination or another; no one has an authentic proof to contradict him on this point. Instead of these fruitless efforts to depict truthfully what one does not know how to depict, let the artist imitate in a vaguer fashion and by noise the commotion of the tempest. Let the drums, the kettledrums reinforce the symphony and augment its tumult; and above all let the melody be such that it not permit anyone who listens to say: *all that is only noise.*

I attended an evening concert on the boulevard one day: the orchestra was numerous and very loud; the overture to *Pigmalion* was being played: the weather foreboded a storm; at the *fortissimo* of the reprise a clap of thunder was heard: everyone, like me, sensed a marvellous connection between the symphony and the weather that roared in the heavens; Rameau found himself, in that moment, to have produced a tableau of which until then neither he nor anyone had suspected the intention or the resemblance.

Musical artists who reflect on your art: does not this example teach you something?

There is an effect in nature that music renders with sufficient verity; it is the roaring of the waves in anger. Many basses playing in unison and making the melody roll like the billows that rise and fall back, create a tumult similar to that of the agitated sea. We all formerly heard a symphony in which the composer, without a pictorial intention, had placed that unison: its imitative effect was so generally felt that this symphony was called the *tempest*, although there was nothing else which could justify that denomination. Would not the reader, in keeping with such facts, be right to call music the *art of portraying without uncertainty*?

Let us speak of another imitation, of that which depicts with one of our senses what is subject to another sense, as when sound imitates light.

Everyone knows the story of the man blind from birth, to whom a painting was presented in which there was seen a mountain, trees, people, and herds of animals. The incredulous blind man carefully ran his hand over all the parts of the canvas, and finding there only a plain surface, could not conceive the representation of so many different objects. This example demonstrates that one sense is no judge at all of what another sense experiences: also it is not properly for the ear that one paints in music what strikes the eyes: it is for the mind, which placed, as we have said, between these two senses, combines and compares their sensations. Tell the musician to paint light taken abstractly and he will acknowledge the impotence of his art: tell him to paint the dawn and he will feel that the contrast of clear, piercing tones placed in opposition to heavy, veiled tones, can resemble the contrast of light and darkness. From this point of comparison, he makes his means of imitation: but what in fact is he painting? Not the day and the night; but only a contrast, and any contrast whatever: the first that one might imagine will be entirely as well expressed by the same music as that of light and darkness.

Let us not hesitate to repeat it for the instruction of artists: the musician who produces such tableaux does nothing if he does not produce them with fortunate melodies. Painting is only the second of his duties; singing is the first. If he does not satisfy in this, what merit will he have? Through the weakness of his art he paints imperfectly; through the weakness of his talent he fails in the resources of his art.

Why does music paint what strikes the eyes while painting does not even try to render what is in the province of hearing? Painting is constrained by its essence to imitate; if it does not imitate, it is no longer anything: able to speak only to the eyes, it can imitate only what is perceptible to sight. Music on the contrary pleases without imitation, by the sensations that it procures; its pictures being nearly always imperfect, and consisting sometimes in an imperceptible analogy to the object that it wishes to depict, such connections easily multiply. In a word, painting imitates only what is proper to it, because it must imitate strictly. Music can paint nearly everything, because it paints everything in an imperfect manner.

CHAPTER VI

WHAT THE ADVANTAGES AND DISADVANTAGES ARE WHICH RESULT FROM THE INTENTION TO PAINT AND TO IMITATE IN MUSIC.

The essential and almost unique advantage of imitation joined to music is to unite to interesting situations that art which lends them a new interest, and which itself receives from this a new charm. Here examples will instruct better than arguments.

That symphony which I mentioned just now and which seemed to make the sea roar in anger, heard at a concert, never excited more than the amusement of the spirit, astonished by an imitative result that it was not expecting. That symphony heard at the theater, and tied to the situation of the young Hero expecting her lover in the night on the shores of the Hellespont, would become a tragic scene. It is in this way that the overture of *Iphigénie en Tauride*[b] announces and commences a majestic and terrible spectacle. Abruptly affected through all his senses at the same time, the spectator hears and sees the tempest; the turmoil and the concern penetrate into his soul through all the paths that can lead to it. In one of the repetitions of this work, it was proposed to silence the machine that imitated thunder, so that the music might be better heard: this was to prefer the illusion to the truth itself, and the musicians maintained that it should be that way; but the truth of the spectacle and the general opinion prevailed.

The overture to *Pigmalion*, worthy of being applauded on all sides, would be so with much more enthusiasm if it participated in the interest of a situation which was appropriately united with it. Chance revealed to us the analogy of certain features of this overture to claps of thunder: it is well if during this symphony an unfortunate creature threatened by the lightning blunders upon the theater with long strides to escape the roaring of the heavens that pursues him; music will receive from the situation an interest it gives to it, and both heightened, the one will live upon the other.

[b]The opera by Gluck.

Transport music away from the stage, and it will gain little by rendering itself imitative: into various arias, into various monologues performed in the concert hall, the interest of the situation will hardly penetrate: stripped of everything that grounds it, prepares it, animates it, and excites it, that interest grows cold like the glowing iron when it is withdrawn from the furnace: what shall I say? Outside the theater, the sole advantage perhaps of music with words over that which has none of them at all, is that the one aids the weak intelligence of the demi-connoisseurs and the ignorant in fixing the character of each piece by indicating the meaning, which they would not conceive without this help; while purely instrumental music leaves their spirit in suspense and in uneasiness over the signification of what they are hearing. The more one has a practised ear, sensitive and endowed with musical instinct, the more one dispenses easily with words, even when there is a singing voice; not one of the instrumentalists who perform in a concert orchestra hears the words articulated by the singer, and yet nobody is so strongly moved by the song of a capable man. I am persuaded that if anyone wanted to explain to these instrumental musicians what the singer meant, they would take up their instrument, and repeating the vocal part, would respond, "This is what the singer said."

But how explain that abuse so great, so general, of desiring that to every simple and tuneful melody words be added; whether they be feeble, mannered, or spiritualized; whether lifeless madrigals, or commonplaces worn out to the point of disgust: it makes no difference, one believes one serves the melody by clothing it in these unbecoming laces: to criticize the abuse would be to accomplish nothing; it is better to look for the cause of it, which perhaps will be its excuse.

Without doubt no instrument pleases our ear as much as the human voice: it is the one which in general the greatest number of people prefer; and we will not admit that the human vocal organ, accustomed to pronounce words, limits itself even in singing to presenting only sounds: from this there probably arises our indulgence for all those words so little singable which people like to sing. The emptiness and the ridiculousness of these not very lyrical follies are as though made up for by the merit that they have of adapting to the human voice that which without them would not be suitable there. We forgive the words for the sake of the instrument that pronounces them. Hardly do these songs without character and without expression deserve to be cited as imitative music; it is on the subject of imitation, however, that we have spoken of them. We have explained the advantages of imitation joined to music; let us explain the unfortunately too common disadvantages that result from the intention of painting and imitating by means of tones.

These disadvantages would not exist if the direct end of music was to imitate. Every musician who adhered to imitation would make art adhere to

306

its natural end, and would run no risk of losing his way; but imitation being only the accessory, and not the principal point, the essential of the art, it is to be feared that in occupying oneself with it too much, one will neglect what is the first necessity. We have already seen how the painting of various natural effects limits and constrains the conduct of the melody: let it not be doubted that outside the theater (where the other arts complete the imitation, and where the interest of the situation seconds its effect), one would not long sustain these crude pictures, which elaborate nothing with much truth, as the endeavors of the melody to express what it can not convey. What kind of concert would it be in which one would wish to present to the listener without respite varied pictures, even if they were designated by words? Either I am very much mistaken, or the listener, wearied by this musical optics, would demand that one spoke a little less to his eyes and more agreeably to his ears. Let us conclude this chapter with some examples that will serve to demonstrate that imitation in the art of music is necessarily only secondary.

The overture of *Pigmalion*, composed without any pictorial intent, becomes a tableau through the sole effect of its melody. The overture of *Acante et Céphise*,[c] in which rockets, fireworks, and cries of *vive le Roi* were painted, is a piece without effect, which neither paints nor sings. The overture to *Naïs*,[d] during which the Titans scale the heavens, does not seek to paint either the crags that rise up, nor those that fall back, and so on. It sings in a manner austere and vigorous, and the piece produces an effect. Mondonville, in one of his motets, wishes to describe the daily journey of the sun: he has the chorus sing the complete scale two times in two different octaves, rising and descending, which conducts the melody circularly and leads it back to the point from which it had departed: in *Tithon*, the same composer, to paint the break of dawn, has his whole orchestra proceed gradually from low to high, and at the end he keeps the instruments hovering at the top of the octave. Here are two tableaux just as perfect, just as faithful, as music might produce: why do these two pieces remain without effect and without fame? In the superb duet of *Sylvain* (a product of Monsieur Grétry, which, like so many others of the same composer, will not give way, among us, before any masterpiece of Italy), I see the same melody applied to these words contradictory to one another: "*Je crains—j'espère— qu'un juge—qu'un père,*" etc. The most avowed partisans of imitation might nevertheless applaud this magnificent duet: as much as melody exercises an irresistible domination in music, so much the preponderance of those who reason about that art have poorly analyzed its means, and give themselves little account of the true causes of their pleasures.

[c]Another Rameau opera.
[d]Still another Rameau opera.

A last consequence that one can not refrain from deducing from what we have just put forward, is that the works of Monsieur Gluck, if they were not filled with a new, touching, and varied melody, would never have produced the effect that we see them produce.

CHAPTER VII

SONG IS NOT AN IMITATION OF SPEECH.

The painting of impressions referred to our senses is called *imitation*; the painting of our feelings is called *expression*; it is of the former that we are now going to speak. First of all, we have to combat an error rather generally established, and from which there arise a multitude of errors; it is that song is an imitation of speech; or, to explain ourselves again with more clarity, that the man who sings should strive to resemble the one who speaks. May we be pardoned if we expatiate a little in the development of our opinion on this point; we have to struggle against the force of a prejudice in which we believe the multitude to be steeped; of a prejudice which the philosophers and men of genius have allowed and extended.

In order that song should be an imitation of speech, it would have to be subsequent to it in its institution; but, let us take care here, it necessarily preceded it.

The employment of speech supposes an established language: but does that not suppose the establishment of a language? I will not repeat what the best metaphysicians have written on this subject. I will not mark out at all the slow and successive degrees by which man had to pass from simple cries of need to various imitative sounds, and from these sounds to various words that might resemble them. To point it out in passing, this formation of languages, probable in some respects, in some others lacks probability. If all languages were derived from the imitation of objects and of natural impressions, they would all, in that common origin, have to have taken on resemblances and a character of uniformity which they do not have. In all languages, the words that express *the sea, a river, a torrent, a brook, the wind, thunder,* and so on would have to be about the same, since they would all have been instituted and chosen to imitate the same things. If one compares the Greek words which correspond to those we have just cited, one will find that they have nothing in common. Let us return to our subject. I accept what

308

Monsieur Rousseau has written on the origin of languages; "it is," he says, "so difficult to explain, that without the help of an established language, we do not conceive how it has been possible for us to have established one."[9] The origin of song does not present these difficulties to us at all; Monsieur Rousseau himself seems to have felt this. He depicts savage man for us, isolated in the forests, "leaning against a tree, and amusing himself by blowing into a sorry flute, without ever knowing how to draw from it a single tone." That which the savage did not know how to do with the flute, he knew without difficulty with his voice: the organ furnished him the tones; and instinct, with which we have recognized the animal, the child, and the savage to be endowed, that musical instinct indicated to him the order in which he should arrange the tones he uttered.

When we suppose that man sang only after having learned to speak (which cannot be admitted), it would still be necessary for him to have made a trial of his voice, his melodic instinct, and to have formed some songs, before dreaming of uniting song and speech: thus in every causal state the one subsisted independently of the other, and instrumental music necessarily preceded vocal; for when the voice sings without words, it is no more than an instrument. All the philosophers, up to the present, have regarded the vocal as anterior to the instrumental, because they have regarded speech as the mother of song, an idea which we believe absolutely false.

The processes of the one and the other differ entirely. Song admits only intervals perceptible to the ear and to calculation; the intervals of speech can be neither perceived nor calculated. That is true for ancient languages as it is for modern ones. Open Aristoxenus, in his *Elements of Harmonics*; see Porphyry's *Commentary on Ptolemy*; interrogate all the Greek musicians; read Cicero, Quintilian, and so on. All have said, "Speech rambles confusedly over steps that one cannot estimate; music has all its intervals estimated and known." I know that Dionysius of Halicarnassus determined the Greek accents as the interval of a fifth. We shall seek to explain the passage elsewhere;[10] let it suffice for us here to state that this same Dionysius of Halicarnassus has transmitted to us the notated melody of a few verses of Euripides, and that he specifies that this melody formally contradicts the prosodic intonation. Accordingly, even among the Greeks, among that people whose language, we are told, was a music, song still differed entirely from speech. Not only does the perceptibility of the intervals distinguish song from other language, but the trills or shakes, the extensions or roulades, the steadiness of a series of measures, the employment of refrains or rondeaux, the return of the same phrases both in the principal key and in the accessory keys, the harmonic co-existence of tones, etc. etc. etc., in short,

---

[9] *Notes sur l'égalité des Conditions.*
[10] In the second part of this work.

all the processes of song, deviate from those of speech, and often contradict them. They have nothing in common with the organ to which they belong.

What! Oratorical accent well imitated is, according to some philosophers, one of the principal sources of expression in music; and Quintilian, whose language is, in their opinion, so musical, forbids the orator to speak as one sings!

Monsieur Rousseau advises the musical artist to study grammatical accent, oratorical or impassioned accent, and then to join musical accent to it. I am very much afraid that the artist who devotes himself to these preliminary studies might not have the time to get to those of his art. Where is the musician who became a grammarian, an orator, and a tragic and comic actor before adapting his melodies to words?

If musical expression is tied to the prosodic expression of language, there can not be for us an expressive music on Latin words: for we are ignorant of the prosody of the Romans. What will become then of the expression of the *Stabat Mater,*[e] the work of a musician who pronounced Latin differently from us? How did that Armenian, whom Monsieur Rameau observed in Italy, enjoy from the very first the music of that country, whose language he did not know?

Italy has abounded for a long time in celebrated composers; it reveals few actors of a very distinguished talent. In France, we excel in declamation, even by the admission of foreigners; and the first lesson we give to our actors, is not to sing: why would we counsel our musicians to imitate our actors? That implies a contradiction.

What shall we say of instrumental music? That plan deprives it of all expression, since instruments have nothing in common with language. What! The ritornello of the *Stabat Mater* is devoid of expression? What! Tambourins and *allemandes* do not contain the expression of gaiety?

The least musical part of music is simple recitative, which tends to approach speech. It is there that song casts off all the melodic embellishments, trills, portamentos, little suspended notes, long holds; finally, the very meter, in the recitative of dialogue, becomes uncertain and fluctuating. In spite of this privation of song, reduced solely to fixed and musical intonations, through this sole property, recitative differs essentially from speech; it calls for a bass throughout, and speech never calls for one.

If you wish to comprehend still better how false is the principle *that the merit of song is to resemble discourse,* see how Monsieur Rousseau is at a loss, and even bewildered, in wanting to establish it. "What one seeks to render by the melody," he says, "is the manner in which the feelings are expressed that one desires to represent: and one should take good care not to imitate in

---

[e]The setting of Pergolesi, which was universally admired.

this the declamation of the theater, which itself is only an imitation, but the. voice of nature speaking without affectation and without art."

What follows from this? What! A musician who desires to set to music the most beautiful arias of Metastasio should not imitate the declamation an excellent actor would give them but the simple and familiar manner of conversation? But the words of these arias are not susceptible of a simple and familiar manner: since it is impossible in an ordinary conversation for anyone ever to utter verses such as those of Metastasio extemporaneously, there is no simple and familiar manner at all that might be applied to these verses: do not search for it; the manner does not exist at all. What is beautiful and perfect declamation? It is the truest manner that one might (in accordance with the various genres) give to the discourse one is pronouncing. If the style is polished, studied, elegant, elevated, and sublime, the declamation should take on its level, and distance itself from the familiar and popular manner. If then the music of operas had to imitate speech, it would be to the declamation of these operas that it would have to conform. In this case, each tragedy of Metastasio would not have been set to music in twenty different ways, for I do not think that there would be twenty ways of declaiming the same thing. Take the air of Alceste, "*Je n'ai jamais chéri la vie*";[f] take the one of Roland, "*Je vivrai, si c'est votre envie*";[g] give them to the most intelligent and sensitive actor to declaim; and you will discover whether the conduct of his voice approximates that of the two composers.

CHAPTER VIII

THE EXPRESSION OF SONG DOES NOT CONSIST IN THE IMITATION OF THE INARTICULATE CRY OF THE PASSIONS.

What extraordinary thing has not somehow been asserted of music from the moment one lost sight of the fact that its constitutive principle is melody? All the power of that art, it has been said, consists in imitating the inarticulate cry of the passions. But from a cry how does one make a song? There is what

[f]From Gluck's *Alceste.*
[g]From Lully's *Armide.*

troubles me. Does the precept reduce to inserting the cry of a passion into a melody? It is then no more than an accident of the art, and of the melody; it is no longer its ground, its foundation, and its essence.

One can not deny, I think, that music is susceptible of gaiety; it is one of the feelings which most closely belong to it. What is then the inarticulate cry of gaiety? Laughter. You would search in vain for the imitation of it in those tambourins, in those *provençales*, in those *allemandes*, which spill the feeling of gaiety out over an assembled multitude, and which excite convulsive movements of joy. Have you observed that the gaiety which arises from music does not at all conduce to laughter? It lightens all of the limbs, and puts the body into an active and alert state. I do not know anything less cheerful in music, than the melodies to which one has the actors in the theater laugh: the actor laughs, but the music does not do its share with him; the imitative intonation of laughter that one desires to give to it, destroys its gaiety, and saddens its character.

The *Stabat Mater* is commonly accepted as bearing an expression of grief; one does not find in it an imitative cry.

Monsieur Gluck, whose genius has more than any other, if I am not mistaken, sought for and attained musical expression, has often in his melodious songs plaintive notes that recall the accent of grief, and on these notes he calls upon the singer to approximate the natural accent. At the first performance of *Orphée*, the principal actor approximated it a little too much. He put too much verity into the heart-rending cry which at intervals broke through the song of the disconsolate Thracians: he noticed it, and softened it. He had in some way departed from his art to make himself fully receptive to nature; the instinct of taste drove him back, and made him begin within his natural limits again: the imitation lost in its verity, but it became musical, and was more enjoyed.

Several of our passions have no cry at all that is proper to them; yet music expresses them. Instruments incapable of the cries of the human voice are no less the eloquent interpreters of its energy and of the expression of music. *"Natura ducimur ad modos: neque aliter enim eveniret ut illi quoque organorum soni, quamquam verba non exprimunt, in alios, atque alios ducerent motus auditorem."* Quintilian, in this passage, does not say: instruments affect us because they imitate words and cries; he says: "Nature has made us sensitive to melody. Otherwise, could it be that instruments which do not articulate a word would instill in us so many different agitations?" There is the true remark, which explains all; "nature has made us sensitive to melody: *natura ducimur ad modos.*" All music that pleases people versed in melody is certainly melodious. But how does music, without imitating speech, or cries, express the passions? It assimilates to our diverse feelings, as much as it is able, the diverse sensations that it produces; it is this that we shall now develop.

312

CHAPTER IX

OF THE MUSICAL FEELINGS APPLICABLE TO OUR DIVERSE FEELINGS, AND OF THE NATURAL MEANS OF EXPRESSION PROPER TO MUSIC.

Such and such a song pleases you, you like to hear it; this cannot be because it produces on you any impression whatever. Study this impression, investigate its nature and its character; it is impossible that you would not recognize whether it is sharp or sweet, ardent or tranquil; the movement alone would indicate it to you. It is gentle and tender: Apply to it words of the same species, and you will render music expressive that you did not suspect previously of being so; of a sensation almost vague and indeterminate you make a feeling of which you can give an account to yourself.

I beg the reader to control his imagination, not to allow it to progress more rapidly than this discussion will permit: he will find a little further on the developments and the clarifications that he has a right to expect from us.

The air that we call *tender* does not perhaps constitute in us exactly the same situation of body and mind that we would have in actually pitying a woman, a father, a friend. But between these two situations, the one actual, the other musical (if we may be pardoned for this way of speaking), the analogy is such that the mind consents to take the one for the other.

Why, one will say, do you require that the effect of such music be only a sensation, and not a distinct feeling?—Reader, I require it so, because in interrogating you after an air without words which has given you pleasure, if I ask you what distinct sensation it awakens in you, you will not know how to tell me. I suppose a tender air, I ask you if it is the tenderness of a happy or unhappy lover that the air instills in you; if it is that of a lover for his mistress, or of a son for his father, etc. etc. etc. If all these different feelings are equally appropriate to the air which is in question, am I wrong in calling the effect rather a slightly vague sensation than a definite feeling? Moreover, I will repeat it again, let us not progress more rapidly than is necessary; what we are bringing forward here in a general and superficial manner, elsewhere will be determined with more exactitude.

What are the natural means that give to the melody a character of sadness or of gaiety, of softness or of resolution? Reader, in engaging to resolve such questions, I advance, so to speak, into the darkness with which nature conceals and surrounds all first causes. I shall go as far as the torch of experience will conduct me; and the more obscure the matter is, the more I will make it a duty to set down only incontestable assertions.

It is the nature of protracted tones to convey a character of sadness. Do not think that this is a fact of convention: no; men have not made a pact between them to find the cry of the turtle-dove plaintive, and the song of the blackbird joyous. Since the nightingale intermingles several tones with one another, and sounds them together, you will attach to this musical language an idea less sad than if the solitary bird caused us to hear in the night a tone that it prolonged for some time. Is it not recognized that a uniform sound, such as that of a voice which reads on the same tone, induces us to sleep? If sound brings about that immediate effect on us, why should we deny other effects which contain nothing more astonishing?

The minor mode produces, in general, a sweeter, softer, and more sensitive impression than the major mode. Do not ask the reason for this; nobody is in a position to tell it to you; but the passage from one of these modes to the other renders that different impression perceptible to every musical ear. In the minor mode, the sixth note of the key is more tender than all the others: every time it makes its appearance, were it even in the gayest allegro, it exacts from the executant a softer and more tender inflection: in the major mode, it is the fourth note of the key that has this property; it is the one which, by its intrinsic virtue, keeps summoning the executant to a pathetic expression, even when the rest of the melody leads him to a different sensation. High tones have some indefinable clarity and brilliance that seem to incite the soul to gaiety. Compare the high strings of the harp with the low strings of the same instrument, and you will feel how the latter more readily dispose the soul to tenderness: who knows whether the large undulations of the long and less taut strings do not communicate similar vibrations to our nerves, and whether that propensity of our body is not the one which will give us tender sensations? Man, you may believe me, is only an instrument; his fibers respond to the strings of the lyrical instruments which assail them and interrogate them: each tone has its properties, and each instrument also, from which the melody profits skillfully, but which it also controls at its pleasure; for the most sensitive instrument can articulate joyous melodies with success.

Tender music employs movements without rapidity: it binds the tones, it does not set them into contrast at all, make them come into collision with one another. In music of this character, the staccato breve does not imperiously dominate the dotted long to which it is joined; and the executant alters his tones by means of liberal vibratos. Those whose taste inclines to sadness, draw out the tones (in accordance with the observation we have already made), their bow is afraid to leave the string; their voice gives to the melody some indefinable indolence and laziness. Joyous music dots the notes, makes the tones skip about: the bow is always in the air, and the voice imitates it.

Such are pretty much the natural means that music employs, and through the aid of which it produces sensations in us. The composer, a man of talent, who has felt all these effects, and who applies them suitably to the words and to the sensations, is an expressive musician. The reader will see with clarity that all the means of expression are within the province of melody, not of harmony.

One essential observation, which is connected with the very foundation of our doctrine, is that in the most expressive air, there are nearly always, I would even say, there are necessarily features, passages, contradictory to the character of expression which is to dominate in it. Let us cite an example. In the first verse of the *Stabat Mater*, I do not see a line, not a word, that does not call for the same nuance of sadness.

> *Stabat Mater dolorosa,*
> *Juxta crucem lacrimosa,*
> *Dum pendebat Filius.*[h]

Music in the commencement deploys all its means of expression. The movement is slow, the tones weak and veiled; they are slowly drawn out, they are slurred: there is the expression, well established. At the tenth measure, everything changes: a *fortissimo* succeeds the *piano*: the tones which were creeping obscurely in the lower part of the scale, suddenly rise up, gather excessive strength; and through a proud, detached articulation, jar with and contradict those that have preceded them. What can this disparity come from? From music in its essence being not at all an art of imitation: it lends itself to imitation as much as it can; but that office of compliance can not distract it from the functions which its very nature imposes on it. One of these necessary functions is to vary its changes at each instant, to associate in the same piece the *gentle* and the *strong*, the *prolonged* and the *detached*, the proud articulation and that which is tender. This art, thus considered, is of an ungovernable inconstancy: all its charm depends on its rapid transformations; I know that in each piece it returns often to the same things, but without ever stopping there. Now, through all these passing and fugitive forms, how do you want the imitation to be one and the same, and to proceed with an even tread? It follows playful and changeable music with a halting step, overtaking it sometimes, and sometimes allowing it to go on alone. If the proof of what I put forward is found in the first couplet

[h]There the grieving mother stood
Weeping beside the cross
On which her son was crucified.

of the *Stabat Mater*, so beautiful, so expressive, so short, and composed with two single ideas, in what Italian aria will this proof not reveal itself still more obviously?

Now, reader, however little a musician you may be, you are in a position to judge the dramatic system of Monsieur Gluck; you will understand why, being devoted to the expression that he regards rightly as the foundation of all theatrical illusion, he permits himself an entire air only when the situation itself permits to music those digressions, those vague deviations in which melody delights. Every time that a periodic and coherent melody would make the action languish, and would transform the actor into a singer at his music-stand, Monsieur Gluck cuts to the quick this melody which has begun; and by another movement, or by a simple recitative, he puts the singing back into the course of the action, and makes it run along with it. It is inconceivable that a system so true, could have been disapproved of in a country where the art of the theater is so well known; it is still more inconceivable that among its disapprovers, there have been men, who by their position and their enlightenment, should defend the rights of the scene against those of the music. In Italy, men of letters have said that music of the theater was almost no longer for the enjoyment of intellectuals. Here, intellectuals, hardly musicians, have affirmed that the operas of Monsieur Gluck were made more for the mind than for the ears; and while they were delivering this judgment, the most fastidious and the most practised ears were feeding with delight upon the music of Monsieur Gluck: I do not think that there have ever been judgments more calculated to astonish.

CHAPTER X

EXTENSION OF THE PROOFS OF THE PRECEDING CHAPTER. UNITY OF THE ART RESULTING FROM OUR SYSTEM.

If you force song to serve the imitation of speech, if you make it depend on the character of the language and of prosodic inflections, you create two arts in place of one. The vocal will have its principles; and the instrumental will also. Music which is *one* for all the people of the earth when they employ in it the voice of the instruments, will be entirely different in consequence of the diverse idioms. The French musician, who knows neither German nor Italian will understand nothing of the song of these two peoples: the foreign virtuoso arriving at Paris, for whom some one will offer to accompany an air of Monsieur Grétry, or of Monsieur Philidor, will be obliged to respond, "Excuse me, I do not know French." More parody: the *Colonie*, composed to Italian words, is necessarily wretched in French. *Orphée, Alceste*, the same, etc. etc. etc. Observe where a poorly established principle leads you. Recognize a truer one. Music is simply song; song differs from speech; it has its separate processes, which do not depend upon the pronunciation of words. Consequently instrumental melody is like vocal; music of the concert like that of the dance; that of the theater like that of the church; that of Europe like that of Asia. Art becomes *one* in all its parts.

Twenty years ago it was not thought at all at the Opéra that the voice could or should do what the instrument did. A ritornello began and said one thing; the voice unexpectedly arrived afterwards to say another. It is no longer that way; the orchestra and the actor speak the same language; the same spirit animates them and identifies them.

I do not think that there exists a truly beautiful instrumental piece that one might not appropriate for the voice by joining words to it. If it is a resounding symphony, we shall make of it a chorus, simplifying for the voice what the violin executes; removing from the midst of the sixteenth-notes the ones that constitute the outline and the framework of the melody. (Those who are versed in music will understand me.) Duets, trios, clavecin pieces, all can be compounded with words, provided that the music has character.

The Italians, like us, seem to acknowledge two different musics for the church and for the theater. I do not admit that distinction. On what should it be based? On the custom of the *fugues* introduced into churches? They are worth no more there than elsewhere; boredom is not good anywhere. The music of the church should move the faithful, so that they direct their holy emotions to God: that music should accordingly be lyrical and expressive. The difference between the sacred and the profane does not exist at all for the composer; whether he has to have the Magi sing, prostrate before the star they worship, or the Hebrews at the foot of Mount Sinai, radiant with the glory of the Lord; these two situations, for his art, constitute only one; they call for the same character of music, noble, august, and religious.

Also let us reflect that the beginning of the *Stabat,* sung in chorus, and very softly, around the tomb of Castor, would be perfectly appropriate to the situation. Also we have seen the most lyrical airs of the motets of Mondonville playing a part marvelously at the dressing-table, arrayed in words that were nothing less than pious.

The dance participates in this unity of musical art. Formerly one would not dance a symphonic *adagio*, an *allegro*: today everything that is melodious and characteristic is danced. At a concert, the auditors are inclined to picture to themselves here *Vestris*, there *Dauberval*, and so on; the imagination transfers to the eyes the pleasure of the ears. In seeing music simplify and generalize its relationships with poetry and dance, who will not believe, on the one hand, that it is perfecting itself, and on the other, that we, who consider it under this head of unity, are forming a just idea of it?

We have just said a word in passing about dance; let us be permitted a digression on that art.

Additional Reading

Batteux, Charles. *Les Beaux arts réduits à un même principe*. Paris, 1746. (reprint of the new edition of 1747: Paris, 1970).

_____ *Cours des belles-lettres*. Paris, 1747.

Boyé. *L'Expression musicale, mise au rang des chimères*. Amsterdam, 1779.

Chabanon, Michel Paul Gui de. *Observations sur la musique*. Paris, 1779.

Ecorcheville, Jules. *De Lully à Rameau, 1690-1730; L'esthétique musicale*. Paris, 1906.

Frässdorf, W. "Der Begriff der Nachahmung in der Ästhetik J.J. Rousseaus." *Archiv für Geschichte der Philosophie* 35, 1923.

Goldschmidt, Hugo. "Die konkret-idealistische Musikästhetik im 19. Jahrhundert." *Zeitschrift für Ästhetik und allgemeine Kunstwissenschaft* 6, 1911.

Morellet, André. *Mélanges de littérature et de philosophie*. 4 vols. Paris, 1818.

Maniates, Maria Rika. *"Sonate, que me veux-tu?*; the Enigma of French Musical Aesthetics in the 18th Century." *Current Musicology* 9, 1969.

Serauky, Walter. *Die musikalische Nachahmungsästhetik im Zeitraum von 1700 bis 1850*. Münster, 1929.

PART EIGHT

The Contest of Language and Mathematics

Language and mathematics constitute two basic explanatory principles of music, for the most part sharply opposed in their nature as well as in the characteristics of music they purport to explain. The conflict is closely related, as we can see in the ideas of Girolamo Mei and in the aesthetics of Mattheson and Krause, to the conflict of simplicity and complexity. In the eighteenth century, language and mathematics were connected respectively with melody and harmony (or counterpoint), which also represented spontaneity and artificiality. Newer and simpler styles, under the banner of nature, replaced Baroque elaboration, in a conflict that increasingly became one of social class as well. It was a conflict also between national style and international style, since melody, akin to language, expressed the genius of each nation, while mathematics was ostensibly unaffected by local and cultural differences. Rameau is fundamentally blind to the possibility that his arguments might have any national or historical limitation.

As the outstanding representative of the view that music is a mathematical science, Rameau produces an eighteenth-century equivalent of the quad-rivial science of harmonics, applied now to the project suggested by Descartes in his *De musica* but abandoned by him, of turning aesthetics into a mathematical science. At the same time, Rameau does not fail to account even for the expressive force of melody on mathematical grounds. His *Observations* (1754) is one of the almost numberless replies to Rousseau's famous *Lettre sur la musique francaise* (1753), which provoked a storm of contention. Rameau draws into his discussion the same operatic recitation from Lully's *Armide* that Rousseau had cited—a famous monologue that Rameau had already used in 1726 (in his *Nouveau système*) to illustrate modulation and the fundamental bass. In the history of specific aesthetic controversy this passage occupies a prominent place alongside the air from Gluck's *Orphée* which Boyé seems to have been the first to discuss and which subsequently played an important part, starting with Hanslick, in nineteenth- and twentieth-century aesthetics.

In spite of Rameau's Pythagorean view of music, and his complete insensitivity, as a corollary, to national, social, and historical differences of style, his position in the controversy has its own progressive aspect. For on the central issue of musical expressiveness, the thesis of the priority of harmony effectively freed music from the shackles of imitation, while melody, on the other hand, even in instrumental music, was closely identified with the imitation of language and of the affections, and therefore subject to the musically restrictive influences of the Enlightenment.

But if harmonic theory had its own implication for the understanding of musical expressiveness, it was nevertheless generally subject to criticism in an age dominated by a rhetorical view of music. Rameau was of course the principal target. Mattheson directs a powerful polemic against the mathe-matical conception and explanation of music in the Introduction of *Der*

321

vollkommene Capellmeister (1739) and Herder is still more persuasive in the fourth of his *Kritische Wälder* (1769), subjecting physics as well as mathematics to his criticism. Finally in his *Kalligone* (1800), he vehemently opposes Kant's *Critique of Judgment* (1790) and withdraws music entirely from the external world of science. The coming century would clearly belong to the conception of music as utterance.

CHAPTER SEVENTEEN

JEAN-JACQUES ROUSSEAU

Essai sur l'origine des langues
(1753)

CHAPTER XII

THE ORIGIN OF MUSIC AND ITS RELATIONS

With the first voices were formed the first articulations or the first sounds, according to the various types of passion which dictated them. Anger arouses menacing cries articulated by the tongue and palate; but the voice of tenderness is gentler, it is the glottis that modifies it, and this voice becomes a tone; only its accents are more rare, the inflections more or less sharp, according to the feeling that is joined to it. Thus cadence and sounds are born with syllables; passion makes all the organs speak, and endows voices with all their luster; thus verse, song, speech have a common origin. Around the fountains of which I spoke, the first discourses were the first songs; the periodic recurrences and measures of rhythm, the melodious inflections of accents, gave birth to poetry and music together with language, or rather all of that was only language itself for those happy climes and happy times, in which the only pressing needs that called for the concurrence of others were those to which the heart gave birth.

The first tales, the first orations, the first laws were in verse; poetry was devised before prose; that had to be so, since passions speak before reason. It was the same with music; there was at first no music at all other than melody, no other melody than the varied tone of speech; accents constituted singing, durations constituted measure, and one spoke as much by tones and by rhythm as by articulations and words. To speak and to sing were once the same thing, says Strabo; which shows, he adds, that poetry is the source of eloquence.[1] We should say that both had the same source, and at first were but the same thing. In view of the manner in which the first societies were held together, is it surprising that the first narratives were put into verse and that the first laws were sung? is it surprising that the first grammarians subordinated their art to music, and were professors of both at the same time?[2]

A language which has only articulations and words thus has only half of its resources; it conveys ideas, it is true; but to convey feelings, images, it must also have a rhythm and tones, that is, a melody; this is what the Greek tongue had, but what ours lacks.

We are always astonished over the prodigious effects of eloquence, of poetry, and of music among the Greeks; these effects do not make sense to us because we no longer experience anything similar; and all that we prevail upon ourselves to do, in seeing them so well attested, is to pretend to believe them out of consideration for our scholars.[3] Burette, having transcribed, as well as he could, certain fragments of Greek music into our musical notation, had the naivety to have these fragments performed at the Academy of Belles-Lettres, and the academicians had the patience to listen to them. I admire that experiment in a country whose music is indicipherable to every other nation. Have a French operatic monologue performed by whatever foreign musicians you please, and I defy you even to recognize it; yet it is these same Frenchmen who would pretend to judge the melody of an ode of Pindar set to music two thousand years ago!

I have read that once the Indians in America, seeing the stupifying effect of firearms, would collect musket balls from the ground; then throwing

---

[1] *Geography*, Bk. 1.

[2] "Archytas and Aristoxenus also considered grammar to be included under music, and the same masters taught both. . . . Then too, Eupolis has Prodamus teaching both music and letters. And Marcias, who is Hyperbolus, admits that he knows nothing of music except letters." Quintilian, Bk. 1, Ch. 10.

[3] Doubtless we must modify Greek exaggeration in everything, but it is also giving way too much to modern prejudice to press these modifications to the point of making all the differences disappear. "When Greek music in the time of Amphion and Orpheus," says Abbé Terrasson, "reached the point at which it is today in the cities most remote from the capitol, it interrupted the course of rivers, it attracted oak trees, and moved cliffs. Today when it has arrived at a very high point of perfection, it is much loved, its beauties have even been penetrated, but it leaves everything in its place. It has been thus with the verses of Homer, a poet born in times which still knew the infancy of the human spirit, compared to those which followed. We are enraptured by his verses, but we content ourselves today with enjoying and esteeming fine poets." One cannot deny that Abbé Terrasson knows something of philosophy, but he certainly does not show it in this passage.

them by hand while making a loud noise with their mouth, they were quite surprised not to have killed anyone. Our orators, our musicians, our scholars, resemble these Indians. The marvel is not that with our music we no longer do what the Greeks used to do with theirs; it would be a marvel, on the contrary, if with instruments so different the same effects were produced.

CHAPTER XIII

ON MELODY

Man is changed by his senses, no one doubts it; but instead of distinguishing the changes, we confuse their causes; we give much too little dominion to sensations; we do not see that often they do not at all affect us only as sensations, but as signs or images, and that their moral effects also have moral causes. Just as the feelings that painting arouses in us do not come at all from colors, the dominion that music has over our souls is not at all the work of tones. Beautiful colors well nuanced are a pleasing sight, but that pleasure is purely one of sensation. It is the drawing, it is the imitation that gives these colors life and soul; it is the passions they express that come to stir ours; it is the objects they represent that come to affect us. The interest and the feeling do not adhere at all to the colors; the features of a picture that touches us touch us still in a print; remove those features in the picture, and the colors will no longer have any effect.

Melody does precisely in music what drawing does in painting; it is melody that betokens the features and the figures of which the chords and the tones are only the colors. But, you will say, melody is only a succession of tones. Without doubt; but drawing is also only an arrangement of colors. An orator makes use of ink to trace out his compositions; is this to say that ink is a highly eloquent liquid?

Imagine a land where no one had any idea of drawing, but where many people, passing their time in combining, mixing, and nuancing colors, thought they excelled in painting. Those people would talk about our painting in precisely the same way that we talk about the music of the Greeks. When we spoke of the emotion that beautiful pictures arouse in us and of the charm of being moved before a pathetic subject, their scholars would compare their colors with ours, would examine whether our green is more tender, or our red more brilliant; they would try to discover which harmonies of colors can produce tears, which others can evoke anger; the Burettes of that country would assemble on rags a few deformed fragments of our pictures; then they would ask themselves with surprise what was so marvellous in this coloring.

And if in a neighboring country, some line was indicated, some rough plan of drawing, some figure still imperfect, all of that would pass for daubing, for a capricious and baroque painting; and people would adhere, to preserve taste, to that simple beauty which actually expresses nothing, but displays beautiful nuances, large highly colored slabs, extended gradations of tints without a single line.

Finally, perhaps, through the force of progress, people would arrive at experiments with the prism. At once some celebrated artist would base a beautiful system on it. Gentlemen, he would say to them, to philosophize truly, it is necessary to go back to physical causes. Observe the decomposition of light; observe all the primary colors; observe their relations, their proportions, observe the true principles of the pleasure that painting gives you. All those mysterious words of drawing, of representation, of figure, are the pure charlatanry of French painters, who by their imitations think they give I do not know what movements to the soul, while we know that these are nothing but sensations. You hear of the marvels of their pictures; but look at my colors.

The French painters, he would continue, have perhaps observed a rainbow; they have been able to obtain from nature some taste for nuance and some instinct for coloring. As for me, I have shown you the great, the true principles of art. What am I saying, of art! Of all the arts, gentlemen, of all the sciences. The analysis of colors, the calculation of prismatic refractions, give the only exact relationships that exist in nature, the rule of all relationships. Now everything in the universe is only relationship. One knows everything, then, when one knows how to paint; one knows everything when one knows how to match colors.

What should we say of a painter sufficiently devoid of feeling and of taste to reason in such a way, and to stupidly restrict the pleasure that painting gives us to the physical nature of his art? What should we say of a musician who, full of similar prejudices, believed he saw in harmony alone the source of the great effects of music? We should assign the first to painting wainscotting, and we should condemn the second to making French operas.

Just as painting, then, is not the art of combining colors in a manner pleasing to the eye, so music is equally not the art of combining sounds in a manner pleasing to the ear. If that was all that was involved, both of them would belong to the natural sciences and not to the fine arts. It is imitation alone which raises them to this level. Now what is it that makes painting an art of imitation? It is drawing. What is it that makes music one also? It is melody.

CHAPTER XIV

ON HARMONY

The beauty of sounds belongs to nature; their effect is purely physical; it results from the concourse of diverse particles of air set into movement by a sonorous object and by all its aliquot parts, perhaps to infinity; the effect of the whole is pleasing. Everyone in the world will take pleasure in hearing beautiful sounds; but if this pleasure is not animated by melodious inflections that are familiar to them, it will not be delightful at all, it will not become at all voluptuous. The most beautiful songs, to our taste, will always barely affect an ear not accustomed to them; they will be a language for which we need a dictionary.

Harmony properly speaking is in a still less favorable situation. Having only conventional beauty, it in no way gratifies ears that are not practiced in it; we must become habituated to it over a long period of time to be sensitive to it and to savor it. Uncultivated ears hear only noise in our consonances. When natural proportions are altered, it is not surprising that natural pleasure no longer exists.

A tone carries with it all its concomitant harmonics, in the relationships of intensity and of interval that they should have between them to produce the most perfect harmony of that same tone. Add to it the third or the fifth or some other consonance; you do not add it, you double it; you do not change the intervallic relationship, but you alter the relationship of intensity. In reinforcing one consonance and not the others, you destroy the proportion; wanting to do better than nature, you do worse. Your ears and your taste are corrupted by an art that is poorly understood. Naturally there is no other harmony at all than the unison.

Monsieur Rameau claims that treble parts of a certain simplicity suggest their basses naturally, and that a man having a true ear that is untrained will naturally intone that bass. This is a musician's prejudice, given the lie by all experience. Not only will the person who has never heard harmony or bass fail to discover harmony or bass for himself, but they will even displease him if he is allowed to hear them, and he will enjoy the simple unison much more.

Though one calculated the relationships of tones and the laws of harmony for a thousand years, how would one ever make of that art an art of imitation? Where is the principle of this supposed imitation? Of what is the harmony a sign? And what is there in common between chords and our passions?

If we apply the same question to melody, the response comes automatically; it is already in the reader's mind. Melody, in imitating vocal inflections, expresses laments, cries of sorrow or joy, threats, moans; all the vocal signs of the passions are within its province. It imitates the accents of languages, and the affective turns in every idiom that are caused by certain movements of the soul; it does not imitate alone, it speaks, and its language—inarticulate but alive, ardent, impassioned—has a hundred times more energy than speech itself. From this arises the force of musical imitation; from this arises the dominion of song over sensitive hearts. Harmony can contribute to this in certain systems, by binding the succession of the tones to laws of progression; by making the pitches more accurate; by conveying to the ear an assurance of this accuracy; in adjusting and determining the connected consonant intervals by inappreciable inflections. But in shackling melody also, it deprives it of energy and expression; it effaces the passionate accent in order to substitute for it the harmonic interval; it subjects songs to only two modes which should have as many of these as there are oratorical tones; it effaces and destroys multitudes of tones or intervals which do not fit into its system; in a word, it so separates song and speech that these two languages combat one another, contradict one another, deprive one another of every characteristic of truth, and cannot reunite without absurdity in a pathetic subject. That is why people always find it ridiculous for powerful and serious passions to be expressed in song, for they know that in our languages these passions have no musical inflections at all, and that northern peoples, no more than swans, do not die singing.

Harmony alone is even insufficient for the expressions that seem to depend on it uniquely. Thunder, murmuring waters, winds, storms, are poorly rendered by simple chords. Whatever one does, noise alone says nothing to the mind; objects must speak to make themselves understood; always, in every imitation, a type of discourse must act as the voice of nature. The musician who wishes to render noise with noise deceives himself; he knows neither the failings nor the strength of his art; he judges it without taste, without insight. Teach him that he must render noise with song; that if he would make frogs croak, he must make them sing; for it is not sufficient that he imitate, he must touch and he must please; without which his unpleasant imitation is nothing; and not interesting anyone, it makes no impression.

CHAPTER XV

THAT OUR MOST LIVELY SENSATIONS OFTEN ACT THROUGH MORAL IMPRESSIONS

As much as one might want to consider tones only in terms of the agitation they excite in our nerves, one would learn nothing of the true principles of music and of its power over the heart. The tones of a melody do not act on us only as tones, but as signs of our affections, of our feelings; it is thus that they excite in us the movements which they express, and the image of which we recognize. Something of this moral effect is perceived even in animals. The barking of one dog attracts another. If my cat hears me imitate a mewing, I immediately see it attentive, anxious, agitated. If it perceives that it is I who am counterfeiting the voice of its kind, it sits down again and remains in repose. Why that difference of impression, since there is none at all in the agitation of the nerves, and since at first he himself was deceived?

If the greatest dominion our sensations have over us is not due to moral causes, why are we then so sensitive to impressions that are nothing for barbarians? Why are our most touching pieces of music only an empty noise to the ear of a Caribbean? Are his nerves different in nature from ours? why are they not agitated in the same way? or why do these same agitations affect some people so much and others so little?

Recovery from Tarantula bites is cited as proof of the physical power of tones. This example proves exactly the opposite. Neither definite tones nor the same tones are required to cure all those who are bitten by this insect; what is required for each one of them are tunes of a piece that is familiar to him and statements that he understands. For an Italian, Italian tunes are required; for a Turk, Turkish tunes would be required. Each is affected only by accents that are familiar to him; his nerves yield to these only insofar as his mind disposes them to; he must understand the language that is spoken to him, in order that what he is told may set him into movement. The cantatas of Bernier, it is said, cured a French musician of fever; they would have given one to a musician of any other country.

In the other senses, even to the crudest of all, the same differences can be observed. If a man with his hand placed and his eye fixed on the same object, successively believes it to be animate and inanimate, although his senses are affected in the same way, what a change in the impression! The roundness, the whiteness, the firmness, the gentle warmth, the elastic resistance, the repeated expansion, would not provide him with more than a soft but insipid touch if he did not think he felt a heart that was full of life palpitating and beating underneath.

I know of only one sense in the effects of which nothing moral is mingled: it is taste. And gluttony is thus the dominant vice only of people who can taste nothing.

Let those who wish to philosophize, then, on the power of sensations, begin by separating from purely sensuous impressions the intellectual and moral impressions which we receive by way of the senses but of which the senses are only the occasional causes; let them avoid the error of endowing sensible objects with a power that they do not possess, or that they owe to the affections of the soul which they present to us. Colors and tones can do much as representations and signs, but little as simple objects of sense. Successions of tones or of chords will amuse me for a moment, perhaps; but to charm me and to touch me, these successions must offer me something that is neither tone nor chord, and that moves me in spite of myself. Even songs that are only pleasing and say nothing are wearisome; for it is not so much that the ear conveys pleasure to the heart, as that the heart conveys it to the ear. I believe that by developing these ideas more fully, we should really be spared foolish arguments over ancient music. But in this century when we are obliged to materialize all the operations of the soul, and to remove all moral ingredients from human feelings, I shall be deluded if the new philosophy does not become just as disastrous for good taste as for virtue.

CHAPTER XVI

FALSE ANALOGY BETWEEN COLORS AND SOUNDS

There are no kinds of absurdity to which physical observations have not given rise in the consideration of the fine arts. The same relationships have been found in the analysis of sound as in that of light. At once this analogy was seized upon eagerly, without concern for experience and for reason.

The systematic spirit confused everything; and not knowing how to paint for the ears, one undertook to sing for the eyes. I have seen that famous harpsichord on which one claimed to compose music with colors; it was certainly to be poorly acquainted with nature not to see that the effect of colors is in their permanence, and that of tones in their succession.

All the riches of coloring are spread simultaneously over the face of the earth; at the first glance everything is seen. But the more we look the more we are enchanted; no more is required than to admire and contemplate ceaselessly.

It is not thus with tone; nature does not analyze it and separate its harmonics at all; she hides them, on the contrary, behind the appearance of the unison; or if she sometimes separates them in the modulated song of man and in the warbling of some birds, it is successively, and one after the other; she inspires melodies and not chords, she dictates melody and not harmony. Colors are the dress of inanimate beings; all material is colored; but sounds announce movement; the voice announces a sensible being; it is only animate bodies that sing. It is not the automaton flutist who plays the flute, it is the mechanic, who measures the wind and causes the fingers to move.

Thus each sense has its domain which is proper to it. The domain of music is time, that of painting is space. To multiply the tones heard at one time, or to develop colors one after the other, is to change their economy, is to put the eye in place of the ear, and the ear in place of the eye.

You say: just as each color is determined by the angle of refraction of the ray that conveys it, so each tone in the same way is determined by the number of vibrations of the sounding object in a given time. Now the relations of these angles and of these numbers being the same, the analogy is evident. Granted; but that analogy is one of reason, not of sensation, and it is not reason that concerns us. First of all, the angle of refraction is sensible and measurable, but not the number of vibrations. Sounding objects, subject to the action of the air, change incessantly in volume and in tone. Colors are durable, tones vanish, and it is never certain whether those that are reborn are the same as those which were extinguished. Further, each color is absolute, independent, while each tone is only relative for us, and is distinguished only by comparison. A tone in itself has no absolute character which makes it recognizable: it is low or high, loud or soft, in relation to another; in itself it is none of these. In the harmonic system, any tone whatever, in its nature, is nothing more; it is neither tonic nor dominant, neither harmonic nor fundamental, because all these properties are only relationships, and since the entire system is able to vary from low to high, any tone will change in its order and in its place in the system according as the system changes in pitch. But the properties of colors do not consist at all of relationships. Yellow is yellow, independent of red and of blue; it is sensible and recognizable everywhere; and as soon as we have determined the angle of refraction that produces it, we are sure of having the same yellow at all times.

Colors are not in colored objects, but in light; for an object to be seen, it must be illuminated. Tones also need a mover, and in order for them to exist, a sonorous object must be agitated. That is another advantage of sight, for the perpetual emanation of the heavenly bodies is the natural instrument which acts upon it; while nature alone engenders few tones; and unless we accept the harmony of the celestial spheres, animate beings are required to produce it.

We see by this that painting is closer to nature, and that music owes more to human art. We feel also that the one concerns us more than the other, precisely because it brings man together more with man and always gives us some idea of our kind. Painting is often dead and inanimate; it can transport you to the center of a desert; but as soon as vocal signs strike your ear, they announce a being like yourself; they are, so to speak, the organs of the soul; and if they also represent the solitude to you, they tell you that you are not there alone. Birds whistle, man alone sings; and one cannot hear either song or symphony without realizing at once, Another intelligent being is here.

It is one of the great advantages of the musician to be able to paint things that one cannot hear, while it is impossible for the painter to represent those that one cannot see; and the greatest marvel of an art which acts only by movement is to be able to shape it even into the image of repose. Sleep, the calm of night, solitude, and silence itself, enter into musical depictions. We know that noise can produce the effect of silence, and silence the effect of noise, as when we fall asleep to a steady and monotonous reading, and when we awaken the instant it stops. But music acts more intimately on us, exciting affections through one sense that are similar to those which can be excited through another; and since the relationship can not be perceptible unless the impression is strong, painting, devoid of that power, cannot return to music the imitations which the latter draws from it. When all of nature has fallen asleep, the one who contemplates it will not be sleeping, and the art of music consists of substituting for the insensible image of the object that of the movements its presence excites in the heart of the contemplator. Not only will it agitate the sea, animate the flames of a conflagration, make brooks run, rain fall, and torrents swell; but it will paint the horror of a frightful desert, cast a gloom over the walls of a subterranean prison, calm a tempest, render the air tranquil and serene, and diffuse from the orchestra a new freshness over the woodlands. It will not represent these things directly, but it will excite in our soul the same feelings that we experience in seeing them.

CHAPTER XVII

AN ERROR OF MUSICIANS HARMFUL TO THEIR ART

See how everything continually leads us back to the moral effects of which I spoke, and how far from knowing wherein the effect of their art resides are the musicians who consider the power of tones only in terms of the action of air and the agitation of fibers. The more they connect it with purely physical impressions, the more they remove it from its origin, and the more they deprive it also of its primitive energy. In abandoning its vocal accent and adhering solely to harmonic principles, music becomes noisier to the ear and less pleasing to the heart. It has already ceased speaking, soon it will no longer sing; and then with all its chords and all its harmony it will no longer have any effect on us.

CHAPTER XVIII

THAT THE GREEK MUSICAL SYSTEM HAD NO RELATION TO OURS

How have these changes occurred? Through a natural change in the character of languages. It is known that our harmony is a Gothic invention. Those who claim to find the Greek system in ours are mocking us. The Greek system had absolutely no harmony in our sense except what was required to determine the tuning of instruments from the perfect consonances. All people who have string instruments are compelled to tune them by consonances; but those who do not have them have inflections in their songs which we call false because they do not fit into our system and we cannot notate them. This is what has been observed about the songs of the American savages, and this is what necessarily would have been observed also about various intervals of Greek music, if that music had been studied with less prejudice in favor of our own.

The Greeks divided their system by tetrachords, as we divide our keyboard by octaves; and the same divisions are repeated exactly in each of their tetrachords, as they are repeated exactly in each of our octaves; a similarity that could not have been preserved in the unity of a harmonic style and that would not even have been thought of. But as we progress by smaller intervals when we speak than when we sing, it was natural that they regarded the repetition of the tetrachords in their vocal melody as we regard the repetition of the octaves in our harmonic melody.

They recognized as consonances only those that we call perfect consonances; they rejected from their number the thirds and the sixths. Why? It is because the interval of the minor tone being ignored by them, or at least proscribed in practice, and their consonances not being tempered at all, all their major thirds were too large by a comma, their minor thirds too small by the same amount, and consequently their major and minor sixths altered reciprocally in the same way. Let us imagine now what ideas of harmony we could have and what harmonic styles we could establish by excluding thirds and sixths from the consonances. If even the consonances they admitted had been known to them through a true feeling of harmony, they would have at least suggested them behind their melodies, the tacit consonance of the fundamental progressions would have lent its name to the diatonic progressions that the fundamental ones had suggested to them. Far from having fewer consonances than we do, they would have had more; and prejudiced, for example, by the bass *ut sol*, they would have given the name consonance to the second, *ut re*.

But, you will say, why the diatonic progressions, then? Through an instinct which in an accented and singing tongue makes us choose the most comfortable inflections: for between the overly great modifications that must be imposed on the glottis to intone continually the large intervals of the consonances, and the difficulty of regulating the intonation in the highly complex relationships of the lesser intervals, our vocal organ adopts an intermediate course and falls naturally into intervals smaller than the consonances and simpler than commas; which does not prevent lesser intervals from having their use also in more pathetic genres.

CHAPTER XIX

HOW MUSIC HAS DEGENERATED

To the degree that language advanced, melody, in subjecting itself to new rules, lost its ancient energy, and the calculus of intervals was substituted for the finesse of inflections. It was in this way, for example, that the use of the enharmonic genus gradually disappeared. When the theaters had taken a regular form, there was no longer singing in them except in prescribed modes; and to the degree that the rules of imitation multiplied, the imitative languages grew weaker.

The study of philosophy and the progress of reason, having perfected grammar, deprived language of that vital and impassioned tone that had originally made it so melodious. From the time of Melanippides and Philoxenus, the symphonists, who originally were engaged by the poets and worked only for them, and to their dictates, so to speak, became independent of them; and it is this license of which "Music" complains so bitterly in a comedy of Pherecrates, of which Plutarch has preserved the passage for us. Thus melody, beginning by no longer adhering so closely to discourse, gradually took up an existence of its own, and music became more independent of words. Then also, those marvels ceased that it had produced when it was only the accent and the melody of poetry, and when it endowed it with that dominion over the passions that the word continued to exercise subsequently only over reason. Also, from the time that Greece was full of sophists and philosophers, there no longer dwelt there either celebrated poets or celebrated musicians. In cultivating the art of persuasion, people lost the art of arousing the emotions. Plato himself, jealous of Homer and of Euripides, decried the one and was not able to imitate the other.

Soon servitude added its influence to that of philosophy. Greece in chains lost that fire which warms only free spirits, and no longer found, to praise its tyrants, the tone in which it had sung its heroes. The intermingling of the Romans weakened still more what remained of melody and accent in the language. Latin, a duller and less musical language, did harm to music by adopting it. The singing employed in the capitol, gradually altered that of the provinces; the theaters of Rome ruined those of Athens. When Nero carried off the prizes, Greece had ceased to deserve them; and the same melody, shared out to two languages, suited the one less than the other.

Finally there occurred the catastrophe which destroyed the progress of the human spirit, without removing the vices of which it was the product. Europe, inundated by barbarians and enslaved by illiterates, lost simultaneously its sciences, its arts, and the universal instrument of both, namely, harmoniously perfected language. Those coarse men engendered by the North gradually accustomed every ear to the roughness of their vocal organ; their hard voice devoid of accent was noisy without being sonorous. The emperor Julian compared the speech of the Gauls to the croaking of frogs. All their articulations, like their voices, were nasal and muffled; they could give only a sort of shout to their song, reinforcing the sound of the vowels to cover up the abundance and the harshness of the consonants.

This noisy song, joined to the inflexibility of the voice, obliged these newcomers and the subjugated peoples who imitated them to slow down all their sounds in order to make them understood. The laborious articulation and the exaggerated sounds contributed equally to expel from the melody any feeling of measure and rhythm. Since what was most difficlt to pronounce was always the passage from one sound to the next, there was nothing better to do than to stop on each as long as possible, to expand it, to make it sound out as much as one could. Song soon became no more than a tiresome and slow succession of dragging and shouted sounds, without sweetness, without measure, and without grace; and if some scholars said that longs and shorts must be observed in Latin song, it is certain at least that verse was sung like prose, and that there was no longer any question of feet, of rhythm, or of any type of measured song.

Stripped thus of all melody, and consisting solely in the force and the duration of sounds, singing was bound to suggest finally the means of rendering itself more sonorous again, with the aid of consonances. Several voices, dragging out tones of unlimited duration in unison, found a few chords by chance, which, augmenting the noise, made it seem pleasing to them: and thus began the practice of discant and of counterpoint.

I do not know how many centuries the musicians deliberated vain questions which the known effect of an unknown principle made them ask. The most indefatigable reader would not endure in Jean de Muris the verbiage of eight or ten long chapters in order to learn, in the interval of the octave divided into two consonances, whether it is the fifth or the fourth which should be on the bottom; and four hundred years afterwards we still find in Bontempi enumerations no less tiresome of all the basses that should carry the sixth instead of the fifth. But harmony gradually took the route that analysis prescribed for it, until finally the invention of the minor mode and the dissonances had introduced into it the arbitrariness of which it is full, and which prejudice alone prevents us from perceiving.[4]

---

[4]Relating all of harmony to that very simple principle of the vibration of the aliquot parts of strings, M. Rameau found the minor mode and dissonance on the alleged experimental observation that a sonorous string in motion makes other, longer strings vibrate at the twelfth and the major seventeenth below. These strings, according to him, vibrate and quiver in their whole length, but they do not resonate sympathetically. Here you have, it seems to me, a singular physical fact; it is as if one said that the sun shines and nothing is seen.

These longer strings, producing only the tone of the higher one, because they divide, vibrate, and resonate in unison, fuse their tone with the first, and seem not to produce any. The error is to have believed they are seen to vibrate in their whole length, and to have overlooked the nodes. Two sonorous strings forming some harmonic interval can make their fundamental tone below audible, but without a third string; this is the experiment known and confirmed by M. Tartini; but a single string has not other fundamental tone at all than its own; it does not make its multiples resonate and vibrate as such at all, but only its unison and its aliquots. As tone has no other cause than the vibration of a sonorous object, and since where the cause acts freely the effect always follows, to separate vibrations from their sympathetic resonance is to predicate an absurdity.

Melody being forgotten, and the attention of the musician being turned entirely towards harmony, everything was controlled gradually by this novel object; the genera, the modes, the scale, everything received new faces; it was harmonic successions that regulated the progression of the parts. That progression having usurped the name of melody, in this new melody, in effect, one could not fail to recognize the features of its mother; and our musical system having thus become, by degrees, purely harmonic, it is not astonishing that its vocal accent suffered and that music lost for us nearly all its energy.

That is how song became, by degrees, an art entirely separated from speech, from which it takes its origin; how the harmonics of tones caused the inflections of the voice to be forgotten; and how, finally, limited to the purely physical effect of the concourse of vibrations, music found itself deprived of the moral effects it had produced when it was the twofold voice of nature.

CHAPTER EIGHTEEN

JEAN PHILIPPE RAMEAU

Observations sur notre instinct pour la musique, et sur son principe
(1754)

PREFACE

The full enjoyment of the effects of music calls for a sheer abandonment of oneself, and the judgment of it calls for a reference to the principle by which one is affected. That principle is Nature itself; it is through Nature that we possess that feeling which stirs us in all our musical activities, she has made us a gift of it that one may call *instinct*: let us consult her, therefore, in our judgments, let us see how she develops her mysteries in us before declaring our sentiments: and if there still are men conceited enough to venture an opinion on their own authority, there is good reason to hope that there will not be others weak enough to listen to them.

A biased mind in listening to music is never in a free enough state to judge it. If in its opinion, for example, it connects the essential beauty of that art with passages from low to high, from soft to loud, from lively to slow, means which one makes use of to vary the sounds, it will judge everything according to that presumption without reflecting on the weakness of these means, on the small merit there is in employing them, and without being aware that they are foreign to harmony, which is the unique basis of music, and the principle of its greatest effects.

How very differently a truly sensitive soul will judge! If it is not affected by the force of the expression, by those vivid depictions of which harmony alone is capable, it is not at all fully satisfied: not that it does not know how to lend itself to everything that can entertain it; but at least it values things only in proportion to the effects it experiences.

It is to harmony alone that there belongs the arousal of the passions; melody draws its force only from that source, from which it emanates directly: and as to the differences of low and high, etc., which are only the surface modifications of melody, they therefore add to it almost nothing, as will be demonstrated by striking examples in the course of this work, in which the principle is verified by our instinct, and that instinct by its principle, which is to say, where cause is verified by the experienced effect, and that effect by its cause.

If the imitation of sounds and movements is not employed as frequently in our music as in the Italian, it is because the dominant object of ours is feeling, which has no determinate movements at all, and which in consequence can not be subjected at all to a regular measure, without losing that truth which constitutes its charm. The expression of the physical is in the measure and the movement, that of the pathetic, by contrast, is in the harmony and the inflections: which must be weighed carefully before deciding on what is to tip the scales.

The comic genre almost never having feeling for its object, it is by consequence the only one that may be constantly susceptible of those cadenced movements with which one does honor to Italian music, without remarking, however, that our musicians have quite fortunately employed them in the small number of essays which the delicacy of the French taste has permitted them to venture: essays in which one has felt, while enjoying oneself, how easy it would be for us to excell in this genre.[1]

One may regard this modest work as the result of all those I have presented on the same subject: and I hope that I may be granted, in that case, a few repetitions which are necessary for the information of anyone who finds himself engaged in these matters for the first time. If I have expanded a little upon certain points which perhaps will not interest all my readers equally, various authors, at least, will be able to recognize here in what respect they have been able to deceive themselves.

While I was working on this tract, in which at first I had in view only our instinct for music and its principle, there appeared several writings on the theory of the art,[2] to which I believed I could respond no better than by profiting from my first ideas to put each writer in a position not only to judge

[1]The *Troquers* represented at the last fairs of Saint Laurent and of Saint Germain, and the *Coquette trompée* represented at Fontainebleau in 1753.
[2]Perhaps the authors of these writings will be grateful to me for not naming them at all.

340

for himself, but also to be able to account to himself for the different effects of harmony, without much trouble either to the mind or to the memory.

To arrive at knowledge that up to the present could appear as almost impenetrable, this was only a matter in effect of attending solely to the products of the sonorous body, products that separate into two types, which types are identified by the position these same products occupy in the order of generation, which position, for its part, is designated by two terms of the art that are, moreover, very significant, namely the *dominant*, the *fifth* above, and the *subdominant*, the *fifth* below: the one indicating that the voice must . rise, the other that it must fall: the one always being assisted by a new *sharp* or *natural*, the other by a new *flat*, the one possessing in general vigor and joy as its lot, the other weakness, gentleness, tenderness, and sadness: both the one and the other, in short, most often serving us as interpreters in our expressions, when, for example, we call upon the *sharp*, or the *natural*, as a sign of vigor or energy, and raise our voice in such a case, and when we lower it and call upon the *flat* as a sign of softness, of weakness: so that indeed the whole, considered with a little reflection, is reduced to the greatest simplicity.

The examples contained in my *Observations* confirm the truth of the precepts that I give to arrive at a knowledge of the causes, and go as far as justifying the taste of the nation for the musical works to which it has accorded its favor.

To give these precepts their whole necessary force, it was necessary for me to test instinct by its principle and this principle by that same instinct: they are, both the one and the other, the work of Nature: let us then no longer desert her, this Mother of the sciences and the arts, let us examine her well, and let us try henceforth to allow ourselves to be conducted only by her.

The principle that is in question is not only that of all the arts of taste, as a *Traité du Beau essentiel dans les Arts, appliqué principalement à l'Architecture*[3] at once confirms, it is also that of all the sciences of calculation: which one can not deny, without denying at the same time that these sciences are founded on proportions and progressions, which Nature announces to us in the phenomenon of the sonorous body, in circumstances so conspicuous that it is impossible to reject the evidence: and how deny it! since there will follow no proportions, no geometry.

Every hypothesis, every arbitrary system, must disappear in the face of such a principle, we must not even hope ever to discover one equally luminous: if we already find in it the germ of all the elements of geometry, of all the rules of music and of architecture, what may we not expect in grounding it still more scrupulously than has so far been done?

[3]By M. Briseux.

OBSERVATIONS ON OUR INSTINCT FOR MUSIC AND ON ITS PRINCIPLE

Music is natural to us, we owe only to pure instinct the agreeable feeling that it makes us experience: that same instinct is operative in us on the occasion of several other objects which may well have certain relationships to music; this is why it should not be a matter of indifference to persons who cultivate the sciences and the arts to know the principle of such an instinct.

That principle is now known: it exists, as one cannot fail to be aware, in the harmony that results from the resonance of every sounding body, such as the sound of our voice, of a string, of a tube, of a bell, etc., and to convince oneself still further, it is necessary only to observe oneself in all the steps one takes in music.

For example, the man without experience in music, just like the one most experienced, ordinarily takes the first sound he intones in the center of his vocal range, from which he sings at his whim, and always rises, although the extent of his voice is nearly equal below to what it is above the first tone: which is absolutely in conformity with the resonance of the sonorous body, all the tones that emanate from which are above that of its totality, which one believes he hears alone.

In another way, no matter how little experience one may have, one hardly ever fails, when one wants to start vocalizing, to intone in succession, always ascending, the perfect chord composed of the harmony of the sonorous body, whose type, which is *major*, is always preferred to the *minor*, at least when the latter is not suggested by some reminiscence.

If one intones ordinarily first in the perfect chord the *third*, in ascending, although the sonorous body gives it only at the double *octave*, which is the *seventeenth*, and thus above the *octave* of the *fifth*, which is its *twelfth*; this is because we naturally reduce all the intervals to their smallest degrees, since the ear appreciates them more promptly and since the voice arrives at them more readily;[4] but it will not be the same for a man without experience, who has never heard music, or who has not listened to it at all; for there is a difference between hearing and listening. If this man intones a slightly low sound, quite clear and quite distinct, and if he then allows his voice to move promptly, without being preoccupied with any object, not even with the interval over which he might like to leap, the operation becoming purely mechanical, he will certainly first intone the *fifth*, in preference to every other interval, according to the experiment that we have done more than once.[5]

---

[4]See my *Réponse à M. Euler sur l'identité des octaves*, p. 13.
[5]The Reverend Father Castel has spoken of this experiment in the *Journal de Trévoux*.

It is quite well known that the *fifth* is the most perfect of all the consonances: the course of these Observations will only serve to confirm it.

The smallest natural degrees, called diatonic, those, in a word, of the scale *do, re, mi, fa,* etc., are instigated only by virtue of the consonances to which they conform, and which they form in succeeding one another, so that these consonances will always present themselves first to every person without experience. For the rest, as soon as one wishes to follow the order of these smallest degrees without the help of any reminiscence one will always ascend by a *tone,* and one will descend by a *semitone,* above all when one wishes to return immediately afterwards to the first tone from which one has departed: for example, if we call *do* that first tone that represents a sonorous body, its *fifth, sol,*[6] which sounds with it, will take over the auditory field, and if one desires to pass from *do* to its closest adjacent degree, this *sol* will therefore present itself as a new sonorous body, which consists in its *major third, ti* and in its *fifth, re,* so that one will be forced by that to ascend by a *tone* from *do* to *re,* and to descend by a *semitone* from *do* to *ti.*

On the other hand, after the *tone* ascending, one will naturally be disposed to intone another such: the *semitone* will present itself only by reminiscence, because the two *tones* form the *major third* that sounds in the vibrating body, whereas the *tone* and *semitone* form only a *minor third* that does not sound there; but also, after these two *tones,* one will feel oneself forced to intone a subsequent *semitone,* to pass to the *fourth,* the third *tone* which is here refused therefore, giving a dissonance: and it is for that reason that it has always been said, because it has been felt, that three *tones* in succession were not natural: after this last *semitone* again, another one will never present itself; the *tone* will prevail in every ear to arrive at the consonance of the *fifth.*

Such is the dominance of the consonances over the ear, which therefore is preoccupied only with the degrees that form them, or that lead to them; these consonances being moreover only the product of the resonance of the sonorous body: which must be well remarked, seeing that one may not additionally insert anything else, so that the principle demonstrated is the instrument of all those faculties that we have just acknowledged to be natural to us.

There is more; and if one has ever so little experience, one finds unaided the fundamental bass of all the cadences of a melody, according to the explanation given in our *Nouveau Système,* etc., page 54; which well proves again the dominance of the principle in all its products, since in this last case the progression of these products recalls to the ear that of the principle which has determined it, and consequently suggested it to the composer.

---

[6]One says *fifth* instead of *twelfth,* and *third* instead of *seventeenth* because of their identity or equivalent sound, which is occasioned by the octave.

This last experience, in which instinct alone is active, just as in the preceding ones, well proves that melody has no other principle than the harmony given by the sonorous body: a principle with which the ear is preoccupied to such a degree without one thinking about it, that it suffices alone to make us find immediately the foundation of harmony on which that melody depends: which happens not only to the composer who has conceived it, but also to every person of ordinary experience: also one finds a large number of musicians capable of accompanying by ear a song that they are hearing for the first time.

Moreover what is the driving force of those beautiful preludes, of those fortunate fantasies, executed as soon as conceived, chiefly on the organ? In vain would the fingers be trained for them in all the possible melodies, and in condition to obey instantly the imagination guided by the ear, if the guide of this last were not of the most natural kind.

That guide of the ear is no other, in fact, than the harmony of an initial sonorous body, by which it is no sooner affected, than it activates all that can follow that harmony, and leads it to it: and this all consists simply in the *fifth* for the less experienced, and in the *third* also when experience has made greater progress.[7]

But let us not go so far, and let us note always that as little experience as one may have, one never fails to follow first of all the *mode* announced by the first harmony, and that the first new *mode* to which one then passes, is generally that of the same *fifth* from which we receive the feeling of the *tone* in ascending, in accordance with what has already been said on this point: the *fifth* on which there is founded all the melody that can be derived with justice from natural instruments, such as the trumpet and the hunting horn, and which has been given to the kettledrums to serve as the bass of this melody:[8] and also as that other bass, the *fundamental bass*, without this having been the intention, since it has been recognized only in our time.

These natural instruments are themselves sonorous bodies, which, in their whole range, contain nothing but just what belongs to their harmony, and to that of their *fifth*: so that when we confirm the instinct that inclines us generally in the direction of this *fifth* or of its harmony, that instinct confirms, in turn, the principle that guides it.

Such a process on our part, a process purely mechanical, should indeed open our eyes to the principle that is its sole and unique driving force: and the persons who cultivate other sciences might do well also to examine the

---

[7]See the *Démonstration du principe de l'harmonie* on the formation of the *mode*, p. 33, on that of the *minor*, p. 62, and on the relationship of the *modes*, p. 42. We leave aside the *enharmonic*, because we can dispense with this genus, absolutely speaking, although it may have its beauties. It is a very short time that it has been in use, and often without pleasing very much, so rare is it to be able to employ it fortunately.

[8]The *fourth*, which the two kettledrums form between them, is an inverted *fifth*.

process which they follow: they would recognize in it, without doubt, that same principle, at least in the proportions upon which they base nearly all their activities. Would one prefer to owe these proportions to chance, rather than to a phenomenon in which Nature has embraced them all, under circumstances that may indeed extend to other objects as well as to music?

Instead of consulting Nature on music, the philosophic mind has approached it, from the earliest times, from the direction of geometry, in order to follow in that Pythagoras, without examining if this author was well or ill grounded: he is made to speak, he is made to act, as one thinks he could have: one conceives with him, or after his fashion, hypotheses to make the relationships he gave to sounds square with the different orders that experience suggests: each reports what he thinks; and all are equally mistaken.

Where is the philosopher, where is the man, who with a modicum of common sense will not recognize as due to Nature, to his pure instinct, this agreeable feeling he experiences in hearing certain relationships of tones? And what sort of person is it who will not therefore profit from the means that he will have discovered in that Mother of the sciences and the arts, to proceed accordingly? But not at all; it is maintained that Pythagoras, after having recognized the *octave* as being composed of two unequal intervals, which are the *fifth* and the *fourth*, of which the *major tone* constitutes the difference, has of his own authority added that *tone* to itself, to form thereby the *major third*: is that logical, and can one suppose such an error in so great a man? What! he finds in Nature an interval composed of two unequal ones, and it is maintained that on his own authority he has composed another of two that are equal? One is assuredly deceived on his account, in this case and at all times. It is much more probable that that author fertile in progressions, as one can judge by what remains to us from him, having recognized the relation of the *fifth* or double *fifth* called twelfth, between 1 and 3, would have formed a triple progression of this first relation, and would have carried it up to its twelfth power, as all the intervals given as belonging to his system will confirm,[9] and particularly his *comma* formed of the ratio of unity to this twelfth power: the *comma* of which the origin has been ignored at all times, even by those of the Pythagorean sect, since it has never been spoken of except by the name Pythagorean *comma*, without any other explanation.

As soon as we do not consult the ear; we will always be seduced by the product of a triple progression in which all the intervals necessary to music are found, with the exception of the *enharmonic*, of which the usage has been known only to our time, although the Ancients spoke of it, but very confusedly: now it is quite possible to believe that Pythagoras no more

[9]One may compare the system of Pythagoras with the triple progression of my *Démonstration*, Example A; everything in the two will be absolutely conformable.

consulted the ear concerning the intervals given by his progression than did all the authors who adopted his system, since there is nothing just in this progression but the *major tone* and the *fifth*, from which the *fourths* are found by inversion, all the rest being false, without *minor tones* being found in it: and from this it arises that the *major third* is composed in it of two *major tones*.[10]

The ear in music obeys only Nature, it takes account neither of measure nor of criterion, instinct alone leads it. We moderns have therefore been wrong to conclude, from the falsity of the system of Pythagoras, that the Ancients did not practise harmony: we have, we ourselves, contributed to that error by too much confidence in those who have preceded us in this regard: and without the idle fancies that are announced every day in music, a reflection so just and so simple would perhaps still have escaped us. The ear in music obeys only Nature, we repeat it again, and all the false systems that have been spread up to this day, the false relationships that are found, even, in the perfect system,[11] have not prevented our musicians from singing truly, and from carrying their art to a very high degree of perfection.

That system of Pythagoras, in spite of all its imperfections, did not cease to exist during a rather large number of centuries, indeed until Ptolemy, if I am not mistaken, who finally discovered the *minor tone*, to form from it, with the *major*, a just *major third*.

Zarlino takes this as his point of departure, and projects in consequence a harmonic division, with the help of which he finds the just relations of the perfect system;[12] but soon afterwards he loses his way: he does not know why it happens that in this system he meets with consonances having false relations,[13] we even think he avoids speaking of them; which was the reason that several authors, following him, thought they had to change the order of the *tones*, without taking care that the defect they wished to avoid did not return elsewhere.

All musicians, both in practice and in theory, have only copied this author up to the most recent times.

Before the systems of which we have just spoken, there was an early one, called the *tetrachord*, because it was composed of only four strings or tones, in the order *ti, do, re, mi*; it was, more correctly, only a half-system, since it was necessary to add it to itself to form from it a complete one; but also, for this very reason, it was sufficient, and the idea was a very happy one.

---

[10]One must judge by this report that the authority of Pythagoras, no more than that of all the Ancients, can hardly carry weight in music.

[11]*Démonstration . . .* , pp. 54-59.

[12]We are concerned here only with diatonic systems, which alone preside in all music in general.

[13]*Démonstration . . .* , pp. 54-59.

Without troubling ourselves about the inventor of this *tetrachord*, let us see what could have led him to it, and let us begin by investigating what tonal relationships the first man who was sensitive to tones could have found striking at once.

In order for a relationship of tones to attract attention the first time we are affected by it, it is necessary as a minimum condition that it be pleasing, or else it will suffer the fate of every other element of discourse, where we are aware of things only to the extent that they give more force and more energy to what we wish to depict; but as to tones in particular, they will never divert us from the ideas with which we are preoccupied if they do not give rise to a sensation sufficiently pleasing to engage and fix the attention. We are dealing here with an involuntary feeling, which is produced by accident and which can be due only to this accident the first time it is experienced.

We leave it to be judged, now that the driving force of all our feelings in music is known, which of the two, consonance or dissonance, is capable of predisposing us in favor of its relationship; considering, and this is to be well noted, that all the tonal relationships in discourse are not simply dissonant, but are even inappreciable to the ear.

The degrees of the *tetrachord* are all dissonant in their order of succession from one to the other, so that in hearing *ti do, do re,* or *re mi* successively, we shall have nothing sufficiently pleasing to arrest us: hearing them together will be still worse: instead of which, in hearing *do mi,* and above all *do sol,* together or in succession, we can only be very pleasantly impressed. Thus it can be only by the feeling of consonance, that the relationship of tones was able to attract attention for the first time; more especially as the principle that propels us makes only consonances audible, and this reason alone could suffice, without adducing others.

If that is so, and one can hardly doubt it, the inventor of the *tetrachord* in question must have been impressed by the relationship of various consonances before contriving those of which he compounded the *tetrachord*; but still more, instinct never will countenance a *semitone* as the first step of an ascending diatonic order: everyone must test this for himself, and it is not at all to custom that the contrary must be imputed, it is alone to the impression of an initial given tone to which a relationship must be set up: custom in no way commands instinct: on the contrary, it is on the basis of instinct that custom is formed: and everyone without experience as well as with experience will always begin an ascending diatonic order with the *tone* from *do* to *re*; and if they continue to ascend, they will sing of themselves that *tetrachord, do re mi fa,* consequent on all our preceding remarks, which may be read again, in the event they have been forgotten.

If consequently the *tetrachord* of the Ancients could not have been inspired in the order in which it is found, and if the acquaintance with certain antecedents was necessary to arrive at that order, there is every reason to presume that its inventor derived it from the very principle upon which we have established it.[14]

But why, one will say, did that inventor reveal only the product, without making known its principle? One could say similarly: why did Pythagoras reveal only the relations of tones, without making known the source from which he drew them? Mystery prevailed quite readily among the Ancients, and they could have had their purposes. However this may be, it will always be surprising that among so many great men who have written about music, none has carried his reflections that far, not even since the phenomenon in question has been known.

The mathematician will excuse himself, perhaps on the basis that he was deprived of the aid of the ear, from being able to derive various advantages from such a phenomenon: he can at least not deny that he should have recognized here the seed of proportions and progressions whose object can not be indifferent to him.

When Father Pardies says, with reference to the harmonic progression, in which the proportion is mixed: "All that has been said up to the present about this progression is not of great use; and I do not wish to undertake here to say things that are out of the ordinary," apparently things must already have been said which seemed out of the ordinary to him; but quite often they would seem so to us only because we do not understand them; and as to the use of the harmonic proportion from which the progression arises, it may turn out that it still has not been well investigated.

The matter concerns a sonorous object, which is no sooner set into motion than it divides itself into all its aliquot parts;[15] it even makes the largest of these sound out; namely, its third (1/3), which sounds its twelfth, or double *fifth*, and its fifth (1/5), which sounds its major seventeenth, or triple *major third*;[16] so that the tone which appears single is nevertheless triple in its nature, and should well be so, in order that the ear might appreciate it, since if the body is sufficiently large so that its seventh part sounds as strongly as its third part and its fifth part, then it is no more than a confused and inappreciable sound: it is the same when the body is so small that its third part can no longer sound: thus the body that is too large, which gives too low a sound, and the body that is too small, which gives too high a sound, equally surpass the scope of the organ of hearing;[17] but what indeed confirms still better the union of these three tones in a single one is that experiment proposed in our *Génération harmonique*,[18] where one sees that the

---

[14]*Démonstration . . .* , p. 46; also Example B.
[15]The aliquot parts are one-half, 1/2, one-third, 1/3, one-fourth, 1/4, one-fifth, 1/5, and so on; they are also called *submultiples*.
[16]The double and the triple are caused by the octaves that are encountered between the two tones compared.
[17]*Génération harmonique*, p. 16.
[18]*Ibid.*, p. 13.

tones of the third part and of the fifth part so constitute that of the total body, that whatever the dissonances may be which occur between the harmonics[19] of different fundamental tones, understood to be simultaneous, one distinguishes only these fundamentals alone, as if they were single and unique: which must appear all the more *extraordinary*—it is the term of Father Pardies—as the experiement is conducted with tubes whose resonance is very much stronger than that of the aliquot parts relative to the fundamental.

The sonorous body is not limited to the generation of its *submultiples*, it engenders also a comparable number of its *multiples*[20] in the same relationship to itself inversely, in making these vibrate, from which there arises the arithmetic proportion 1, 3, 5, it being noted that beyond the quintuple, bodies already give sounds that are too low, and that the body which sets them in motion does not have sufficient power in addition to make their vibration perceptible to the eye. In a word, there exists with these *multiples* as with the *submultiples*, that which, beyond the quintuple and the fifth part, one can see on the one hand, and hear on the other, disappear from the eye and from the ear; there is no longer anything distinct nor appreciable.

Not only do the multiples vibrate, but they also divide into all the unisons of the body that sets them into motion; which happens to them only by means of the proportion in which they stand: thus that proportion gives them their law, and must necessarily concur with anything new.

If they divide, these multiples, it is only so that all may unite again in the heart of the body that calls them to its aid in making them vibrate, and so that they may show thereby that they rely entirely on it for all the fruit that may be drawn from the proportion by means of which it recalls them to memory. See the section on the "Minor mode" in the *Demonstration*, etc., p. 62.

These two proportions, the harmonic and the arithmetic, each form a kind of harmonic group, to which one adds as many *octaves* as one wishes, and which, by means of this addition, can combine in every possible fashion. There ensue, moreover, two progressions, the one descending, in which the generator divides into an infinitude of parts without ceasing to exist as a whole; the other ascending, in which the generator is multiplied to infinity:[21] so that in forming only a single progression of the two, one finds in it neither beginning nor end.

[19]One calls the tones that compose the harmony of the sonorous body *harmonics*, namely, its *fifth*, called *twelfth*, 1/3, and its *major third*, called *seventeenth*, 1/5. And one calls the tone of the totality of that same sonorous body the *fundamental*.

[20]If the *submultiples* are aliquot parts, the multiples are on the contrary aliquant parts, that is to say that they are formed of bodies larger than the one that sets them in motion.

[21]The descending progression, in which the body is divided, is on the contrary ascending in practical music, because one always passes in it from low to high: and for the same reason, the ascending, in which the body is multiplied is descending, because one always passes in it from high to low.

Yet all the proportions are manifested in the sonorous body at the first instant that it sounds; one hears in it the harmonic, one infers in it the geometric in the *octaves* 1, 2, 4, and one sees in it the arithmetic in the vibration of the multiples.

Harmony is given by the resonance of the sonorous body, and if there is lacking no more than to find its succession, we see that this presents itself perfectly naturally in the progressions which form of themselves between the submultiples on the one hand and the multiples on the other, where it is a question only of regarding as sonorous bodies all the tones that we shall choose for that purpose: which cannot be understood otherwise.

One chooses then, for that purpose, the first tone which presents itself after that of the totality of the sonorous body, which is approximately found to be its *fifth*, leaving aside its *octave* which does nothing but represent it: and from the alternating succession of these two sonorous bodies there arises among their harmonic tones that very *tetrachord* of the Greeks, *ti do re mi*, of which only a minute ago we sought to discover where those Greeks could have found the origin,[22] and of which the order presents itself almost entirely in the necessity to which instinct subjects us of ascending by a *tone* and of descending by a *semitone* after an initial given tone:[23] and if one reflects carefully upon this, one will see that it can be only by virtue of the alternating succession of two sonorous bodies a *fifth* apart that there arises in us the feeling of this difference between the steps we traverse.

Let us remark again that the first tone of this tetrachord is a harmonic of the *fifth*, and that every *fifth* can be suggested only by its generator; thus we do not possess the power to imagine it, this *fifth*, without being affected beforehand by what produces it.

As soon as this tetrachord is given, we feel that the same order can be continued constantly ascending, and to obtain from the principle what the ear requires in this case, it is sufficient to recall that this principle is equally to be obtained a *fifth* below as well as above, the one by the vibration of the multiples, the other by the resonance of the submultiples: so that in forming a new sonorous body of this *fifth* below,[24] we shall have a new tetrachord similar to the first, but on other degrees of the voice, with the names *mi fa sol la*, which gives all the smallest natural degrees contained within the compass of the *octave* of the first generator called *do*, namely *ti do re mi fa sol la*.

One would not be able to reflect too much on these last remarks, in which it is a matter of revealing in their full light the consequences which the principle furnishes in the order of its products, in order to derive convincing illumination for all that we have put forward up to the present.

---

[22]P. 29 [p. 347 in the present translation].
[23]Pp. 6-7 [p. 343 in the present translation].
[24]An account will be given in what follows of the necessity of this resonance.

If one looks first of all into the resonance of the sonorous body, from which there comes to us the natural feeling of harmony, one will see the same by the tones common to the harmony of different fundamental tones that succeed one another directly, from which there comes to us the feeling of the succession of harmony, called melody in each part in particular: of which there follows the explanation.

When *do* sounds, its *fifth sol* sounds with it: accordingly this *sol* is present for us in hearing *do*, and in the instant that the ear is engaged by it, its harmony is naturally understood also: so that everything invites us then to pass from *do* to *sol*, or to one of its harmonic tones: the return of this *sol* to *do* is perfectly simple; thus we have a presentiment of the *fifth* below as well as above: from which it follows that in hearing *do*, we can have a presentiment equally of the *fa* of which it is the *fifth*: there is a common tone on each side, which is the *fifth* above or below; and it is by such resorts that the ear is guided from one tone to another.

Since the presentiment of a fundamental tone entails that of its harmony, there follows naturally for us the liberty of choice between all the harmonic tones which then succeed one another; and it is from the choice dictated by good taste that the most pleasing melody is formed.

As it is only by virtue of the arithmetic proportion, formed by the totality of the multiples, that these multiples vibrate and divide, this totality must at least be supposed: and if from the same proportion there arises a harmony almost as pleasing, if not as pleasing, as that of the harmonic proportion, not only must the totality be supposed, but also its resonance must be understood.

Do we not see, moreover, that the source calls its multiples to its aid only to open up a route in that direction just as it opens one up in the direction of its submultiples? We shall forbid it that route on our own authority, when it takes its place at the center of both directions, from which it can depart only when we pass from one side or from the other.

EXAMPLE

Harmonic Proportion			Arithmetic Proportion	
$\frac{1}{5}$	$\frac{1}{3}$	1	3	5
Third above	Fifth above	Source	Fifth below	Third below

What is recognized in this example is a succession of two generations, in which one sees again that they cannot communicate with one another

351

without the mediation of the source which remains at their center.[25] It does more, this source, and to fix their succession within limits proportional to those of our senses, it takes its two fifths separately, with which it forms this triple proportion: 1/3, 1, 3,—or 1, 3, 9 in whole numbers—a proportion called geometric, from which arises the most perfect and at the same time the most pleasing order between the tones, that which is called *diatonic*, known under the name *scale*, and of which what we call *mode* is composed.[26]

That proportion is almost the general basis of all of music: because each of the tones can no longer appear in it except as a sonorous body, or a fundamental, it follows that each of them can have the same right over its *fifths* that the first sonorous body, the source and generator, acquired in this respect: so that the same proportion subsisting between these new sonorous bodies and their *fifths*, there will arise *modes* similar to the first: all of which, however, does not exceed the given limits; that is to say, that the province of generator does not extend beyond its two *fifths* in everything that must be related to it, and consequently in everything that can please us relative to the first impression received of this generator, an impression by which alone the ear is guided; which further constitutes three similar modes, called *major*, to which are joined three others called *minor*, in all of which the *fifths* also appropriate the right that the generator acquires of forming a new *mode* of this genus in its multiples.[27]

This new *mode* takes the name of the genus of the *minor third* that the source forms in it, in order to reserve to itself the right it acquired up to then of ordering the different effects that result from harmony, and from its succession; for the whole difference between the *major mode*, which it first generated, and this one, consists only in the *third*.

In order that the source form the *minor third*, it is forced to choose a fundamental tone which it charges with the whole conduct of the new *mode*, founded nevertheless on the *major* that it first generated; which ties these two *modes* in a very intimate relationship: and from this there follows a fundamental succession by *thirds*.[28]

All these discoveries lead to observations that are all the more necessary as the series above rolls along unconditionally.

---

[25]*Démonstration* . . . , pp. 46-52.

[26]The source is sensible as the generator of every *mode*, we call it *tonic* in the nomenclature of the art, its *fifth* above, *dominant*, and its *fifth* below, *subdominant;* these three tones always bear the title *fundamental* everywhere the bass is in question, unless they are no more than *octaves, fifths*, etc.

The *dominant* and the *subdominant* introduce all the melodic pauses that end on the *tonic*, pauses that are called cadences, that is to say, closes: the first introduces the *perfect* cadences in descending a *fifth*, and the second the *imperfect* or *irregular cadence* in ascending a *fifth*: every other *cadence* presupposes the *perfect*, which may be *broken*, or *interrupted*.

It is quite necessary to remember the terms *dominant* and *subdominant*, their position with respect to the *tonic*, and their use; because everything of interest in the rest of these Observations revolves almost solely around these same terms.

[27]See the section on the *minor mode* in the *Démonstration* . . . , p. 62.

[28]*Démonstration* . . . , pp. 79 and 81.

If it were a matter here of comparisons, would one not attribute naturally to joy this throng of descendents presented by the submultiples, whose resonance indicates their existence? It is there also that the *major third*, the *major mode*, the *sharp*, the melody whose force redoubles in ascending, and the *dominant*, the *fifth* above, justly have their origin. And for a reason exactly opposite, would one not attribute to sorrows, tears, and so on those multiples of which the gloomy silence is aroused only by the divisions in unison with the body that makes them vibrate, to signal that it falls to this to represent them? Now it is from this quarter, then, that there arise the *minor third*, the *flat*, the melody that becomes gentle in descending, the *subdominant fifth* below, and what is more, the *chromatic* and the *enharmonic*, with which we shall soon be concerned.

These things have still perhaps not been well considered, yet ascriptions are made every day in this sense, when the *sharp* or *natural* is cited as a sign of force, of joy, when one's voice is raised in the same instances, in anger, and so on, and when the *flat* is cited as a sign of softness, of weakness, and so on, and finally when one's voice is lowered in the same instances.

Everyone perceives also something of these differences, however little experience he may have in music, when the *major mode* and the *minor mode* succeed one another on the same *tonic*.

But to judge for ourselves the feeling that these two different spheres, that of the *dominant* and that of the *subdominant*, can inspire, we have taken a look at a parenthetical passage of Lully, who has led us to these observations from which even composers will be able to draw some fruits.

When Armide says: *"le vainqueur de Renaud . . . "* and then upon reflection she adds: *"Si quelqu'un le peut être!"* the music seems to make her pronounce that reflection with a species of humiliation, of mortification, as though at once the fear of not being able to triumph over this hero entered her mind, consequent upon the first nine verses of her entrance, of which the last two are:

Non je ne puis manquer, sans un dépit extrême,
La conquête d'un coeur si superbe e si grand.

In fact such a conquest is a great victory for a coquette: so that Armide can very well be considered one when she says to herself: *"Puis-je me flatter, moi-meme, d'en être le vainqueur?"* Such is without doubt the sense that guided Lully; for if one would have it that Armide had only intended simply to exalt the glory of her hero, without recalling at the same time the fear of not being able to triumph over him, Lully would not have failed to make us feel it by means of a different foundation for the harmony. See example A.[29]

---

[29]The terms *tonic, dominant,* and *subdominant* are used only for the bass; one says third, fourth, fifth, etc. when it is a question of comparing the parts among themselves.

Example A

to the subdominant, descending: Lully's original

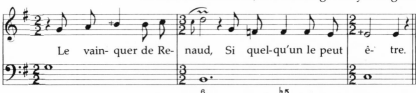

or:

the same, ascending

to the dominant, descending

or:

the same, ascending

It is necessary first to sing this music with the motion the words require, without adding them to it and without concerning oneself with any other feeling but that which the melody is able to give rise to of itself, while remarking in it the aspect towards which one will feel more inclination to softness or to pride: and then, all bias aside, the new *flat* that derives from the sphere of the subdominant, either in descending or in ascending, will be inclined naturally towards softness: whereas the new *sharp*, given by the resources of harmony from the sphere of the dominant, will demand the animation of the melody, and render it susceptible of all the pride with which one would wish to accompany it.

When one desires to experience the effect of a melody it is always necessary to support it with all the harmony from which it derives; it is in that harmony itself that the cause of the effect resides, by no means in the melody, which is only its product: a truth that will be recognized in a moment in the subject of the *chromatic*; it is necessary in addition to sing what preceded this song, because it is the impression received from the *mode* in which one starts that occasions the feeling one experiences from the *mode* which follows it.

Three means cooperate, then, in the difference of the expressions. Lully's way descends, passes to the subdominant, and to a new *flat*, and keeps to the idea that I have supposed in it: the other way on the contrary ascends, and passes to the dominant and to a new *sharp* in the resources of harmony: a *sharp* which is expressly noted above the bass. It is true that there is an ascent and a descent in each approach; but we shall discover the reason for this in a moment.

Two of these means are only one, namely, the *dominant* with the *sharp* on the one hand, and the *subdominant* with the *flat* on the other: they are moreover the only ones on which the principal expression here produced of feelings and passions depends: the other means, namely, the difference of high and low, is only accessory in this, it strengthens that expression, but it can do nothing here of itself; for proof of that, the sphere of the *subdominant* will produce a nearly equal effect either in ascending or in descending, and the same is true for that of the *dominant*: we shall always feel, on the one hand, that species of humiliation that we have supposed there, and on the other, that pride that can be expected there: what is more, the sphere of the *dominant* in descending always holds to the pride, and does not give any feeling of softness like the sphere of the *subdominant* in ascending, where the new *flat* compels a softening of the song in spite of what one may do; at least let one not seek to impose the torture upon oneself here of extracting an expression contrary to the feeling which that *flat* gives rise to, as happens sometimes to those persons who, prejudiced in favor of a certain expression, wish to make it square, at whatever price may be, with a melody that is entirely opposed to it: and it is this we must guard against.

Often that which is due only to the words is believed to derive from the music, or one tries to comply with the expression one wishes to ascribe to the words by means of forced inflections, but this is not the route to the ability of judging music: it is necessary, on the contrary, to let oneself be carried along by the feeling it inspires, this music, without thinking about it, without thinking, in a word; and then that feeling will become the instrument of our judgment. As to reason, it is at present within everyone's grasp, we have just drawn it from the very womb of Nature;[30] we have proven, in fact, that instinct recalls it to us at every moment, both in our actions and in our discourse. Now, as soon as reason and feeling are in accord, there will no longer be a means of appealing their verdict.

Modulation, fixed first of all in the two *fifths*[31] of the generator, is not restricted to them: and to extend the limits, that generator has also kept in reserve its two *major thirds*, of which it makes, with itself, a quintuple proportion, in the order, taken in whole numbers, 1, 5, 25, where 5 represents it at the center, a place that it occupies in every context: so that from the products of its harmony and of that of one of its extremes, no matter which, 1 or 25, there arises the minor *semitone*, called *chromatic*: and from the harmonic products of these two extremes, 1 and 25, there arises a *quarter-tone*, called *enharmonic*, which is absolutely not perceptible. Which well confirms the superiority of the *fifth*, in accordance with our opening remarks, since it is the unique source of natural truth, of true beauty, of that which alone can provide us with a sufficiently pleasing music: for the proof, we appeal to the operas of Lully,[32] and even to the Italian music of his time, which was hardly more varied than his: and to judge of this equitably, we must transport ourselves into those times. For the rest, just as one can never interrupt the diatonic order except by a single chromatic or enharmonic interval, which then serves for the translation from one mode to another whose relationship is more or less distant, and just as this transition is generally feasible by means of the diatonic, except that which depends on the enharmonic, which has still occurred in French opera only in a monologue of *Dardanus*; one must necessarily conclude that whatever advantage one might derive from these last intervals, all of music is able to please without their aid: and this reflection should always be kept in mind so that we may not permit ourselves to be prevailed upon by high flown words that signify nothing.

Is it not said every day, by some to find fault, by others to praise: that is chromatic music; although often there may be no question of this at all: on the

---

[30]Pp. 52-54 [pp.   in the present translation].
[31]There is a *fifth* and a *third* below as well as above.
[32]There is no descending *chromaticism* at all in Lully, if I am not mistaken, but only ascending, and generally from a *minor third* to the *major*, which very much approaches the diatonic, because the same *tonic* always subsists and becomes a common tone for these two *thirds*.

other hand, the *chromatic* is not suspected in music in which it abounds, because it is again represented only in the melodic interval, when this interval is only the accident caused by the products of a fundamental succession from which arises the feeling that one experiences: examine, for that effect, the Rondeau of the monologue *Tristes apprêts*, etc. in the opera *Castor et Pollux*: the feeling of dismal sorrow and of the lugubrious that reigns here depends entirely on the *chromaticism* provided by the fundamental succession, while there is not a single interval of this genus in all the parts:[33] a feeling that is not the same in the previous chorus, where the *chromatic* intervals, which abound in descending, elaborate the tears and moans caused by pangs of sorrow.

We cite this *chromaticism* principally to make known that if the feeling one experiences is always confined to sadness, sometimes to softness, to tenderness, it will take its origin equally well from the *enharmonic* in the *minor mode*,[34] the sphere of the multiples, as we have already stated: a new additional proof in support of the resonance of the totality of the body, from which there arises the arithmetic proportion, on which this *mode* is based and from which there arise also the *minor third*, the *subdominant*, and the *flats*, which one can not repeat too often: but we shall perhaps gain more from examples than from words, and that will properly furnish us with the occasion to restore to Lully the justice which is due him, and of which it was intended to deprive him through a criticism the more poorly founded as it was generally contradictory to the principles that its author himself had professed in the *Encyclopédie*: let us accordingly see what is in question:

Enfin il est en ma puissance.[35]

"Here is a trill, and what is worse, a perfect cadence in the very first verse."

The trill[36] creates beauty in our music, especially in the present case, where it adds force to the word *puissance*, on which the whole sense of the verse rests: and if several abuse it, it is wrong to lay the blame on the thing itself.

Armide is congratulating herself here on having Renaud in her power, and to express her exultation over this, nothing is better conceived than the *trill* she employs here: a *trill* justly similar to that of the trumpets in songs of victory. Example B.

---

[33]The feeling that one experiences of chromaticism, which formally does not exist at all in this monologue, proves the necessity of joining to the melody all the harmonic foundations on which it depends, in accordance with the remark on page 58 [page   in the present translation], in order to be able to judge its full effect.

[34]*Démonstration . . .* , pp. 28 and 92.

[35]Page 81 of the *Lettre sur la musique françoise* of M. Rousseau.

[36]This term (*trill*) is more suitable than that of *cadence*, which we made use of improperly in a similar case.

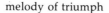

melody of triumph

As to the *perfect cadence*, there is not a trace of it in the music according to the very principles of it that the author has given.[37]

M. Rousseau can not be ignorant that to the extent that a song unfolds over the same harmony, the variety of tones one uses in it serves only for the embellishment of the melody, and that to that extent this variety basically never represents anything but a single tone, as one sees in the bass of Example B: now how was he able to imagine that there was a cadence, still more, a *perfect cadence* on *puissance*, when not only the same *tonic*, and its same harmony, subsists throughout the verse, but even up to the hemistich of the second? what has become of the principles set down on this subject in the *Encyclopédie*?

A compelled pause to take a breath, compelled really to detach the first *ce*, with which puissance ends, from the *ce* that begins the following verse, just as every actor will be compelled equally here, a cadence of that nature, I say, can it be taxed with that name in music, and *what is worse*, with *perfect cadence*? Does the *trill* have this character in itself, when on the contrary, it is generally

---

[37]In the *Encyclopédie*, under the word *cadence*, one finds nearly throughout the word *repos* [*pause, close*] for the word *cadence*: and specifically, on the penultimate line of page 514, there is: "To establish a perfect close, etc." Now, perfect close, absolute close, perfect cadence, final ending, after which one no longer desires anything, all these are synonymous.

Then on the second line one reads: "What one calls the cadential progression always results from two fundamental tones of which one announces the cadence and the other terminates it."

On the third line: "The chord formed on the first tone of a cadence," properly the one that announces it, "must accordingly always be dissonant." There is consequently an error at the end of the first line, where it is said precisely: "It follows that all harmony is properly only a series of cadences;" since the tonic never carries dissonances, it consequently can never announce *cadences*: also there will never be one in the progression from a *tonic* to whatever note may be: unless from the *tonic* it was it becomes a *dominant* or a *subdominant*: which must be carefully noted before deciding, and this reflection will not be unserviceable in what follows.

employed only to announce the cadence. Is such a contradiction with the given precepts pardonable?

Ce fatal ennemi, ce superbe Vainqueur.

An author who has done me the courtesy of adopting my principles is without doubt not ignorant of the intimate relation already cited between the *major mode* and the *minor*, he will not be ignorant, no more so, that the latter owes its origin to the first, that it depends on it, and that if it has softness as its lot, the other is on the contrary masculine, vigorous.[38] If that is so, why reproach Lully by saying: "I would gladly pardon, etc." for what is most admirable in the conduct of the first two verses? To avoid any cadence from the opening to the end of the second verse, in order to make the connection of the meaning perceptible, since the same *tonic* subsists up to the hemistich of the second, where it passes to another *tonic*, that is already a great deal; but to employ first the *minor mode*, so that its softness opposed to the vigor of the *major* adds a new spur here, and redoubles it, so to speak, at the moment that this *major* will terminate a perfect cadence, on these words, *ce superbe Vainquer*, here is the great stroke of the master: for ultimately it is only on these last words that all the defiance of Armide rests, it is not at all *ce fatal Ennemi* that occupies her, no more than his delivered captives, as she says subsequently to prod herself to an act that her heart disowns, it is only the contempt of Renaud for her charms that wounds her pride.

Let us reflect on this, after being well informed of the facts on which the art is founded, and we shall see what instinct alone is capable of; for Lully, led by feeling, and by taste, had no knowledge of these facts, unknown in his time.

In seeing what instinct alone can do, we see at the same time the simplicity of the principle that guides it: two *tonics* of which the one is subject to the laws that the other imposes on it, here is all that is employed to render an expression with the greatest perfection we might desire.

For the rest, one should always mistrust one's judgment, when, ignorant of the principles, one wishes to separate it from the impressions that one has received, or that one is receiving. Let us give ourselves over to pure feeling, let us listen without thinking about it, and we shall see that the *trill* in question strikes us only as a simple suspended cadence, in which there is expressed the triumph that Armide claims to enjoy: we shall similarly feel the force of expression that falls on those words, *ce superbe Vainqueur*, without knowing that it arises from the art with which the modulation is observed here; but what does it matter: if we are truly sensitive, and if we judge only according to feeling, we shall always judge well.

. . . . .

---

[38]One may see on pages 54 and 55 of the *Lettre* . . . that the author recognizes these kinds of differences, and should appreciate in consequence the use one may make of them for the purpose of contrast.

Additional Reading

Ecorcheville, Jules. *De Lully à Rameau, 1690-1730; L'Esthétique musicale.* Paris, 1906.

Herder, J.G. "Viertes Wäldchen." In his: *Kritische Wälder.* Vol. IV of *Herders Sämmtliche Werke,* ed. B. Suphan. Berlin, 1878.

Jansen, Albert. *Jean-Jacques Rousseau als Musiker.* Berlin, 1884.

Jullien, Adolphe. *La Musique et les philosophes au dix-huitième siècle.* Paris, 1873.

Masson, Paul Marie. "Les Idées de J.J. Rousseau sur la musique" *Revue musicale S.I.M. 8,* 1912.

Rameau, Jean Philippe. *Observations sur notre instinct pour la musique, et sur son principe.* Paris, 1754.

Rousseau, Jean-Jacques and Johann Gottfried Herder. *On the Origin of Language,* tr. J.H. Moran and A. Gode. New York, 1966.

PART NINE

The Aesthetics
of Opera

Operatic history is marked by ceaseless discussion and controversy concerning the proper nature of opera. After the early confrontation of ancient and modern which furnished the initial aesthetic basis of opera, operatic aesthetics in Italy is distinguished chiefly by satire, which Marcello's *Teatro alla moda* (1720) brought to a sudden and lasting popularity. Less natively Italian, doubtless, was the sharp criticism of men of letters, who could not brook the interference of music with poetry or the restrictions it imposed on the drama, and who regularly echo the disapproval expressed by Saint-Evremond. Muratori's *Della perfetta poesia italiana* (1706) is the most influential critique written from such an unfavorable literary point of view, while even less specifically Italian in its outlook is Algarotti's famous *Saggio* of 1755, which is notable for its comprehensive and judicious discussion.

One of the reasons for the controversy surrounding French opera was certainly the existence of an impressive spoken drama and of the neoclassical aesthetics that accompanied it, which found the source of its tradition—just as opera had done, and with comparable inaccuracy—in Aristotle and in ancient Greek tragedy. Another reason for the controversy was the existence of Italian opera, obviously thriving and successful and obviously quite different from the French. Thus two very different theatrical forms suggested themselves as models for French opera, which also had to make its way, to some extent, as their competitor. And along with the question of good taste, which became a central conception of eighteenth-century aesthetics, and the problems endemic to opera (the kind of subject matter that was appropriate, the relative weight of music and text or of music and dramatic action, and the principles of combination of the diverse constituent arts), two persistent tendencies of French operatic thought are to take spoken drama as a basis of evaluation and to hold French opera up to comparison with Italian.

In the seventeenth century, Lully's librettist Quinault was criticized by Boileau and Saint-Evremond, among others, for the central role that love played in the action of his librettos and for his happy endings, things that departed from the character of classical tragedy. Instead of undertaking to improve morality, it was urged, opera had devoted itself to sensuous pleasure, spectacle, and entertainment.

In the eighteenth-century comparison of the two national types of opera, the French controversy became a contest of ancient and modern, with French opera as ancient and Italian as modern. This antithesis, which we have come upon in the ideas of Girolamo Mei, constitutes a pattern of thought and argument in various fields from the sixteenth century to the eighteenth. The most numerous and important operatic tracts in France were those belonging to the mid-century War of the Buffoons, which was precipitated by a performance of Pergolesi's *La serva padrona*, and those occasioned somewhat later by the operas of Gluck, who was pitted against

363

Piccini, and it is these two centers of controversy that are illustrated by the passages from Diderot and from Lacépède.

Operatic aesthetics in Germany had to wage a protracted battle first against the moral strictures of Pietism and then, very much as in France, against neoclassic conceptions of spoken drama, which were represented by Gottsched, but it manifested an increasingly enthusiastic response to operatic achievements and an increasing interest in the possibilities of combining music and drama. The eighteenth-century effort to define the peculiarities of each art, which can be observed in Krause's treatise and which is so widely known in the example of Lessing's *Laocoön*, was exerted largely so that the knowledge it produced of the individual arts could become the basis of a successful combination of the arts in opera. In spite of this crescendo of interest in Germany, however, which carried over into the nineteenth century, Wagner in particular seems to have derived his operatic theories more from France than from Germany. The similarities between Wagner's ideas and Lacépède's are much more striking than the resemblances between Wagner's operas and those of Gluck and Spontini. Yet in either case, the powerful international influence of French thought and of Parisian opera—an influence that continued well into the nineteenth century— cannot be questioned. Nor is it surprising, in view of the originality and fertility of French ideas on the one hand and the international complexion of Parisian opera on the other, for French opera was to a considerable extent the creation of Italians and Germans.

In the last three decades of the eighteenth century, opera and operatic aesthetics underwent important changes which paralleled and may even have provoked the changes in musical aesthetics in general. France and England were joined by Germany in their rejection of musical imitation, for Germany followed developments in France and England closely, translating and publishing French and English tracts on both general and musical aesthetics. Imitation, however, was replaced by expression and by artistic autonomy. Strength of feeling became a major new value, both in France and in the German "Sturm und Drang." This was nothing less than a musical parallel to the increasing emphasis on sublimity in general aesthetics, which was placed beside beauty as the first step in expanding the range of aesthetics to include the characteristic and even the ugly in art. Descriptions of the expressive power of music, which are found more in literary than in philosophical works, are particularly prominent in the writings of Herder and in Heinse's *Musikalische Dialogen* and his novel *Hildegard von Hohenthal* (1796). And another expansion of expressiveness occurred also, with the appearance of the early Romantic conception of the irreality and unworldliness of musical feeling, of its cosmic quality and provenance.

These new conceptions of strong or sublime feeling were coincident with the discovery of the autonomy of art. For if art was not the imitation of an external object, its nature must reside in itself. Musical feelings were in a world of their own; they were only apparent. And the work of art was self-contained; it possessed an internal unity and coherence. It may in fact have been in opera rather than in the symphony that this alternative to imitation was first discovered, for verisimilitude and probability, as dramatic imitation was called, were clearly inadequate to explain it. In any event, artistic apparency, or semblance, and artistic autonomy were the counterparts in experience of the autonomy of aesthetics itself, which was revealed at the same time by Kant's *Critique of Judgment* (1790), and in a radically different way—and for music in particular—by Herder's "Viertes Wäldchen" (1769) and his *Kalligone* (1800).

CHAPTER NINETEEN

DENIS DIDEROT

Le Neveu de Rameau
(c. 1760-1764)

. . . . .

I: (After a moment of silence on his part and mine, during which he walked up and down whistling and singing, I tried to get him back to his own talent by saying:) What are you doing now?

HE: Nothing.

I: Very tiring.

HE: I was silly enough as it was; I have been to hear this music by Duni and our other youngsters, and that has finished me off.[a]

I: So you approve of this style of music?

HE: Of course.

I: And you find beauty in these modern tunes?

HE: Do I find beauty? Good Lord, you bet I do! How well it is suited to the words! what realism! what expressiveness!

I: Every imitative art has its model in nature. What is the musician's model when he writes a tune?

HE: Why not go back to the beginning? What is a tune?

I: I confess the question is beyond me. That's what we are all like: in our memories we have nothing but words, and we think we understand them through the frequent use and even correct application we make of them, but in our minds we have only vague notions. When I pronounce the word 'tune' I have no clearer idea than you and most of your kind when you say

[a]Duni (1709-75), Italian operatic composer, settled in Paris in 1757 and after that date composed some twenty operas of a 'light' type. (Annotations are the the Tancock Translation.)

'reputation, blame, honour, vice, virtue, modesty, decency, shame, ridicule'.

HE: A tune is an imitation, by means of the sounds of a scale (invented by art or inspired by nature, as you please), either by the voice or by an instrument, of the physical sounds or accents of passion. And you see that by changing the variables the same definition would apply exactly to painting, eloquence, sculpture or poetry. Now to come to your question: what is the model for a musician or a tune? Speech, if the model is alive and thinking; noise, if the model is inanimate. Speech should be thought of as a line, and the tune as another line winding in and out of the first. The more vigorous and true the speech, which is the basis of the tune, and the more closely the tune fits it and the more points of contact it has with it, the truer that tune will be and the more beautiful. And that is what our younger musicians have seen so clearly. When you hear *Je suis un pauvre diable* you think you can tell it is a miser's plaint, for even if he didn't sing he would address the earth in the same tone when hiding his gold therein: *O terre, reçois mon trésor*.[b] And that young girl, for example, who feels her heart beating, who blushes and in confusion begs his lordship to let her go—how else could she express herself? There are all kinds of characters in these works, and an infinite variety of modes of speech. Sublime, I tell you! Go and listen to the piece when the young man, feeling himself on the point of death, cries: *Mon coeur s'en va*.[c] Listen to the air, listen to the instrumental setting, and then try and tell me the difference there is between the real behaviour of a dying man and the tune of this air. You will see whether the line of the melody doesn't coincide exactly with that of speech. I am not going into time, which is another condition of song; I am sticking to expression, and nothing is more obvious than the following passage which I have read somewhere: *Musices seminarium accentus*. Accent is the nursery-bed of melody. Hence you can tell how difficult the technique of recitative is, and how important. There is no good tune from which you cannot make a fine recitative, and no recitative from which a skilled person cannot make a fine tune. I would not like to guarantee that a good speaker will sing well, but I should be surprised if a good singer could not speak well. Believe all I say on this score, for it is the truth.

I: I should be only too willing to believe you if I were not prevented by one little difficulty.

HE: What difficulty?

I: Just this: if this kind of music is sublime, then that of the divine Lully, Campra, Destouches and Mouret, and even, between ourselves, of your dear uncle, must be a bit dull.[d]

[b]Airs from Duni's *L'Isle des fous* (1760).
[c]From *Le Maréchal ferrant*, by Philidor (1761).
[d]Musicians of the 'French' school, from Lully to Philippe Rameau.

HE (whispering into my ear): I don't want to be overheard, and there are lots of people here who know me, but it *is* dull. It's not that I care twopence about dear uncle, if 'dear' he be. He is made of stone. He would see my tongue hanging out a foot and never so much as give me a glass of water, but for all his making the hell of a hullaballoo at the octave or the seventh—la-la-la, dee-dee-dee, tum-te-tum—people who are beginning to get the hang of things and no longer take a din for music will never be content with that. There should be a police order forbidding all and sundry to have the *Stabat* of Pergolesi sung. That *Stabat* ought to have been burned by the public hangman. Lord! these confounded Bouffons, with the *Serva Padrona*, their *Tracallo*, have given us a real kick in the backside.[e] In the old days a thing like *Tancrède, Issé, L'Europe galante, Les Indes* and *Castor, Les Talents lyriques* ran for four, five or six months.[f] The performances of *Armide*[g] went on for ever. But nowadays they all fall down one after the other, like houses of cards. And Rebel and Francoeur[h] breathe fire and slaughter and declare that all is lost and they are ruined, and that, if these circus performers are going to be put up with much longer, national music will go to the devil and the Royal Academy in the cul-de-sac will have to shut up shop. And there is some truth in it, too. The old wigs who have been going there every Friday for the past thirty or forty years are getting bored and beginning to yawn, for some reason or other, instead of having a good time as they used to. And they wonder why, and can't find the answer. Why don't they ask me? Duni's prophecy will come true, and the way things are going I'll be damned if, four or five years after *Le Peintre amoureux de son modèle*, there will be as much as a cat left to skin in the celebrated Impasse. The good people have given up their own symphonies to play Italian ones, thinking they would accustom their ears to these without detriment to their vocal music, just as though orchestral music did not bear the same relationship to singing (allowances being made for the greater freedom due to range of instrument and nimbleness of finger) as singing to normal speech. As though the violin were not the mimic of the singer who in his turn will become the mimic of the violin one of these days, when technical difficulty replaces beauty. The first person to play Locatelli was the apostle of modern music. What nonsense! We shall become inured to the imitation of the accents of passion and of the phenomena of nature by melody or voice or instrument, for that is the whole extent and object of music; and shall we keep our taste for rapine,

[e]Operas by Pergolesi. Term *Bouffons*, applied to these Italian composers in the famous *Guerre des Bouffons* in the fifties of the eighteenth century in Paris, was derived from the Italian *buffi*.
[f]*Tancrède* by Campra, *Issé* by Destouches, *L'Europe galante* by Campra, *Les Indes galantes, Castor et Pollux, Les Talents lyriques*, musico-dramatic works of Rameau.
[g]*Armide* (1686), opera by Lully to libretto by Quinault, the dramatic poet with whom Lully had a long and fruitful collaboration.
[h]Directors of the Paris opera, threatened by the Italian vogue.

lances, glories, triumphs and victories? *Va-t-en voir s'ils viennent, Jean.*[i] They supposed they could weep or laugh at scenes from tragedy or comedy set to music, that the tones of madness, hatred, jealousy, the genuine pathos of love, the ironies and jokes of the Italian or French stage could be presented to their ears and that nevertheless they could still admire *Ragonde* and *Platée*.[j] You can bet your boots that even if they saw over and over again with what ease, flexibility and gentleness the harmony, prosody, ellipses and inversions of the Italian language suited the art, movement, expressiveness and turns of music and relative length of sounds, they would still fail to realize how stiff, dead, heavy, clumsy, pedantic and monotonous their own language is. Well, there it is. They have persuaded themselves that after having mingled their tears with those of a mother mourning the death of her son, or trembled at the decree of a tyrant ordering a murder, they won't get bored with their fairy-tales, their insipid mythology, their sugary little madrigals which show up the bad taste of the poet as clearly as they do the poverty of the art which uses them. Simple souls! It is not so, and cannot be. Truth, goodness and beauty have their claims. You may contest them, but in the end you will admire. Anything not bearing their stamp is admired for a time, but in the end you yawn. Yawn, then, gentlemen, yawn your fill, don't you worry! The reign of nature is quietly coming in, and that of my trinity, against which the gates of hell shall not prevail: truth, which is the father, begets goodness, which is the son, whence proceeds the beautiful, which is the holy ghost. The foreign god takes his place unobtrusively beside the idol of the country, but little by little he strengthens his position, and one fine day he gives his comrade a shove with his elbow and wallop! down goes the idol. That, they say, is how the Jesuits planted Christianity in China and the Indies. And the Jansenists can say what they like, this kind of politics which moves noiselessly, bloodlessly towards its goal, with no martyrs and not a single tuft of hair pulled out, seems the best to me.

I: There is a certain amount of sense in everything you have been saying.

HE: Sense! It's as well, for devil take me if I have been trying. It just comes, easy as wink. I am like those musicians in the Impasse, when my uncle arrived; if I hit the mark, well and good. A coal-heaver will always talk better about his own job than a whole Academy and all the Duhamels in the world. . . .

(And off he went, walking up and down and humming some of the tunes from *L'Ile des Fous, Le Peintre amoureux de son modèle, Le Maréchal ferrant* and *La Plaideuse,* and now and again he raised his hands and eyes to heaven and exclaimed: 'Isn't that beautiful! God, isn't it beautiful! How can anyone wear a pair of ears on his head and question it?' He begain to warm up and sang, at

[i]Refrain of a popular song.
[j]Operatic works by Mouret and Rameau respectively.

first softly, then, as he grew more impassioned, he raised his voice and there followed gestures, grimaces and bodily contortions, and I said: 'Here we go, he's getting carried away and some new scene is working up.' And indeed off he went with a shout: *Je suis un pauvre misérable... Monseigneur, Monseigneur, laissez-moi partir.... O terre, reçois mon or, conserve bien mon trésor.... Mon âme, mon âme, ma vie! O terre!... Le voilà le petit ami, le voilà le petit ami! Aspettare e non venire... A Zerbina penserete.... Sempre in contrasti con te si sta....* He sang thirty tunes on top of each other and all mixed up: Italian, French, tragic, comic, of all sorts and descriptions, sometimes in a bass voice going down to the infernal regions, and sometimes bursting himself in a falsetto voice he would split the heavens asunder, taking off the walk, deportment and gestures of the different singing parts: in turn raging, pacified, imperious, scornful. Here we have a young girl weeping, and he mimes all her simpering ways, there a priest, king, tyrant, threatening, commanding, flying into a rage, or a slave obeying. He relents, wails, complains, laughs, never losing sight of tone, proportion, meaning of words and character of music. All the chess-players had left their boards and gathered round him. Outside, the café windows were thronged with passers-by who had stopped because of the noise. There were bursts of laughter fit to split the ceiling open. He noticed nothing, but went on, possessed by such a frenzy, an enthusiasm so near to madness that it was uncertain whether he would ever get over it, whether he should not be packed off in a cab straight to Bedlam. Singing a part of the Jomelli *Lamentations* he rendered the finest bits of each piece with incredible accuracy, truth and emotion, and the fine accompanied recitative in which the prophet depicts the desolation of Jerusalem was mingled with a flood of tears which forced all eyes to weep. Everything was there: the delicacy of the air and expressive power as well as grief. He laid stress upon the places where the composer had specially shown his great mastery, sometimes leaving the vocal line to take up the instrumental parts which he would suddenly abandon to return to the voice part, intertwining them so as to preserve the connecting links and the unity of the whole, captivating our souls and holding them in the most singular state of suspense I have ever experienced. Did I admire? Yes, I did. Was I touched with pity? Yes, I was. But a tinge of ridicule ran through these sentiments and discoloured them.

But you would have gone off into roars of laughter at the way he mimicked the various instruments. With cheeks puffed out and a hoarse, dark tone he did the horns and bassoons, a bright, nasal tone for the oboes, quickening his voice with incredible agility for the stringed instruments to which he tried to get the closest approximation; he whistled the recorders and cooed the flutes, shouting, singing and throwing himself about like a mad thing: a one-man show featuring dancers, male and female, singers of both sexes, a whole orchestra, a complete opera-house, dividing himself into twenty different stage parts, tearing up and down, stopping, like one possessed, with flashing eyes and foaming mouth. The weather was terribly hot, and the sweat running down the furrows of his brow and cheeks mingled with the powder from his hair and ran in streaks down the top of his coat. What didn't he do? He wept, laughed, sighed, his gaze was tender, soft or furious: a woman swooning with grief, a poor wretch abandoned in the depth of his despair, a temple rising into view, birds falling silent at eventide, waters murmuring in a cool, solitary place or tumbling in torrents down the mountain side, a thunderstorm, a hurricane, the shrieks of the dying mingled with the howling of the tempest and the crash of thunder; night with its shadows, darkness and silence, for even silence itself can be depicted in sound. By now he was quite beside himself. Knocked up with fatigue, like a man coming out of a deep sleep or long trance, he stood there motionless, dazed, astonished, looking about him and trying to recognize his surroundings. Waiting for his strength and memory to come back, he mechanically wiped his face. Like a person waking up to see a large number of people gathered round his bed and totally oblivious or profoundly ignorant of what he had been doing, his first impulse was to cry out 'Well, gentlemen, what's up? What are you laughing at? Why are you so surprised? What's up?' Then he went on: 'Now that's what you call music and a musician. And yet, gentlemen, you mustn't look down on some of the things in Lully. I defy anyone to better the scene *Ah, j'attendrai*, without altering the words. You mustn't look down on some parts of Campra, or my uncle's violin airs and his gavottes, his entries for soldiers, priests, sacrificers ... *Pâles flambeaux, nuit plus affreuse que les ténèbres ... Dieu du Tartare, Dieu de l'oubli. ...* '[k] At this point he raised his voice, held on to the notes, and neighbours came to their windows while we stuck our fingers in our ears. 'This,' he went on, 'is where you need lung-power, a powerful organ, plenty of wind. But soon it will be good-bye to Assumption, Lent and Epiphany have already come and gone. They don't yet know what to set to music, nor, therefore, what a musician wants. Lyric poetry has yet to be born. But they will come to it through hearing Pergolesi, the Saxon,[l] Terradeglias, Trajetta and the rest; through reading Metastasio they will have to come to it.')

I: You mean to say that Quinault, La Motte, Fontenelle didn't know anything about it?[m]

HE: Not for the modern style. There aren't six lines together in all their charming poems that you can set to music. Ingenious aphorisms, light,

[k]From *Castor et Pollux* by Rameau.

[l]'The Saxon' in this list of Italian composers may be Hasse or Handel.

[m]Quinault, La Motte, Fontenelle all wrote operatic libretti. Fontenelle (1657-1757) was, of course, also an important literary figure in other fields, particularly as a popularizer of scientific ideas and the great champion of the Moderns in the Quarrel of the Ancients and Moderns in the last years of the seventeenth century.

tender, delicate madrigals, but if you want to see how lacking all that is in material for our art, the most exacting of all, not even excepting that of Demosthenes, get someone to recite these pieces, and how cold, tired and monotonous they will sound! There is nothing in them that can serve as a basis for song. I would just as soon have to set the *Maximes* of La Rochefoucauld or the *Pensées* of Pascal to music. It is the animal cry of passion that should dictate the melodic line, and these moments should tumble out quickly one after the other, phrases must be short and the meaning self-contained, so that the musician can utilize the whole and each part, omitting one word or repeating it, adding a missing word, turning it all ways like a polyp, without destroying it. All this makes lyric poetry in French a much more difficult problem than in languages with inversions which have these natural advantages . . . *Barbare, cruel, plonge ton poignard dans mon sein. Me voilà prête à recevoir le coup fatal. Frappe. Ose. . . . Ah! je languis, je meurs. . . . Un feu secret s'allume dans mes sens. . . . Cruel amour, que veux-tu de moi? . . . Laisse-moi la douce paix dont j'ai joui. . . . Rends-moi la raison. . . .* The passions must be strong and the sensibility of composer and poet must be very great. The aria is almost always the peroration of a scene. What we want is exclamations, interjections, suspensions, interruptions, affirmations, negations; we call out, invoke, shout, groan, weep or have a good laugh. No witticisms, epigrams, none of your well-turned thoughts— all that is far too removed from nature. And don't imagine that the technique of stage actors and their declamation can serve as a model. Pooh! we want something more energetic, less stilted, truer to life. The simple language and normal expression of emotion are all the more essential because our language is more monotonous and less highly stressed. The cry of animal instinct or that of a man under stress of emotion will supply them.

(While he was saying all this the crowds round us had melted away, either because they understood nothing he was saying or found it uninteresting, for generally speaking a child like a man and a man like a child would rather be amused than instructed; everybody was back at his game and we were left alone in our corner. Slumped on a seat with his head against the wall, arms hanging limp and eyes half shut, he said: 'I don't know what's the matter with me; when I came here I was fresh and full of life and now I am knocked up and exhausted, as though I had walked thirty miles. It has come over me all of a sudden.')

I: Would you like a drink?

HE: I don't mind if I do. I feel hoarse. I've no go left in me and I've a bit of pain in my chest. I get it like this nearly every day, I don't know why.

I: What ill you have?

HE: Whatever you like. I'm not fussy. Poverty has taught me to make do with anything.

(Beer and lemonade are brought. He fills and empties a big glass two or three times straight off. Then, like a man restored, he coughs hard, has a good stretch and goes on:)

But don't you think, my lord Philosopher, that it is a very odd thing that a foreigner, an Italian, a Duni should come and teach us how to put the stress into our own music, and adapt our vocal music to every speed, time, interval and kind of speech without upsetting prosody? And yet it wouldn't have taken all that doing. Anyone who had ever heard a beggar asking for alms in the street, a man in a towering rage, a woman mad with jealousy, a despairing lover, a flatterer—yes, a flatterer lowering his voice and dwelling on each syllable in honeyed tones—in short a passion, any passion, so long as it was strong enough to act as a model for a musician, should have noticed two things: one, that syllables, whether long or short, have no fixed duration nor even a settled connexion between their durations, and the other, that passion does almost what it likes with prosody; it jumps over the widest intervals, so that a man crying out from the depths of his grief: '*Ah, malheureux que je suis!*' goes up in pitch on the exclamatory syllable to his highest and shrillest tone, and down on the others to his deepest and most solemn, spreading over an octave or even greater interval and giving each sound the quantity required by the turn of the melody without offending the ear, although the long and short syllables are not kept to the length or brevity of normal speech. What a way we have come since we used to cite the parenthesis in *Armide: Le vainqueur de Renaud (si quelqu'un le peut être)*, or: *Obéissons sans balancer* from *Les Indes galantes* as miracles of musical declamation! Now these miracles make me shrug my shoulders with pity. The way art is advancing I don't know where it will end! Meanwhile let's have a drink.

CHAPTER TWENTY

JOHANN JAKOB WILHEM HEINSE

Musikalische Dialogen
(1776 or 1777)

SECOND DIALOGUE
THE PRINCESS***, METASTASIO,
AND THE GRACES[a]

. . . . .

Princess. . . . . . Opera is reproached with being unnatural in that it is ridiculous when Hercules and Alexander sing their heroic thoughts accompanied by all the pomp of music. One can answer nothing to this reproach except—that the ridiculousness, in the case of an excellent performance, can be felt only by cold philosophers, whose heads and ears contain vital spirits that are insusceptible of warmth and have no connection with the heart. This reproach cannot be directed to your accomplished Graces as well. For a Grace one doubtless can not maintain that song is unnatural.

Metastasio. But I think that there are still many reasons to question whether the singing Alexander and Hercules are indeed not really ridiculous.

[a]The Graces (Aglaia, Euphrosyne, and Thalia) do not really appear in the dialogue itself, but only in a short dramatic poem intended for musical setting that Heinse appends to the dialogue. In the earlier part of the dialogue, which I have omitted, the Princess comes upon Metastasio while she is out walking. She offers him a lovely rose in exchange for the poem on which he has been working (the Italian original of the appended one), and she is overcome by its beauty. After a brief discussion of the musical quality of the Italian language, the talk naturally turns to opera.

When opera was invented, people must undoubtedly have thought so, for the poets did not venture to place human beings on the stage, but had gods and Satan and nymphs and fairies appear, and even when they did venture to, a god still had to untie the so-called knot. The fools did not have enough common sense to realize that gods were still more ridiculous in this than men.

The gods appearing among men were already more ridiculous in the times when people still believed in them, honored them, and brought them sacrifices; Euripides himself brought his gods and goddesses into the theater only so that he might make fun of them. Nothing is more ridiculous than when the old Zeus must descend from his ancient heaven to make up for the lack of genius in a poet and by the discovery of a piece of folly in a horribly tragic action, to cut the knot asunder.

Princess. Your Graces doubtless cannot be reproached with this. They lead us into the paradise of the Homeric heaven, and permit us to look at the most beautiful of their goddesses there. They do not untie any knot. The action is so modest, so beautiful, so excellently worked out, and the phantasy at the same time so probable, that it can only deceive us and surprise us with the actual presence of the Graces. They transport us to the Greek heaven, the way a fine Greek poet or painter magically transported his contemporaries. Herr Metastasio, must we not be just as advanced in dramatic art as the Greeks?

Metastasio. A fine opera is the high masterpiece of dramatic art. Its invention was reserved for the moderns, for the ancients did not possess it.[b] The Greek tragedy was really not an opera at all, as a number of scholars have wished to represent it. We cannot assert more than that Greek tragedies in their performance had at the most a similarity to our recitatives. The Greeks achieved the highest degree of perfection in their music, and we perhaps the highest degree of perfection in ours. The musical instruments of the Greeks were more imperfect by far than ours. They could use them only for accompaniment, and in their accompaniment they without doubt arrived at the highest degree of perfection, just as in their singing. But I believe I can now draw the conclusion from this that our music is more perfect to the extent that our instruments excell the Greek ones. At least our instrumental music is that much more perfect. Our virtuosi without any

[b]In the countless comparisons of ancient and modern art, which extend from the sixteenth century to the nineteenth, opera is sometimes identified with ancient music or tragedy and sometimes with modern, depending mostly on the attitude of the writer towards opera and on his conception of ancient music. Heinse's Metastasio—whose views are not really those of the historical Metastasio—obviously has a very high regard for opera, and he is no longer subject to a blind enthusiasm for Antiquity. His conception of ancient tragedy, in addition, does not permit him to equate it to opera. As a result, opera becomes a distinctively modern genre of dramatic art that is superior both to ancient tragedy and to spoken tragedy in general.

doubt can play their clavecins and violins just as excellently as the Greeks their barbitons, for with a number of virtuosi no higher degree of perfection can any longer be imagined. Their barbiton could at the most be no more perfect an instrument than our harp. And thus to the same extent that an excellent clavecin is more perfect than a harp, our instrumental music also is more perfect.

Princess. The argument seems to be quite conclusive; but skeptical heads will doubtless still not consider it to be conclusive. They will say, who knows whether the barbiton was not just as perfect an instrument as our clavecin? for there are scholars who are not embarassed to assert that the ship of Ulysses was a large as a great English man-of-war.

Metastasio. The comparisons of our arts with the arts of the ancients are always foolish. Modern music is something entirely different than the music of the ancients. That is obvious. But we cannot exactly determine the various degrees of its perfection, because we have no remnants of the music of the ancients.

Princess. This can doubtless not be denied: that our instrumental music is more perfect; but how does it stand with vocal music?

Metastasio. I believe that our famous cantatrici and singers are at least as excellent as the singers and cantatrici of the Greeks. Their song was beautiful Nature, and our song is beautified Nature. Their cantatrici probably did not make such a particular study of it as our Faustinas and Luzzonis do. Perhaps they sang just as excellently as these; but what is a little song compared to the tender, the moving representations of a whole opera!

Princess. This argument is too strong. Excellent song tied to an excellent action must indeed produce more effects than song alone, or than song tied to the action that is required for a little song. But the cold northern admirer of the Greeks will always say: your opera is unnatural, and consequently Greek music still excels modern after all! For to want to excel the natural through the unnatural is just like wanting to set above Petrarch the imitators who snatch at antitheses.

Metastasio. One could first of all have these cold northern heads demonstrate that the production of the Greek tragedies was as natural as they suppose. Their declamation, their choruses, and their pipes and other instruments also, would perhaps make their demonstration very difficult, and when they produced one, they would perhaps likewise have diminished the unnatural aspect of our opera as a result.

Princess. But whence does it come that the song of these heroes on the stage does not at all seem unnatural to us, since we must imagine it as unnatural in the living room.

Metastasio. Princess, spare me the explanation of this question! An abstract cold German head will perhaps better be able to explain this matter to you than I. My soul does not depart from my phantasy, and consequently it also can not contemplate this from a distance and come to conclusions about it.

Princess. This excuse will not do. Warm heads can philosophize on certain matters better than cold; and fiery ones better than both. This matter is suitable for you.

Metastasio. I do not know the way into the sanctuaries of the goddesses Music and Philosophy; there it is dark. How can I find a path that I do not know? How can I see where it is dark?

Princess. I remark already now why you do not wish to do this; you think I would surely not understand your explanation. Is that not so?

It is true I am still an unknowing girl; but I still believe I can understand very well that which is understandable. Your philosophy is certainly understandable. Each little word in your language has an image, and I understand the little words very well with which I can connect images.

Metastasio. Your fervent desire for knowledge would be a demonstration of the radiance of the nobility of your soul if your countless, deep thoughts did not already demonstrate it. Indeed I thank the Father of existence for the bliss that nations under your future governance will enjoy. Princess, your soul is truly an emanation of divinity, even if no other human soul be such.

Princess. You are a man of quality, Metastasio. Your tongue is as equal to your heart as it is to your head. I will seek to cultivate myself in such a way that you shall not have thanked the Father of existence in vain for the bliss of the nations. But, dear Metastasio, we do not want to let ourselves be blinded by these lightning flashes in our conversation. Why, Metastasio, does the song of heroes on the stage not seem unnatural to us, since it seems to be unnatural off it? Should we be unable to explain this? We want to try: you begin, I also want to help work along. You will certainly not refuse to work with so clever a girl as I am?

Metastasio. You humble yourself too much before the poet Metastasio.

Princess. And you humble the Princess too much when you speak to her in this way.

Metastasio. You compel me to, Princess! You will therefore be so gracious as to pardon me if my philosophy should be forced.

He who has seen an excellent opera performed in Naples will not doubt the possibility that an opera can deceive and set the spectator into such a forgetfulness of the improbability that he believes he sees the real Alexander, the real Dido, the real Hercules. The frequent tears that roll over faces full of violent emotion, the deeply respiring bosoms, in which fear is at work, of the Italian women will demonstrate it to him. If there should be even one head with such witnessing eyes that wanted to regard these tears as proofs of the fanaticism of the Italians, then he may consider the faces of the Frenchmen and Englishmen in such operas, and their tears will tell him that he is not a man, still less a god—but that he is nothing more than a thinking machine without humanity. Even the often inappropriate figure of the castrati for the personae they represent does not interfere with the deception. When perhaps Faustinas, Luzzonis, Porporas have the roles suitable to them, when at the same time an Apostolo Zeno expresses the passion of the personae in the language of the Muses, and a Pergolesi has experienced in his soul the accents for that purpose—oh! how little must he then know Nature who can deem the song of these persons to be unnatural! He is not worthy to feel bliss! Let him have the fame of a stoic, of a man whose soul remains forever impassive, like a stone.

Princess. But how must things proceed so that the most enlightened heads, the people with the best taste, without attending to the improbability, are yet so much deceived that they can not keep it in mind?

Metastasio. Where Nature is, the poet and the composer can easily charm the improbability out of the heads of the listeners. The improbability in operas is not much greater than in tragedies and comedies. Caesar, Cato, Brutus, Alexander, Medea, and Lucretia speak in French, English, and Italian verses in the theater. When the poet has drawn their characters well and powerfully, when the actors and actresses are excellent, Nature banishes the improbability.

Princess. Then did Pergolesi, Vinci, and Leo have to bring the unnatural element to opera; the more excellent, the more ravishing their melodies were, the more unnatural did they have to be? What a foolish assertion! One should cut off the ears or pierce the eardrum of those who can assert something of this kind.

Metastasio. In operas the passions are presented in the highest degree of beauty of which they can possibly be capable. Everything must accord with the passion: tone, action, and expression. The persons acting in operas are ideals of perfect human beings.

Why is song in the invention of an opera held to be natural for gods and unnatural for men?

Princess. Without any doubt, because the gods were imagined as the most perfect men.

Metastasio. The tone of the usual utterance of a person who is in a certain passion is coarse; the passion itself brings it forth still crude and imperfect. The composer simply adapts it, and gives it the pleasantness, the beauty that the poet has given to the rough speech, the unpolished expression of the impassioned person.

When a person who is in a violent passion only narrates, or even, if I may thus express myself, treats of the history of the passion, the tone of the usual utterance will not change much; but as soon as he expresses his feelings about it, as soon as he groans over his fate, or as soon as two persons are in a scene in which they no longer act, but can only feel, there the tone changes very noticeably, the accents become now faster, now slower; now words fail them for the expression of their feeling, it thus expresses itself simply in tones; now it can no longer do even this, and the all too violent feeling chokes off tone and words. The narration or the described history of the passion makes up the recitative, and the feelings expressed about it arias and choruses. This takes place with most of the passions: anger, love, fear, horror, jealousy mount up from their beginnings to their greatest height, and with their growth the accents of threats, tenderness, laments, sighs, rage, and horror continuously change.

The poet makes Nature more perfect, and the composer perfects it still more. When they both are equal geniuses, are equally excellent, they will heighten the strength, the beauty of the passion to such a degree that simply in looking at and listening to the persons acting, those present must feel more than when they themselves are in the same passion.

The spectators see and hear persons actually behaving; their feeling, their senses do not permit them to think of the unnatural, but prove to them only too much that the sung feeling is natural. Only so much of the history of Dido occurs to them as is necessary to understand her passion.

The composer must know perfectly the nature of the tones together with their effects on the nerves of the ear, and the shocks that these produce throughout the entire human being; the melody must harmonize perfectly with the feeling.

And thus an opera is nothing less than unnatural; much more is there an addition made here of that which natural beauty and perfection still lack. Thence it comes that an aria affects the heart a hundred times more strongly when it is sung than when it is only declaimed in a tragedy. I have seen the finest tragedies of Corneille and Racine performed, and the almost superhuman action and declamation of the most famous actress have not lured forth so many tears by far from the spectators as an excellent cantatrice can produce with the transporting song of an aria in which the most profound degree of a melancholy tenderness is expressed in the divine language of the Italians. Her tender, sighed accents sung by a mouth suffused with melancholy grace, the tears of her eyes looking up to heaven, her anxiously heaving breast with which the heart can speak more than with the tongue! bound to the activity of a beautiful body—Who will feel nothing here? Even behavior is more natural in the opera than in a tragedy; here it is often so rapid that it makes the whole action unnatural; the battle of the mind with the passions in their full strength is often not finished in as short a time as an actress in a tragedy allows it to last in order to avoid emptiness.

Poet and composer must both have one and the same final aim: the poet may put nothing into his action that the composer can not treat, and the composer may not interrupt the action or diminish its interest through the pomp and the empty noise of his music.

Therefore the poet may do nothing more than gradually realize the passions in actions from their interesting beginnings up to their highest point. Their fire may not entirely die out, the flame must always grow little by little. Cold, deliberated sentences, thoughts without feelings, syllogisms, political subtleties, in short, witticism and understanding must not force their way into the language of feeling and the heart. The composer can not express these. Music either expresses passions and feelings or it is nothing more than a pleasant noise for the ears. The spectator must feel continuously;[c] as soon as the feeling is interrupted, as soon as the soul can think as it pleases, that soon is at least the interest in the action weakened, if it has not totally disappeared. Hence the first and the somewhat later operas were nothing more than a concert of recitative and arias intermixed. The music was a thing in itself, and the poetry also. At the most they set up an alliance, like a not too loving married couple. They should be connected, however, like the parts of a human being; one must be able to distinguish separately neither poetry nor melody; they must flow together, fuse together with one another. And then the deception will be produced with complete certainty, and the opera will always be with respect to tragedy and comedy what tragedy is with respect to the real actions of men.

Princess. I have listened to you with pleasure, and you seem to be perfectly right when you elevate the opera so far above the tragedy.

Men are raised up by the opera to an ideal of perfection which they surely have still not achieved in Nature; the acting persons in opera are improbable, but not unnatural. The improbability vanishes because men always wish for beautiful Nature in actuality, and when they are given even the slightest opportunity to do so, they really perceive it. Nature endows human beings in particular with this basic impulse to become always more perfect. From this there arises the love of supernal beauty; for the supernal, the ideal beauty is a perfectly natural one; and thence arises our love of seeing each thing in its highest perfection. We have hardly made the wish when phantasy at once contributes what is lacking for full perfection; if it does not do so itself, it is exceedingly delighted if a painting of the highest perfection of a thing is presented to it. All the senses are directed upon the object, and everything is removed that is contrary to this painting of the highest perfection. Thus one looks upon a beautiful painting as though it were alive; the Titian Venus sleeps, Christ is transfigured, the Medici Venus leaves her bath, Laocoön groans as the serpents crush him; the power of our phantasy goes still further, we see before our eyes the persons that poets allow to act in their poems; and in just this way we see with our eyes the conquering heroes bodily present, our real eyes are transformed into the eyes of the phantasy, we see them as they are and not as

---

[c]Continuity of feeling was to be emphasized more and more in the future as an important requirement of opera. Lacépède discusses it at length in his *Poétique de la musique* of 1785.

they are said to be according to their history. Song is nothing more than speech brought to the highest perfection. The unharmonious tones of everyday utterance have become harmonious.

Metastasio. But why do we look upon the caricatures, the exaggerated ugliness in paintings as just as much alive as the beauty?

Princess. Because the ugliness is more perfect than the beauty. But when I see an ugly object portrayed, I look upon it immediately after the first glance merely as a painting and not as alive, and I will not allow the painter to arouse aversion in my senses. I will always prefer to see everything beautiful rather than ugly and deficient. We should also call the artists who cultivate the ugly not fine artists, but ugly ones.

Metastasio. Princess, at times poets and painters must develop ugly characters in order to set the other persons in a brighter light through this contrast. One must often only describe Nature, allow it to show itself as it is, if one wishes to make a painting interesting; too great a perfection will become a burden to us if we can not attain it. Too beautiful a Nature, especially passions too purified of the human, receive through the excessive improbability a touch of the unnatural, so that they wound our self-love and we take the passion for something affected, for hypocrisy.

Princess. Human nature must be adhered to; the passions natural to it, human nature beautified to the highest degree with true, authentic human passions, will always remain an object of our love. We indeed may not elevate our heroes to the status of gods, extracting the humanity from them; we must endow them not only with exalted nobility, but also with anger, licentious love, and other human passions. They must have blood and nerves. I believe that we may never place on the stage an ugly character, until he increases the tears that we must shed over the person made unhappy by him. The stage is destined more for the spiritual pleasure of men than for instruction, just as all the fine arts are. Moral philosophy is supposed to show the consequences that vices and virtues have. We are interested in the virtuous persons on the stage, and the vice-ridden we shun; but we must already know what virtue and vice are before we can do this. We admire a fine poet's great knowledge of human beings in his dramatic pieces, indeed we learn to know men better from him, we study the nature of the passions in his acting characters; but we do not go to the play in order to be shown the consequences of vice and virtue through an action three hours long. Consequently the chief purpose of a fine artist is to beautify Nature and to make it more perfect, in order to elicit spiritual pleasure in those for whom he works.

Now because in a perfect opera the spiritual pleasures are elicited in the spectators and listeners not only more strongly but also more frequently, it is also precisely for that reason far to be preferred to tragedy and comedy. And consequently you, Herr Metastasio, are to be preferred to the Greek and English and French tragic authors, because you write operas just as perfect as their tragedies are; for a poem in which there may be nothing other than passion, nothing other than action and feeling, is very much more difficult to construct than another in which one has the permission of the art critics to pour the cold water of sententiousness over the spectators and listeners.

Metastasio. Princess, I do not know how I have come to deserve that you be so extraordinarily gracious to me today. I will apply all my talents to how I can make myself worthy in the future of your extraordinary kindness.

Princess. No compliments and professions of thanks to my praise! Metastasio, you know how highly I esteem you! Your Graces have further increased the deep respect I already had for you. They are the most lovely girls, together with their Cupid. They make the entire soul serene with their naive and innocent tales; and even their revenge, and the nature of the revenge, is full of grace. If the composer only follows this naive innocence, and only does not desire to display his art in its artifice, and if then the cantatrici can lend grace to their action and their song, this little poem must set the spectators and listeners into the sweetest rapture. There will be a bright stillness in our soul such as in the most beautiful spring surround of Elysium.

CHAPTER TWENTY-ONE

BERNARD GERMAIN LACÉPÈDE

La Poétique de la musique
(1785)

VOLUME I BOOK II
ON THEATER MUSIC

We are entering the sanctuary of vocal music; she will show us the children who owe to her their life. At their head the *Tragédie lyrique*, proud, terrible, majestic, sublime, advances with a dagger in one hand and the lyre in the other; her stride is lordly and animated; her hair is disheveled; often she sheds tears. At her side the *Comédie lyrique*, gay, alive, playful, appears in the center of the games; the Graces scatter flowers around her, a smile is on her lips, and shyness in her eyes; her stride is noble, but lively, her manner affable and familiar; she portrays morals and the ridiculous with the colors gaiety supplies to her, and if occasionally she sheds some tears, they are soon wiped away by pleasure. In their train comes the *Pastorale*; she sings only shepherds; she portrays only rustic scenes; she is happy only in the midst of the woods and at the margin of fountains; musettes and oboes make the echoes resound everywhere she turns her steps. Between her and the *Tragédie lyrique* appears the *Heroic Pastorale*, who along paths strewn with flowers, approaches the shepherds, the heroes, and the gods; the trumpet and the pipe are in her hands; warriors precede her, and gentle shepherds accompany her.

Further away, one perceives the Music uniquely consecrated to sing the praises of the Eternal: her august and religious stride is, however, full of grace; she scarcely raises her voice except in temples: the sacred trumpet announces her approach; she loves above all to hear around her voices singing in chorus; the celestial chords of the saintly harp that sounds under her fingers accompany the soft, noble, and touching melody that she makes use of to send forth her affections. Sometimes she sighs; sometimes, holding up her majestic head, she celebrates the Most High and his saints; nearly always in a tender voice and in a meditative air, she addresses to Heaven the prayers of the multitudes.

Finally there appears the Music whose use is to diffuse a thousand charms in our dwellings, either when assembled in great number, we would like to enjoy in common the gentle and innocent pleasures of melody and harmony, or when in solitude, we would seek to enliven the days that we pass there alone, and when we would interrupt with pleasing and tranquil songs the silence of a pleasant retreat. Let us approach all these daughters of vocal music, the better to receive their lessons and their sweet presents. Let us begin by listening to the *Tragédie lyrique*.

ON THE TRAGÉDIE LYRIQUE
ON THE GENERAL EFFECT OF THE
TRAGÉDIE LYRIQUE

We can not better indicate the different means the musician must employ to produce in the tragedy all the effects that one may expect of him; we can not better reveal the beauties he is able to distribute there and the defects he must avoid there, than by following in detail the different parts of the tragedy, at least those that the musician must originate, or embellish. But let us precede these particular considerations with a general view: let us examine the tragedy in itself, and let us cast our glance over the whole that it must present: the most important object of all those with which the musician must occupy himself, and the one that presents him with the greatest difficulties to be overcome.

It is not necessary that the musician join to his talents the art of writing verse; that art is essential only to the poet with whom he works, and from whom he derives the subject that he must animate. But he must in some way possess to the same degree as the poet the talent of revealing and placing before his eyes the subject of the tragedy, the art of presenting only one action, of showing it always in the large, of grounding it in the scenes and in the acts, in such a way that no act ends without our having been conducted nearer to the denouement, and that no new scene appears only to present or announce an event, a plan, or a new feeling. He should, like the poet, know the means of making the wonder, the terror, and the pity grow from the beginning of the work to the end, the three great passions that the tragedy must depict; he should, like the poet, know how to avoid boredom, useless episodes, all that which could dampen the spectator. Like the poet, he should know how to motivate the entrances and the exits of the characters; see to it that none of them appears uselessly; that all those who play an important role are announced necessarily, either by an occurrence or by an actor. He should know, like the poet, the art of establishing and of painting vividly the characters, of making them contrast without affectation, of sustaining them from the beginning to the end, of rendering the situations agonizing, terrifying, moving, etc., and finally, of producing a dialogue broken by pauses more or less long, according as the feeling that animates the characters is more or less rapid, more or less concentrated, more or less restrained.

Why should the musician combine the talents and skills we have just indicated? Primarily, to enter readily into the spirit of the poet, not to harm his work in any way, to efface none of its beauties, even to give his tragedy a new brilliance; and in the second place, to be able to replace it to some extent, when particular circumstances have prevented the poet from observing fully what is necessary to the perfection of a dramatic work; and when nevertheless a large substratum of interest or of highly attractive situations has induced the musician to work on the poet's product. But how will the musician be able with his art to make good the deficiency of the poet, when the latter has not fulfilled at all the different duties of which we have just spoken, and which were set forth long ago? I say *with his art*; for if he seeks to correct the poem in itself, it is no longer as a musician that he works, it is as a poet, and our tract can not consider him.

Primarily, the musician should substitute for the poet with respect to the exposition of the subject. In truth, if the poet has constructed absolutely no exposition, it will be impossible for the musician to conceal this great deficiency; but if the poem presents an imperfect exposition, it will most often be simple for the musician to complete it. If the poet has only glossed over some important occurrence, the musician will have to bring out with the greatest care the weak expression which points to that merely forgotten event. He will sacrifice in some way to the section he would like to make visible some of the measures that precede it; he will stop at the place where the occurrence is spoken of; he will deploy there all the power of melody, and all that of harmony: if the occurrence is of such a nature as to demand a somewhat lengthy depiction, and if the words that the poet has made use of to speak of it cannot be spoken several times without affectation, the musician will have the art to keep the voice silent for some time, and to place in the orchestra the repetitions necessary to the expression he desires. If this same occurrence must be depicted with a highly varied melody, a strengthened harmony, a clamorous ensemble; the musician to render it more perceptible will present surrounding it, for some measures, only a very simple and in some degree monotonous melody, for which most often he will even provide no accompaniment. If on the contrary this interesting occurrence calls for a simple melody and a gentle harmony, his tableau will have to be preceded only by a shock of notes that will rush noisily and rapidly through very wide intervals.

If the poet has not neglected in his exposition the events already past, or those which must take place during the course of the piece, he may have drawn in an inexact or too feeble manner the characters of the various personae, either of those who give the exposition, or of those who are discussed in it. The musician will then be able to substitute for him in portraying the characters, not only with colors analogous to the expression of the poet, but even with colors a little stronger, so as to compensate on the one side for what is lacking on the other. It is necessary, however, that he take care not to carry his expression to excess, for fear that he may create too great a contrast between the tone he employs and that of the poet, and that he may render more striking the deficiency of the poem instead of concealing it. For the rest, the musician will make use, for the portrayal of the characters, of the means that we shall shortly indicate to him.

But not only must the musician observe what we have just pointed out when the poet has left something to be desired in his exposition; he must observe it also when the exposition is what it should be, so as to reinforce the intentions of the poet well, and to make the piece produce all the effect it can create; but let him not employ, then, colors stronger than those that the tone of the poem may require. See in the *Iphigénie en Tauride* of M. le chevalier Gluck, with what art he has presented the exposition constructed by the poet, and followed the design of the latter! One must similarly admire the manner in which M. Sacchini has set to music, in the opera *Chimène*, the narration of the battle against the Moors. A narration is for the musician only a more or less animated exposition.

The author of a dramatic work should never cease attending to the excitement of curiosity of the mind, to the circumspect treatment of its laziness, to the anticipation of its agility and inconstancy. The subject of a dramatic work should thus be interesting, single, and varied. In a tragedy, where one always expects great things, the subject can be of interest only in so far as it presents a quality of grandeur; the action of the *tragédie lyrique* should thus be great, single, and varied. How will the musician be able to make good the deficiency of the poet, at least up to a certain point, when the latter has depicted an action interesting and touching in itself, but which does not provide the quality of grandeur that it should present? He will be able to attain this in two ways: first of all, in giving more force to the occurrences, I would say, in portraying them more horribly or more pleasantly, in enlarging the effects that issue from them; and secondly, in employing a means more potent than the one we have just proposed to him, in animating in his depictions all the passions that agitate the characters, in giving more vivacity to the fires of hate and to those of love, in representing in a manner more energetic than that of the poet, all the feelings that are to appear on the stage. Every feeling raised to a very high degree becomes a great object, just as it is ennobled by its cause.

With regard to the unity of action, the musician can, by means of his colors, enfeeble the occurrence that could interrupt that unity at the point at which it is grounded, at which it is concealed, so to speak, in the principal occurrence, and at which it is almost impossible not to merge the two together. The musician will similarly reinforce the unity of interest, if he does not present in an equally vivid manner the traits of the characters from whom attention and interest could be diverted, and if on the contrary he searches for the strongest nuances for depicting the traits of the character whom one should have uniquely in view. He will succeed in attaining this last end, if he sacrifices to his project in some degree the role of the character he would like to keep from stealing attention, or better stated, if he endeavors to render that role as perfect as another one of its kind, but if he weakens the feelings of the character, if he depicts his love only as a tenderness, his grief only as a sorrow, his anxiety only as a concern, etc. Similarly, when he has to show the event that could prejudice the unity of the action, he will not deploy all the force with which he can represent the objects. For the rest, the musician must equally observe all that we have just said when he has only to reinforce the poet. See how M. Gossec in his opera *Thésée* has weakened everything that could have been connected with tenderness in the character of Médée, so that we might see in some way to some extent in the love of this sorceress only vanity, jealousy, and fury; that she might not change the direction of the interest, and that all hearts might be with Eglé, who every time she sings, expresses through fervent but gentle melodies the tender agitations of her soul.

As for the variety that the subject should present, the musician will find in this tract different means of producing it.

The gradation in the scenes and in the acts, so necessary to the effect of a dramatic work, is perhaps the object of dramatic art for which it is easiest for the musician to take the place of the poet, and to make up for his omissions or his unavoidable negligence. A scene which neither offers us nor informs us about any interesting occurrence, and in which the feelings are the same as those that have already been expressed, can only harm the dramatic work of which it is a part; not only does it not produce an effect superior to that of the scene that has preceded it, and in consequence it interrupts the gradation that is desired; but it absolutely destroys that gradation: it is absolutely cold, it can only diffuse boredom: it consequently diminishes the interest that one had already succeeded in creating. It is, however, possible for the musician to make up here for the deficiency of the poet; not only will he cause this scene to be heard with pleasure; but he will make it more interesting than the preceding one. He will not be able to relate any action in it, to develop any new feeling in it, to depict any new occurrence in it; but everything one already knows he will tell in a manner so novel, he will tell in a manner so touching, he will tell with so much charm, he will infuse with so many musical beauties, that he will make the most complete illusion arise: we shall believe we see or hear new things, because those that we shall see or that we shall hear will appear in a form absolutely novel. If we come to perceive that we have before our eyes only the same things concealed behind new ornaments, we shall nevertheless not be able to prevent ourselves from seeing them with an interest almost as keen as if they were new: so difficult it is in all things, and especially in the arts, not to transfer to the subject the charm of its accessories! There will even be, in a certain way, events and feelings that are really new, since they would not yet have been expressed in so strong a manner, and since they still in consequence would not have existed as an entire whole for the spectator.

In general, the musician will succeed in establishing between the musical pieces, between the scenes and the acts, the gradation that one should find there, if when he is able to choose between two manners of representing an object, he always reserves the strongest expression for the piece of the same type which will have to appear last; and even if he weakens the traits of the tableaux presented at the beginning of the work, when every other means is denied him. He will keep for the end of the tragedy, or for the scenes which will be nearest to it, the most agonizing harmonies, the most daring transitions, the most expressive accompaniments, the most distinctive orchestral features, the most extended, the most beautiful, the most pathetic melodies, the strongest contrasts, those renunciations, those sublime violations of most of the rules, those moving cries, all those sources of the true beauties and the great effects of music. Perhaps M. Rousseau had good reason to write M. Gluck that his opera *Alceste* would have been still more beautiful and would have produced more of an effect if he had restrained his colors at the beginning, and if he had reserved for the end the strong colors of sadness, of desolation, and of grief.

When the poet has neglected to establish between the passions he will produce on the stage, the gradation so necessary for the effect of a tragedy, or when he has not been able to create that same gradation, what will the resource of the musician be in substituting for the solicitude of the poet?

The poet has two means of making the passions appear more or less forceful. He can depict them as extreme by not contenting himself with having the characters say that they are animated by a violent passion of hate, of amibition, of jealousy, etc.; but primarily by making them speak like truly impassioned men; and secondly, by employing a means with which he will produce still more of an effect, in making them act like those who are transported by a violent passion.

When the poet has neglected to make the actors speak in a manner the more impassioned as the action advances the more towards the denouement, it will be easy for the musician to make up his deficiency; has not the musician at his command a language much more expressive than ordinary language when it comes to feelings and consequently to passions? He has only to give the more force to the musical language as the end of the work is the nearer, and we shall certainly not perceive that the language of the poet is not steadily increasing its force.

When it is the deficiency of action on the part of the characters that makes the passions languish in a tragedy, it is very difficult for the musician to veil that deficiency, and to eliminate its bad effect. He can indeed paint vividly all that is offered him, he can indeed represent actions that do not exist, but he can not confer them upon those who are seen not to act: he can not make an actor who discourses when it might be necessary to go to battle appear nevertheless in the middle of a battle with weapons in his hand: he can only in such a case have recourse to the means that we have already indicated to him. Let him give to the actors a manner of speaking more animated than the one that they owe to the poet; he will create a certain illusion in the heart of the spectators: affected, even transported by the vehement accents of the actor, they will perhaps not perceive that actions were demanded at the time, not words. When a hero should be going to take his place at the head of his troops, they will not see that he is remaining uselessly on the stage, if the manner in which he expresses himself breathes military ardor, and kindles in their hearts the noble fire of glory. It is thus that a great poet may salvage scenes that are cold and stripped of action, by a charm of style so seductive, by expressions so animated, that we may not perceive that the actors should be acting instead of speaking.

May musicians never neglect the means that we have just indicated to them, even though they may have no deficiency with which to reproach the poet, even though they may desire solely to have the beauties of his work appear in the full light of day, if they wish at least that the tragedy which occupies them might obtain for them all the glory to which they aspire. See how, in *Iphigénie en Aulide*, M. Gluck has put into the mouth of Clytemnestra, expressions the more terrible and the more harrowing the nearer is the denouement; and how he has observed that desired gradation even from the moment when Clytemnestra is aware of the frightful sacrifice that threatens the days of her daughter. With regard to the colors which the musician should use for all the depictions we have just indicated to him, we shall speak of them in treating the manner of representing the passions.

When the poet has left in his work some moment that is cold, devoid of action or of feeling, let the musician redouble his efforts to prevent it from being perceived: let him sustain alone the attention of the spectator that is about to lessen. If that spectator is bored for a moment, all the bauties that may have preceded that fatal spot could be forgotten, all those that may follow it could produce only half of the effects they would have created. Let the musician deploy all the magic of his art, then, let him sound the most beautiful songs, the sweetest and freshest melody, the most pleasing accompaniments, the most seductive instruments; let him even be prodigal with musical science, in order to furnish the auditor with all kinds of objects of attention, provided only that this science does not prejudice the charms that he has spread out elsewhere: let him recall, without the spectator being in doubt about it, the most touching pieces of those that have already been heard; let him by this adroit means prolong, so to speak, the sensations that have been experienced, the emotion that has been felt; and let him cover with this renewed emotion the place that by itself must create only coldness: provided that the spectator is moved, he will argue about nothing, he will not ask who is making his tears flow.

The musician may recall these touching pieces already heard, either by placing in the midst of the melodies of his characters the most marked melodies of the air he desires to recall, and of which he desires to have the effect revived, or by diffusing these melodies in the accompaniments he sounds, or simply by recalling the accompaniments of the piece whose aid he is invoking, and by making them serve as accompaniments or as melody at the moment when he needs outside beauties. In addition, will he not further bind together by this means the different pieces that will compose his opera? Often, if the musician employs with skill the power of his art, the cold place in the tragedy will be the one where the spectator will be attracted by more charms, carried along by more variety, seduced by a melody more entrancing, touched by accents more pathetic: so much will the melodies that are heard have acquired a great power for having been connected, in the same opera, with a moving situation!

This manner of recalling pleasing phrases, expressive melodies already heard, or tableaux already presented, will be able to serve the musician in binding to the work the episodes that the poet has introduced into it; he will have to have recourse to it above all, when those episodes are too long or too distant from the subject, in order not to detract from the unity of the action, and not to interrupt the interest. He will still be able to arrive at the same goal, in mixing with the expression of the situations and the feelings that the episode contains, the depiction of the feelings and the situations that he will be able to imagine in the principal action, during the interval filled by the episode: in that way, the action or the interest will be only half suspended.

The musician will however need a certain art to employ these two, often opposed depictions; without that, the auditor too occupied with the one or the other, too divided between the tableaux, will not be able either to see or to grasp either of them: no expression will rule; and in place of an episode foreign to the principal action, but which might have been very pleasing and give rise to very great pleasure, there would remain only a piece often too long, and at the worst always cold and boring.

Most frequently, the musician who desires that these two depictions not harm each other at all, will be able to place in the melody the tableau provided by the episode, and represent by the accompaniments the portion of the principal action that may be supposed to transpire at the same time.

All the entrances and all the exits of the actors should be motivated; when they have not been by the poet, the musician will be able to fill his place, in depicting, by means of his orchestra, some occurrence parallel to the drama, which it will be easy to divine, which will be supposed to take place behind the scenes, and which will be of such a nature as to oblige one of the actors to appear on the stage, or to leave it.

When the reasons for an entrance or for an exit assigned by the poet are too weak, the musician will strengthen them by painting with more vivid colors the events introduced or narrated by the poet, or by expressing with more energy the feelings that he has placed on the stage.

The theater should never remain empty, that is to say, that for the greatest connection of the scenes, an actor should never depart without having left on the stage a second actor, with whom he may even have conversed in one fashion or another. When the poet has been forced to break this rule of the theater, the musician will be able to represent, by means of the instruments, some noteworthy event related to the drama, to the action, or in place of the scene, easy to divine, and which the composer will portray as passing at the very moment when he presents the image of it. The tableau that the musician will present of it will be able, in some sense, to take the place of an actor: it will occupy the stage alone for a moment, and it it is on a large scale and well made, it will take hold of the spectators so much the more, as they will enjoy not only the pleasure of seeing the tableau itself, but also that of guessing, at least half way, the subject of the depiction. The actor who must exit will be held by this tableau, while the spectator begins to enjoy it; the tableau alone will then dominate, and the actor who comes onto the stage will have to be able to occupy himself with it for some time, before seeing it disappear. In this way, the tableau put in the place of an actor who would have been introduced will follow exactly the same rules to which the latter would have been subjected.

The musician should make use only rarely, however, of the resource that we have just pointed out to him. He should include it among those whose magic depends in large measure on their rarity, which in a certain way can please only through their novelty, and which in consequence should never be employed frequently.

Will the musician be able to make necessary to the action an unnecessary character placed on the stage? No; but if he cannot remove the defect introduced by the poet, he can veil it; he can have this unnecessary character sing so beautiful a melody; he can have him sing pieces so touching or so pleasing, that it will be impossible for the spectator to become aware of his lack of utility. And why indeed would the spectator be offended to see an actor who in fact does not come to satisfy his curiosity, or to appease the anxiety of his soul, but who comes to speak to him in a captivating manner, who in some way deploys the means of seduction within the power of music; who quiets with the sweetest charms the fearful distress of hearts that are tortured by too painful a grief; who comes to create a happy contrast between situations that are too intense; and who augments the effect of the pathetic situations that must follow, by moving the heart in advance with the most expressive accents, by softening it with a plaintive melody, and by disposing it thus to tender pity?

The musician will be able to employ the delicate means that we have just proposed to him only when he is able to have a certain confidence in his powers, when he is assured of portraying the principle characters with colors sufficiently vivid for them not to be dulled by the proximity of the bright colors in which he will have presented the unnecessary character.

He will also be able to bind this last character to the action of the tragedy to some extent by placing skillfully in the melody that the character will sing, or in the accompaniments that will be joined to it, musical phrases which recall some striking part of the action that we have already had in front of our eyes, or better expressed, some phrase which we may already have heard during the interesting occurrence, some phrase which consequently may have been tied to it, and which may have acquired in that way the power of causing the same feelings to be experienced.

Such is the advantage of music over many arts of imitation: having several parts at its disposal, each one susceptible of painting feelings and events in a manner more or less powerful, it can, when it wishes, express several different things at once, even without these dissimilar expressions getting in each others way very much, and without it being difficult to distinguish them. In truth, it is necessary for this that the artist have a certain skill, that he know how to present them together; but most often that he make them occur successively, and replace the one by the other with such delicacy and rapidity that we think we are receiving the impression of them at the same time.

Musicians cannot see to it that a character who appears in the later acts of the tragedy has been announced in the earlier ones; but they can to some extent give a presentiment of his arrival, by offering in the piece of the earlier acts in which the announcement of the character would be best placed, some depiction of the action that he will come to relate, or in which he will come to take part. When the character whose name has not been announced in the earlier acts appears on the stage, the musician will recall the melody or the accompaniment he used for the depiction of which we have just spoken: and in this way, will the character not be connected with what has preceded by the resemblance of the feelings that he will arouse to those that have already been experienced?

With regard to the characters who have not been drawn by the poet in a sufficiently strong manner, and who are not sufficiently distinct from one another, the musician will give them the degree of force that they lack, by making use of the means we shall indicate to him in a special section.

But how will the musician be able to embellish the situations imagined and presented by the poet? Interesting and striking situations, either through the character of the personae who meet on the stage, or through the nature of the feelings that the events instill in them.

If the situations draw their beauty from the character of the personae, the musician will only have to add by his colors to the force of the design of the poet, and the sitaution will be embellished. For example, when two heroes, proud, intractible, and mortal enemies of one another meet on the stage, the situation is excellent; but it will become still more so if the musician employs all his power to represent, in the most vivid manner, the pride, the arrogance, and the ardent courage of the two heroes: the more redoubtable they appear, and the more we are attracted by the situation, the more it will appear and actually will be glorious.

If that same situation draws its force from the feelings that the events inspire in the characters; then the musician may redouble his efforts to depict the same feelings, to enlarge and animate their image, to incite them more keenly in the soul of the spectators.

If the interest of a situation comes from one character not knowing what is most important for him to know, and if it depends on the opposition of the feelings that the actor experiences to those he should have, then the musician may give to the character feelings still more opposed to those by which he should be affected. For example, in *Cyrus*, the *tragédie lyrique* of Metastasio, when Mandane sees her son Cyrus for the first time, she takes him for the murderer of that son so dear to her; she believes that the maternal love which rises in her heart is only a feeling of pity; she betrays that Cyrus she so desires; she pretends to recognize him as her son; under the pretext of supporting him fearlessly, she has him betake himself to a wild and lonely spot where he is to meet death at the hand of Cambyse, his own father, who will not know him and whom he has never seen; she no longer hears anything but her hatred of the supposed murderer of her son; she breathes only vengeance; and instead of dreaming that she herself has just deprived herself, in the most fatal manner, of the single blessing that binds her to life; instead of thinking that she has delivered to death that son for whom she would shed her blood a thousand times, she addresses herself to Mithridate, whom she believes to be the father of the murderer, and the author of the death of Cyrus; she paints for him, with the bitterness of a cruel irony, all the horror of the situation into which she believes he is going to be plunged; to avenge herself on him in the most frightful manner, she searches for the moment somehow to drive a dagger into his breast; and at the moment when the spectators, beside themselves, are ready to cry out to her, "Unfortunate one! you are speaking of yourself," she says to him, "Learn what it costs to lose, to mourn a son."[1]

Is the musician unable to add some new measure of force to this situation, one of the most heart-rending and most lofty that has been seen on any stage? Let him exalt the feeling of hate and vengeance that takes hold of the heart of that unfortunate mother; let him give her that kind of contentment so distant from the horrible despair to which she is going to be delivered, when all her misfortune is unveiled to her; let him permit the cry of maternal tenderness contained in Mandane's heart to dominate only to show how the rage that transports her chokes off all the feelings that should reign in her heart, how this same mother's love, misled by a fatal error, extinguishes all the fires it should ignite: and nevertheless, so that the spectator never may lose sight of all that the situation contains of agony and horror, let the accompaniments make heard the voice of revolted nature that cries out to her in a terrible and plaintive tone, "Unfortunate one! you are immolating your own son."

When the dialogue of the poet does not maintain the rapid pace that it should have, the musician may discard everything that could hinder his depictions from succeeding one another with rapidity; he may replace the one of them by the other promptly, and he may be certain nearly always that the spectator, struck by the rapidity with which his images succeed one another, will not perceive the slowness with which those of the poet appear in their succession.

Such are the means that the musician seems to me to be able to employ to do duty for the poet when the latter has been in some way compelled not to introduce into his tragedy all the beauties that one desires with so much justification in a dramatic work.

The musician may also make use of these same means, as we have already indicated, when he must work on a perfect product: how, without that, could

[1]These two verses are taken from a French opera entitled *Cyrus*, which is based on Metastasio by M. Paganel, and which has not yet been published.

he second the intentions of the poet, render all the sources of interest more abundant, instead of drying them up; increase the vivacity of expression, and the vividness of the colors employed.

We have seen what the concerns of the musician should be with respect to the work of the poet; let us now seek out what he should do so that the work that belongs only to him may present that connection and that wholeness without which it will never obtain all the success to which it may aspire.

Let us search first for how he should tie together the different pieces of music that compose his work, the recitatives, the airs, the duets, the choruses, the ballets, and so on. Let us still consider all these different objects only as pieces of music that are part of a single work, and pay no attention to the diverse manner in which we shall see they should be composed when we examine them in themselves.

First of all, all the musical parts of a *tragédie lyrique* should form a whole, and be tied together by their manner of being, that is to say, by the character they present, by the colors they offer, by the particular texture one may remark in them, still not considering them at all as diversified in their nature, not regarding them at all as choruses, as duets, and so on.

In recommending the connection of which I have just spoken, I do not wish to say solely that the different pieces of music that compose a tragedy should be united by chains of harmony of such a kind that one piece begins in the same key in which the preceding one has ended, or in a closely related key: neither do I wish solely that they be bound by melody in such a way that one melodic phrase which ends a piece begins the following piece, and that it is common to both. That may be an attraction in many circumstances: it is partly in that that the art of musical transitions consists, with which we shall soon concern ourselves; but it is not the type of connection that we are calling for here.

That connection which we make the first means of uniting all the parts of the *tragédie lyrique* should not depend uniquely on the beginning and the end of the pieces, but on all the portions presented by these same pieces; and in that, it is very different from the connection produced by the art of transitions.

Not only should the pieces of music be held in their place by their beginning and by their end; but they should be attached to that same place by all their parts. It is necessary then that all the different parts that compose one piece be suited to the different parts that compose another one; that all the musical pieces that form a tragedy have to some extent a family quality, that one may be able to see easily that they have been invented by the same composer, and destined for the same drama.

Is it not necessary, according to this, that they have something in common, either in the melody properly so-called, or in the manner in which the songs are fashioned, or in the quantity of notes they present, or in the nature of the instruments employed by preference, or in the manner in which the basses are constructed, whether they sing or are reduced to simple notes; or in the nature of the harmony, full and presenting all the chords it may offer, or sounding only those whose effect is most pronounced; or finally in the type of simple or full accompaniments, mixing and merging with the vocal part, or separating from it and presenting tableaux more or less different from the depictions offered by the melody?

But in giving to the diverse pieces he will produce that family quality and that great resemblance, the musician may never cease to diffuse everywhere the greatest variety; without that, instead of having constructed a tragedy of which all the parts concur, he will have composed only a single piece that is very long, very monotonous, very boring. Let him never forget that the first rule is to please, and that it is worth more to create a work that interests and that touches with incoherent parts, than a tragedy of which all the parts will be perfectly tied together, but which will produce only disgust and boredom.

Fortunately the musician has a very great number of means to bind, in a common chain, all the pieces of which he composes his opera. When he has chosen some one of these means, there will still remain to him a very large number of which he will be able to, of which he should make even an opposite use: he will make use of them to diffuse among all the pieces as much variety as he will have bestowed resemblance by the particular resource he has adopted.

It is above all between the different pieces that compose an act that the musician should establish that unity of which we are speaking; it is over these diverse pieces that he must diffuse those uniform colors and those varied colors about which we will not cease to speak to him. An act is a whole that nothing may divide: no part of it is separated even by the smallest space of time: moreover it is never so long that one may not easily see the beginning, the middle, and the end, that all the parts are not present together, and that one is not easily able to judge their relationships, their resemblances, and their differences.

One can to some degree compare an act of a tragedy with one of the façades of a building: this is a side of the edifice that one easily sees together, whatever its extent may be: it is a side all of whose portions must observe between them the greatest relationship, present a great resemblance, and yet offer a great variety, so that one may be able to say that the architect deployed in it all the beauties of his art.

Perhaps someone will stop me here, and will say to me: why is the resemblance so strongly necessary in music? Is it not sufficient that one may be able to pass easily from one piece to the other, that the art of transitions has been well observed, that one finds great variety, and that a great number of detailed riches have been spread out?

Without doubt this would be much, but it would not suffice. Let us except those sublime beauties which transport and enrapture wherever they may be placed, but which appear so rarely, and which even lose a great part of their merit when they do not enter into the general effect of a work; we shall see that in music, much more than in all the other arts, the soul is truly moved only when it has had, so to speak, the time to familiarize itself with the objects being presented to it: it truly rejoices in the tableau offered to it only when this has been before its gaze for some time. If the diverse musical pieces that compose an act lack that family countenance which makes us think that they already have affected us although we may in fact have heard only ones that resemble them, the soul does nothing but run through objects always new to it: it doubtless does not have time to become bored; it perhaps rejoices; it may even experience a great pleasure; but no sensation has time to become profound: the soul does nothing but pass from one impression to an unknown impression; wandering about ceaselessly, it is to some extent in perpetual error; if we wish, it is enchanted, but it does not have time to be touched, still less to be profoundly moved. And can we then flatter ourselves to have attained the goal of *tragédie lyrique*?

Moreover, must not the soul suffer in not uncovering the source of its enjoyments when it begins to be acquainted with it and to enjoy all the charms that it can give rise to, and in seeing itself thus deprived without being presented, in its place, with anything that resembles what is being taken away? If too long a constancy bores it, must not too rapid and too marked a change affect it in a disagreeable manner, make it impatient, torment it?

Not only should the different portions that compose the acts present that connection of which we have spoken, but also the acts should be united by some common element; it is thus that one truly causes that general effect of a dramatic work to arise; it is thus that, after having begun to create it by the union of the portions which form the principal parts of the tragedy, one succeeds in producing it by the connection of these same parts among themselves. A *tragédie lyrique* is like a great building the general effect of which is truly beautiful only when, to begin with, all the architectural members that compose a façade present the type of accord which should rule among them, and following this, all the façades observe among themselves the relationships which are suitable to them.

But the acts are separated by a rather large interval of time, and by an absolute cessation of everything that can give rise to or sustain the illusion: moreover, an act makes up just about the extent that the spectator can grasp all at once, and see with a single glance. Accordingly the musician should not apply himself to uniting the different parts of one act with those of another in the same manner as he should connect the portions of each act considered as isolated; he would only be taking needless pains. But when he has followed for each act in particular the route that we have indicated to him, the musician no longer sees in each of these acts the parts that form it: when, for example, there are five acts, he considers them only as five large musical pieces between which he must establish a connection and a relationship like those he has created between the portions of each act: it is in some measure a new act the five parts of which it is necessary to unite; and although at first glance it seems more difficult to produce a whole of five acts than of one act in particular, will the musician not achieve this with much more facility at least when he has to work only on acts whose portions are already connected? He need employ, to succeed, only the means he has already used to unite the portions of each act in particular; and here there are only five pieces to which he must give a quality of resemblance, while it is nearly impossible that he did not previously have a very much greater number of them to connect.

If one pictures the building that has already been an object of comparison for us, one will see without difficulty why it is not necessary to make the parts of one act agree with the parts of another: in this building, one does not seek to connect the architectural members of one façade with those of another, because these two façades are entirely distinct from one another, and one can see them together only obliquely and in a very imperfect manner: but must these two façades, considered uniquely as two architectural members, not be united by certain relationships, without which they could not come together in the same building?

We have just seen the manner of connecting not only the little parts that a tragedy includes, but even the large portions that compose it: there are further pains that the musician should take so that his work may present the most perfect whole.

Not only must the different pieces that form a tragedy have a family quality to be able to belong to the same work; but they must present an appearance which is common to all of them, and according to which one may be able to some extent, without the help of words, to divine the diverse objects of which we are going to speak. That appearance, that general form must be analogous to these objects, not only to produce the association which is the object of our reflections, but also to create the illusion, or at the least to augment it, to prevent the spectator from seing that he is watching only a theatrical representation, to persuade him that he is really witnessing what is presented to him, and that he really has before his eyes the occurrence of which the painting is being offered to him.

Independently of the particular nuances of the situations, all the pieces of a dramatic work should present colors proper to the subject that is treated. A tragedy which has to do principally with battles should not be composed by the musician like a tragedy in which one sees only touching actions and events particular to a small number of people: not only should the musical pieces that are heard in it be harrowing when the situation demands it, but also they should always present a military character, because in this tragedy everything should be related to battles, and because battles, or actions dependent on a battle, are to some extent its whole subject.

If, for example, the first three acts of Corneille's *Horaces* constituted the basis of a *tragédie lyrique*, it would be necessary that the music have quite a different color than in an opera drawn from Racine's *Phèdre*; in each part, the musician would have to join to the expression of the event narrated, of the situation offered, or of the feeling presented, a type of martial tone which would not be appropriate in an opera about Phèdre.

All the pieces that compose a *tragédie lyrique* should have a further feature of resemblance; they should indicate the location of the scene. It will be necessary for the music to have quite a different tone when the action transpires in civilized Greece, in Athens, among the most spiritual and the most polished people in the world, or in a Greece still semi-barbaric; in Rome, or in the milieu of the perfidious Parthians; among the effeminate Persians, or among the Turks, conquerors of a part of Asia and of Europe, etc. When the musician wishes to depict fury, he must employ very different nuances if that passion is transporting an American savage, if consequently it is deployed with all its force, with all the energy that a brute nature which nothing constrains can give it, or if it rules over an effeminate Sybarite, where everything breathes softness and bears its imprint, where degraded nature has been able to produce only a character without vigor, where all the feelings present nothing but obliterated traits, and where fury is scarcely the beginning of a weak anger.

Observe that difference in general tone which M. Gluck was able to establish between *Iphigénie en Aulide, Iphigénie en Tauride*, and *Armide*, and notice in this last opera how the tone of the music changes when the scene is moved from the realm of Damascus to the abode of the sorceress Armide who seeks to bewitch Renaud, and how from this moment everything presents an illusory or enchanting character.

The diverse musical pieces that compose the *tragédie lyrique* should also present an expression which is relative to the purpose of the work and which is common to all of them; the musician may, for example, wish to excite terror more particularly than pity, pity more than terror, admiration more than pity; to succeed in this more surely, the musician must not neglect, in each piece in particular, to try to create that unique feeling which he has in view: he must take care, however, not to detract in this way from the depiction of the particular feelings that each piece should present; if indeed he can introduce into each piece the depiction of the passion he has before his eyes during the whole course of the work only by detracting from the expression of the particular feelings that offer themselves successively to his pen, it would be better for him not to consider creating the general feeling: otherwise it would happen that the general feeling would dominate in the particular tableaux, and that the musician could compose only a monotonous opera; or that the two expressions would be equal, would mutually destroy one another, would leave nothing in their place, would produce a piece that would not mean anything and in consequence be cold and tiresome; and the first rule in the theater is to please and to amuse.

Each piece of a *tragédie lyrique* should moreover present a color proper to the station of the character who will perform it; it must not be composed for a king as it would be for a shepherd, even though, in appearance, the two may have the same feelings to express. I say in appearance; for these feelings, which may appear so similar, are nevertheless very different in reality: the anger of a shepherd is not that of a king: it is mingled in the shepherd with many half-feelings that are very different from those with which it is mixed in the king. And here there are two factors to consider. The first is that each piece in particular should present a color proper to the character who appears for the purpose of singing it; and the second is that all the pieces of a *tragédie lyrique* should present, independently of that particular color, a common physiognomy, analogous to the station of the principal characters; and it is this second consideration that is truly essential for the general effect of the work.

When, for example, the principal characters of a tragedy rule over great empires, the general complexion of the work should be different than when the principal characters are of a less elevated station: all the passions, all the feelings, should present in the first a larger air of dignity, and if I may make use of the term, a more imposing apparel; the same magnificence, then, that appears in the decoration, in the dress of the actors, and in the numerous followers who accompany them, should in some way reign in the musical pieces that we hear; and for example, an army general who is animated by the same passion, who experiences the same violence of it, and who is placed exactly in the same situation, should not sing altogether in the same manner in a work in which the principal characters are kings, as in a tragedy in which their estate is in no way equally illustrious.

But how will the musician be able to give the different pieces of his work that appearance of dignity and that brilliance which they should present? By employing proportions more grand than ordinary in the singing; by placing more often in the accompaniments, in the bass parts, or in others, firm lineaments, decisive passages; by employing from time to time instruments that most announce the accessories of royalty and power, such as kettle-drums, etc; by not allowing the words he sets to music to appear crowded together or too much repeated, which above all would be very contrary to the dignity of the characters; and finally by having recourse to several other means that will be divined without difficulty when we treat of the characters.

There still remain a great many general observations for the musician to make. He should search for the feelings that dominate in each character, and the passion that enslaves him, not only so that each role bears in particular the imprint of this passion that rules over the actor with more sovereignty than the others (This belongs to the art of delineating the characters), but also in order that all the portions of his work present some feature of the passion that most controls the principal characters. The influence of this passion controls the poet in the composition of the whole work; should it not rule also in the manner of shading all the musical pieces?

The composer must consider the different actions distributed in the tragedy with which he is concerned, and above all the catastrophe, the most important occurrence, the one in which the whole work is going to culminate, the one for the sake of which the whole work is constructed, and which decides the fate of all the characters. Let the musician treat the different subjects that are offered to him in the course of the work in a manner more or less different, according to the nature of these events: the same character subject to the same passion and controlled by the same circumstances, will have to sing differently in an opera on *Atrée et Thieste* than in one on the Clemency of Titus. Even though indeed the anger which in this latter opera sometimes agitates Vitellia might equal that of Atrée, it would have to be expressed very differently; it would have to present always, although faintly, a certain character that accorded with the general tone of the work and the events that occur in it.

The musician will easily be able to cast over the diverse tableaux that he presents that nuance drawn from the most notable occurrences. He will only have to consider if that nuance, or better said, if the feeling that these occurrences give rise to, if that affection which alone can depict them, and the passion he wants to represent in the specific piece he is working on are of the same type or of an opposed type or of a different type. If the feeling inspired by the occurrences is of the same type as the passion that the musician wants to display in a particular piece, he strengthens this passion; the musician will only have to make his colors more vivid. If the feeling produced by these occurrences is of a type opposed to the passion proper to the particular piece, he will lessen the passion; the musician will have to weaken the traits he presents. If finally the two feelings are of a different type, the musician will paint both, always watchful, however, to allow the superiority to the passion of the moment, to the one for which the piece is composed.

Here is one of those occasions that it is easy to observe after all we have said, where music shows a certain superiority over poetry, and a certain equality with painting, in the facility with which it can express several things at the same time, a facility that it owes to the union of the melody and the accompaniments, and to the power which every composer of skill can enjoy: to the power of having each part of these same accompaniments looked upon as a melody.

To make more clearly perceived all that we have just said relative to the similar appearance which the diverse pieces of a tragedy should present, let us again make use of the help of the comparison we owed to architecture.

In order that a building may do the greatest honor to its architect, all the parts that we can see at the same time, not only in each of its façades, should resemble one another sufficiently for us to judge them made for one another, and nevertheless be sufficiently different to offer the most pleasing variety; not only should the different façades, regarded then as particular portions, resemble each other and differ from one another in certain points, like the parts that compose them; but it is also necessary that the building considered in its entirety, or better said, that all the parts it presents inform us by their character, their decoration, their dimensions, etc., whether the building is the palace of a king or the dwelling of a subject; whether it is destined to house warriors or to serve as the sanctuary of ministers of justice. For whatever purpose one may wish to use the building, one will always find in it columns, peristyles, galleries, etc.; but these peristyles, these galleries, these columns will resemble each other very little, in accordance with the diverse usages of the building; will they not present ornaments and accessories of a sufficiently different type, so that the purpose of the edifice may be designated and to a certain point clearly perceived?

Similarly, in a perfect *tragédie lyrique*, not only should the diverse pieces which compose an act and which form that part of the tragedy which the spectator to some degree can grasp all at once present a family quality and yet a very large and very pleasing variety; not only should the acts, considered then as so many particular pieces, resemble each other and yet differ sufficiently from one another to prevent monotony from arising and to make the interest grow at each instant; but it is also necessary that the whole general effect of the tragedy, that all the parts that one may remark in it, obtain from their accessories, owe to some one of their portions, or receive by whatever means may be, a color that is common to all of them, that makes easily divined the subject of the work, the location of the scene, the principal feeling which the musician wishes to produce, the station of the characters that the poet has introduced, the nature of the feelings that reign with the most force in their souls, and the most notable events distributed in the tragedy.

Let no one fear, if the musician is adroit, that a great number of different expressions do not grade into one another, if they clash, if they are too allowing in their place only a cold source of boredom. In truth, if the expressions do not grade into one another, if they clash, if they are too distinct, if they are all equally vivid, they will divide the attention, draw it aside too much, and weaken it in that way to the point of annihilating it: but if the principal color of the subject dominates the others, and if these latter are grounded with art in the diverse nuances of the first, it will readily happen

404

that this principal color is different from what it would have been if it had appeared entirely alone; but it offers only an increased beauty; this altered color does not appear in some way less unique; one has before his eyes no less a unique object towards which the attention must necessarily be directed in its full entirety.

For example, let a beautiful flower, let a beautiful lily rise up in the middle of a field: if it was isolated, its whiteness would continue to affect us alone; but it is placed under an arbor of roses and of foliage that is always green; the green and the soft red are going to mingle pleasing nuances with the whiteness of the lily: the sun, lighting up peacefully with its golden rays a sky pure and serene, comes to add the color of a beautiful yellow to those which are already changing the whiteness of the flower; and the azure of the heavens, reflecting itself in it, comes also to turn it blue. Look at this lily; it has changed for you; it is no longer the same object; its whiteness is no longer the same; it has been altered by all that surrounds it. But these are not at all several different objects that divide and destroy the attention; it is not at all an azure sky, the purest sunshine, roses, and green foliage that you are obliged to see simultaneously: you remark only the colors that they have created; you see only those that they transmit to the lily; you have before your eyes only a single object, you perceive only a lily that mingles with its sparkling white the pleasing nuances of the soft red of roses, of a beautiful green, of a celestial azure, and of a golden yellow. Similarly, if the musician wants to use the resources of his art, one will not be obliged to pay attention to the personality of the character, to the location of the scene, and to the other objects represented in the same piece; one will hear, in truth, an air different from what it would have been if the musician in composing it had had before his eyes only a single object; but this air will never present more than a single image. And in painting, would not that difference be one between presenting several tableaux simultaneously, or displaying only one of them in which several objects were disposed in an orderly way?

Musicians, everything that you are obliged to represent will give you in some way only feelings to display: examine then in what respect the passions you have to depict resemble one another, or differ; in what respect they reinforce each other, or destroy each other: suppress all that is destroyed; give a new force to all that has been augmented by the intermixture of some new affection, and do not touch at all that which has suffered no alteration. You will produce in this way, and you will create, so to speak, a new feeling; this new feeling will be in truth the affection that results from all those you have to display, the passion which floats on the surface of all the others, and which arises from their contention.

The means that we have just recommended to composers demand sagacity for their employment; perhaps no musician has yet considered them; but it is nevertheless not so difficult to make use of them as one might believe; moreover, it seems to me that it is necessary to have recourse to them in order to present only a clear representation, in order not to offer perpetually mixed traits, confused portraits, in which one would be able to discover no resemblance,[2] and so that the art might arrive at the eminence which it should attain.

The general effect of a *tragédie lyrique* would not be perfect if the musician did not add further precautions to those we have just indicated to him.

He should in each act, at least if he is not diverted from it for some reason, he should, I say, make such a distribution of musical pieces of different genres, such as recitatives, airs, duets, choruses, etc., that all those of the same genre not be placed in succession one after the other; that one does not see, for example, several airs, several duets in succession, but that these diverse pieces be intermixed with taste; that, for example, from an air one passes to a recitative, from a recitative to a duet, and so on.

If the poem is well made, it will be easy for the musician to observe this pleasing and varied order, because if the poem is in no way devoid of the beauties it should offer, it will present feelings or passions throughout, and because everything that is passion or feeling can easily be represented by an air, and often by a duet, as we shall see in what follows. But when the poem on which the musician will work contains only scenes that are cold and devoid of feeling, how will the composer place in it airs, duets, and so on?

He will have to choose, in each scene, the pieces that come closest to the painting of feeling, that most have the appearance of it; he will have to apply himself to those in which a past but violent feeling is recalled, those in which there is announced a feeling that is still to come, but that is to have great intensity. He will make use of these pieces to have his characters sing, at least for a moment, to have an air heard, however short it might be; he will give that air all the luster with which he can endow it; he will seek to redeem, in this way, the long monotony of the rest of the scene, which he is able to treat only in recitative; or if it is absolutely impossible for him to place the smallest air in the dispassionate scenes he encounters, let him at least miss no opportunity to interrupt his recitative with rhythmical, brilliant, and varied orchestral passages, so that he replaces in this way as much as possible the airs that he is not able to insert, and so that he presents, in short, what has been called an obbligato recitative, with which we shall be concerned.

The musician must also manage so that in regarding each act simply as a scene, or better said, in considering all the acts of a tragedy simply as a whole, one may not see in one place too many airs, in another too many duets, or too many choruses, recitatives, etc. The best thing would be that the subject permits the musician to distribute in the acts considered as forming

---

[2]See the sample we shall give bearing on this subject before the end of our discussion of the *tragédie lyrique.*

simply a whole, that pleasing variety which he must try to present everywhere; but that he never constrains his subject, and that he allows himself no false reading at all to obtain this increase in beauty; that he does not have sung by two or by several characters what can be appropriate only to a single one; that he does not set in recitative that which depicts a very vivid, very decided feeling, and so on. It is rather difficult to see at a single glance all the acts of an opera, so that it is entirely open to the musician to deviate, with respect to these acts, from the kind of rule we have just indicated to him.

Will it not also be advantageous for the musician to be careful about the extension he gives to his duets, choruses, recitatives, etc. considered solely as musical pieces, so that when his expression will not suffer by it, he may be able to establish between the lengths of these pieces a certain proportion which may render them analogous to one another, and produce in them at the same time a sufficiently great variety to provide every species of pleasure to the listener?

There is still another path the musician should follow to make the greatest general effect rule in his tragedy, and to uncover in it the most abundant sources of beauty and illusion. Let him subject the diverse pieces that compose an act to a musical connection: the art of this connection is nothing other than that of transitions, as we have said to him.

For the connection to exist, it is not sufficient for each musical piece to conclude with a chord very close to the one with which the following piece begins: the connection would be too weak; it is necessary also, for the greatest perfection of the transitions, that the end of a piece may in some way serve as the beginning of the following piece, at least when they are of the same tempo and the same type; or really (since the exact observation of what we have just prescribed for the musician could soon give rise to monotony and boredom), it is necessary that there be between the close of one piece and the start of the following one the same relationship which we shall see should be set up between the two parts of an air: that is to say, it is necessary to announce the second piece, and to make it desired, whether it be by the modulation, by the kind of accompaniments, or by the nature of the melody used in the close of the first. We shall explain in detail, in speaking of the airs, the means that music provides for this matter.

But the composer must make observations here that are exceedingly delicate, exceedingly fine, and that call for the boldness of genius joined to justice of taste and prudence of mind. We have just seen that the pieces that compose an act should be tied together; but in an opera which is well made, and in which there is consequently a great variety of feelings, one does not always need these connections; often the musical pieces, very far from having one grounded in the other, should be cut off and separated in a very distinct manner. The general effect of the work must then depend on everything but musical connection; it must be produced uniquely by the diverse means of which we already have treated.

Two pieces that touch and follow each other are each the painting of a feeling. The first thing that the musician will have to do is to consider carefully the two feelings represented, compare them, and examine well their resemblances and the distance that separates them. When he has determined the degree of their remoteness, let him try to place between the two pieces of music the same distance as there is between the feelings that he must depict; he will be able to achieve this by means of the melody, the accompaniments, the modulation, and so on. When the two feelings are very close, let all the art of transitions be employed, let the whole be graduated, let one pass, without any doubt, from the first piece to that which follows it in the same way that we allow ourselves to go from one feeling to another that borders on it without being aware of the change we experience; the more imperceptible the passage is, the more skill the musician will have shown, at least if the feelings are separated by only a slight nuance. But when these same feelings are opposed to one another, when the fire of hate must be made to follow all the tenderness of love, whether it be that the same character passes thus, with rapidity, from one feeling to a contrary passion, or that two different characters, of which the one loves as much as the other hates, yield one after the other to the frenzies that animate them, let the musician abandon all musical connections; the more removed the motion of the second piece is from the preceding one, the more different its melody is from the one which has been used, the more unexpected its accompaniments are, the greater will be the effect it produces, the more complete the illusion it creates, the more faithful its depiction.

In the opera on Armide, Renaud has just been cast under a spell on a grassy bank; demons of the most pleasing form encircle him with chains of flowers; music sounds the most gentle tones, it reveals the charm that diffuses around the hero, the fatal rapture in which he is immersed, the lovely spot in which his steps are delayed. See how M. Gluck has suddenly depicted the arrival of Armide, who, a dagger in her hand, and breathing only hate and vengeance, advances in a terrifying manner to immolate Renaud: there is no transition at all to connect the two scenes; nothing is more sharply distinct than the two musical pieces; nothing contrasts more strongly and produces more of an effect.

It is necessary to take care, however, not to carry the contrast that should separate the two pieces to excess; otherwise the opening of the second would shock the ear by its harshness, so much would the chords, the melodies, and the accompaniments in it differ from the accompaniments, the melodies, and the chords that have preceded them: one must never cease to please, or to say it better, one must never revolt the spectator, if one does not wish the illusion to be destroyed.

There is still another consideration to keep in mind, which is basically, however, only an extension of what we have already said. When the opposed feelings that follow each other do not succeed one another in a brusque manner, but abate by insensible nuances and merge in a manner in which it is impossible to separate them by a really distinct line, the two pieces composed by the musician must fall away and coalesce in the same fashion. Do not all these nuances through which these opposed feelings pass form a series of several feelings, of a very short duration and very close to one another, and should they not, in consequence, be represented by a series of little pieces that are very close, very short, or what is the same thing, by two pieces which, although opposed in their nature, fuse and mingle with one another insensibly?

A great number of musicians, without thinking much about uniting the melodies or the accompaniments, have hardly concerned themselves with anything but the manner of connecting the pieces by means of modulations, in the same way that one joins together the parts that make up an air. Instead of establishing solely what the modulations may be which, after certain modes, might shock the ear least, give it the most pleasure, appear to it the most pleasing, and which, in consequence, one should use most often after those same modes, the musicians perhaps should have busied themselves with a species of table which could be very useful to composers and of which here is the idea:

One would determine with care the distance of all the modes from a given mode: one would consult and follow for that the greater or lesser pleasure with which the ear would hear them after that same mode. One would place them along one side of the table, ranged according to the order that had been discovered.

One would try also, and this would be more difficult and would demand really great sagacity, one would try, I say, to determine the different degrees of removal of all the feelings relative to some feeling one could take at random for the first of the scale, for example, relative to pity. One would arrange the feelings according to their greater or lesser removal from pity, and one would place them along the other side of the table. When one wished to determine the key in which a musical piece should begin, one would find out in what key the preceding piece had finished, and what feeling the first and the second piece had to depict. If the two feelings assigned by the subject were removed in the table, for example, by four degrees, one would choose for the key or for the mode of the second piece the one that was four degrees removed from the mode that had terminated the first piece; and one would easily find it by means of the column that expressed the order of the modulations. I do not need to insist on the utility of such a table.

When the musician has followed all the different routes that we have just indicated to him, he will have put into his work all the interconnection of which it is susceptible, he will have carried out the largest part of that which can have a bearing on the general effect; and if the richness of the details is in keeping with the beauty of the whole, his tragedy will have to have a very great success: but it will still remain for him to make some general observations.

It is not sufficient for the musician to be acquainted with all the resources of his art, to have a fortunate facility of conceiving novel and pleasing melodic turns, to be able to create easily a beautiful and touching melody which is captivating even independently of its accessories, to know how to distribute over all the pieces he composes the types of chord that will be most appropriate to them, and not to be ignorant of the means of producing an imposing harmony when he has need of its help; it is not enough that he know how to give to all the parts of the acts of his tragedy, and to the acts themselves, the resemblance which should unite them, and yet the large variety which is necessary for them to please, that he know how to make his colors proportionate to the more or less tragic subject of the work, to the location of the scene, to the end of the tragedy, to the station of the characters, to the feelings which rule with the greatest dominion over their souls, to the occurrences distributed by the poet in his work; it is not enough that the length of the various pieces which he produces, and the place which they occupy in the different acts, offer precisely that analogy and that variety which they should present, and that finally he know and employ appropriately the art of merging together two pieces of music, or of opposing them to one another, of making them contrast and of separating them by a very distinct line. Not only must he know how his tragedy should be composed, but also how it should be performed: without that, how could he achieve the completion of his task? He should to some degree know the size of the theater for which his work is destined, know which are the pieces that a delivery conformable to the laws of nature calls for one to say rapidly or slowly, to repeat, or to be content to state once; so that he may regulate according to this the length of his various pieces, of his choruses, of his duets, of his airs, and above all of his ritornellos, one of the things in which one should most pay attention to the manner in which it is performed, because it is one of those in which the performance of the actor may be thwarted the most, and in which, consequently, one may most detract from the effect of the tragedy.

A musician who has no idea of the true manner of representing a dramatic work, but who is endowed with a refined judgment and a sensitive soul will without doubt easily see if an air is necessary in the situation that is presented to him, if the feeling demands that one sing, or simply that one recite; but it is uniquely according to an acquaintance with the art of performing dramatic works that one may decide the length of the piece. The

410

musician will know without its aid if he should depict fury by an air; but if he is not acquainted with the violent acting, the alarming pantomime which must necessarily accompany the depiction of that fury and render it more expressive, either he will compose too short a piece, and he will not give this terrifying acting the time to be deployed and to produce all its effect, or he will compose too long a piece, and the actor, worn out or embarrassed in varying his acting, will become cold or will provoke annoyance, and destroy the whole illusion he was able to create previously.

May we not say as much of the duets, the choruses, etc., and above all of the ritornellos, that is to say, of that kind of symphony which begins or terminates a piece of a *tragédie lyrique*, or any one of its principal parts? Sensitivity and discernment will be able to make the musician suspect the place where they should be employed, in the same way as he will be able to compose them with the aid of musical art, in the manner most appropriate. to bring out the piece that they will follow or that they will precede; but it is uniquely an acquaintance with dramatic performance that must serve to decide absolutely upon their necessity, and to determine their place and their length. If the composer is not endowed with this knowledge, the actor, pressed to give forth his passion, and more involved, perhaps, in the depiction through his discourse than the feeling alone is able to make the musician imagine, will be obliged to wait coldly or in a constrained manner for a ritornello that is misplaced or too long to be heard: and when he must deploy only little by little the feeling which affects him and agitates him but whose expression must be given forth only after having been contained for a long time and only after a great number of efforts to suppress it, what will he do if there is no ritornello at all, or if it does not have a length proportionate to the manner in which he must allow the fire that devours him to escape, a length that the musician can not determine solely according to a knowledge of the feeling he must depict? Or indeed the actor will not be able in any way to make visible that succession of nuances, that chain of feelings more or less restrained, more or less exalted, so proper to project the trouble into the soul of all the spectators, and the situation will lose a great part of its beauty; or he will be able to develop only half way the feelings that must appear only successively, or better, all the gradations of the same feeling that must be replaced by one another; instead of embracing all hearts, he will spread among them only coldness and boredom.

For the rest, it is easy to see that it is not necessary that the musician be able to represent his operas himself, like the Barons, the Garricks, the Lekains would perform tragedies: it is not necessary that his arm lend itself to all gestures, his voice to all inflections, his body to all movements; but is it not necessary to some extent that he not be ignorant of any of these inflections, that none of these movements be unknown to him? Is it not necessary that he be able to determine their place, to assign their duration, to indicate their force, in a word, that he be in a position to foresee the whole performance that a great actor would employ in a given situation?

Is it not necessary in addition, and this is perhaps more necessary than one would think, that he know to some extent not only what the pantomime of an actor in such and such a situation should be, but also what the number of steps is that this actor should take before beginning a new piece? Is it not necessary that he know the best manner of having his actors arrive on the scene, of satisfying the eye at the same time as the ear, of engrossing all the senses, of presenting the most magnificent spectacle, of disposing with taste the numerous followers who sometimes accompany his actors, of distributing a numerous court, an army, or a whole people, of conducting their multitudes onto the stage with art, while still giving them an air of spreading out there by chance, of amassing them there in more or less time, of composing of them the most beautiful tableaux? The number of measures of the various musical pieces, must it not be proportioned to all of these things? and how could it be if the musician is ignorant of them?

How many precautions to take, how many cares to take upon oneself, how many observations to make, how many details to discharge! How will the musician, occupied by all that his tableau considered in itself demands of him, be able to give his different depictions that color which we have seen they should have? Why do so many considerations not extinguish his genius? How will enough fire remain over to him to depict forcefully, when he is always constrained by multifarious rules, by precepts that seem to contend with each other and to destroy one another? How, always surrounded by precipices, will he dare to advance with that assurance which alone is able to win over to his following those whom he wishes to conquer? Ah! may the musician who strains to produce a great and beautiful work in which genius has ignited all the fires of feeling take good care not to think of what we have just explained to him in these moments of enthusiasm and of rapture in which he is going to create; but may he meditate profoundly on his subject prior to these happy moments when man truly enjoys all his grandeur and all his privileges, when he can be proud to be man: let him recall then our principles, let him apply them to the tableau that he is going to construct before his head is exalted and the heat of creation has yet embraced his soul; let him penetrate into the situation that he has to depict; let him see what the person is whom he is going to have speak; let him transport himself to the location of the scene; let him put himself in the place of the character; let him be, like him, king, general, leader of a great people, hero, etc., let him clothe himself in his whole character, let him embrace all the feelings, let him be inflamed by all his passion: insensibly his soul will be embraced, and his exalted genius will elevate his ideas. Let him deliver himself then without reflection to the fire that consumes him and to the transport that dominates him; let him no longer imagine that he is a musician and that he is composing a tragedy, but let him think himself into the frightening situation in which he is going to depict his hero; let him, in the middle of the tears or of the transports of anger, give vent to the feelings that are too powerful for him to be able to contain any longer; let him write all that which this state of enthusiasm will inspire in him, let him not reject any of the images that will present themselves to him, let him seize all the traits he will see, or better said, let him trace out all that he will experience himself, and let him place no limit on the expression of the transports that he is no longer able to moderate.

Insensibly that violent state will be appeased; the feeling will be dissipated by dint of being diffused; his fatigued genius will refuse to elevate and to animate his ideas, calm will again arise in his soul and in his heart, his tears will cease to flow, the illusion in which he was plunged will evaporate; he will distinguish little by little the hero he has just depicted from the artist who has made the tableau; he will see his work with composure, he will remark in it with a sane view the beauties and the defects, he will judge to some extent a work foreign to his genius and to his heart.

Let the severe finger of criticism come to retrace for him then the rules on which he has meditated, and which we have tried to establish here; let him polish his work according to these same rules, let him suppress in it that which will be too opposed to them; but let him know that everything which produces the greatest effect is always that which is most beautiful; that all the rules must give way to that sublime *élan* of genius; that genius itself can sometimes justify them only in relating them to the magical power that has carried it away. Let him sacrifice to those gleaming pieces, and let him abandon all the rules rather than dull their ardent light. But also, when he is not arrested by that august and sacred badge of genius, or by the burning imprint of a sublime feeling, let him come again to give his work the degree of perfection that the rules will offer to him; let him add to them if it is necessary; but when he has great changes to make, let him not amuse himself by polishing a statue of which so many parts are defective; let him rekindle the fire of his genius and of his feelings, let him take a new mold, and let him refound his statue.

Additional Reading

Dahlhaus, Carl. "Romantische Musikästhetik und Wiener Klassik." *Archiv für Musikwissenschaft* 29, 1972.

_____ "Karl Philipp Moritz und das Problem einer klassischen Musikästhetik." *International Review* 9, 1978.

Deditius, Annemarie. *Theorien über die Verbindung von Poesie und Musik: Moses Mendelssohn, Lessing.* Liegnitz, 1918.

Diderot, Denis. *Rameau's Nephew, and D'Alembert's Dream,* tr. L.W. Tancock. Baltimore, 1966.

Evans, R.L. *Diderot et la musique.* Birmingham, 1932.

Gilg-Ludwig, R. "Die Musikauffassung Wilhelm Heinses." *Schweizerische Musikzeitung* 91, 1951.

Heinse, J.J.W. *Hildegard von Hohenthal.* 3 vols. Berlin, 1795-96.

——————— *Musikalische Dialogen.* Leipzig, 1805.

Herder, J.G. *Kalligone.* Vol. XXII of *Herders Sämmtliche Werke,* ed. B. Suphan. Berlin, 1880.

——————— "Viertes Wäldchen." In his: *Kritische Wälder.* Vol. IV of *Herders Sämmtliche Werke,* ed. B. Suphan. Berlin, 1878.

Hilbert, Werner. *Die Musikästhetik der Frühromantik.* Remscheidt, 1911.

Hirschberg, Eugen. *Die Encyklopädisten und die französische Oper im 18. Jahrhundert.* Leipzig, 1903.

Huber, Kurt. "Herders Begründung der Musikästhetik." *Archiv für Musikforschung* 1, 1936.

Jacoby, G. *Herders und Kants Ästhetik.* Leipzig, 1907.

Jansen, Albert. *Jean-Jacques Rousseau als Musiker.* Berlin, 1884.

Jullian, Adolphe. *La Musique et les philosophes au 18e siècle.* Paris, 1873.

Kretzschmar, Hermann. "Immanuel Kants Musikauffassung und ihr Einfluss auf die folgende Zeit." *Jahrbuch der Musikbibliothek Peters für 1904.*

Lacépède, Bernard Germain. *La Poétique de la musique.* 2 vols. Paris, 1785.

Maecklenburg, A. "Die Musikanschauung Kants." *Die Musik* 14, 1914-15.

Marks, Paul F. "Aesthetics of Music in the Philosophy of 'Sturm und Drang': Gerstenberg, Hamann and Herder." *Music Review* 35, 1974.

Masson, Paul-Marie. *L'Opéra de Rameau.* Paris, 1930.

Meyer, Kathi. "Kants Stellung zur Musikästhetic." *Zeitschrift für Musikwissenschaft* 3, 1920-21.

Mornet, D. "La Véritable signification du 'Neveu de Rameau'." *Revue des deux mondes,* August 15, 1927.

Müller, H. "Wilhelm Heinse als Musikschriftsteller." *Vierteljahrsschrift für Musikwissenschaft* 3, 1887.

Müller-Blattau, Joseph. "Zur Musikübung und Musikauffassung der Goethezeit." *Euphorion* 31, 1930. (also: *Musik und Kirche* 2, 1930.)

Nufer, W. *Herders Ideen zur Verbindung von Poesie, Musik und Tanz.* Berlin, 1929.

Oliver, Alfred R. *The Encyclopedists as Critics of Music.* New York, 1947.

Prodhomme, Jacques Gabriel. "Diderot et la musique." *Zeitschrift der internationalen Musikgesellschaft* 15, 1914.

Schering, Arnold. "Zur Musikästhetik Kants." *Zeitschrift der internationalen Musik-gesellschaft* 11, 1909-10.

Schubert, Giselher. "Zur Musikästhetik in Kants 'Kritik der Urteilskraft.' " *Archiv für Musikwissenschaft* 32, 1975.

Schueller, H.M. "Immanuel Kant and the Aesthetics of Music." *Journal of Aesthetics* 14, 1955.

Seifert, Wolfgang. *Christian Gottfried Körner: Ein Musikästhetiker der deutschen Klassik.* Regensburg, 1960.

Strauss, A. *Zur Musikästhetik der deutschen Frühromantik.* Prague, 1935.

Strich, Fritz. *Deutsche Klassik und Romantik, oder Vollendung und Unendlichkeit.* Munich, 1922.

Terras, Rita. *Wilhelm Heinses Ästhetik.* Munich, 1972.

Vexler, F. *Studies in Diderot's Aesthetic Naturalism.* New York, 1922.

Wieninger, Gustav. *Immanuel Kants Musikästhetik.* Munich, 1929.

Wiora, Walter. "Herders und Heinses Beiträge zum Thema 'Was ist Musik?' " *Die Musikforschung* 13, 1960.

Bibliography

Besseler, Heinrich. "Grundfragen der Musikästhetik." *Jahrbuch der Musikbibliothek Peters für 1926.*

Bücken, Ernst. *Geist und Form im musikalischen Kunstwerk.* Potsdam, 1929.

Dahlhaus, Carl. *Musikästhetik.* Cologne, 1967. (tr. W.W. Austin as *Esthetics of Music.* Cambridge, 1982.)

Dammann, Rolf. *Der Musikbegriff im deutschen Barock.* Cologne, 1967.

Ehrlich, Heinrich. *Die Musikästhetik in ihrer Entwicklung von Kant bis auf die Gegenwart.* Leipzig, 1882.

Gatz, Felix M. *Musik-Ästhetik in ihren Hauptrichtungen.* Stuttgart, 1929.

Goldschmidt, Hugo, *Die Musikästhetik des 18. Jahrhunderts.* Zurich, 1915.

Graf, Max. *Composer and Critic; Two Hundred Years of Musical Criticism.* New York, 1946.

Huber, Kurt. *Musikästhetik.* Ettal, 1954.

International Review of the Aesthetics and Sociology of Music. vol. 1 - , 1970 - . (Referred to as *International Review.*)

Jullien, Adolphe. *La Musique et les philosophes au dix-huitième siècle.* Paris, 1873.

Le Huray, Peter and James Day, eds. *Music and Aesthetics in the Eighteenth and Early-Nineteenth Centuries.* Cambridge, 1981.

Lippman, Edward A. *Musical Thought in Ancient Greece.* New York & London, 1964.

Markus, Stanislaw A. *Musikästhetik.* 2 vols. Leipzig, 1959-1977.

Moos, Paul. *Die Philosophie der Musik.* Stuttgart, 1922.

Moser, Hans Joachim. *Musikästhetik.* Berlin, 1953.

Die Musik in Geschichte und Gegenwart. (Articles on individual authors and subjects.)

The New Grove Dictionary of Music. (Articles on individual authors and subjects.)

Pfrogner, Hermann. *Musik: Geshichte ihrer Deutung.* Freiburg, 1954.

Salmen, Walter, ed. *Beiträge zur Geschichte der Musikanschauung im 19. Jahrhundert.* Regensburg, 1965.

Schäfke, Rudolf. *Geschichte der Musikästhetik in Umrissen,* 2nd ed. Tutzing, 1964.

Serauky, Walter. *Die musikalische Nachahmungsästhetik im Zeitraum von 1700 bis 1850.* Münster, 1929.

Striffling, Louis, *Esquisse d'une histoire du gout musical en France 1929. 18e siècle.* Paris, 1912.

Strunk, Oliver, ed. *Source Readings in Music History.* New York, 1950.

Zoltai, Dénes. *Ethos und Affekt: Geschichte der philosophischen Musikästhetik,* tr. B. Weingarten. Budapest, 1970.

List of Texts

1. *The Dialogues of Plato,* tr. B. Jowett. 4 vols. 4th ed. Oxford, 1963. Vol. IV, pp. 218-242.

2. Saint Augustine. "On Music," tr. R.C. Taliaferro. In: Vol. IV of *The Fathers of the Church.* New York, 1947. pp. 324-379.

3. *The Confessions of Saint Augustine,* tr. E.B. Pusey. New York, 1952. pp. 255-277.

4. Girolamo Mei. *Letters on Ancient and Modern Music,* ed C.V. Palisca. American Institute of Musicology 1960. pp. 90-101.

5. Marin Mersenne. *Harmonie universelle.* Paris, 1636. *Traitez des Consonances, des Dissonances, des Genres, des Modes, & de la Composition: Livre premier, des Consonances.* pp. 10-19.

6. Johann Mattheson. *Der vollkommene Capellmeister.* Hamburg, 1739. pp. 133-160.

7. Christian Gottfried Krause. *Von der Musikalischen Poesie.* Mit einem Register vermehrt. Berlin, 1753. pp. 25-45.

8. James Harris. *Three Treatises.* 4th ed. London, 1783. pp. 53-69, 95-103.

9. Charles Avison. *An Essay on Musical Expression.* 2nd ed. London, 1853. pp. 1-7, 20-28, 56-75, 107-119.

10. Daniel Webb. *Observations on the Correspondence between Poetry and Music.* London, 1769. pp. 1-14, 28-48, 124-145.

11. James Beattie. *Essays.* 3rd ed. London, 1779. pp. 113-169.

12. Thomas Twining. *Aristotle's Treatise on Poetry, and Two Dissertations, on Poetical, and Musical, Imitation.* 2nd ed. 2 vols. London, 1812. Vol. I, pp. 66-93.

13. Charles Batteux. *Les Beaux-arts réduits à un même principe.* Paris, 1747. pp. 259-286.

14. André Morellet. *Mélanges de littérature et de philosophie.* 4 vols. Paris, 1818. Vol. IV, pp. 366-404.

15. Boyé. *L'Expression musicale, mise au rang des chimères.* Amsterdam, 1779. pp. 1-24.

16. Michel Paul Gui de Chabanon. *Observations sur la musique.* Paris, 1779. pp. 13-83.

17. Jean-Jacques Rousseau. *Essai sur l'origine des langues, où il est parlé de la mélodie, et de l'imitation musicale,* ed. Ch. Porset. Bordeaux, 1970. pp. 138-195.

18. Jean Philippe Rameau. *Observations sur notre instinct pour la musique, et sur son principe.* Paris, 1754. pp. iii-xvi, 1-78.

19. Denis Diderot. *Rameau's Nephew, and D'Alembert's Dream,* tr. L.W. Tancock. Baltimore, 1966. pp. 97-107.

20. Johann Jakob Wilhelm Heinse. *Musikalische Dialogen.* Leipzig, 1805. pp. 113-141.

21. Bernard Germain Lacépède. *La Poétique de la musique.* 2 vols. Paris, 1785. Vol. I, pp. 106-180.

419

List of Authors

1. Plato. B.C. 427-347. Greek philosopher. He deals extensively with the ethical influence of music on the character of the state and of the individual.

2 and 3. Saint Augustine. 354-430. Bishop of Hippo, in ancient Numidia. He is the most influential and the most profound of the Fathers of the Church.

4. Girolamo Mei. 1519-1594. Italian humanist, born in Florence and died in Rome. He was an editor of ancient Greek texts and a historian of Greek music.

5. Marin Mersenne. 1588-1648. French philosopher, theologian, mathematician, and musical theorist. He was vitally interested in mechanics and in scientific experimentation. His immense correspondence with philosophers and scientists includes letters exchanged with Descartes and Doni on musical matters.

6. Johann Mattheson. 1681-1764. Hamburg composer, critic, and lexicographer. He was a prolific and influential music theorist and aesthetician.

7. Christian Gottfried Krause. 1719-1770. Berlin song composer and musical aesthetician.

8. James Harris. 1709-1780. English grammarian; author of *Hermes*, a philosophic inquiry concerning universal grammar. He was a nephew of Shaftesbury, who influenced his aesthetic views.

9. Charles Avison. 1709-1770. English composer, conductor, organist, and writer on music.

10. Daniel Webb. c.1719-1798. British writer on music and poetry.

11. James Beattie. 1735-1803. Scottish poet and philosopher.

12. Thomas Twining. 1735-1804. English classical scholar.

13. Charles Batteux. 1713-1780. French philosopher and aesthetician.

14. André Morellet. 1727-1819. French economist and miscellaneous writer, one of the last of the *philosophes*.

15. Boyé. Nothing is known of this writer.

16. Michel-Paul-Gui de Chabanon. 1729 or 1730-1792. French classical scholar, composer, and musical aesthetician. An enlarged version of the *Observations* was published in 1785, with the title *De la Musique considérée en elle-même et dans ses rapports avec la parole, les langues, la poésie, et le théâtre.*

17. Jean-Jacques Rousseau. 1712-1778. Swiss philosopher, author, and composer, of French Protestant descent. His views on music had a strong impact throughout Western civilization.

18. Jean-Philippe Rameau. 1683-1764. French composer, organist, and musical theorist. Born in Dijon, settled in Paris in 1723, where he died.

19. Denis Diderot. 1713-1784. French philosopher, encyclopedist, critic, and man of letters. He was the founder and chief editor of the *Encyclopédie*. His views and ideas, including those on music and on opera, were highly influential.

421

20. Johann Jakob Wilhelm Heinse. 1749-1803. German novelist and writer on the aesthetics of visual art and music. Heinse combined the frank voluptuousness of Wieland with the enthusiasm of the "Sturm und Drang." He had considerable influence on the romantic school.

21. Bernard Germain Lacépède. 1756-1825. French naturalist, composer, and musical theorist and aesthetician.

INDEX

423

428

430